Panasonic Lumix GX7 and GM1: From Snapshots to Great Shots

Rob Knight

Peachpit Press

Panasonic Lumix GX7 and GM1: From Snapshots to Great Shots
Rob Knight

Peachpit Press
www.peachpit.com

To report errors, please send a note to errata@peachpit.com

Peachpit Press is a division of Pearson Education

Senior Editor: Susan Rimerman
Production Editor: Tracey Croom
Copyeditor: Scout Festa
Proofreader: Elaine Merrill
Composition: WolfsonDesign
Indexer: James Minkin
Cover Image: Rob Knight
Cover Design: Aren Straiger
Interior Design: Mimi Heft

ISBN-13: 978-0-321-99640-4
ISBN-10: 0-321-99640-2

9 8 7 6 5 4 3 2 1

Printed and bound in the United States of America

Dedication

I could not have written this book without the love and support of my wife, Becky.

Acknowledgements

Thanks to Giulio Sciorio for introducing me to the Lumix family and making this project possible. Thanks to Tom Curley and Darin Pepple for your consistent encouragement and support. Working with you guys and the Lumix Luminary team is a real pleasure.

Thanks to Ted Waitt for deciding to pull the trigger on a Lumix book, and thanks to Frederick Van Johnson for introducing me to Ted in the first place. The gang at Peachpit Press has made this process very smooth and a lot of fun. Thanks to Susan Rimerman, Scout Festa, Tracey Croom, Elaine Merrill, and James Minkin for all of your hard work. I also want to thank Jeff Revell for creating such a great foundation for the Snapshots to Great Shots series.

Thanks to Rick Sammon and Juan Pons. Your friendship and advice have been invaluable. You guys have helped me open a lot of doors, and I really appreciate it.

Contents

Introduction

There is a lot of buzz these days about mirrorless cameras. Mirrorless cameras are generally much smaller than traditional DSLR cameras, but the camera body is only part of the equation. The Lumix GX7 and GM1 use a smaller image sensor than most DSLRs, which allows the lenses to be smaller and lighter as well. It's the combination of outstanding image quality and smaller gear that attracted me to Lumix cameras in the first place. You obviously see the same advantages in the GX7/GM1, because you're reading this book! There are hardly any resources like this for Lumix camera owners, and I'm really excited to write the first Lumix book for Peachpit Press. This book is not a rehash of the owner's manual, but rather a resource to teach photography with the specific technology present in the camera that you now own. I have put together a short Q&A to help you get a better understanding of just what it is that you can expect from this book.

Q: Why does this book cover two cameras?

A: The GX7 is a natural choice for a book like this because it has many features that make it a great camera for beginners and serious photo enthusiasts alike. It may seem strange to include the little GM1 in the same book, but the two cameras have the same sensor, processor, autofocus, and more. Since the cameras share so many functions and produce the same great image quality, I thought GM1 users would benefit from the same tips and techniques as GX7 users. When you see tutorials throughout this book, you will see the settings for the GX7 followed by the same settings for the GM1.

Q: Where can I find the GX7 and GM1 manuals that you reference in this book?

A: The basic owner's manual that is included in the box with your camera doesn't cover a lot of the functions that I will discuss. The page number references in this book are for the "Owner's Manual for advanced features," which is available in PDF form. I like to download the advanced manuals to my smartphone or tablet so I can access them when I'm out shooting. I have uploaded both manuals to my website so you can find them easily. You can download them at http://robknightphotography.com/GX7guide.pdf and http://robknightphotography.com/GM1guide.pdf.

Q: If I have the advanced manual, why do I need this book?

A: The advanced owner's manual is a great resource that covers every feature of your camera. The manual does a good job of telling you what a feature does or how to turn it on in the menus, but it doesn't necessarily tell you *why* and *when* you should use it. If you really want to improve your photography, you need to know the whys and whens to put all of those great camera features to use at the right time. To that extent, the manual just isn't going to cut it. It is, however, a great resource on the camera's features, and it is for that reason that I treat it like a companion to this book. As you read through the book, you will see callouts that point you to specific pages in your advanced owner's manual that are related to the topic being discussed. These are meant to expand upon the feature or function that I cover as it applies to our specific needs.

Q: What can I expect to learn from this book?

A: Hopefully, you will learn how to make great photographs. My goal, and the reason the book is laid out the way it is, is to guide you through the basics of photography as they relate to different situations and scenarios. By using the features of your GX7/GM1 and this book, you will learn about aperture, shutter speed, ISO, lens selection, depth of field, and many other photographic concepts. You will also find plenty of full-page photos that include captions, shooting data, and callouts so you can see how all the photography fundamentals come together to make great images. All the while, you will be learning how your camera works and how to apply its functions and features to your photography.

Q: What are the assignments all about?

A: At the end of all of the chapters, you will find shooting assignments, where I give you some suggestions as to how you can apply the lessons of the chapter to help reinforce everything you just learned. Let's face it—using the camera is much more fun than reading about it, so the assignments are a way of taking a little break after each chapter and having some fun.

Q: Should I read the book straight through or can I skip around from chapter to chapter?

A: Here's the easy answer: yes and no. No, because the first four chapters give you the basic information that you need to know about your camera. These are the building blocks for using the camera. After that, yes, you can move around the book as you see fit, because the later chapters are written to stand on their own as guides to specific types of photography or shooting situations. You can bounce from portraits to shooting landscapes and then maybe to a little action photography. It's all about your needs and how you want to address them. Or, you can read it straight through. The choice is up to you.

Q: Is that it?

A: One last thought before you dive into the first chapter. My goal in writing this book has been to give you a resource that you can turn to for creating great photographs with your Lumix GX7/GM1. Take some time to learn the basics and then put them to use. Photography, like most things, takes time to master and requires practice. One of the most important things I tell my students and others about my own photography work is that I'm still learning. Always remember that it's not the camera that makes beautiful photographs—it's the person using it. Photography is one of those activities that let you explore, no matter if you are traveling or shooting your child's birthday party. So enjoy the experience, learn from your mistakes (which I encourage you to make), and take your snapshots to another level—to great shots.

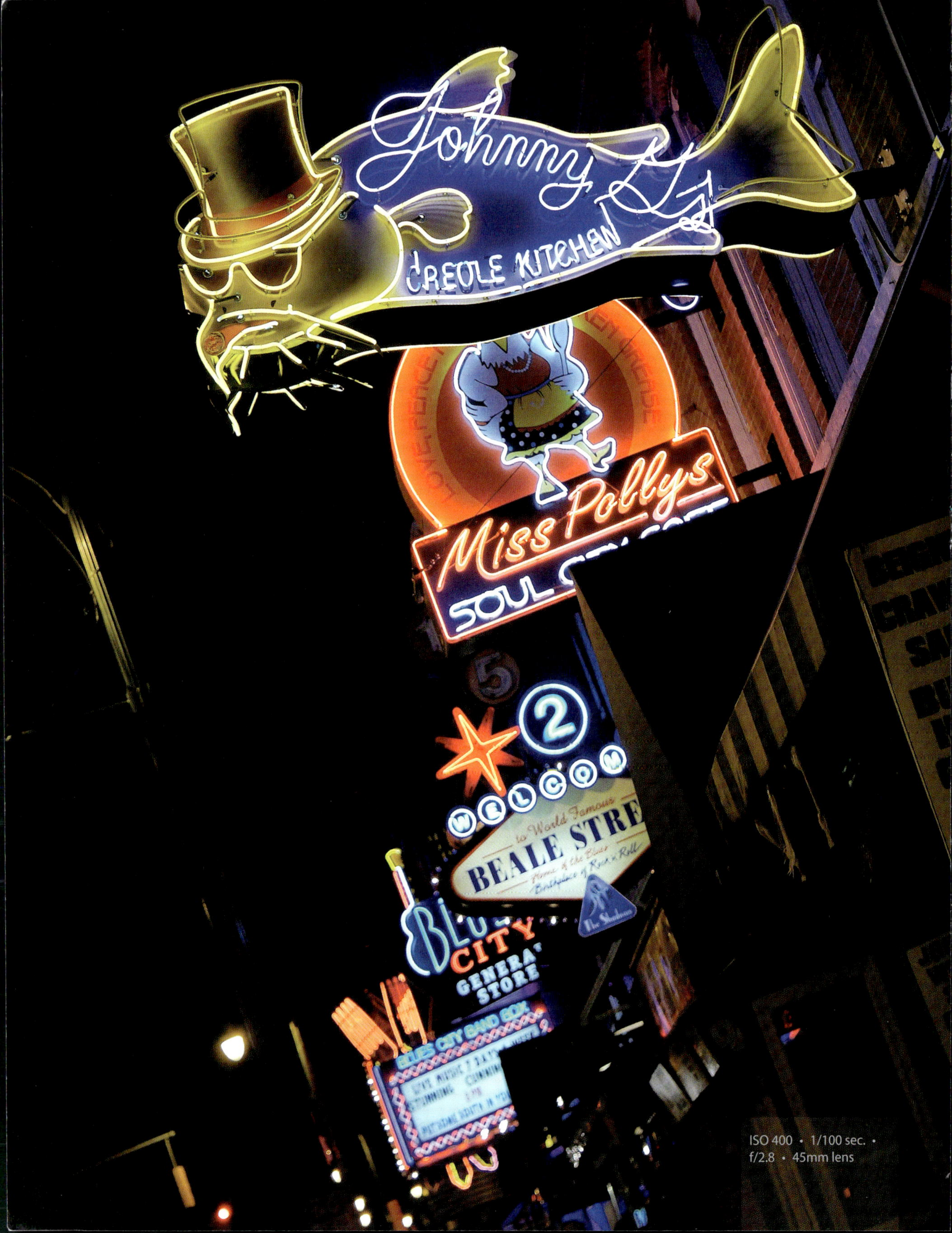

ISO 400 • 1/100 sec. • f/2.8 • 45mm lens

1

The NEX-6 Top Ten List

Ten Tips to Make Your Shooting More Productive Right Out of the Box

Ah, you have to love that new camera smell, right? I'm always excited to unbox a new piece of equipment, especially a camera. I just want to unwrap the packaging, put the lens on, insert a new memory card, and start rediscovering the world photographically. Sound familiar? Instead of being patient and at least glancing at the owner's manual, I'm always eager to break in the shutter on my new camera!

Of course, this behavior always leads to frustration in the end—there are always issues that could have been easily addressed had I known about them before I started shooting. Maybe if I had a top ten list of things to know, I could be more productive without having to spend countless hours with the manual. So this is where we begin.

The following list will get you up and running without suffering many of the "gotchas" that come from not being at least somewhat familiar with your new camera. So let's take a look at the top ten things you should know before you start taking pictures with your Lumix GX7/GM1.

Poring Over the Camera

GX7 Front

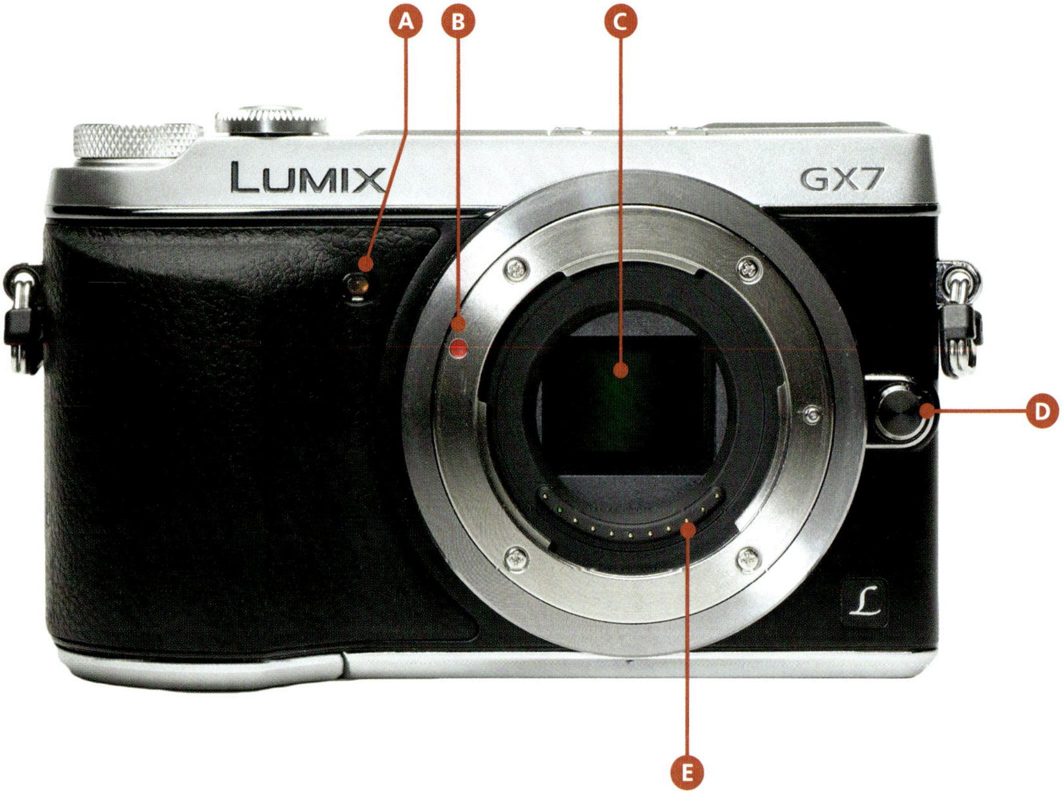

A AF Illuminator/ Self-Timer Indicator

B Lens Fitting Mark

C Sensor

D Lens Release Button

E Lens Contacts

GX7 Back

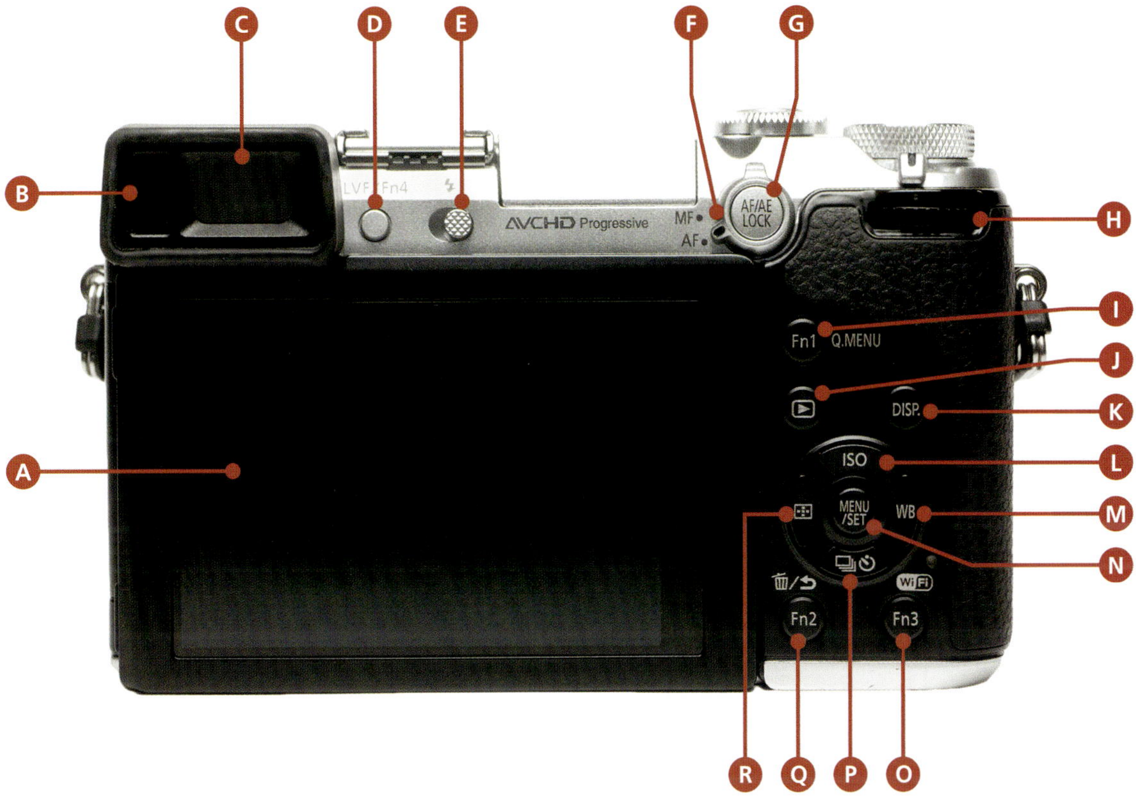

A LCD Screen	G AF/AE Lock	M White Balance Button (▶)
B Eye Sensor	H Rear Dial	N Menu/Set Button
C Viewfinder	I Fn1 – Q.Menu	O Fn3 – Wi-Fi Button
D LVF/ Fn4	J Playback Button	P Drive Mode Button (▼)
E Flash Pop-Up Button	K DISP Button	Q Fn2 – Trash/ Return
F Focus Mode Lever	L ISO Button (▲)	R AF Area Mode Button (◀)

Poring Over the Camera

GX7 Top

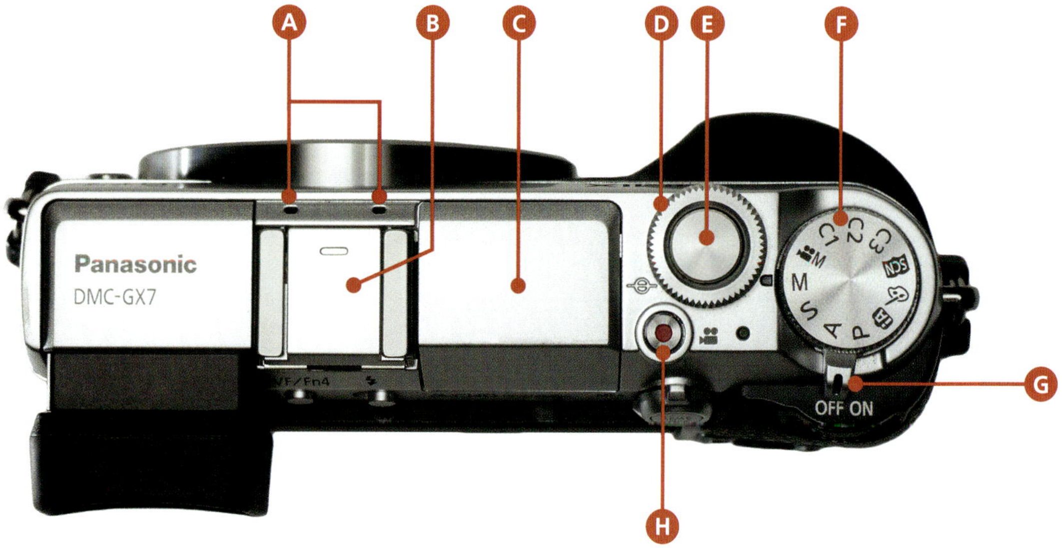

A Stereo Microphones
B Hot Shoe
C Pop-Up Flash
D Front Dial
E Shutter Button
F Mode Dial
G Power Switch
H Motion Picture Button

GM1 Front

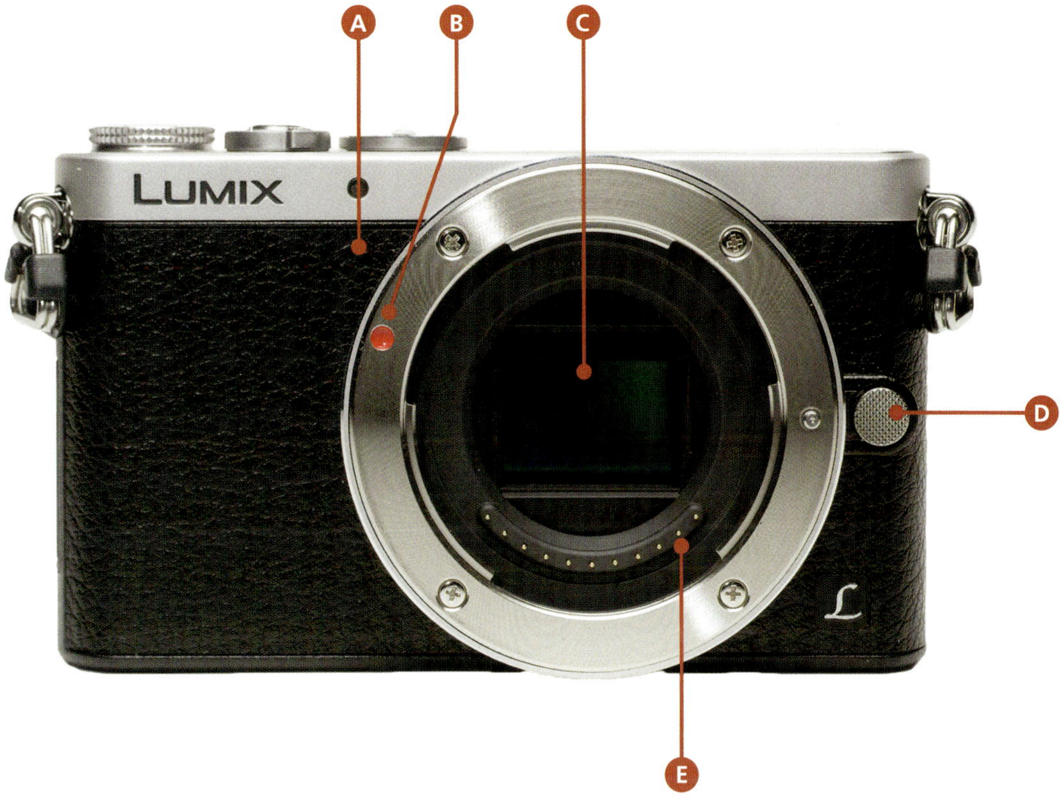

A AF Illuminator/ Self-Timer Indicator
B Lens Fitting Mark
C Sensor
D Lens Release Button
E Lens Contacts

GM1 Back

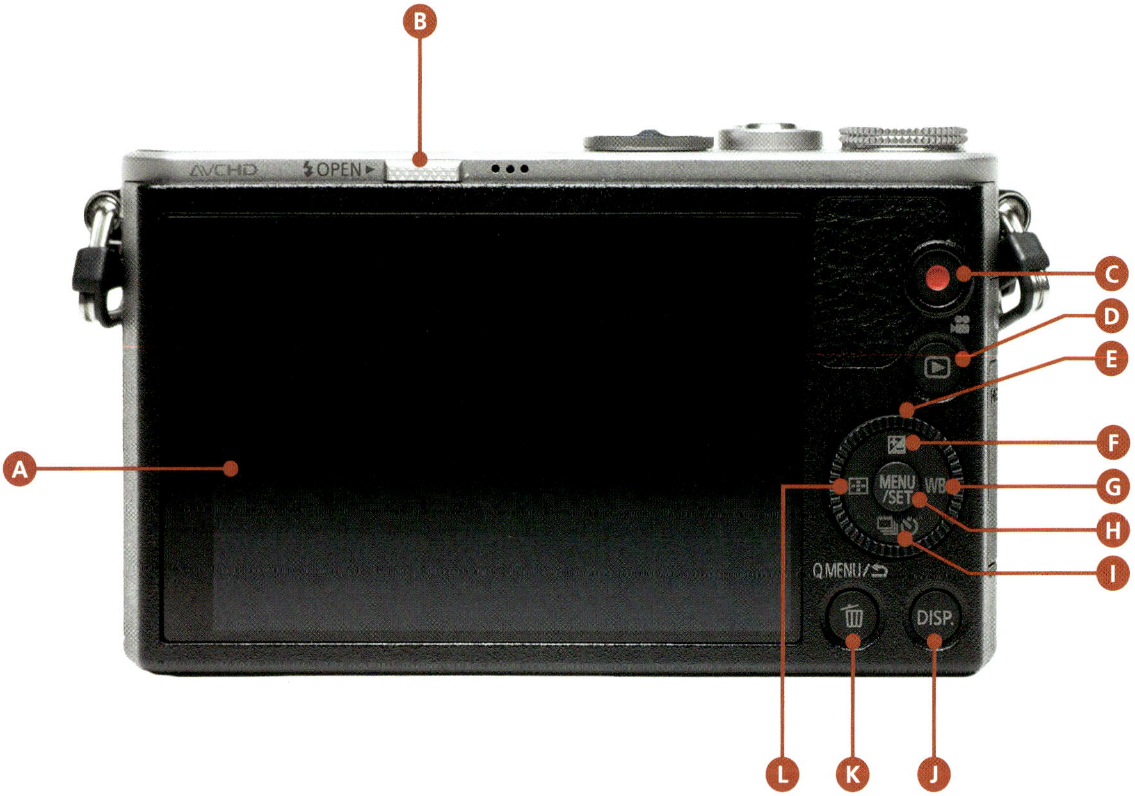

A LCD Screen
B Flash Pop-Up Button
C Motion Picture Button
D Playback Button
E Control Dial
F Exposure Compensation Button (▲)
G White Balance Button (►)
H Menu/Set Button
I Drive Mode Button (▼)
J DISP Button
K Q.Menu/ Trash/ Return Button
L AF Area Mode Button (◄)

GM1 Top

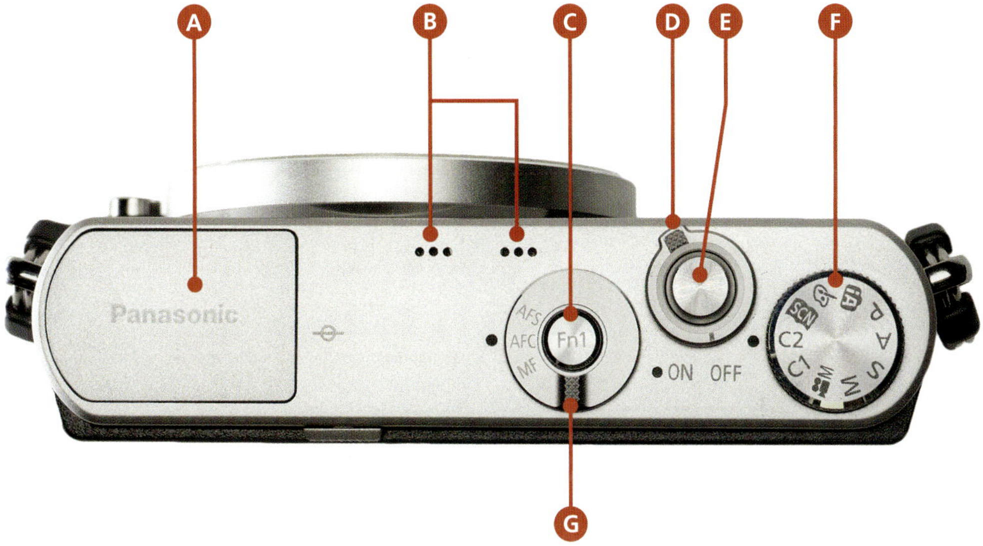

A Pop-Up Flash
B Stereo Microphones
C Function ButtonFn1
D Power Switch
E Shutter Button
F Mode Dial
G Focus Mode Lever

1. Charge Your Battery

I know that this will be one of the hardest things for you to do because you really want to start shooting, but a little patience will pay off later.

When you first open your camera and slide the battery into the battery slot, you will be pleased to find that there is probably juice in the battery and you can start shooting right away. Resist the temptation, and instead get out the battery charger and give that power cell a full charge. Not only will this give you more time to shoot later on, but it will also start the battery off on the right foot. No matter what claims the manufacturers make about battery life and battery memory, I always find I get better life and performance when I charge my batteries fully and then use them right down to the point where they have nothing left to give. To check your battery's level, insert it into the camera, turn on the camera, and look for the battery indicator in the upper-right corner of the LCD screen (**Figure 1.1**).

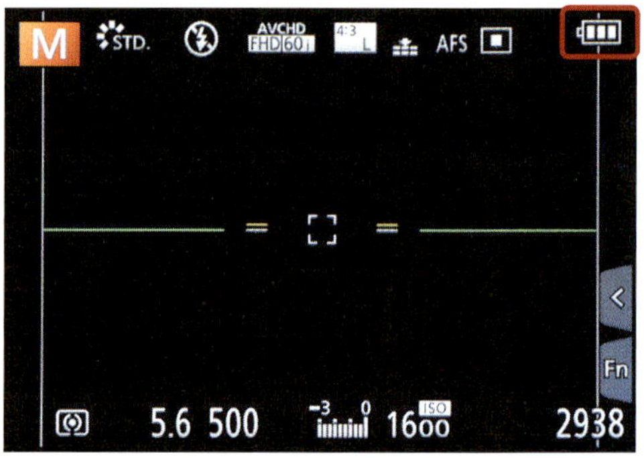

Figure 1.1 The LCD screen shows how much charge is left on your battery.

Keeping a backup battery

If I were to suggest just one accessory that you should buy for your camera, it would probably be a second battery. Nothing stinks more than being out in the field and having your camera die. Keeping a fully charged battery in your bag will give you the confidence that you can keep on shooting without fail. Not only will this extend your shooting time, but alternating between batteries will help lengthen their lives. Rechargeable batteries have a lifespan, and using them half as much will only lengthen their usefulness.

2. Take Advantage of the Touchscreen

There are more and more cameras using touchscreen LCDs. Some let you use the touchscreen to choose a focus point or fire the shutter, and others use onscreen buttons to augment the physical buttons and dials on the camera. Your GX7/GM1 uses the touch-sensitive LCD for all of that and more. The physical buttons on the GM1 are limited by its small size, but the touchscreen allows you to adjust your settings quickly and easily.

Even with the excellent external controls on the GX7, the touch interface makes focusing, changing settings, and navigating the menus much quicker and easier than on a conventional control setup.

Here are my favorite touchscreen tips divided into three sections: shooting mode, playback mode, and navigating the menus. Many of the controls are obvious, but there are some cool tricks you can do with your LCD that you might not realize.

Shooting mode

The most obvious use for the touchscreen is assigning the focus point. I will discuss the different autofocus (AF) area modes later in this chapter, but all the AF modes can take advantage of touchscreen focusing. All you have to do is touch the screen where you want the camera to focus. If you are using Face Detection or 1-Area focus, you can change the size of the focus point by turning the Rear dial (GM1: Command dial) after you touch the screen to set the focus point.

You can also use the touchscreen to activate the shutter and take a photo. Touch the < on the screen to find the touch shutter control (**Figure 1.2**), and touch the icon to activate it. With the touch shutter on, the camera will focus and take a photo when you touch the LCD.

The touchscreen lets you change settings very quickly while you're shooting. When you press the Q.menu button to access menu items, you can simply touch your choices on the LCD (**Figure 1.3**). The same thing goes for AF modes, white balance, exposure compensation, and so on.

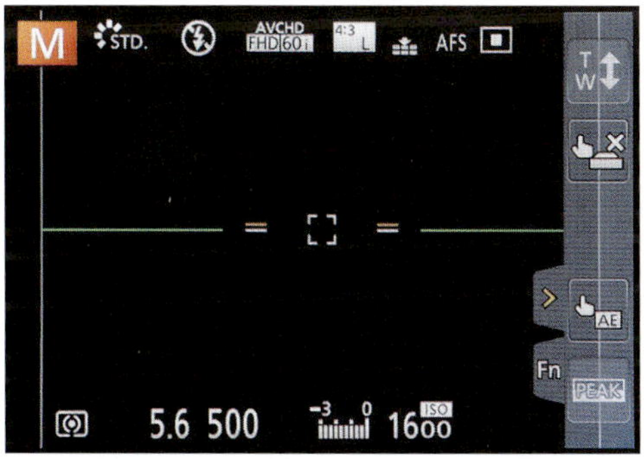

Figure 1.2 **Find the touch shutter function under the > icon on the right side of the LCD.**

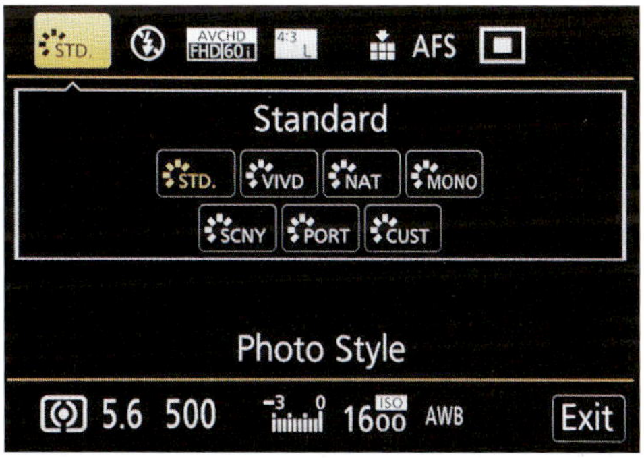

Figure 1.3 **The touchscreen lets you change settings quickly and easily.**

Playback mode

When you're reviewing your images, the touchscreen on your GX7/GM1 behaves much like your smartphone. Once you press the playback button, swipe with your finger to go from one photo to the next. You can also pinch to zoom in to the image and make sure the photo is in focus. While the image is zoomed in, move the enlarged part of the photo by dragging with your finger. When you're done, double-tap the screen to zoom out to full size.

Navigating the menus

Along with touch focus, I find that navigating the menus on the GX7/GM1 is one of the most useful functions of the touchscreen. Touching the menu items to change settings is much faster than using the cursor buttons to scroll through the menus. You must press the Menu/Set button to bring up the menu, but after that the touch interface is the way to go (**Figure 1.4**).

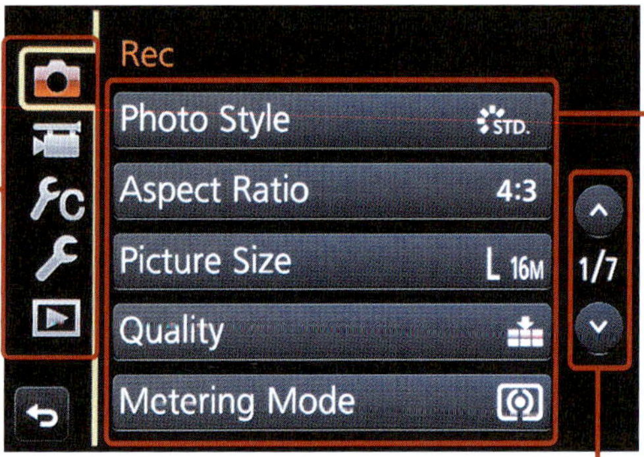

Figure 1.4

3. Custom Functions

I don't recommend worrying too much about all the custom functions and settings when you get a new camera. You should concentrate on learning about exposure and composition a lot more than your camera's bells and whistles. That said, there are a few settings that will improve your GX7/GM1 out of the box. I don't have the space in this book to go over every menu option, but these suggestions will help you make the most of your GX7/GM1. Press the Menu/Set button to open the menus. We will start with the Rec menu and go down the list. (Some of these options are not available in the automatic modes.)

The Rec menu

On page 5/7 you'll find ISO increments. Change this to 1/3EV so you have the same controls for ISO that you have for aperture and shutter speed (**Figure 1.5**).

Find Color Space on page 6/7 and change it from sRGB to Adobe RGB (**Figure 1.6**). I recommend using the Adobe RGB color space because it captures more color information and makes the most of the camera's sensor; it is the largest color space your camera offers. sRGB is rather small, and its purpose is to produce colors consistent with those on most computer monitors.

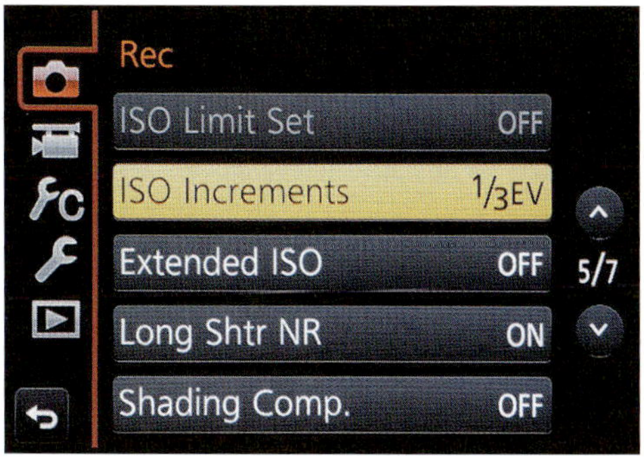

Figure 1.5 **Adjust the ISO in 1/3-stop increments.**

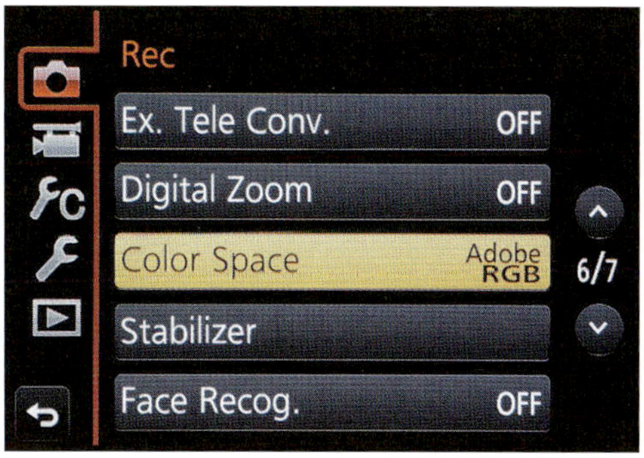

Figure 1.6 **Change your color space to Adobe RGB.**

The Custom menu

Navigate to page 4/8 (GM1: 4/7) and turn Highlight on (**Figure 1.7**). This will activate the highlight overexposure warning, or "blinkies," when you are reviewing your images.

On page 5/8 (GM1: 4/7) you will see Constant Preview (**Figure 1.8**). Turn this on to see the effect of your aperture and shutter speed settings on the LCD before you take a photo in Manual exposure mode. I usually keep this on unless I'm using very long shutter speeds.

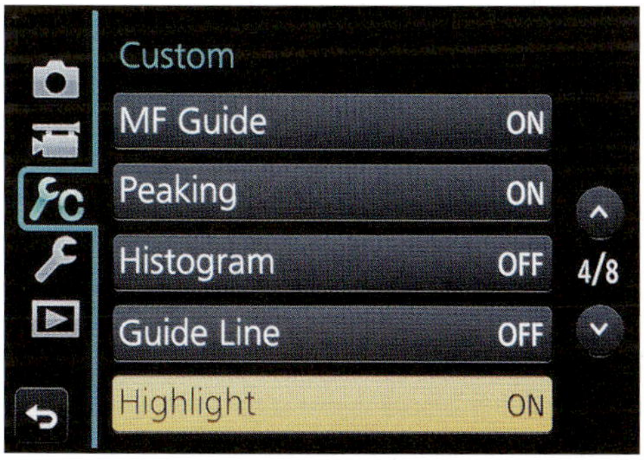

Figure 1.7 **Turn on the "blinkies."**

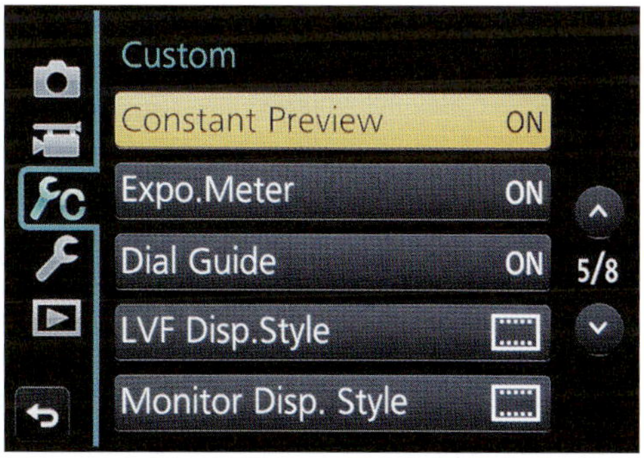

Figure 1.8 **Use Constant Preview to see the effect of your exposure changes.**

Go to page 7/8 (GM1: 6/7) and find Q.Menu. Change this from Preset to Custom (**Figure 1.9**). I discuss setting up the custom Q.Menu in the next section.

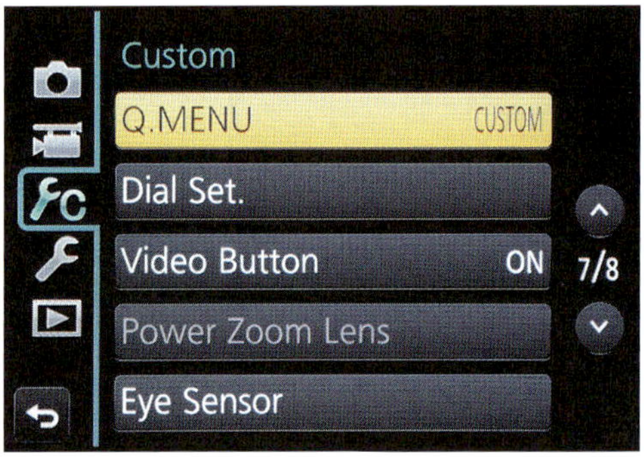

Figure 1.9 Turn on the custom Q.menu.

The Setup menu

There is only one setting in the Setup menu that I would change before I start shooting, and it's the same thing I do when I get any new camera: turn off the focus beep. By default, the camera makes a loud beep to let you know that it has locked focus. You can forget about taking candid shots of people with the beep on, and it is a definite no-no for shooting wildlife. I can see the focus point turn green when the camera locks focus, so I turn the beep off and forget it. Go to page 1/6 of the Setup menu and select Beep, then Beep Volume (**Figure 1.10**). Choose the speaker with the X through it to silence the beep. While you're at it, select E-Shutter Volume and silence it as well.

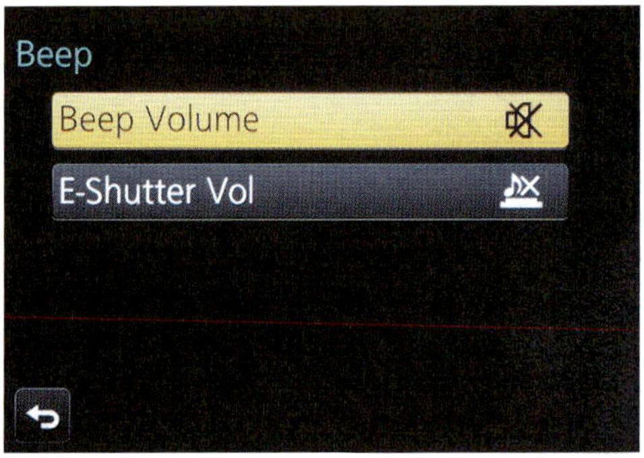

Figure 1.10 Turn off the beep!

4. Configure Your LCD and Viewfinder

If you are used to looking through the viewfinder of an older film camera or a more traditionally styled DSLR, you might find using an LCD or electronic viewfinder (EVF) a bit odd. Instead of looking through the lens via a series of mirrors and glass, with both the LCD and EVF you are looking at an electronic display akin to a computer monitor. Shooting with this takes some getting used to, but after a few rounds of shooting with the camera, you might never want to go back to an optical viewfinder.

One feature common to both the LCD and the EVF that makes the camera appealing and very usable is the set of different display modes you can activate. When you turn the camera on, you'll notice that the LCD on the back of the camera projects the scene that the lens is pointed at, along with some basic exposure information. When you put your eye up to the EVF (GX7 only), it automatically switches on and shows you the same information as the LCD. If you press the DISP button, you can cycle through the five display modes (the GM1 has four display modes). All modes display shutter speed, aperture, ISO, and exposure compensation along the bottom of the screen. The default mode displays exposure mode, photo style, flash setting, movie format, image size, image quality focus mode, drive mode, and battery life along the top of the display, and metering mode and shots remaining along with the exposure information at the bottom of the display (**A**).

Press the DISP button once, and the screen will display only the basic exposure information (**B**).

A second press of the button shows all of the camera settings along with the tilt sensor (**C**). The tilt sensor helps you keep your camera level and plumb.

Press the DISP button a third time to show only the basic exposure information and the tilt sensor (**D**).

A

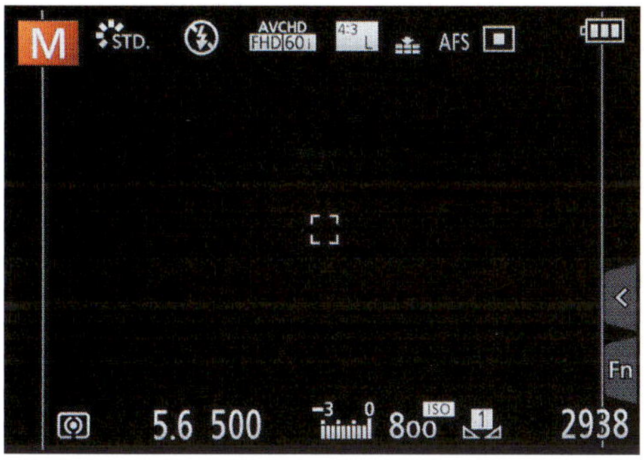

B

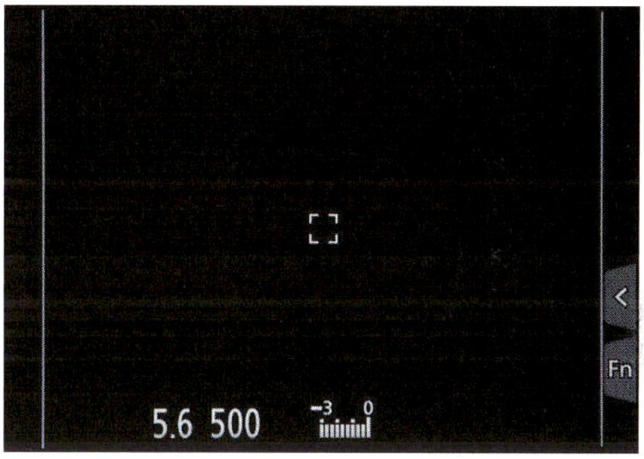

C

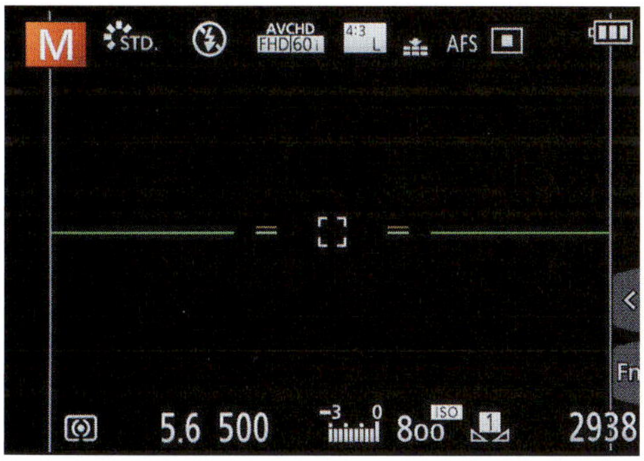

D

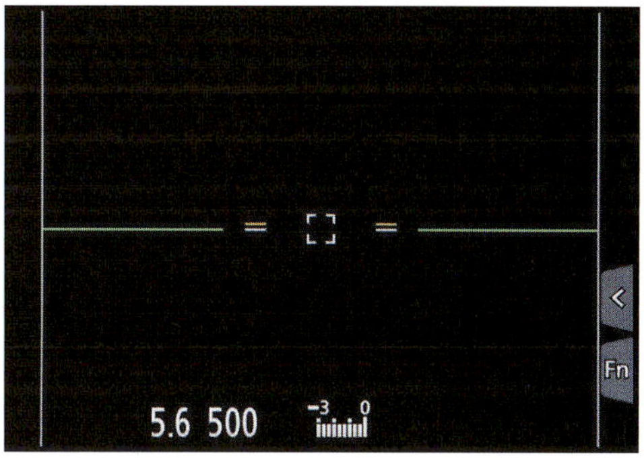

On the GX7, the fourth press of the DISP button shows only the camera settings on the LCD without a Live View image (**E**). In this display mode, you can see a Live View image only by looking through the EVF. Touch any of the settings on the LCD to make adjustments, and the LCD automatically turns off when you use the EVF to prevent accidentally touching the screen and changing your settings.

E

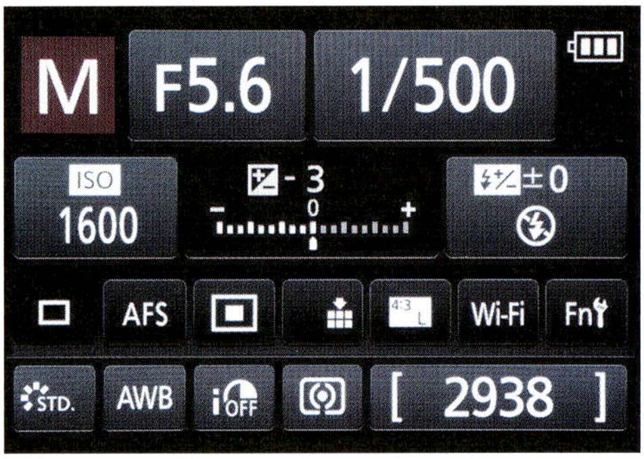

Press the DISP button once again to turn the LCD monitor off and use the EVF with a basic exposure information overlay. This display is reminiscent of what you might see while looking through the viewfinder of a traditional DSLR.

Custom Q.Menu

I suggested you turn on the custom Q.Menu in the previous section. By default, the Q.menu is activated by pressing the Fn1 button on the GX7 or the trashcan button on the GM1. The preset Q.menu gives you convenient access to many camera settings, but by using the Custom setting you can tailor the Q.menu to the settings that are most important to your personal shooting style.

The custom Q.menu allows you to drag and drop the settings that you want to include in the menu and arrange them so they are in just the right order (**Figure 1.11**). Don't worry if you don't know how you might want to rearrange the Q.menu yet—when you first turn on the custom Q.menu it is set up just like the preset Q.menu. As you use your camera, you may find settings that you frequently go into the menu to change. For example, if you find yourself using the electronic shutter a lot you can add the electronic shutter control to the custom Q.menu. You'll find a complete list of functions available in the custom Q.menu on page 45 in your GX7 owner's manual, or on page 41 for the GM1.

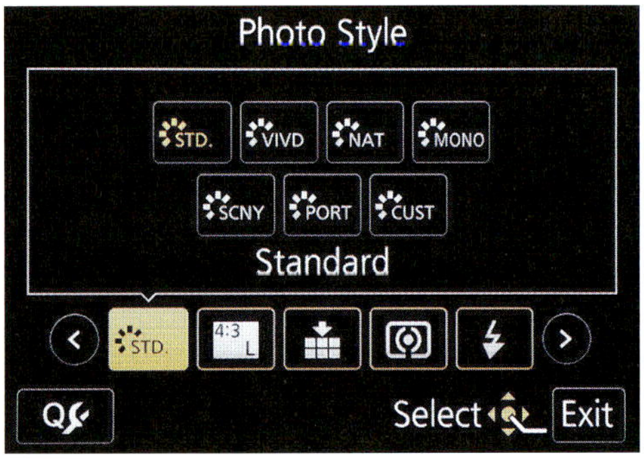

Figure 1.11 The custom Q.menu lets you put your most-used functions within easy reach. Touch the wrench icon in the lower-left corner of the LCD to edit the menu.

Function buttons

The GX7/GM1 has five function (Fn) buttons on the LCD (**Figure 1.12**). You can assign a variety of settings to these Fn buttons, and they stay out of your way until you touch the Fn icon on the right side of the touchscreen. Assigning the Wi-Fi function to one of these onscreen buttons is a great way to keep that function handy while freeing up one of the physical buttons on your camera for a function you use more often. To assign the Fn buttons, press Menu/Set > Custom > Fn Button Set. The GX7 has the option to assign different functions in Rec (shooting) mode and playback mode. From there, simply touch the Fn button you would like to assign and choose a function from the list. For a list of available Fn button settings, look on page 48 of your GX7 owner's manual, or page 43 for the GM1.

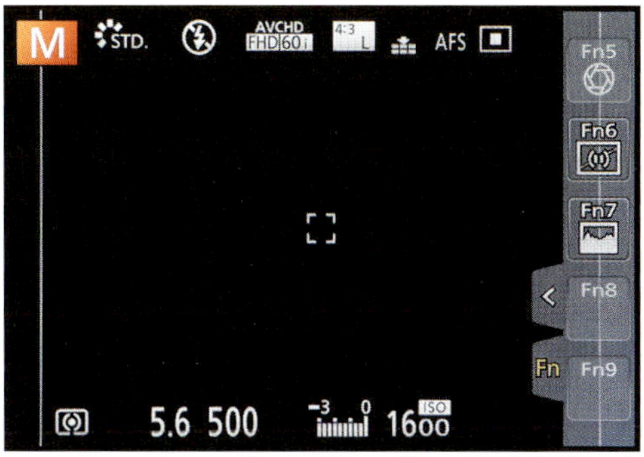

Figure 1.12 Use the five onscreen function buttons for settings you use frequently.

5. Set Your JPEG Image Quality

Your new GX7/GM1 has a number of image quality settings to choose from, and you can adjust them according to your needs. Most people shoot with the JPEG option because it allows them to capture a large number of photos on their memory cards. The problem is that unless you understand how JPEG works, you might be degrading the quality of your images without realizing it.

The JPEG (Joint Photographic Experts Group) format has been around since about 1994 and was developed as a method of reducing large file sizes while retaining the original image information. (Technically, JPEG isn't even a file format—it's a mathematical equation for reducing image file sizes—but to keep things simple, we'll just refer to it as a file format.) The problem with JPEG is that, in order to reduce file size, it has to throw away some of the information. This is referred to as "lossy compression." This is important to understand, because while you can fit more images on your memory card by choosing a lower-quality JPEG setting, you will also be reducing the quality of your image. This effect becomes more apparent as you enlarge your pictures.

The JPEG file format also has one other characteristic: To apply the compression to the image before final storage on your memory card, the camera has to apply all of the image processing first. Image processing involves such factors as sharpening, color adjustment, contrast adjustment, noise reduction, and so on. Many photographers now prefer to use the RAW file format to get greater control over the image processing. We will take a closer look at this in Chapter 2, but for now let's just make sure that we are using the best-quality JPEG possible.

The GX7/GM1 has three sizes for the JPEG format and two quality settings. Picture size is the physical size of the image: Large (L), Medium (M), or Small (S). Large takes advantage of all 16 megapixels of the GX7/GM1's sensor, Medium provides you roughly half of that, and Small provides you an image that is 4 megapixels. The two quality settings are Fine and Standard; I encourage you to use only the Fine option. Standard is more compressed and does not capture the image with as high a quality as Fine. The default settings use the highest quality and the largest size: Fine and Large. After all, our goal is to make big, beautiful photographs, so why start the process with a lower-quality, smaller image?

Setting the picture size and image quality

1. Press the Menu/Set button and select the Rec menu.
2. To select the picture size, navigate to Picture Size and press Menu/Set.
3. Touch L on the screen to select the Large picture size (**A**).
4. To select the JPEG quality, navigate to Quality and press Menu/Set.
5. The Fine JPEG setting is the arrow with two rows of blocks (**B**). The other option I recommend is the RAW+Fine JPEG setting.
6. Press the shutter button halfway to return to shooting.

A

B

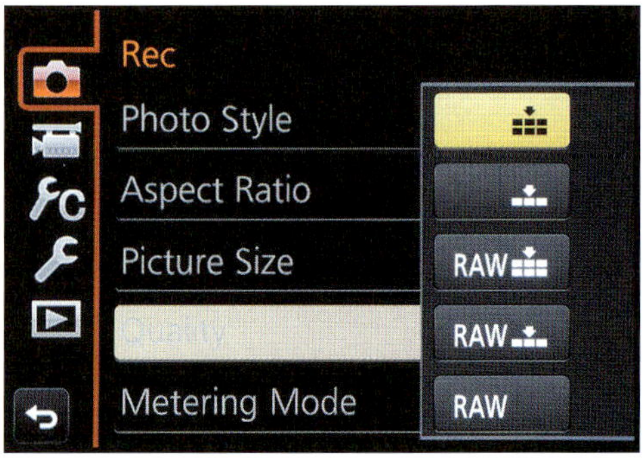

Manual callout

There are four different aspect ratios to suit different printing or playback methods. There is a chart of the dimensions for each aspect ratio on page 139 in your GX7 manual, or on page 128 for the GM1.

For a chart that shows the image quality settings with the number of possible shots for each setting, turn to page 36 in your GX7 owner's manual, or to page 33 for the GM1.

6. Turn Off the Auto ISO Setting

The ISO setting in your camera allows you to choose the level of sensitivity of the camera sensor to light. The ability to change this sensitivity is one of the biggest advantages to using a digital camera. In the days of film cameras, you had to choose the ISO by film type. This meant that if you wanted to shoot in lower light, you had to replace the film in the camera with one that had a higher ISO. So not only did you have to carry different types of film, but you also had to remove one roll from the camera to replace it with another, even if you hadn't used up the current roll. Now all we have to do is go to the menu and select the appropriate ISO.

Having this flexibility is a powerful option, but remember that the ISO setting has a direct bearing on the quality of the final image. The higher the ISO, the more digital noise the image will contain. Since our goal is to produce high-quality photographs, it is important that we get control over all of the camera controls and bend them to our will. When you turn your camera on for the first time, the ISO will be set to Auto. This means that the camera is determining how much light is available and will choose what it believes is the correct ISO setting. Since you want to use the lowest ISO possible, you will need to turn this setting off and manually select the appropriate ISO.

Which ISO you choose depends on your level of available or ambient light. For sunny days or very bright scenes, use a low ISO such as 200. As the level of light is reduced, raise the ISO level. Cloudy days or indoor scenes might require you to use ISO 400. Low-light scenes, such as when you are shooting at night, will mean you need to bump up that ISO to 1600 or higher. The thing to remember is to shoot with the lowest setting possible for maximum quality. Later we will cover some other specifics of exposure so that you know how and why to raise your ISO.

Give your GM1 an ISO button

The GM1 is a great little camera, but it doesn't have as many external controls as the GX7. The Fn1 button on top of the camera activates the Wi-Fi function by default, but I recommend that you change the function to something that you will almost certainly use more often. Press the Menu/Set button and select the Custom menu. Scroll down to Fn Button Set, and press Menu/Set to see all the available Fn buttons (**Figure 1.13**). The Fn1 button is an actual button on the camera, and the others are accessed on the touchscreen.

Select the Fn1 button and assign the ISO function to it. While you're at it, assign the Wi-Fi function to one of the touchscreen buttons for easy access. For the rest of the book, I will refer to the Fn1 button on the GM1 as the ISO button.

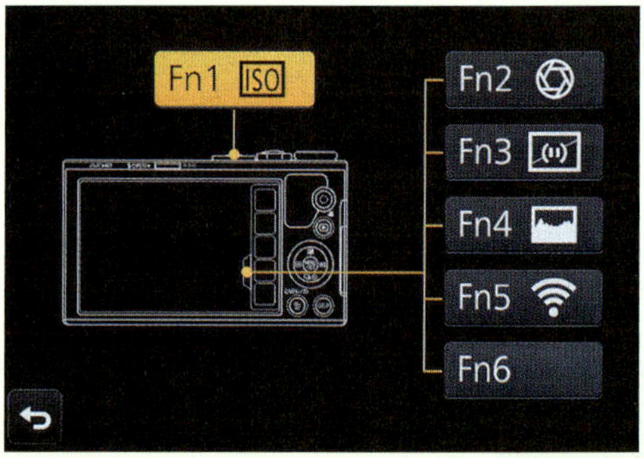

Figure 1.13 Turn the Fn1 button on your GM1 into an ISO button.

Setting the ISO

1. Activate the camera by pressing the shutter release button halfway.
2. Press the ISO button (▲) on the back of the camera.

   GM1: See the sidebar "Give your GM1 an ISO button," then press Fn1 to adjust the ISO.
3. Rotate the Rear dial to highlight the desired ISO (GM1: Control dial) (**A**).
4. Press Menu/Set to lock in your selection and return to shooting.

A

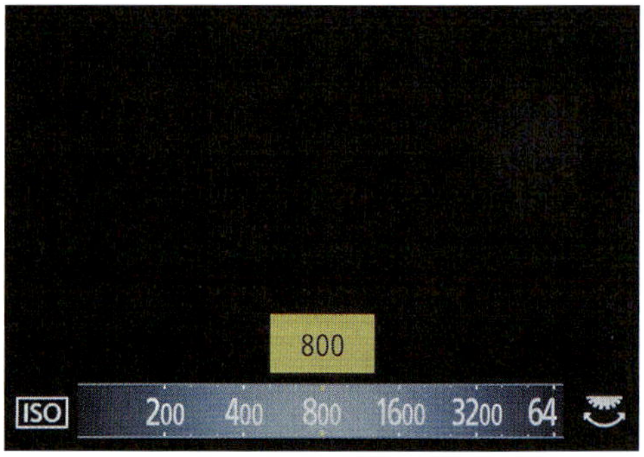

Noise

Noise is the enemy of digital photography, but it has nothing to do with the loudness of your camera operation. It is a term that refers to the electronic artifacts that appear as speckles in your image. They generally appear in darker shadow areas and are a result of the camera trying to amplify the signal to produce visible information. The more the image needs to be amplified—e.g., raising the sensitivity through higher ISOs—the greater the amount of noise there will be.

Set your ISO on the fly

By following the steps above, you can change the ISO without taking your eye from the viewfinder. When you press the ISO button on your GX7, the ISO information will appear in the EVF. You can turn the Rear dial and press it in to set the ISO. This will get easier to do as you become more familiar with the camera buttons. In fact, anything that can be displayed on the LCD can be displayed in the viewfinder, so you can make many more changes while keeping your eye to the viewfinder. Try it out!

7. Set the Correct White Balance

White balance correction is the process of rendering accurate colors in your final image. Most people don't even notice that light has different color characteristics, because the human eye automatically adjusts to changes in color temperature—so quickly, in fact, that everything looks correct in a matter of milliseconds.

When color film ruled the world, photographers would select which film to use depending on what their light source was going to be. The most common film was balanced for daylight, but you could also buy film that was color balanced for tungsten light sources. Most other lighting situations had to be handled by using color filters over the lens. This process was necessary for the photographer's final image to show the correct color balance of a scene.

Your camera has the ability to perform this same process automatically, but you can also choose to override it and set it manually. Guess which method we are going to use? You are catching on fast! Once again, your photography should be all about maintaining control over everything that influences your final image.

Luckily, you don't need to have a deep understanding of color temperatures to control your camera's white balance. The choices are given to you in terms that are easy to relate to and that will make things pretty simple. Your white balance choices are:

- **Auto (AWB):** The default setting for your camera. It is also the setting used by all the automatic modes (see Chapter 3).
- **Daylight:** Most often used for general daylight/sunlit shooting.
- **Cloudy:** The choice for overcast or very cloudy days. This and the Shade setting will eliminate the blue color cast from your images.
- **Shade:** Used when working in shaded areas that are still using sunlight as the dominant light source.
- **Incandescent:** Used for any occasion where you are using regular household-type bulbs for your light source. Tungsten is a very warm light source and will result in a yellow/orange cast if you don't correct for it.
- **Flash:** Used whenever you're using the built-in flash or a flash on the hot shoe. You should select this white balance to adjust for the slightly cooler light that comes from using a flash. (The hot shoe is the small bracket located on the top of your GX7; it rests just to the right of the viewfinder. This bracket is used for attaching a more powerful flash to the camera; see Chapter 8.)
- **Custom:** Uses a white balance determined by your input (explained below). You can save two custom white balance settings.
- **Color temperature:** Used to manually select your camera's color temperature in Kelvin. If you know what the color temperature of your light source is, you can manually create a white balance setting that is specifically for that light source. In order to take advantage of this setting, you must press ▲ after you highlight it. From there, you can use the ▲ and ▼ buttons to manipulate the white balance.

Setting the white balance

1. After turning on or waking the camera, select one of the professional exposure modes, such as P (you can't set the white balance when using the auto modes).
2. Press the WB button (▶) and turn the Rear dial (GM1: Command dial) to select a WB preset (**A**).

A

3. Press Menu/Set to lock in your selection.
4. Check the LCD or electronic viewfinder to ensure that the proper white balance is selected.
5. To set a custom white balance, select one of the custom presets and press ▲. Fill the square on the screen (**B**) with a white balance target (you can use a gray card or even a white piece of paper), and touch Set to save the custom setting.

B

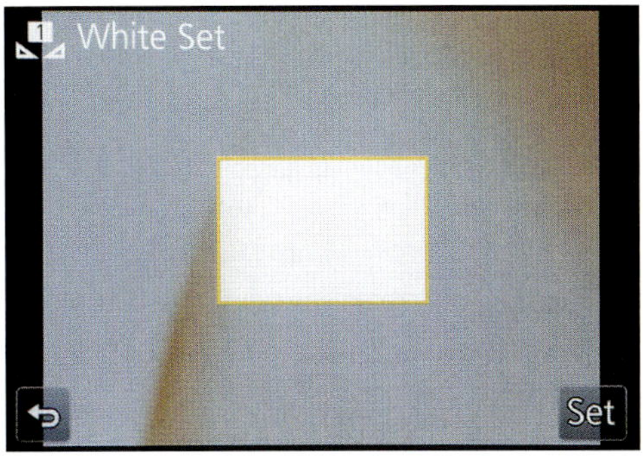

White balance and the temperature of color

When you select white balances, you are selecting changes in the color temperature of your frame, which is measured along the Kelvin (K) temperature scale. Kelvin temperatures refer to colors in the visible spectrum. The visible spectrum is the range of light that the human eye can see (think of a rainbow or the color bands that come out of a spectrum). The Kelvin temperature scale identifies the thermodynamic temperature of a given color of light. Put simply, reds and yellows are "warm" and greens and blues are "cool." Even more confusing can be the actual temperature ratings. Warm temperatures are typically lower on the Kelvin scale, ranging from 3000 degrees to 5000 degrees, while cool temperatures run from 5500 degrees to around 10000 degrees. Take a look at this list for an example of Kelvin temperature properties.

Kelvin Temperature Properties			
Flames	1700K–1900K	Daylight	5000K
Incandescent bulb	2800K–3300K	Camera flash	5500K
White fluorescent	4000K	Overcast sky	6000K
Moonlight	4000K	Open shade	7000K

The most important thing to remember here is how the color temperature of light will affect the look of your images. If something is "warm," it will look reddish-yellow, and if something is "cool," it will have a bluish cast.

8. Set Your Focus Mode

The GX7/GM1 focusing system is renowned for being very fast and very accurate. Like most camera functions, you get the best results if you learn how to take control and choose your own settings. The GX7/GM1 has three autofocus (AF) modes and five AF Area modes. It can be a bit confusing since both settings are referred to as autofocus modes. Basically, the three AF modes (AFS, AFF, and AFC) determine how the camera focuses, and the five AF Area modes (Face Detection, AF tracking, 23-Area, 1-Area, and Pinpoint) determine where the camera focuses.

The GX7 and GM1 have focus mode controls on the outside of the camera. The GX7 has an AF/MF lever to switch from autofocus to manual focus, and the GM1 has a lever that switches between AFS, AFC, and MF. Changing the AF mode on the GX7 affects the AF setting on the focus mode lever. The GM1 allows you to assign either the AFS or AFF setting to the AFS position on the focus mode lever.

Throughout this book I will mention different AF settings and how they relate to different subjects. I generally use AFS and 1-Area focus for my everyday focus settings. The AFS mode locks focus when I press the shutter button halfway and stays locked until I either take the shot or release the shutter button. The 1-Area AF area mode allows me to pick a specific spot I want to focus on by touching the LCD.

Setting the autofocus mode and autofocus area mode

1. To select the AF mode, press Menu/Set and then select the Custom menu.
2. Navigate to AFS/AFF/AFC (GM1: AFS/AFF) and choose AFS (**A**).
3. To select the 1-Area AF Area mode, press the AF Area mode button (◀) and touch 1-Area on the screen (**B**).

A

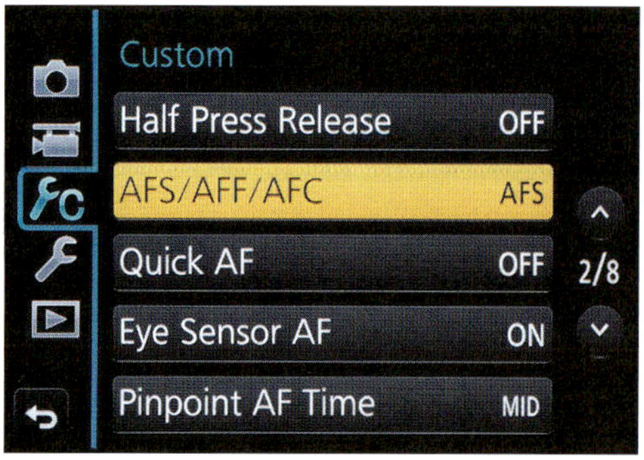

B

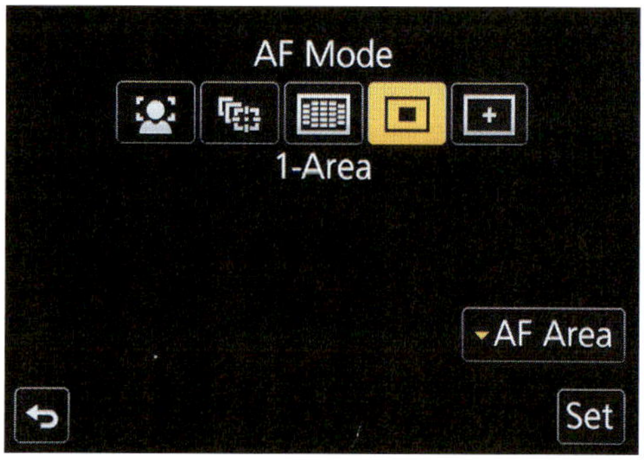

4. Press the shutter button halfway to return to shooting mode.
5. You can touch anywhere on the LCD to pick a focus point, and turn the Rear dial (GM1: Control dial) to change the size of the focus point. Press the shutter button halfway to focus.

Manual focus

I'll be honest: Autofocus is awesome! It truly rocked the photography world in the late 1970s and early 1980s. I'm in autofocus 90 percent of the time, and I'm willing to bet that many other photographers are the same. The technology has developed so much in the past few decades that we now talk about focusing in milliseconds and we are frustrated when it doesn't lock on. This latter situation—and when shooting macro images or static subject matter—is when switching to manual focus comes in handy.

The GX7 and GM1 make it easy to switch to manual focus by moving the focus mode lever to MF. In manual focus mode with most lenses, you turn the focus ring on the lens to focus. With the GM1's tiny kit lens, you use a sliding focus switch on the touchscreen to manually focus (**Figure 1.14**).

The GX7 and GM1 have two features that aid in manually focusing. Focus peaking shows a colored highlight on the EVF or LCD around the in-focus area of the image. You can change the focus peaking level and the color of the highlight by pressing Menu/Set > Custom > Peaking > Set (**Figure 1.15**).

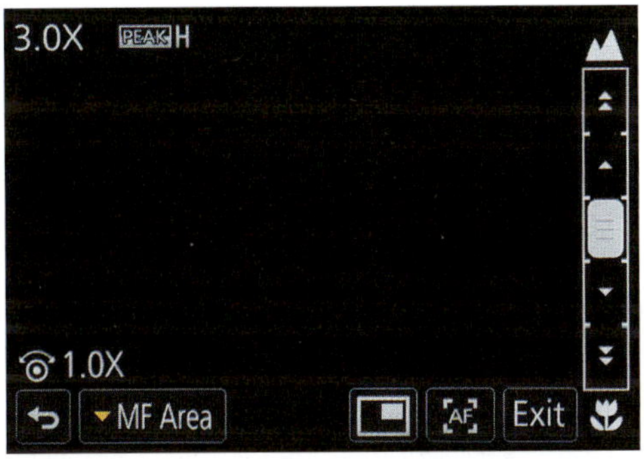

Figure 1.14 Use the touchscreen to manually focus the GM1's kit lens.

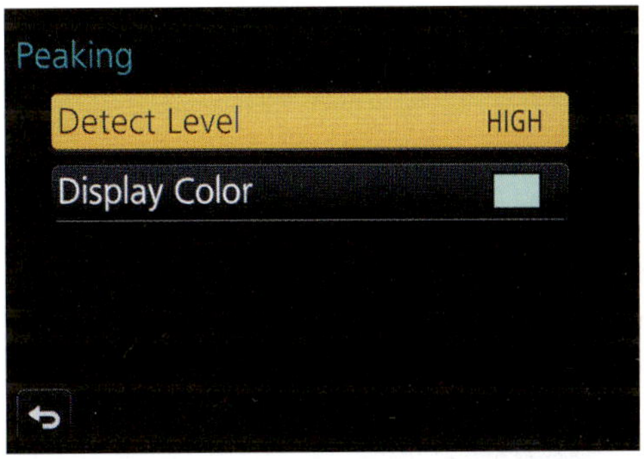

Figure 1.15 You can adjust your focus peaking settings.

The other function that aids in manually focusing is called MF Assist. This feature enlarges a portion of the image so you can focus more accurately. I find the default MF Assist function a bit distracting, as it blows up part of the image when you turn the focus ring on the lens. I recommend you change the MF Assist function by pressing Menu/Set > Custom > MF Assist (**Figure 1.16**). I like to assign the function to the AF Area mode button so I can activate it when I need it.

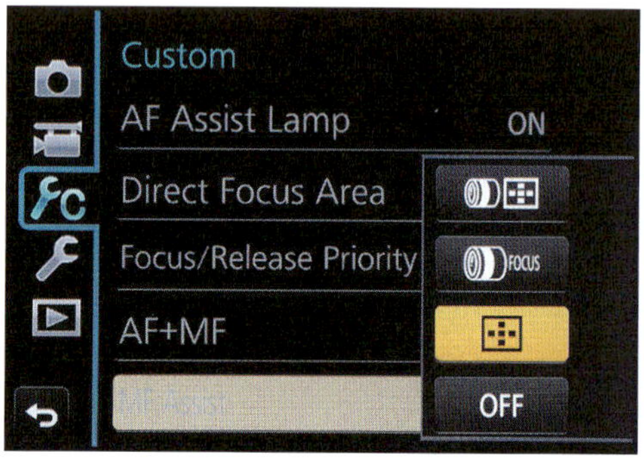

Figure 1.16 **I like to assign the MF Assist function to the AF Area mode button.**

9. Review Your Shots

One of the greatest features of digital cameras is their ability to give us instant feedback. By reviewing your images on the camera's LCD screen, you can instantly tell if you got your shot. This visual feedback allows you to make adjustments on the fly and make certain that you nailed the shot before moving on.

When you first press the shutter release button, your camera quickly processes your shot and then displays the image on the rear LCD display. The default duration setting for that display is 2 seconds. I don't mind this "quick glance" method, because it allows me to get back to shooting more quickly. But if you want more time for visual feedback, you can always set your review time to 3, 4, or 5 seconds.

Changing the image auto review duration

1. Press the Menu/Set button and select the Custom menu.
2. Scroll down to Auto Review, and press Menu/Set (**A**).
3. Use the Rear dial (GM1: Control wheel) or the ▲ and ▼ buttons to highlight and select the desired duration (**B**).
4. Press the Menu/Set button to make your selection, and press the shutter button to continue shooting.

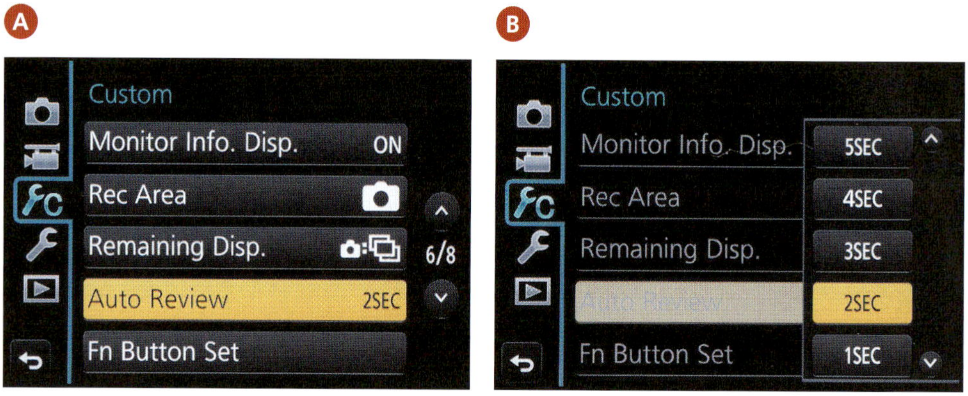

Now that you have the image review time set, let's check out some of the other visual information that will help you when shooting.

Press the Playback button to review your images on the LCD. There are five display modes, and each gives you a different amount of information. The default view (**Figure 1.17**) displays your image with basic exposure information.

To get more visual feedback, press the DISP button. Press it once to get detailed exposure information, plus camera settings like exposure mode, image quality, and so on (**Figure 1.18**).

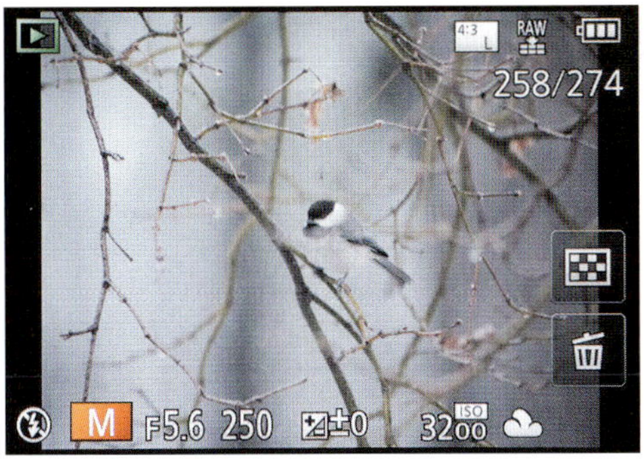

Figure 1.17 **The default display mode on the GX7/GM1**

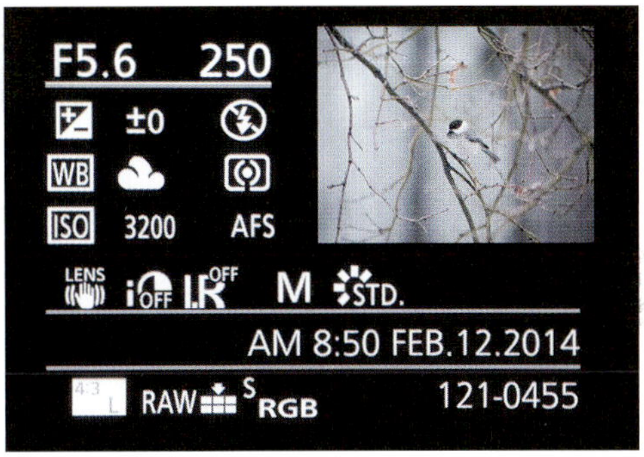

Figure 1.18 **Press the DISP button once to see the detailed information display.**

Pressing the DISP button a second time displays your image along with four histograms (one for each color used to process digital images—red, green, and blue—and one for luminance). The image thumbnail will show areas of overexposure, known as highlight clipping, as blinking black and white. This is commonly referred to as the "blinkies" (**Figure 1.19**).

Press the DISP button again to see your image full-screen with the highlight clipping warning (if you turned on Highlight in the Custom menu).

The final playback screen displays your image full-screen with no information overlay. The trash can and grid icons will disappear after a few seconds (**Figure 1.20**).

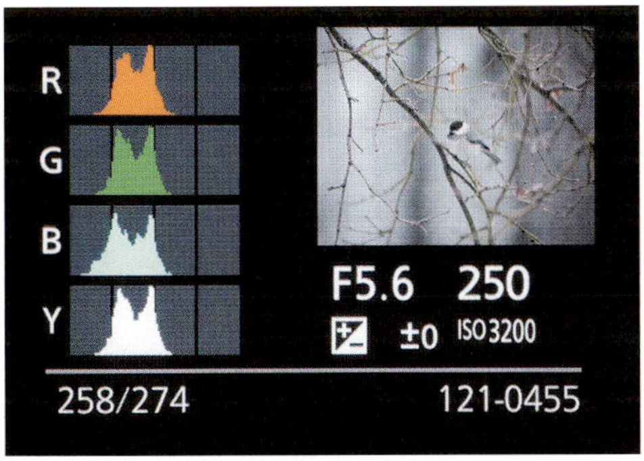

Figure 1.19 **This mode displays your histograms and an overexposure warning.**

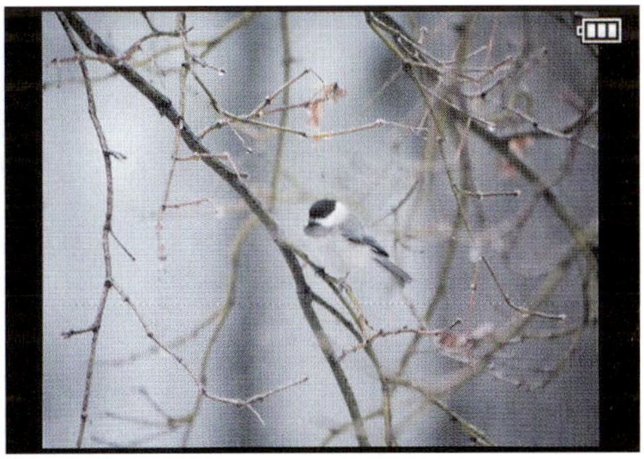

Figure 1.20 **The final monitor screen shows only your image.**

That's a huge amount of information available on a 3-inch screen! Pressing the DISP button while an image is displayed on your LCD screen activates the different display modes. That display mode will remain for all future images until you press the DISP button again. Also, pressing the shutter release button or the Menu button closes the image display. To get your image back up on the LCD screen, simply press the Playback button on the back of the camera.

Deleting Images

Deleting or erasing images is a fairly simple process that is covered on page 80 of your manual (GM1: page 71). To quickly get you on your way, simply press the Playback button and find the picture that you want to delete by turning the Rear dial (GM1: Control dial) or swiping with your finger. Press the Trash button and select Delete Single, Delete Multi, or Delete All (**Figure 1.21**). To delete multiple images, simply touch the images you want to delete and then touch OK on the screen. Touch Yes on the screen to confirm your choice and delete the image(s).

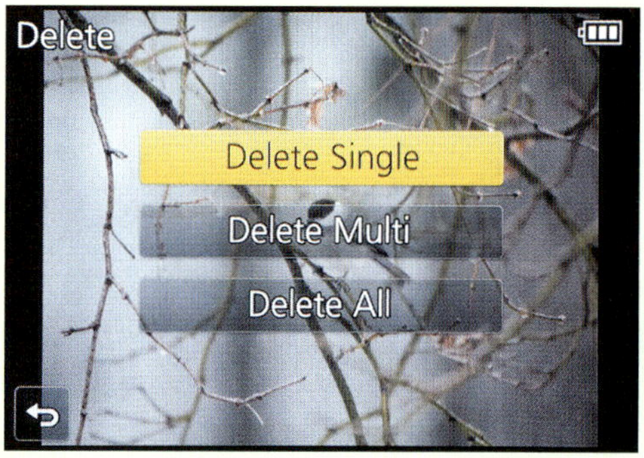

Figure 1.21 **Deleting images on the GX7/GM1 is simple.**

Caution: Once you have deleted an image, it is gone for good. Make sure you don't want it before you drop it in the trash.

The value of the histogram

Simply put, histograms are two-dimensional representations of your images in graph form. There are two different histograms that you should be concerned with: luminance and color. A luminance histogram displays pixel brightness and is most valuable when evaluating your exposures. In **Figure 1.22**, you see what looks like a mountain range. The graph represents the entire tonal range that your camera can capture, from the whitest whites to the blackest blacks. The left side represents black, and the right side represents white.

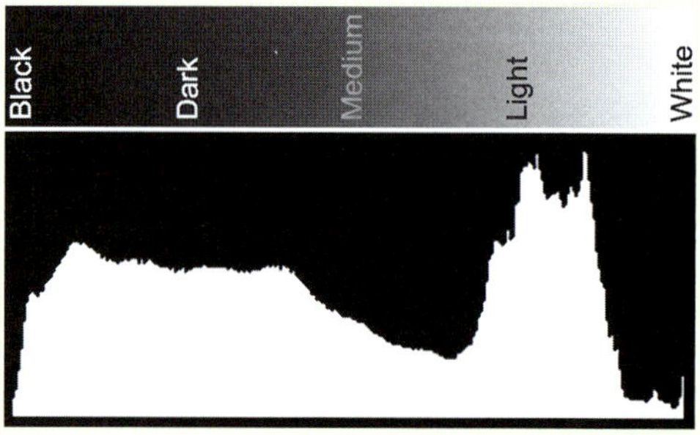

Figure 1.22 **This is a typical histogram, where the dark-to-light tones run from left to right. The black-to-white gradient above the graph demonstrates where the tones lie on the graph and does not appear above your camera's histogram display.**

continues

The value of the histogram *continued*

The heights of the peaks represent the number of pixels that contain those luminance levels (a tall peak in the middle means your image contains a large number of medium-bright pixels). Looking at an image, it can be hard to determine where all of the ranges of light and dark areas are and how much of each I have. If I look at the histogram, I can see that the largest peak of the graph is just to the right of the middle and trails off as it reaches the edges. In most cases, you would look for this type of histogram, indicating that you captured the entire range of tones, from dark to light, in your image. Knowing that is fine—but here is where the information really gets useful.

A histogram that has a spike or peak riding up the far left or right side of the graph means that you are clipping detail from your image. In essence, you are trying to record values that are either too dark or too light for your sensor to accurately record. This is usually an indication of over- or underexposure. It also means that you need to correct your exposure so that the important details will not record as solid black or white pixels (which is what happens when clipping occurs). There are times, however, when some clipping is acceptable. If you are photographing a scene where the sun will be in the frame, you can expect to get some clipping, because the sun is just too bright to hold any detail. Likewise, if you are shooting something that has true blacks in it—think coal in a mineshaft at midnight—there are most certainly going to be some true blacks with no detail in your shot. The main goal is to ensure that you aren't clipping any "important" visual information, and that is achieved by keeping an eye on your histogram.

It is important to realize that the "correct" histogram will depend on the tonality of your subject. In **Figure 1.23**, the histogram shows more information on the left side of the graph because the image is made up of mostly dark tones. You want to make sure that there is not a spike against the left side of the histogram that would indicate clipped shadows.

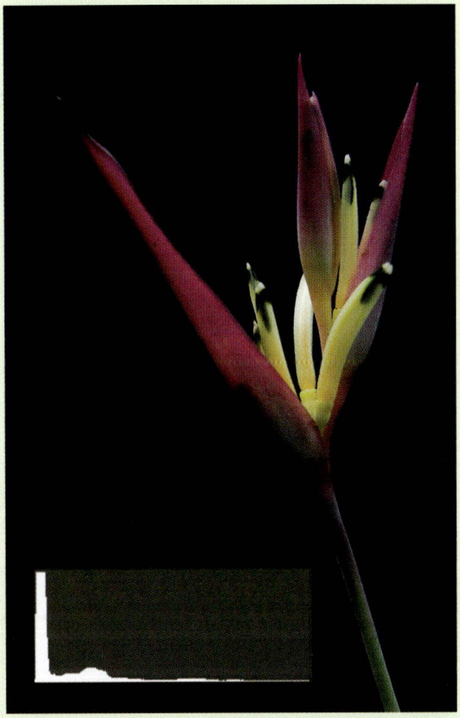

Figure 1.23 This image contains mostly dark tones, so the histogram is skewed to the left.

continues

The value of the histogram *continued*

On the other end of the scale, the histogram for **Figure 1.24** has most of the spikes toward the right side of the graph because the image contains mostly bright tones. For an image like this, you want to keep an eye on the right edge of the histogram and make sure you don't clip your highlights. Both histograms indicate a correct exposure, but the tonality of each image makes the histograms look dramatically different.

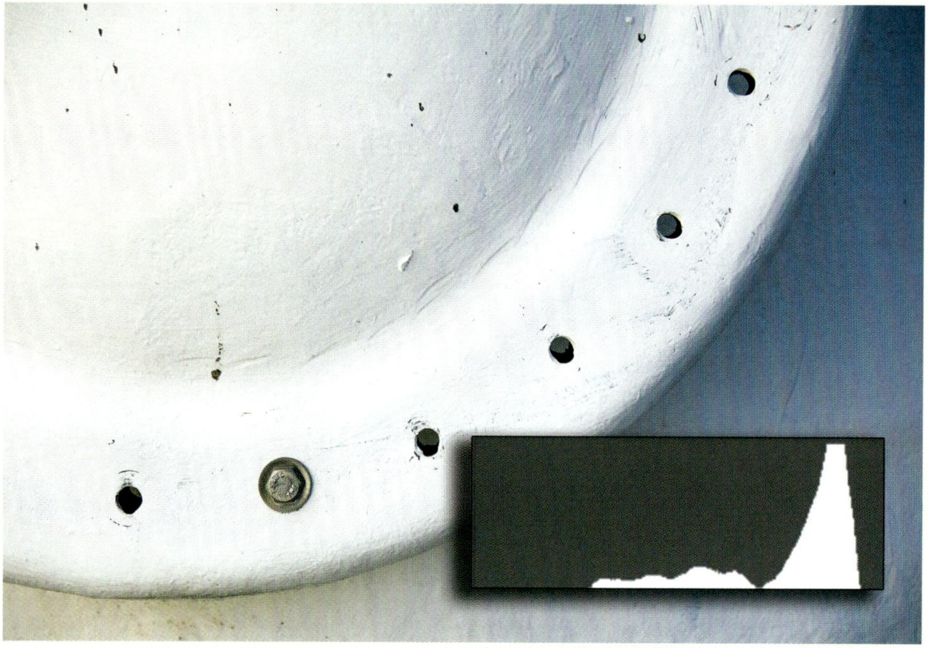

Figure 1.24 This histogram reflects a correctly exposed high-key image.

10. Hold Your Camera for Proper Shooting

Mirrorless cameras, along with most cameras out there, are made to favor the right-handed individual. The basics of properly holding the camera begin with grasping the camera body with the right hand. You will quickly find that most of the important camera controls are within easy reach of your thumb and forefinger. The next step is to create a stable base for your camera to rest on. This is accomplished by placing the camera body in the up-facing palm of your left hand (**Figure 1.25**). With a small camera like the GX7/GM1, you can wrap the fingers of your left hand over the knuckles of your right hand for more support.

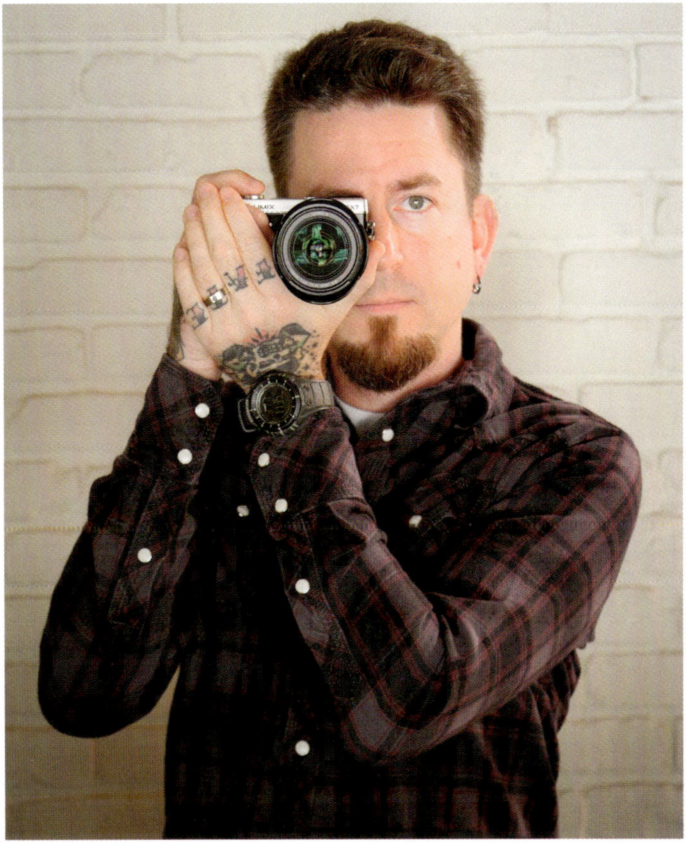

Figure 1.25 The proper way to hold your camera to ensure sharp, blur-free images (Photo by Becky Grace Knight)

Now that you know where to put your hands, let's talk about what to do with the rest of your body parts. By using the underhand grip, your elbows will be drawn closer to your body. You should concentrate on pulling them in close to your body to stabilize your shooting position. You should also try to maintain proper upright posture. Leaning forward at the waist will begin to fatigue your back, neck, and arms. Nothing ruins a day of shooting like a sore back, so make sure you stand erect with your elbows in. Finally, place your left foot in front of your right foot, and face your subject in a slightly wide stance. By combining all of these aspects into your photography, you will give yourself the best chance of eliminating self-imposed camera shake (or hand shake) in your images, resulting in much sharper photographs.

Chapter 1 Assignments

Let's begin our shooting assignments by setting up and using all of the elements of the Top Ten list. Even though I have yet to cover the professional shooting modes, you should set your camera to the P (Program Auto) mode. This will allow you to interact with the various settings and menus that have been covered thus far.

Basic camera setup

Charge your battery to 100% to get it started on a life of dependable service. Next, using your newfound knowledge, set up your camera to address the following: LCD and electronic viewfinder display modes, image quality, and Auto ISO.

Selecting the proper white balance

Take your camera outside into a daylight environment and photograph the same scene using different white balance settings. Pay close attention to how each setting affects the overall color cast of your images. Next, move inside and repeat the exercise while shooting in an incandescent lighting environment.

Focusing with 1-Area focus

Change your camera setting so that you are focusing using 1-Area mode. Try moving the focus spot around the frame to see how it works in focusing your scene. Try selecting a focus point and then using the Rear dial (GM1: Control dial) to change the size of the focus point. Try doing this with subjects at varying distances.

Evaluating your pictures with the LCD display

Review some of your assignment images using the different display modes. Review the shooting information for each image, and take a look at the histograms to see how the content of your photo affects their shapes.

Get a grip: proper camera holding

This final assignment is something that you should practice every time you shoot: proper grip and stance for shooting with your camera. Use the described technique and then shoot a series of images. Try it with improper techniques to compare the stability of the grip and stance.

Share your results with the book's Flickr group!
Join the group here: flickr.com/groups/panasonicGX7_fromsnapshotstogreatshots

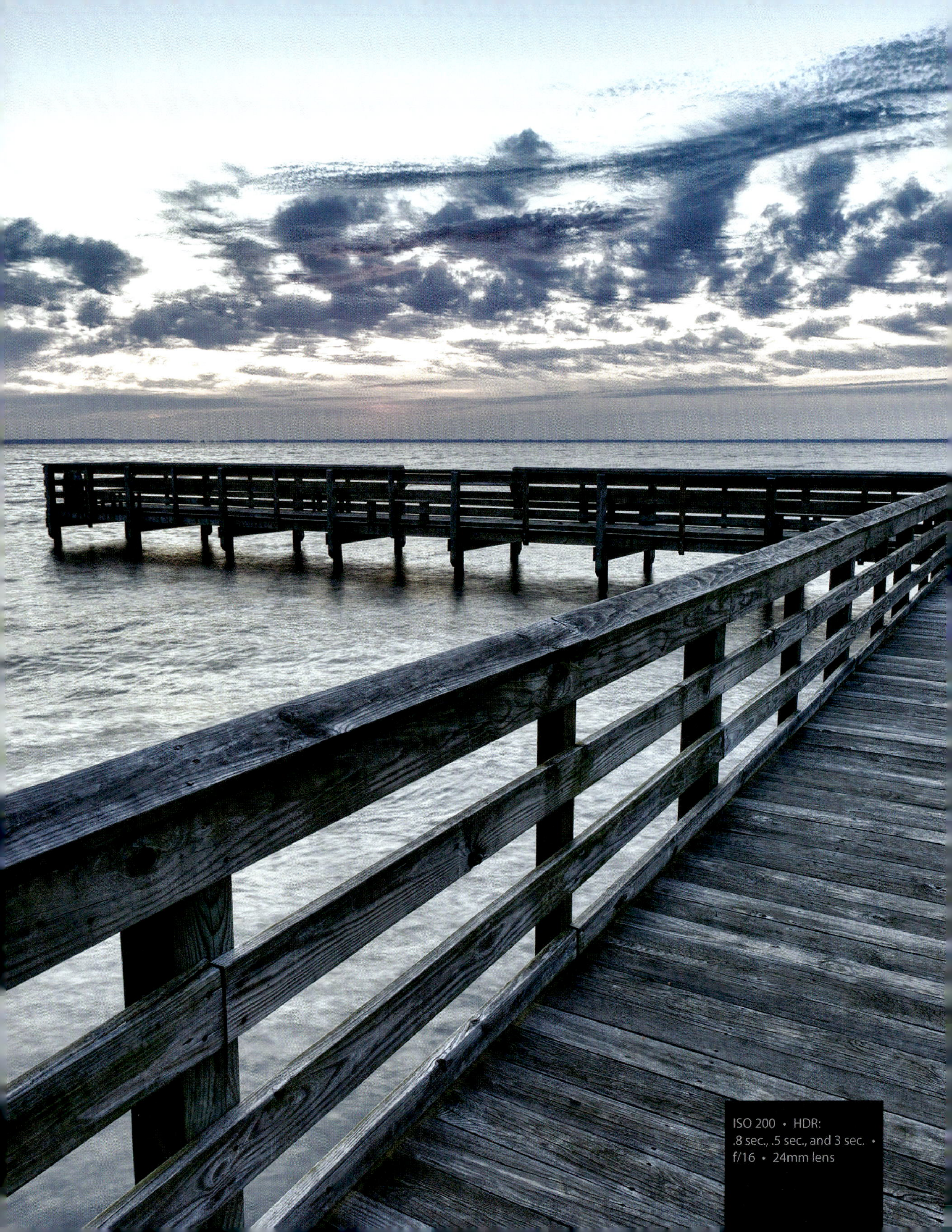

ISO 200 • HDR:
.8 sec., .5 sec., and 3 sec. •
f/16 • 24mm lens

2

First Things First

A Few Things to Know and Do Before You Begin Taking Pictures

Now that we've covered the top ten tasks to get you up and shooting, we should probably take care of some other important details. You must become familiar with certain features of your camera before you can take full advantage of it. Additionally, we will take some steps to prepare the camera and memory card for use. So to get things moving, let's start off with something that you will definitely need before you can take a single picture: a memory card.

Poring Over the Picture

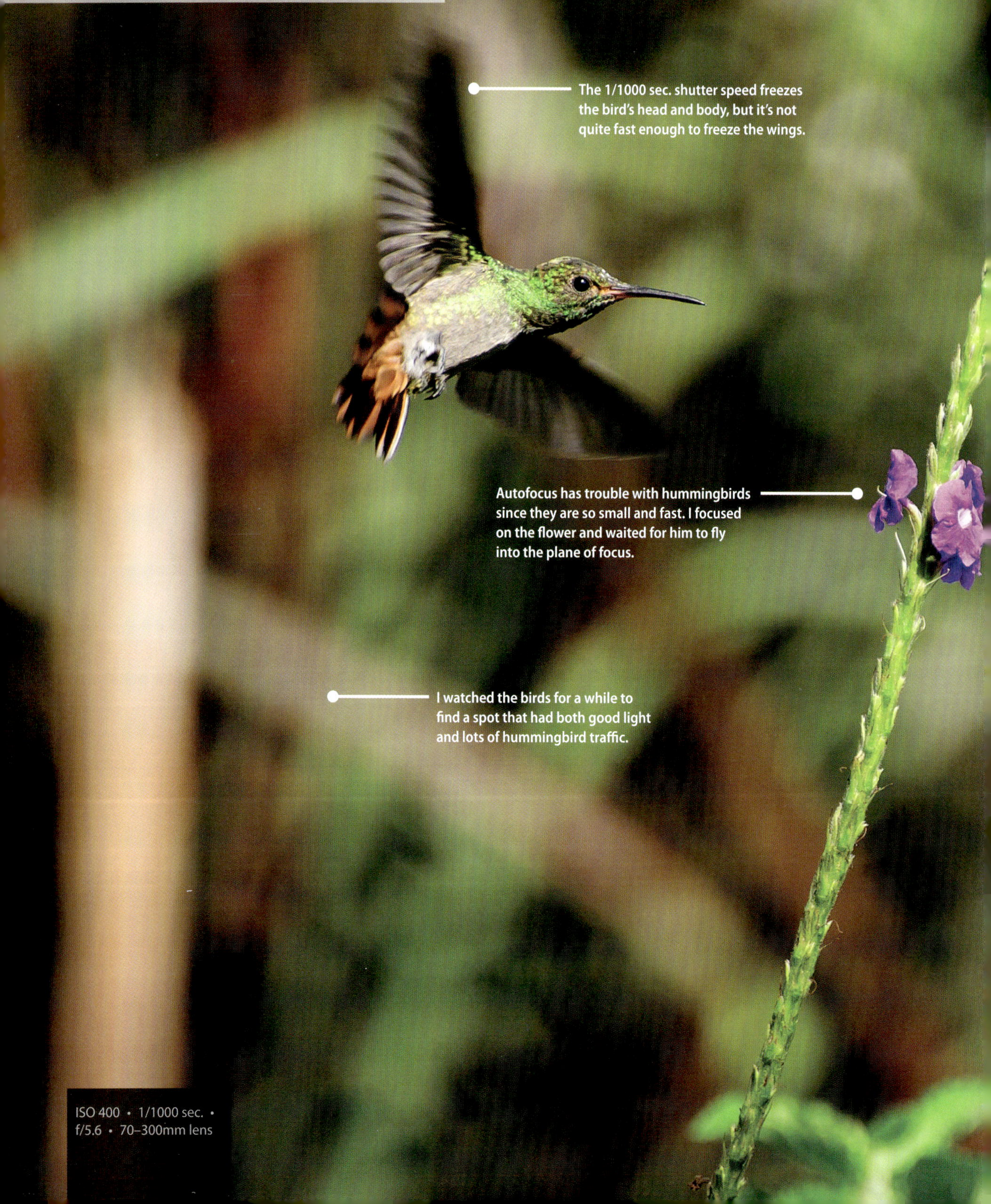

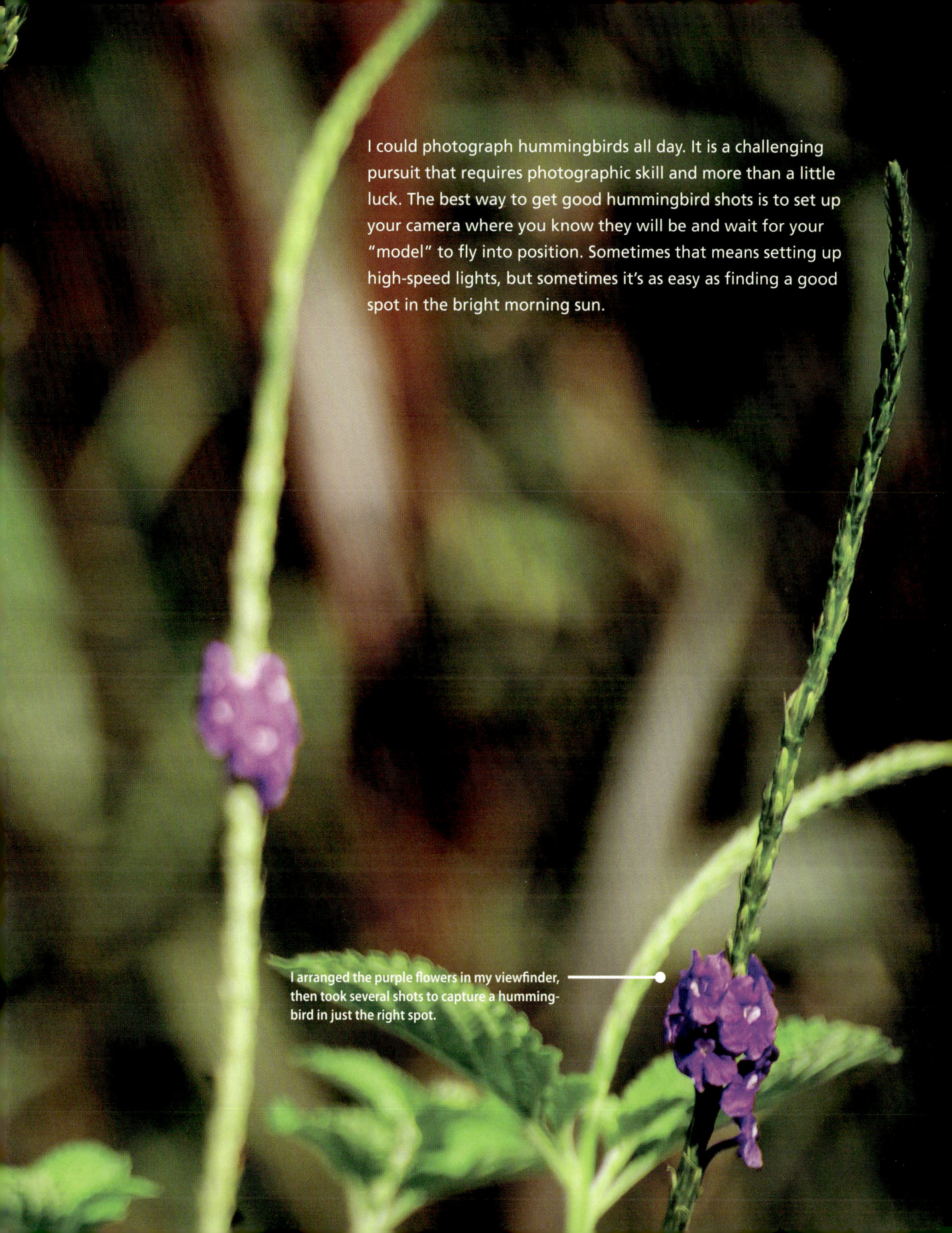

I could photograph hummingbirds all day. It is a challenging pursuit that requires photographic skill and more than a little luck. The best way to get good hummingbird shots is to set up your camera where you know they will be and wait for your "model" to fly into position. Sometimes that means setting up high-speed lights, but sometimes it's as easy as finding a good spot in the bright morning sun.

I arranged the purple flowers in my viewfinder, then took several shots to capture a hummingbird in just the right spot.

Choosing the Right Memory Card

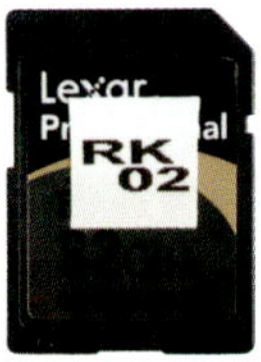

Figure 2.1
I like to label my SD cards with my initials and a serial number so I can keep track of them more easily.

Memory cards are the digital film that stores every shot you take until you move it to a computer. The cards come in all shapes and sizes, and they are critical for capturing all your photos. It is important not to skimp when it comes to selecting your memory cards. The GX7 and GM1 use Secure Digital (SD) memory cards (**Figure 2.1**).

If you have been using a point-and-shoot camera, you may already own an SD media card. Which brand of card you use is completely up to you, but here is some advice about choosing your memory card:

- Size matters, at least in memory cards. At 16 megapixels, the GX7/GM1 will require a lot of storage space, especially if you shoot in the RAW or RAW+JPEG mode (more on this later in the chapter) or shoot HD video. You should definitely consider using a card with a storage capacity of at least 8 GB.
- Consider buying high capacity (SDHC) cards. These cards are generally much faster, both when writing images to the card and when transferring them to your computer. If you are planning on using the Burst mode (see Chapter 5) for capturing fast action, you can gain a boost in performance just by using an SDHC card with a class rating of at least 6. The higher the class rating, the faster the write speed. Having a fast card will also benefit your video capture by keeping the flow of video frames moving quickly to your card.
- Buy more than one card. If you have already purchased a memory card, consider getting another. It's a bad day when your card is almost full and you have to either erase shots or choose a lower-quality image format so you can keep on shooting. With the cost of memory cards what it is, keeping a spare just makes good sense.
- To get the fastest memory possible, you could consider purchasing an SDXC memory card. Although they appear to be the same as SD and SDHC cards, they are made to new specifications that allow memory capacities above 32 GB. Your camera is SDXC compliant, but if you plan to share SDXC cards between devices such as your GX7/GM1 and a video camera, make sure the other device is SDXC compatible too. SDXC cards will work only in SDXC devices. Also, you should format your SDXC card only in your camera.

Panasonic recommends a speed rating of at least Class 4 for shooting video. What you need to know is that all cards are not created equal. In the past, I have had issues with Class 4 cards that could not keep up with the demands of video recording and have caused the camera to stop in the middle of a recording session. My recommendation is that if you know you are going to be shooting video with your camera, you should use a Class 6 or 10 card to keep the pixels flowing.

Formatting Your Memory Card

Now that you have your card, let's talk about formatting for a minute. When you purchase any new SD card, you can pop it into your camera and start shooting right away—and everything will probably work as it should. However, what you *should* do first is format the card in the camera. This process allows the camera to set up the card to record images from your camera. Just as a computer hard drive must be formatted, your card needs formatting to ensure that it is properly initialized. The card may work in the camera without first being formatted, but that makes the chances of failure down the road much higher.

As a general practice, I always format new cards or cards that have been used in different cameras. I also reformat cards after I have downloaded my images and want to start a new shooting session. Note that you should always format your card in the camera, not in your computer. Using the computer could render the card useless in your camera. You should also pay attention to the manufacturer's recommendations with respect to moisture, humidity, and proper handling procedures. It sounds a little cliché, but when it comes to protecting your images, every little bit helps.

Formatting your memory card

1. Press the Menu/Set button and select the Setup menu (the wrench icon).
2. Navigate to Format and press Menu/Set (**A**).

   You can also touch Format on the screen to select it.
3. You'll be prompted by another screen, letting you know that all of the data on your card will be deleted. This screen is a safety feature, ensuring that you want to format the card. Touch Yes on the screen to complete the formatting process (**B**). If you choose not to format, touch No.
4. Once the formatting is complete, the camera will return to shooting mode.

A

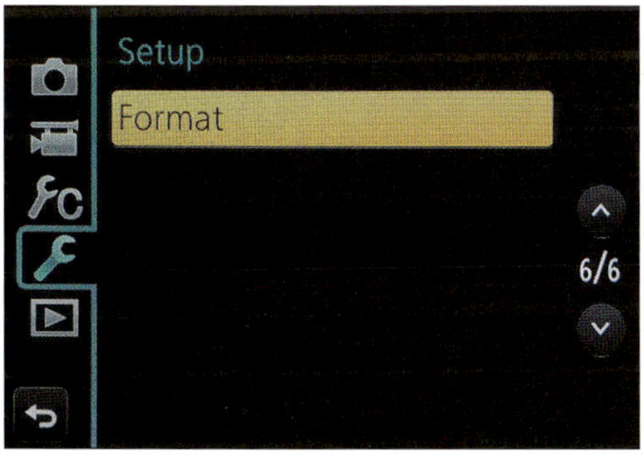

B

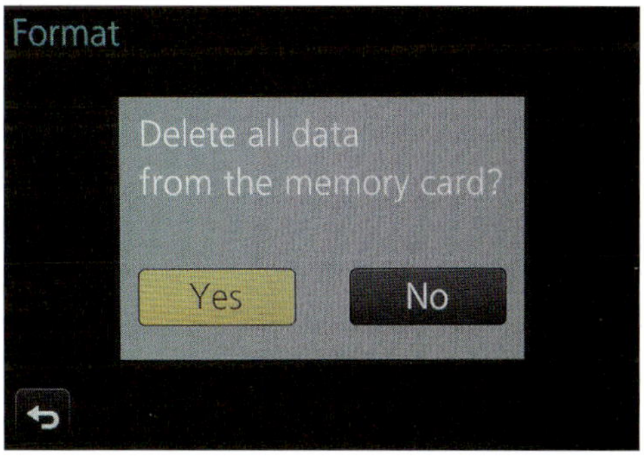

Updating the GX7/GM1's Firmware

I know that you want to get shooting, but having the proper firmware can affect the way the camera operates. It can fix problems as well as improve operation, so you should probably take care of it sooner rather than later. The firmware of your camera is the set of computer operating instructions that controls how your camera functions. Updating this firmware is a great way to not only fix little bugs but also gain access to new functionality. You will need to check out the information at Panasonic joint update service (http://panasonic.jp/support/global/cs/dsc/download/fts/index.html) to review the latest updates. Accept the conditions at the bottom of the page and follow the instructions to get to your camera model. It is always a good idea to be working with the most up-to-date firmware version available.

Checking the camera's current firmware version

1. Press Menu/Set and navigate to the Setup menu.
2. Select Version Disp to see the firmware version for the body and the attached lens (**A**).
3. If these versions are not the latest ones listed on the Panasonic joint update website, follow the steps in the next section to load the latest version.

A

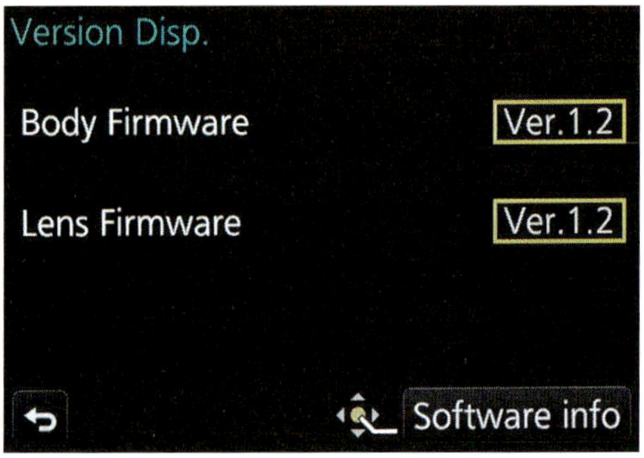

Updating the firmware

1. Access the Panasonic joint update service website (http://panasonic.jp/support/global/cs/dsc/download/fts/index.html). Click the Accepted button at the bottom of the page to accept the license agreement and access the firmware page.
2. Find your camera model, and click the link to go to the download page. (If there is no firmware update available for your camera, the Firmware item will not appear in the list.)
3. Choose your computer's operating system and click Download. After you click the Download button, you can close the download window.
4. Back on the firmware list page, you will find instructions for copying the update to a memory card. Scroll down to the bottom of the page and click "Continue to Step 2. Procedure for G series camera body update." There you will be provided very detailed instructions on how to prepare your camera for the update and how to download and install it.

Cleaning the Sensor

Cleaning camera sensors used to be a nerve-racking process that required leaving the sensor exposed to scratching and even more dust. Now cleaning the sensor is pretty much an automatic function. Your GX7/GM1 vibrates the sensor every time you turn the camera on to remove any dust particles that might have landed on it.

Every now and then, though, there will just be a dust spot that is impervious to the anti-dust vibration technology. If this happens, you have two more options to clean the sensor. First, you can activate the Sensor Cleaning function. Doing so essentially does what the automatic anti-dust vibration technology does when you turn the camera on.

Using the Sensor Cleaning feature

1. Press the Menu/Set button and choose the Setup menu.
2. Select Sensor Cleaning (**A**).
3. Select Yes to start the cleaning process. That's it. After the vibration technology does its thing, press the shutter button halfway to return to shooting mode.

A

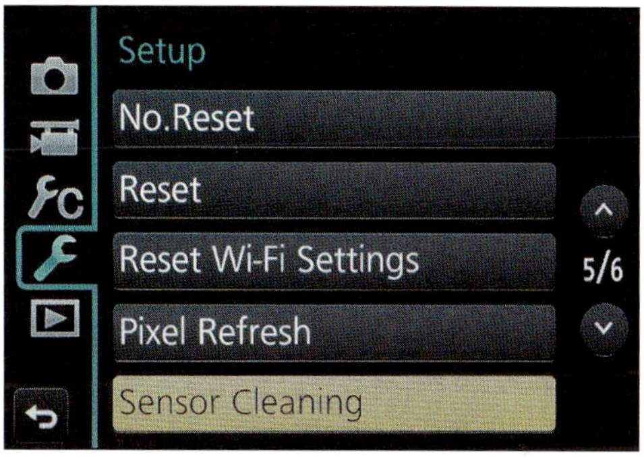

After you perform a cleaning, however, pesky pieces of dust might still persist. This will require manual cleaning of the sensor. If you choose to manually clean your sensor, please use a device that has been made to clean sensors (not a cotton swab from your medicine cabinet). There are dozens of commercially available devices—such as brushes, swabs, and blowers—that will clean the sensor without damaging it. To keep the sensor clean, always store the camera with a body cap or a lens attached.

The camera sensor is an electrically charged device. This means that when the camera is turned on, there is a current running through the sensor. This electric current can create static electricity, which will attract small dust particles to the sensor area. You should always turn off the camera prior to removing a lens.

You should also consider having the lens mount facing down during lens removal so there is less opportunity for dust to fall into the inner workings of the camera. Since the GX7/GM1 is a mirrorless camera, the sensor is immediately exposed when you remove a dust cap or lens. Keep this in mind when you are changing lenses the next time. But keeping your camera's sensor clean is part of owning and using the camera, so don't let the idea of a little dust keep you from shooting.

Using the Right Format: RAW vs. JPEG

When shooting with your GX7/GM1, you have a choice of image formats that your camera will use to store the pictures on the memory card. JPEG is probably the most familiar format to anyone who has been using a digital camera. RAW images contain more image data and require post-processing in a computer.

There is nothing wrong with JPEG if you are taking casual shots or you don't plan to edit your photos in the computer. JPEG files are ready to use, right out of the camera. Why go through the process of adjusting RAW images of the kids opening presents when you are just going to email them to Grandma? For journalists and sports photographers who are shooting ten frames per second and transmitting their images across the wire, JPEG files are necessary. If you can get the images you want using the controls in the camera, then JPEG files are usually fine.

So what does RAW have to offer?

First and foremost, RAW images are not compressed. (Some cameras offer a compressed RAW format, but it is lossless compression, which means there is no loss of actual image data.) Note that RAW image files will require you to perform post-processing on your photographs. This is not only necessary—it is the reason that most photographers use it.

RAW images have a greater dynamic range than JPEG-processed images. This means that you can recover image detail in the highlights and shadows that just aren't available in JPEG-processed images.

There is more color information in a RAW image because it is a 12-bit image, which means it contains more color information than a JPEG, which is almost always an 8-bit image. More color information means more to work with and smoother changes between tones.

Shooting RAW definitely has its advantages if you will be making a lot of changes to your photos using image editing software, especially if you need to recover highlight or shadow detail, but the benefits are not as cut-and-dried if you don't plan to do any post-processing. Remember that any changes you make using the in-camera settings (except exposure) will not apply to your RAW files. Those changes will apply only to your JPEGs.

Advice for new RAW shooters

Don't give up on shooting RAW just because it means more work. Hey, if it takes up more space on your card, buy bigger cards or more smaller ones. Will it take more time to download your images? Yes, but good things come to those who wait. Don't worry about needing to purchase expensive software to work with your RAW files; you already own a program that will allow you to work with your RAW files. SILKYPIX Developer Studio software comes bundled in the box with your camera and gives you the ability to work directly on the RAW files and then output the enhanced results.

My recommendation is that you shoot in JPEG mode while you are using this book. This will allow you to practice using the creative features in the camera to adjust your images. Once you have become comfortable with all of the camera features, you should try shooting in RAW mode so that you can start gaining more creative control over your image processing.

Image resolution

When people discuss digital cameras, image resolution is often used to describe pixel resolution, or the number of pixels used to make an image. This can be displayed as a dimension, such as 4593 x 3448. This is the physical number of pixels in width and height of the image sensor. Resolution can also be referred to in megapixels (MP), such as 16 MP. This number represents the number of total pixels on the sensor and is commonly used to describe the amount of image data that a digital camera can capture.

Selecting RAW+JPEG

Your camera has the added benefit of being able to write two files for each picture you take: one in RAW and one in JPEG. This can be useful if you want to use the controls in the camera to pre-process a JPEG, and you want a RAW version for more advanced processing.

It should be noted that using both formats requires more space on the memory card. I regularly use RAW+JPEG so that I have the flexibility of both formats.

Selecting your image quality setting

1. Press the Menu/Set button, and select the Rec menu.
2. Select Quality and press Menu/Set.

   You can also touch Quality on the screen to select it.
3. Select the RAW+Fine JPEG setting (**A**). Fine and Standard are two JPEG compression formats—Fine is higher quality than Standard.
4. Press the shutter button halfway to return to shooting mode.

A

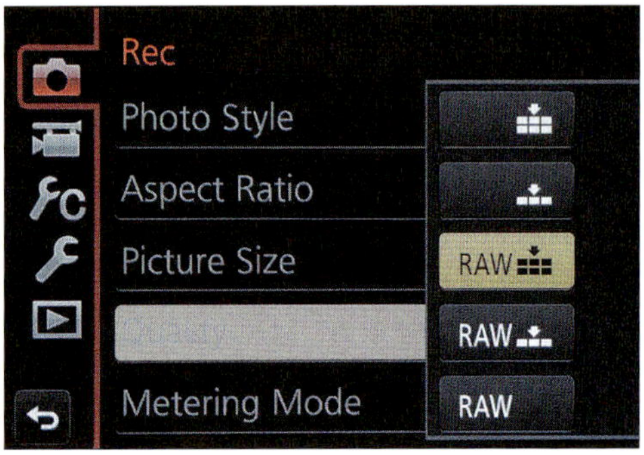

Lenses and Focal Lengths

If you ask most photographers what they believe to be their most critical piece of photographic equipment, they would undoubtedly tell you that it is their lens. The technology and engineering that go into your camera are a marvel, but they aren't worth a darn if it can't get the light from the outside world onto the sensor. The GX7/GM1, as a mirrorless camera that depends upon an interchangeable lens system, uses the lens for a multitude of tasks, from focusing on a subject to metering a scene to delivering and focusing the light onto the camera sensor. The lens is also responsible for the amount of the scene that will be captured (the frame). With all of this riding on the lens, let's take a more in-depth look at the camera's eye on the world.

Lenses are composed of optical glass that is both concave and convex in shape. The alignment of the glass elements is designed to focus the light coming in from the front of the lens onto the camera sensor. The amount of light that enters the camera is also controlled by the lens, the size of the glass elements, and the aperture mechanism within the lens housing. The quality of the glass used in the lens will also have a direct effect on how well the lens can resolve details and the contrast of the scene (the ability to deliver great highlights and shadows). Most lenses now routinely include things like an autofocus motor and, in some cases, an image-stabilization mechanism.

There is one other aspect of the camera lens that is often the first consideration of the photographer: lens focal length, which determines the angle of view delivered through the lens. Lenses are typically divided into three or four groups, depending on the field of view they cover.

Wide-angle lenses cover a field of view from around 110 degrees to about 60 degrees **(Figure 2.2)**. There is also a tendency to get some distortion in your image when using extremely wide-angle lenses. This will be apparent toward the outer edges of the frame. As for which lenses would be considered wide angle, anything 16mm or smaller could be considered wide.

Wide-angle lenses can display a large depth of field, which allows you to keep the foreground and background in sharp focus. This makes them very useful for landscape photography. They also work well in tight spaces, such as indoors, where there isn't much elbow room available (**Figure 2.3**). They can also be handy for large group shots, but due to the amount of distortion they're not so great for close-up portrait work.

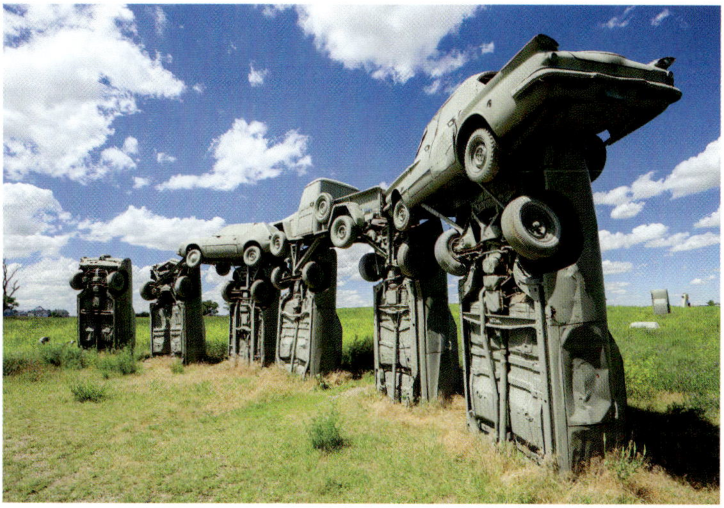

Figure 2.2
A wide-angle lens emphasizes the distance between foreground and background elements in this scene.

ISO 200 • 1/125 sec. • f/16 • 16–35mm lens

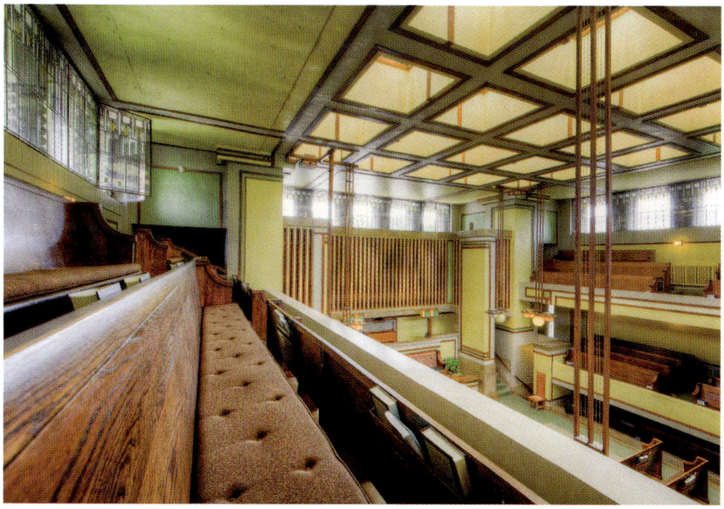

Figure 2.3
When you are shooting in tight spaces or want to exaggerate attractive lines, a wide-angle lens helps capture more of the scene.

ISO 200 • 1/2 sec. • f/11 • 16–35mm lens

A *normal* lens has a field of view that is about 45 degrees and delivers approximately the same view as the human eye (not in angle of view but in size and perspective of subjects). The perspective is very natural, and there is little distortion in objects. The normal lens for full-frame and 35mm cameras is the 50mm lens, but for the GX7/GM1 and its cropped sensor, it is more in the neighborhood of a 25mm lens (**Figure 2.4**).

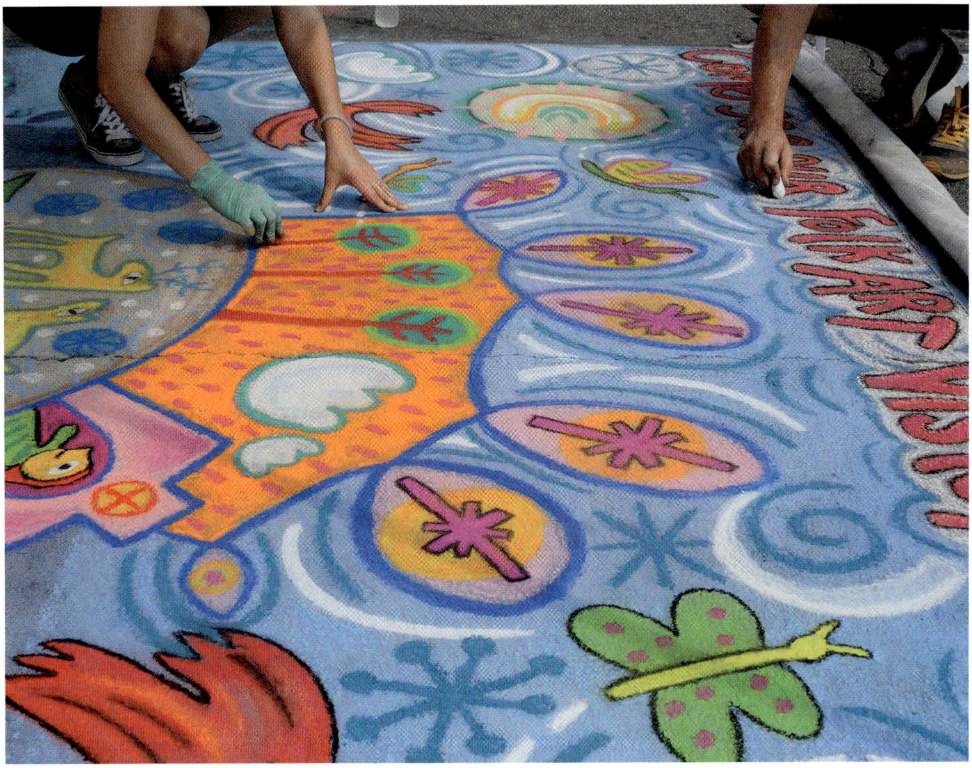

Figure 2.4
A 25mm lens on your GX7/GM1 gives you the same field of view as a 50mm "normal" lens on a full-frame camera.
ISO 200 • 1/1600 sec. • f/8 • 25mm lens

Normal focal length lenses are useful for photographing people, architecture, and most other general photographic subjects. They have very little distortion and offer a moderate range of depth of field (**Figure 2.5**).

Longer focal length lenses are referred to as *telephoto* lenses. On your GX7/GM1 they can range in length from 35mm up to 300mm or longer and have a field of view that is about 35 degrees or smaller. These lenses have the ability to greatly magnify the scene, allowing you to capture details of distant objects, but the angle of view is greatly reduced (**Figure 2.6**). You will also find that you can achieve a much narrower depth of field. They also demonstrate something called distance compression, which means they make objects at different distances appear to be much closer together than they really are.

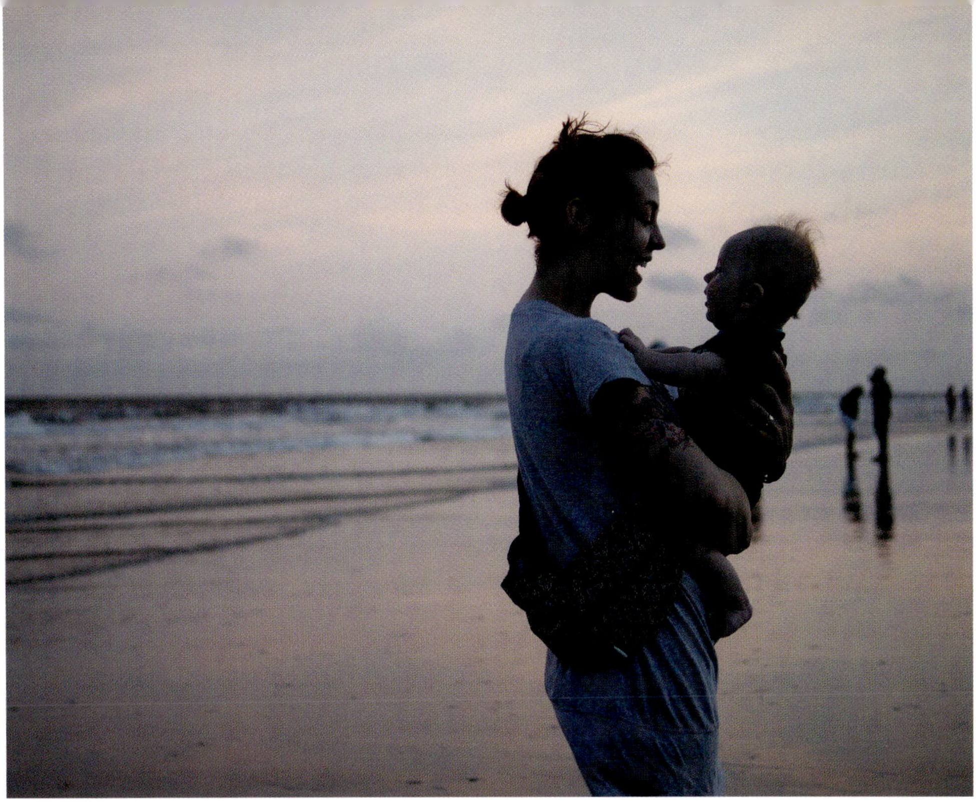

Figure 2.5
Normal lenses are handy for a wide variety of subjects, such as this environmental portrait.

ISO 200 • 1/250 sec. • f/1.4 • 25mm lens

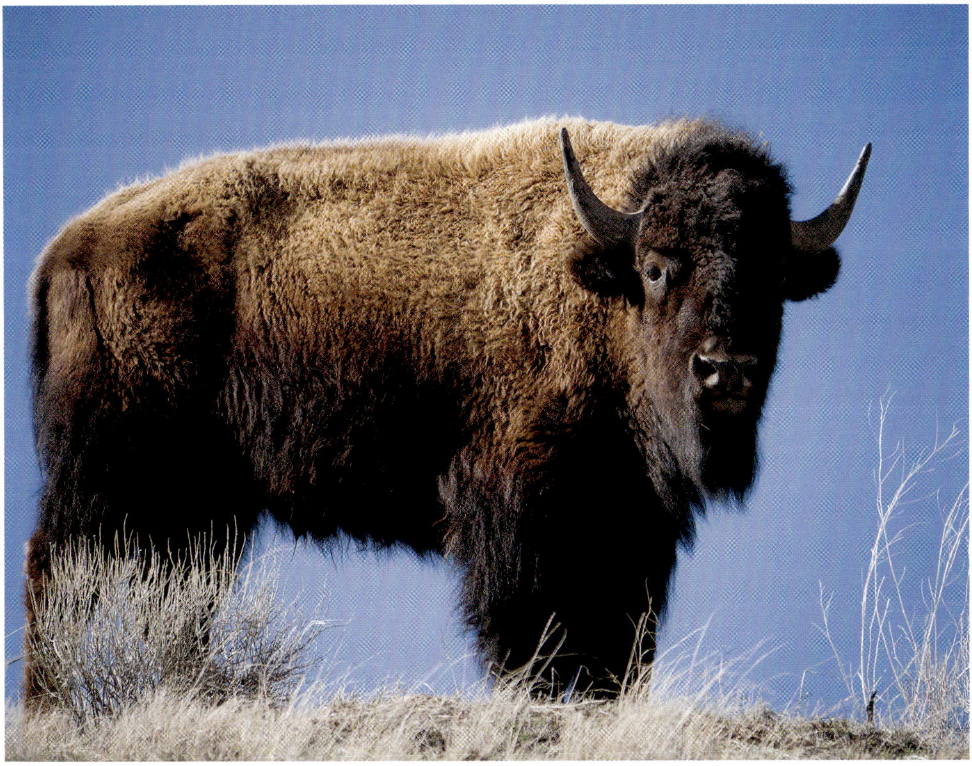

Figure 2.6
A telephoto lens helps bring distant subjects closer.

ISO 200 • 1/500 sec. • f/5.6 • 100–300mm lens

Telephoto lenses are most useful for sports photography or any application where you just need to get closer to your subject. They can have a compressing effect—making objects look closer together than they actually are (**Figure 2.7**)—and a very narrow depth of field when shot at their widest apertures.

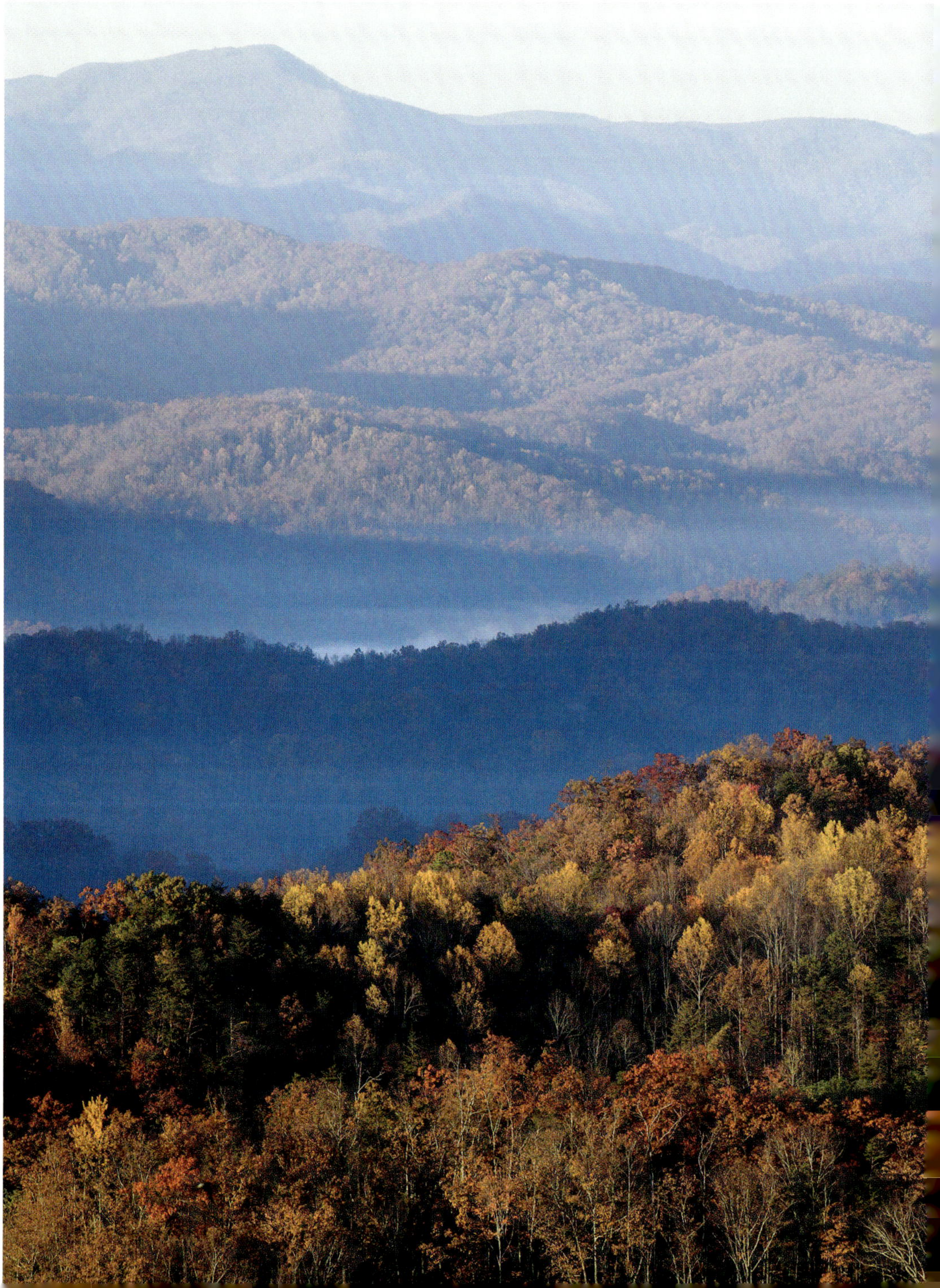

Figure 2.7

The longer the focal length, the more compressed the distance between foreground and background objects will be.

ISO 200 • 1/160 sec. • f/8 • 100–300mm lens

A *zoom* lens is a great compromise to carrying a bunch of single focal-length lenses (also referred to as "prime" lenses). They can cover a wide range of focal lengths because of the configuration of their optics. However, because it takes more optical elements to capture a scene at different focal lengths, the light must pass through more glass on its way to the image sensor. The more glass, the lower the quality of the image sharpness. The other sacrifice that is made is in aperture. Zoom lenses typically have smaller maximum apertures than prime lenses, which means they cannot achieve a narrow depth of field or work in lower light levels without the assistance of image stabilization, a tripod, or higher ISO settings. (We'll discuss all this in more detail in later chapters.)

There are several Lumix lenses that break the zoom lens stereotype. The 12–35mm f2.8 and the 35–100mm f2.8 offer professional image quality, built-in Optical Image Stabilizer technology, and a fast maximum aperture. The 7–14mm f4 is a very sharp ultra-wide lens with a relatively fast maximum aperture. The Lumix 14–140mm is a great all-around lens that provides a range of focal lengths, from the very wide to the medium telephoto. Combine that with great Optical Image Stabilizer technology and you have what I like to call the perfect vacation lens.

What Is Exposure?

In order for you to get the most out of this book, I need to briefly discuss the principles of exposure. Without this basic knowledge, it will be difficult for you to move forward in improving your photography. For our purposes, I will just cover some of the basics of exposure. This will give you the essential tools to make educated decisions in determining how best to photograph a subject.

So what is exposure? It is the process whereby the light reflecting off a subject reflects through an opening in the camera lens for a defined period of time onto the camera sensor. The combination of the lens opening, shutter speed, and sensor sensitivity is used to achieve a proper exposure value (EV) for the scene. The EV is the sum of these components necessary to properly expose a scene. The relationship between these factors is sometimes referred to as the "exposure triangle."

At each point of the triangle lies one of the factors of exposure:

- **ISO:** Determines the sensitivity of the camera sensor. ISO stands for the International Organization for Standardization, but the acronym is used as a term to describe the sensitivity of the camera sensor to light. The higher the sensitivity, the less light is required for a good exposure. These values are a carryover from the days of traditional color and black-and-white films.
- **Aperture:** Also referred to as f-stop, this determines how much light passes through the lens at once.
- **Shutter speed:** Controls the length of time that light is allowed to hit the sensor.

So here's how it works. The camera sensor has a level of sensitivity that is determined by the ISO setting. To get a proper exposure—not too much, not too little—the lens needs to adjust the aperture diaphragm (the size of the lens opening) to control the volume of light entering the camera. Then the shutter opens for a relatively short period of time to allow the light to strike the sensor before the shutter closes and ends the exposure.

ISO numbers for the GX7/GM1 start at 200 and then double in sensitivity as you double the number. So 400 is twice as sensitive as 200. If you select your ISO manually, you are able to select in full-stop increments (ISO 200, 400, 800, and so on up to ISO 25,600). If you place the camera in Auto ISO, it will determine the proper ISO from 200 and up in 1/3-stop increments. There are also a wide variety of shutter speeds that you can use to achieve a proper exposure. The speeds on the GX7 range from as long as 60 seconds to as short as 1/8000 of a second. Typically, you will be working with a shutter speed range from around 1/30 of a second to about 1/2000, but these numbers will change depending on your circumstances and the effect that you are trying to achieve. The lens apertures will vary slightly depending on which lens you are using. This is because different lenses have different maximum apertures. The typical apertures that are at your disposal are f/4, f/5.6, f/8, f/11, f/16, and f/22.

When it comes to exposure, a change to any one of these factors can require changing one or more of the other two. This is referred to as a reciprocal change. If you let more light in the lens by choosing a larger aperture opening, you will need to shorten the amount of time the shutter is open. If the shutter is allowed to stay open for a longer period of time, the aperture needs to be smaller to restrict the amount of light coming in.

How is exposure calculated?

We now know about the exposure triangle—ISO, shutter speed, and aperture—so it's time to put all three together to see how they relate to one another and how you can change them as needed.

Stop

You will hear the term *stop* thrown around all the time in photography. It relates back to the f-stop, which is a term used to describe the aperture of your lens. When you need to give some additional exposure, you might say that you are going to "add a stop." This doesn't just equate to the aperture; it could also be used to describe the shutter speed or even the ISO. So when your image is too light or dark or you have too much movement in your subject, you will probably be changing things by a "stop" or two.

When you point your camera at a scene, the light reflecting off your subject enters the lens and is allowed to pass through to the sensor for a period of time dictated by the shutter speed. The amount and duration of the light needed for a proper exposure depends on how much light is being reflected and how sensitive the sensor is. To figure this out, your camera utilizes a built-in light meter that looks through the lens and measures the amount of light. That level is then calculated against the sensitivity of the ISO setting, and an exposure value is rendered. Here is the tricky part: There is more than one way to achieve a perfect exposure, because the f-stop and shutter speed can be combined in different ways to allow the same amount of exposure. See, I told you it was tricky.

Here is a list of reciprocal settings, known as exposure equivalencies, which would all produce the same exposure result. Let's use the "Sunny 16" rule, which states that, when using f/16 on a sunny day, you can use a shutter speed that is roughly equal to the ISO setting to achieve a proper exposure. For simplification purposes, we will use an ISO of 100.

Reciprocal Exposures: ISO 100

F-STOP	2.8	4	5.6	8	11	16	22
SHUTTER SPEED	1/4000	1/2000	1/1000	1/500	1/250	1/125	1/60

If you were to use any one of these combinations, they would each have the same result in terms of the exposure (i.e., how much light hits the camera's sensor). Also take note that every time we cut the f-stop in half, we reciprocated by doubling our shutter speed. For those of you wondering why f/8 is half of f/5.6, it's because those numbers are actually fractions based on the opening of the lens in relation to its focal length. This means that a lot of math goes into figuring out just what the total area of a lens opening is, so you just have to take it on faith that f/8 is half of f/5.6 but twice as much as f/11. A good way to remember which opening is larger is to think of your camera lens as a pipe that controls the flow of water. If you have a pipe that is 1/2" in diameter (f/2) and one that is 1/8" (f/8), which would allow more water to flow through? It would be the 1/2" pipe. The same idea works here with the camera f-stops; f/2 is a larger opening than f/4 or f/8 or f/16.

Now that we know this, we can start using this information to make intelligent choices in terms of shutter speed and f-stop. Let's bring the third element into this by changing our ISO by one stop, from 100 to 200.

Reciprocal Exposures: ISO 200							
F-STOP	2.8	4	5.6	8	11	16	22
SHUTTER SPEED	1/8000	1/4000	1/2000	1/1000	1/500	1/250	1/125

Notice that, since we doubled the sensitivity of the sensor, we now require half as much exposure as before.

So why not just use the exposure setting of f/16 at 1/250 of a second? Why bother with all of these reciprocal values when this one setting will give us a properly exposed image? The answer is that the f-stop and shutter speed also control two other important aspects of our image: motion and depth of field.

Motion and Depth of Field

There are distinct characteristics that are related to changes in aperture and shutter speed. Shutter speed controls the length of time the light has to strike the sensor; consequently, it also controls the blurriness (or lack of blurriness) of the image. The less time light has to hit the sensor, the less time your subjects have to move around and become blurry. This can let you do things like freeze the motion of a fast-moving subject (**Figure 2.8**) or intentionally blur subjects to give the feel of energy and motion (**Figure 2.9**).

The aperture controls the amount of light that comes through the lens, but it also determines what areas of the image will be in focus. This is referred to as depth of field, and it is an extremely valuable creative tool. The smaller the opening (the larger the number, such as f/22), the greater the sharpness of objects from near to far (**Figure 2.10**).

A large opening (or small number, like f/2.8) means more blurring of objects that are not at the same distance from the camera as the subject you are focusing on (**Figure 2.11**).

As we further explore the features of the camera, we will learn not only how to utilize the elements of exposure to capture properly exposed photographs, but also how to make adjustments to emphasize our subject. It is the manipulation of these elements—motion and focus—that will take your images to the next level.

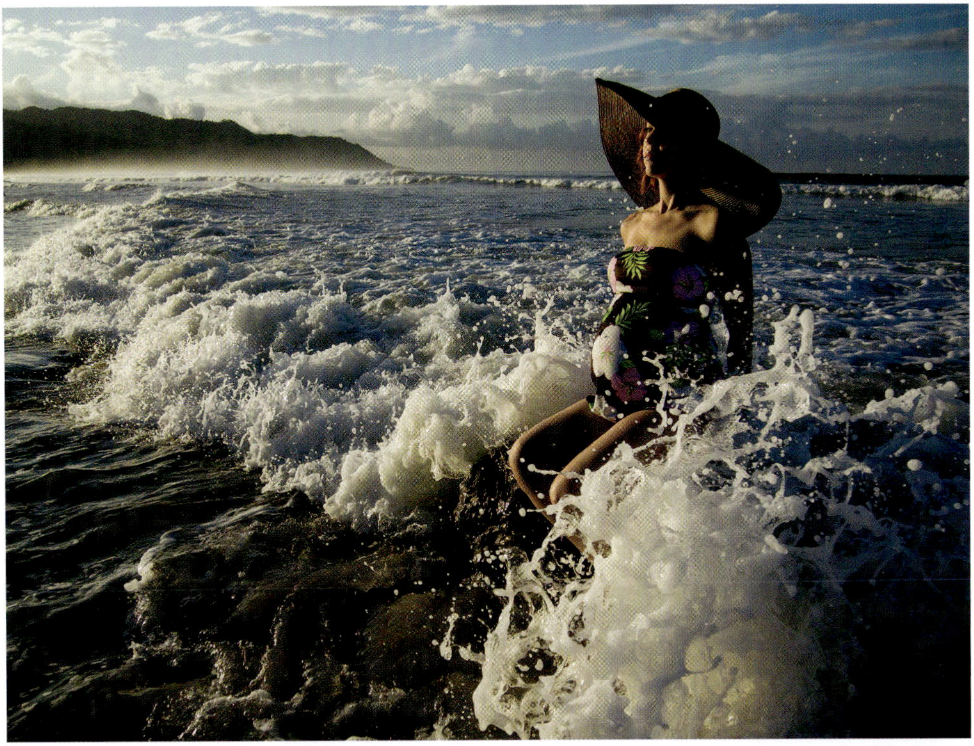

Figure 2.8
A fast shutter speed was used to freeze the water drops in the crashing wave.

ISO 200 • 1/2000 sec. • f/3.5 • 14–42mm lens

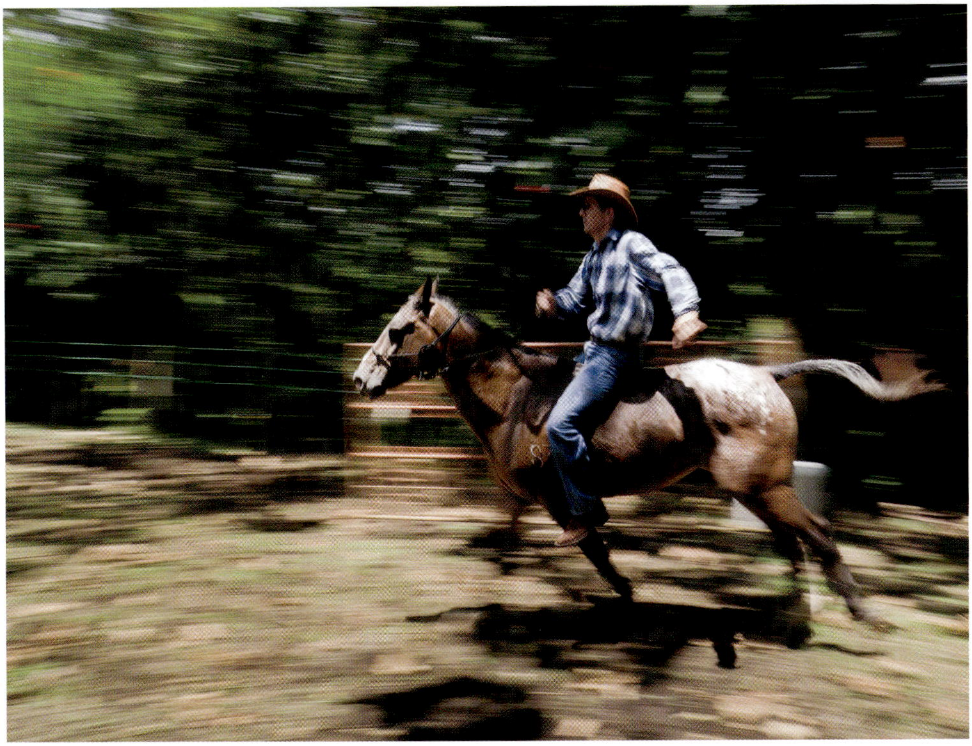

Figure 2.9
The slower shutter speed creates motion blur to depict the energy in the scene.

ISO 200 • 1/30 • f/13 • 12–35mm lens

Figure 2.10
Because I used a small aperture, the area of sharp focus extends from the church all the way out to the trees in the distance.

ISO 200 • 1/160 sec. • f/16 • 16–35mm lens

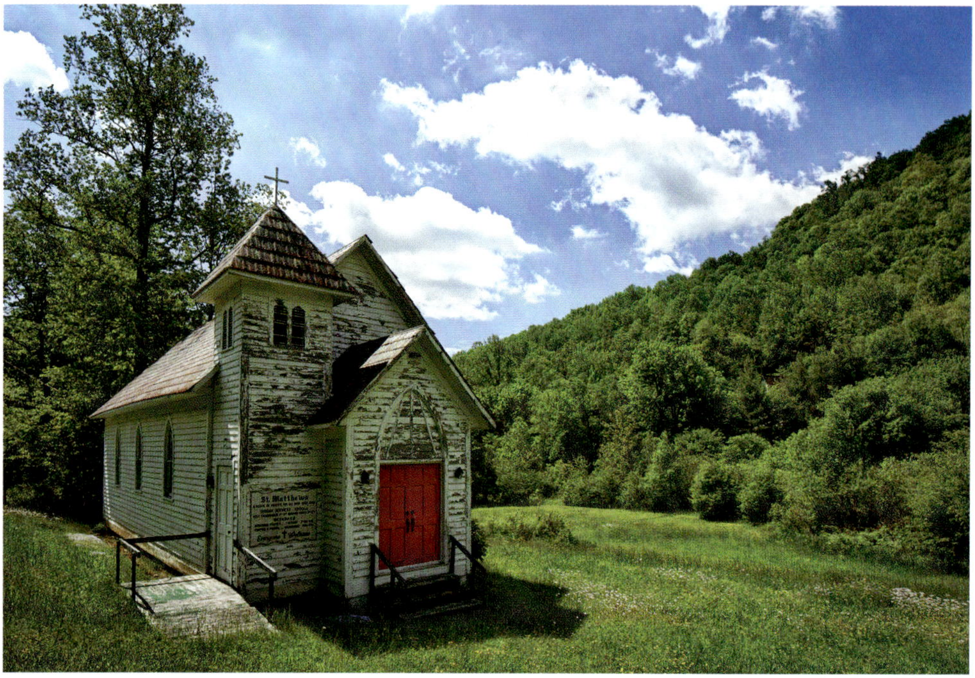

Figure 2.11
The depth of field is very shallow because of the large aperture and my close distance to the subject.

ISO 400 • 1/100 sec. • f/4 • 45mm lens

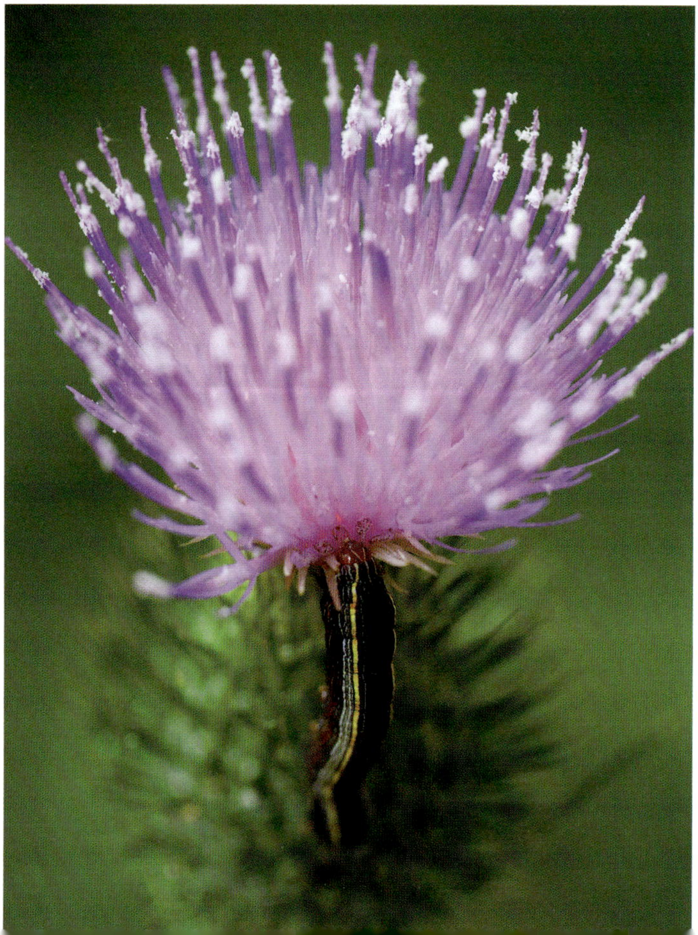

Chapter 2 Assignments

Formatting your card

Even if you have already begun using your camera, make sure you are familiar with formatting the SD card. If you haven't done so already, follow the directions given earlier in the chapter and format as described (make sure you save any images that you may have already taken). Then perform the Format function every time you have downloaded or saved your images or use a new card.

Checking your firmware version

Using the most up-to-date version of the camera firmware will ensure that your camera is functioning properly. Use the menu to find your current firmware version, and then update as necessary using the steps listed in this chapter.

Cleaning your sensor

Make sure you are familiar with the Sensor Cleaning function so you can use it every time you change a lens.

Exploring your image formats

I want you to become familiar with all of the camera features before using the RAW format, but take a little time to explore the Quality and Image Size menus so you can see what options are available to you.

Exploring your lens

If you are using a zoom lens, spend a little time shooting with all of the different focal lengths, from the widest to the longest. See just how much of an angle you can cover with your widest lens setting. How much magnification will you be able to get from the telephoto setting? Try shooting the same subject with a variety of different focal lengths to note the differences in how the subject looks, and also the relationship between the subject and the other elements in the photo.

Share your results with the book's Flickr group!
Join the group here: flickr.com/groups/panasonicGX7_fromsnapshotstogreatshots

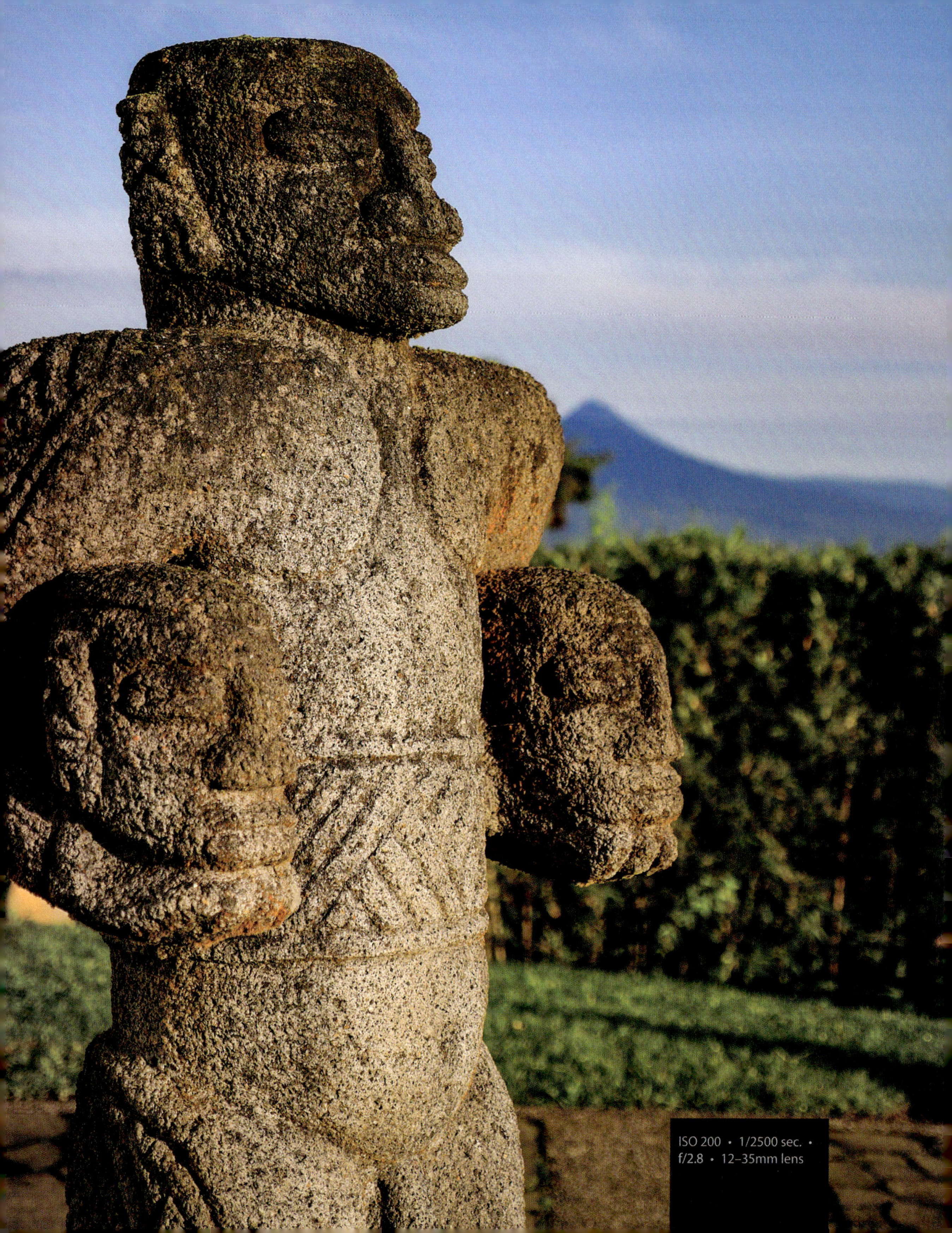

ISO 200 • 1/2500 sec. • f/2.8 • 12–35mm lens

3

The Auto Modes

Get Shooting with the Automatic Camera Modes

The Lumix GX7/GM1 is an amazing camera that has some incredible features. In fact, with all of the technology built into it, it can be pretty intimidating for the person new to photography. Its features allow it to operate just like a DSLR camera but without the size and, of course, the mirror. Fortunately, Panasonic has made it a little easier for you to get great-looking photographs without having to do a lot of thinking. Enter the automatic modes. The icon-labeled automatic camera modes on the Mode dial are set up to use specific features of the camera for various shooting situations. Let's take a look at the different modes and how and when to use them.

Poring Over the Picture

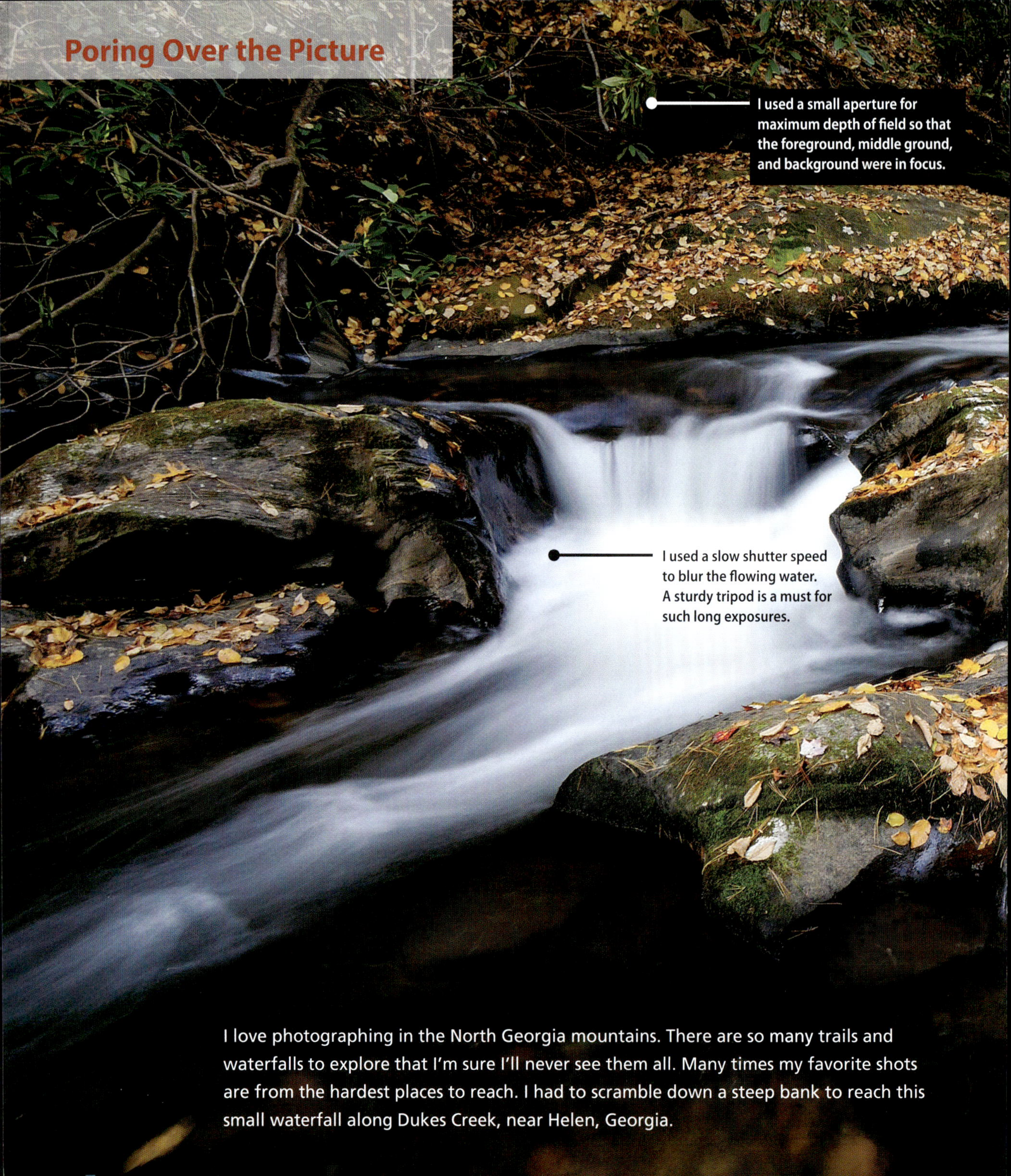

I love photographing in the North Georgia mountains. There are so many trails and waterfalls to explore that I'm sure I'll never see them all. Many times my favorite shots are from the hardest places to reach. I had to scramble down a steep bank to reach this small waterfall along Dukes Creek, near Helen, Georgia.

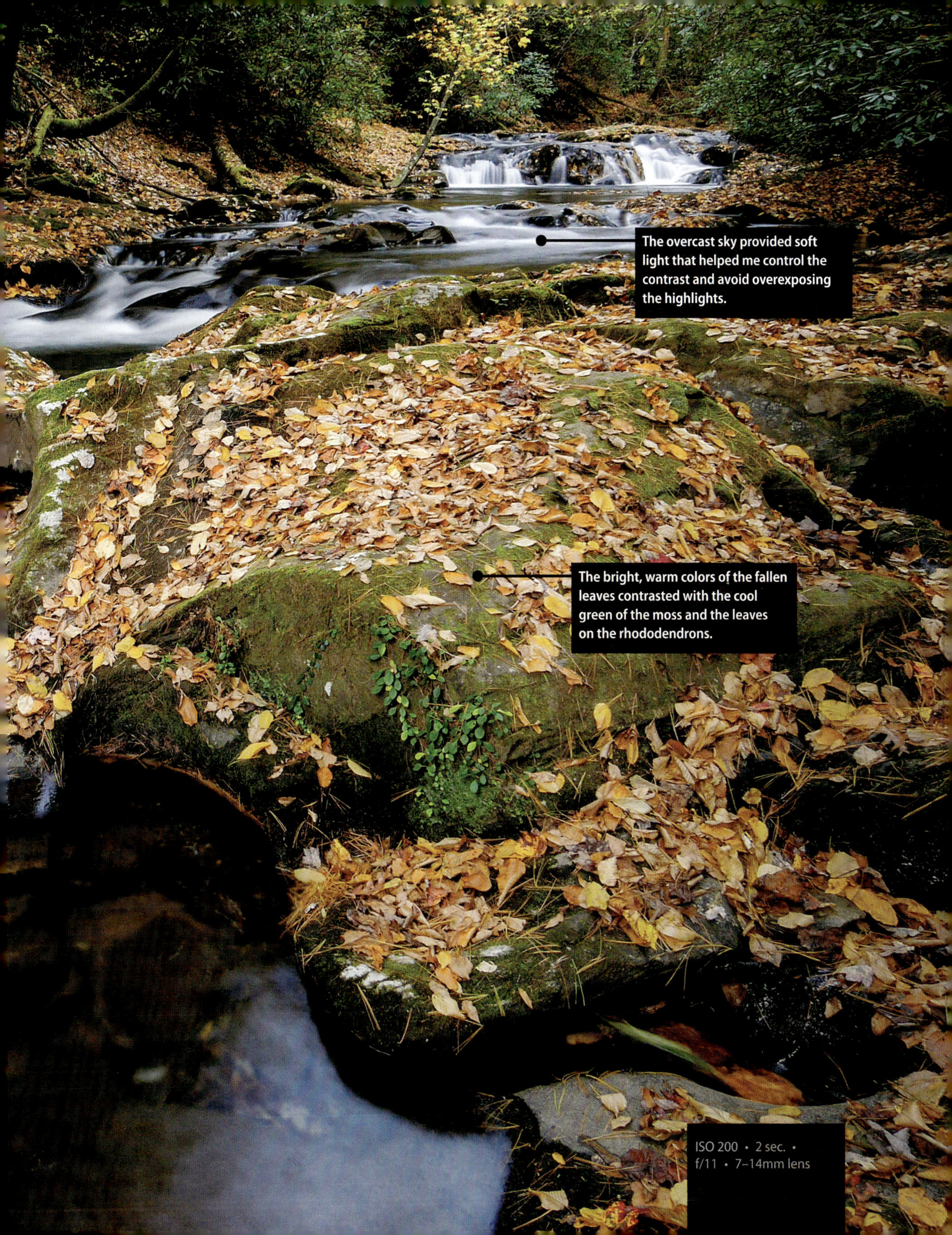
The overcast sky provided soft light that helped me control the contrast and avoid overexposing the highlights.
The bright, warm colors of the fallen leaves contrasted with the cool green of the moss and the leaves on the rhododendrons.
ISO 200 • 2 sec. • f/11 • 7–14mm lens

Intelligent Auto Mode

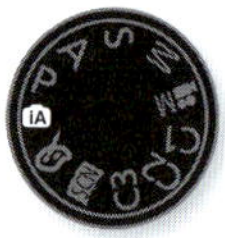

Intelligent Auto mode is all about thought-free photography. There is not much for you to do in this mode except point and shoot. It even determines what type of scene you're pointing the camera at, from a macro setting to portraiture. Your biggest concern when using Intelligent Auto mode is focusing. The camera will utilize the automatic focusing modes to achieve the best possible focus for your picture. Naturally, the camera is going to assume that the object that is closest to the camera is the one that you want in sharpest focus. Simply press the shutter button down halfway while looking through the viewfinder, and you should see one or several focus points light up over the subject. Now just press down the shutter button the rest of the way to take the photo. It's just that easy (**Figure 3.1**). The camera will take care of all your exposure decisions, including ISO. You do have a few options while using this mode. You can control the background defocus, the flash, the autofocus, and the self-timer. Above the LCD display, there is a button that has a lightning bolt icon next to it—slide it to enable the built-in flash. Press the Auto Focus Mode button (◀) to switch between regular AF and AF tracking. And finally, press the Drive Mode button (▼) to activate the self-timer.

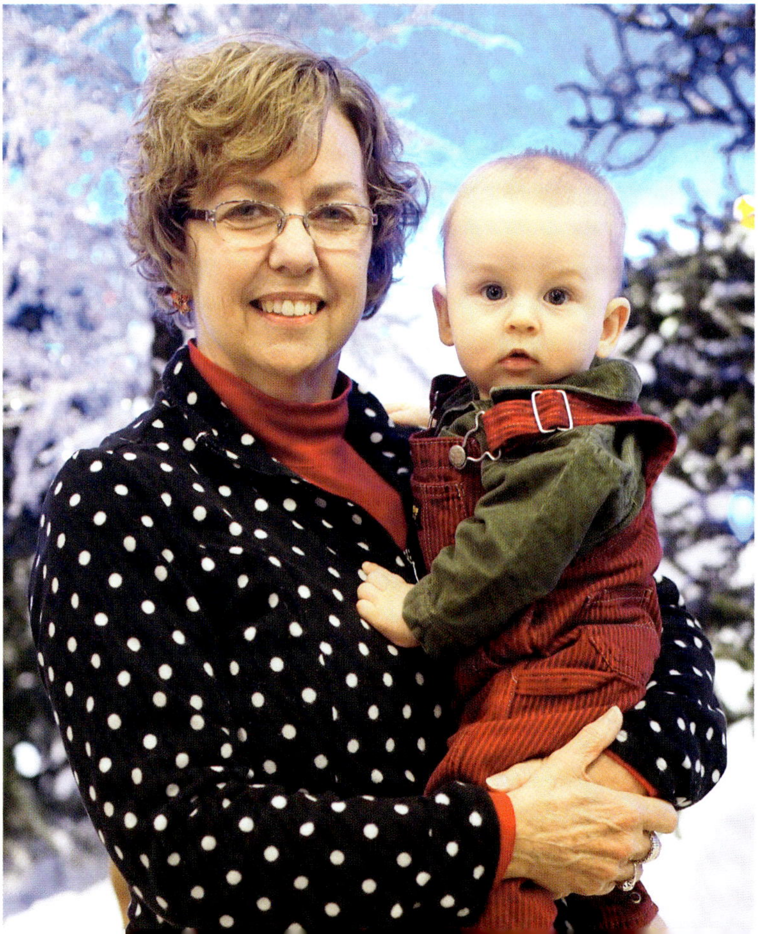

Figure 3.1
Intelligent Auto mode is great when you just want to shoot without thinking too much, as with this holiday snapshot.

ISO 1600 • 1/80 sec. • f/1.8 • 45mm lens

Defocus Control

This setting forces the camera to use either a larger or smaller aperture setting to change the depth of field in your image (**Figure 3.2**). A large aperture (low f-stop number) creates more blur in the background, and a small aperture (high f-stop number) creates less blur in the background. You can adjust Defocus Control by pressing and turning the Rear dial (GM1: press ▲ and turn the Control dial).

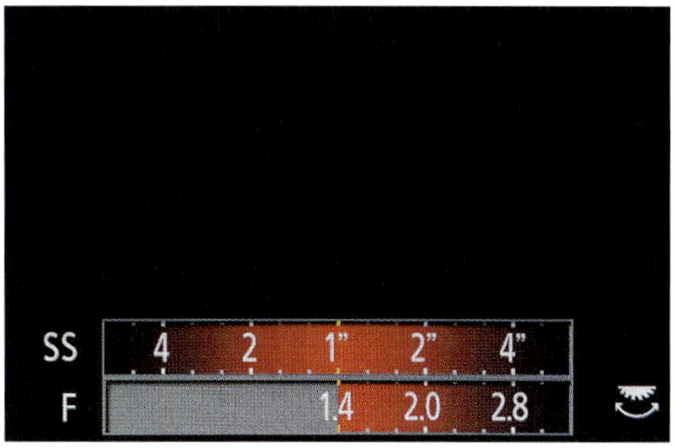

Figure 3.2 Defocus Control

Intelligent Auto Plus Mode

If Intelligent Auto does most of the work for you, Intelligent Auto Plus does just a little more. To switch between the Intelligent Auto and Intelligent Auto Plus modes, press the Menu/Set button and touch your choice on the screen (**Figure 3.3**). Like Intelligent Auto, this mode detects the type of scene you are shooting and determines all exposure settings. Intelligent Auto Plus has the same options as Intelligent Auto, but it adds the ability to adjust the brightness (exposure compensation) and color tone (white balance).

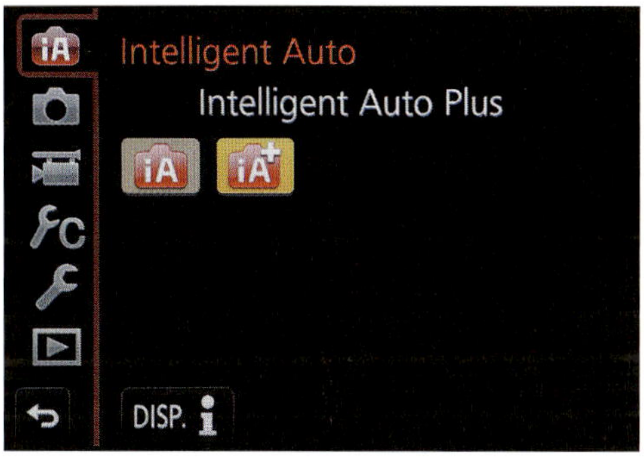

Figure 3.3 Intelligent Auto Plus mode

Flash during auto modes

The built-in flash on your GX7/GM1 does not pop up automatically when you're using the Intelligent Auto or Intelligent Auto Plus mode. If you feel that your primary subject needs more light (especially if you are photographing people), slide the flash pop-up button on the back of the camera (the button has a lightning bolt next to it). Once the flash is up, the mode will do the rest for you. It's not until you switch into P, S, A, or M mode that you have to exert a bit of control over the flash. The use of the built-in flash and flash compensation are covered in Chapter 8.

Brightness

The Brightness control in Intelligent Auto Plus Mode is our first introduction to exposure compensation (**Figure 3.4**). Press and turn the Rear dial (GM1: press ▲ and turn the Control dial) to make the image brighter or darker. You will see the effect of the adjustment in the EVF (GX7 only) or on the LCD.

Pressing the Rear dial (GM1: pressing the ▲ button) switches between Defocus Control and the Brightness setting.

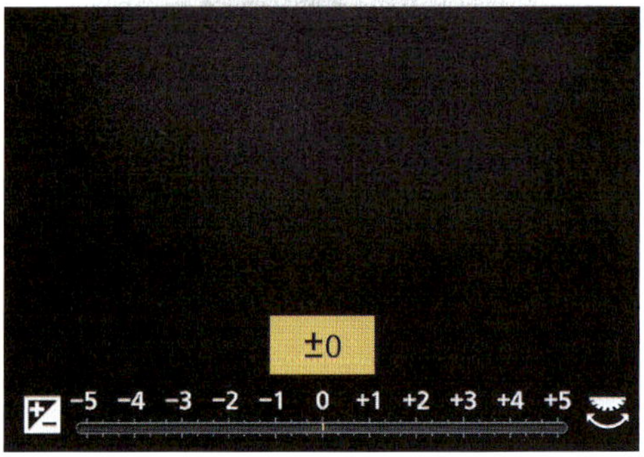

Figure 3.4 **Brightness**

Color

The Color effect simply augments the color temperature of the image, allowing you to make the scene warmer or cooler (**Figure 3.5**). Press the WB button (▶) and turn the Rear dial (GM1: Command dial) to adjust the color.

Making adjustments on the touchscreen

You can adjust the Color, Defocus, and Brightness settings using the touchscreen. Touch the iA+ icon on the LCD (**Figure 3.6**), and then touch the adjustment you want to make.

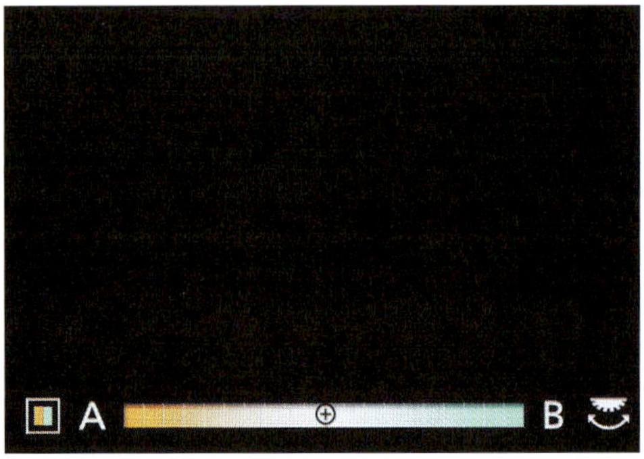

Figure 3.5 **Color**

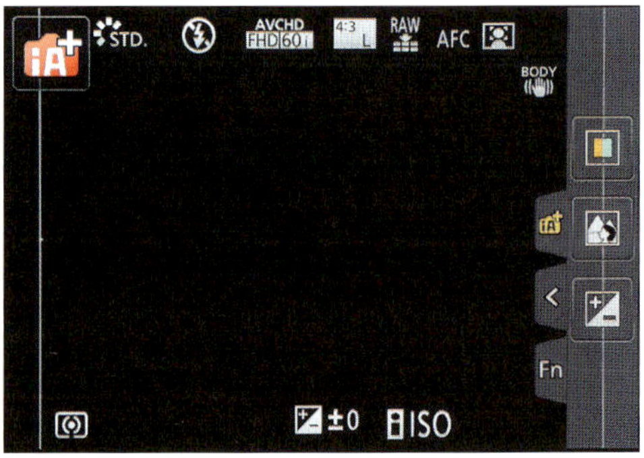

Figure 3.6 **The touchscreen gives you easy access to your image adjustments.**

Exposure compensation

Exposure compensation allows you to fine-tune your exposure in the automatic and semi-automatic modes to make your images brighter or darker. The camera thinks that the "correct" exposure for every scene is medium, but that medium exposure can be quite boring or just plain wrong. You can adjust the exposure in 1/3-stop increments and see the effects in the viewfinder (GX7 only) and on the LCD. To adjust exposure compensation, click and turn the GX7's Rear dial or, on the GM1, press ▲ and then the Control dial. Exposure compensation is not available in Manual (M) or Intelligent Auto (iA) mode, but it is available in Intelligent Auto Plus (iA+) mode.

Creative Control Mode

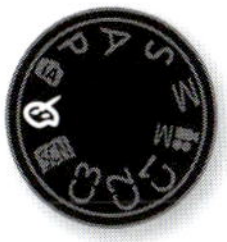

Creative Control mode is a set of filters that lets you add creative looks to your images and videos inside the camera. The GX7/GM1 has 22 different Creative Control filters to spark your creativity. I like to use the in-camera filters because I can see what my image will look like before I take the shot, and I don't have to wait to apply filters in my computer. I use the image effect adjustments to dial in the settings and create my own version of each filter (**Figures 3.7** and **Figure 3.8**).

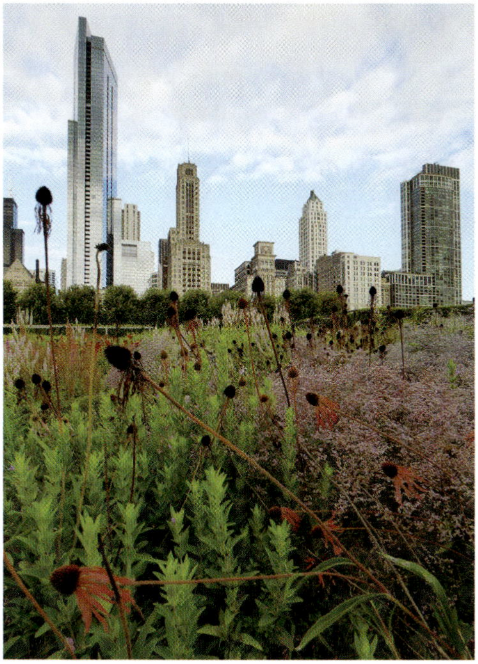

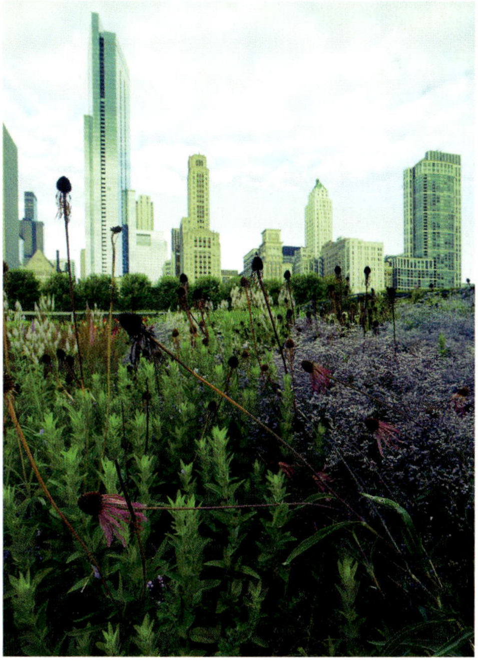

Figure 3.7 (left) **The High Dynamic filter compresses the highlights and shadows in this scene.**

ISO 640 • 1/160 sec. • f/5.6 • 7–14mm lens

Figure 3.8 (right) **The Cross Process filter changes the colors in the scene for a more artistic look.**

ISO 200 • 1/160 sec. • f/5 • 7–14mm lens

You cannot adjust the white balance and ISO in Creative Control mode, but your GX7/GM1 gives you quite a bit of control over your images. You can change the aperture setting with Defocus Control and use exposure compensation to fine-tune your exposure. Each filter also has its own unique image effect adjustment based on how the filter affects your image.

Choosing a filter

1. Set the Mode dial to Creative Control.
2. Press the Disp button to change the selection screen display: Normal display shows the filter list with a live preview (**A**). Guide display explains what the filters do (**B**). List display shows all the filters in a grid (**C**).
3. Touch the filter you want to use and press Menu/Set to make your selection. To switch between filters, touch the red filter icon in the upper-left corner of the LCD.

A

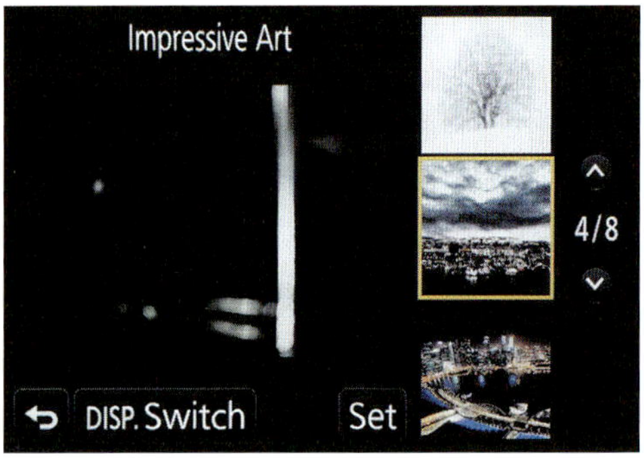

B

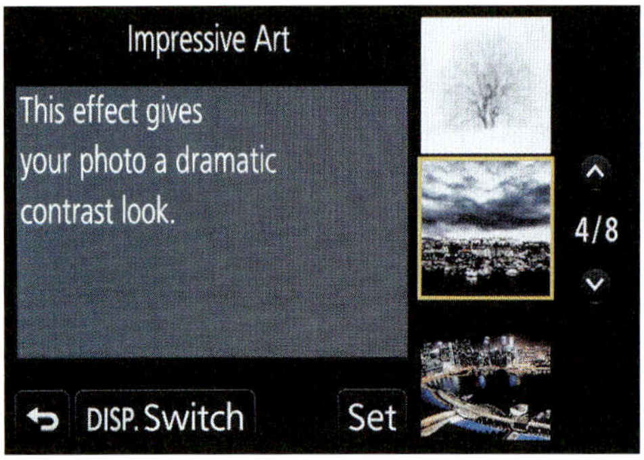

C

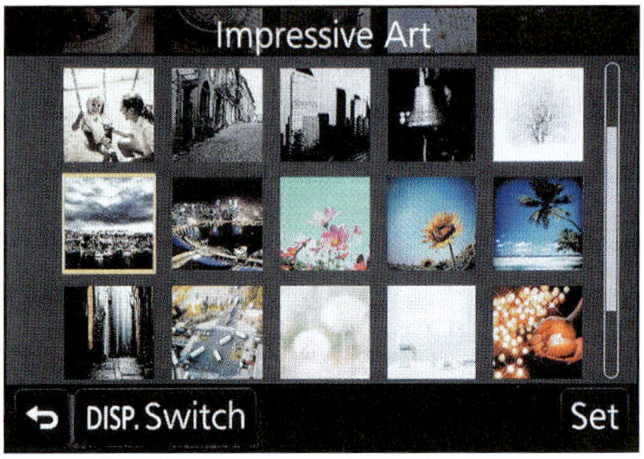

Adjusting the effect

You can adjust the brightness, defocus, and image effect of each Creative Control filter to suit your taste and shooting situation.

1. Press and turn the Rear dial (GM1: press ▲ and turn the Control dial) to make the image brighter or darker.
2. Press and turn the Rear dial again to adjust Defocus Control (GM1: press ▲ and turn the Control dial).

   Pressing the Rear dial (GM1: pressing the ▲ button) switches between Defocus Control and brightness setting.
3. Press the WB button (▶) and turn the Rear dial (GM1: Control dial) to adjust the image effect.

   You can also touch the Creative Control icon on the touchscreen to access the image effect, defocus, and brightness (**Figure 3.9**).

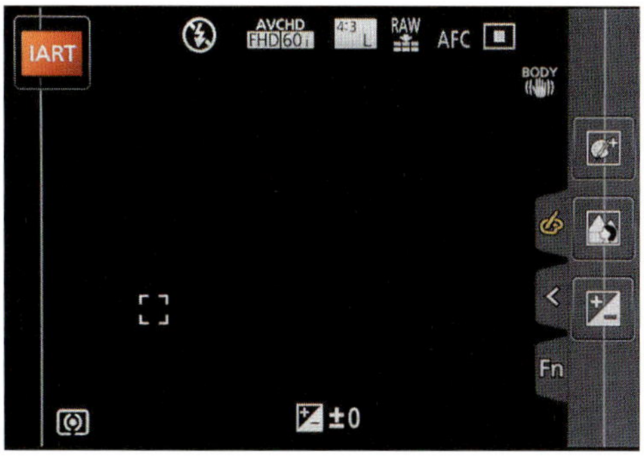

Figure 3.9 You can reach the filter adjustments by touching the palette icon on the LCD.

The image effect adjustment will be different depending on which filter you are using. For example, the Monochrome filter allows you to add a warm or cool tone to your black and white image (**Figure 3.10**), the Cross Process filter gives you the choice of four different color filters (**Figure 3.11**), and the Impressive Art filter adjusts from black and white to bold color (**Figure 3.12**). Filters like Miniature Effect, One Point Color, and Sunshine have additional controls for special effects.

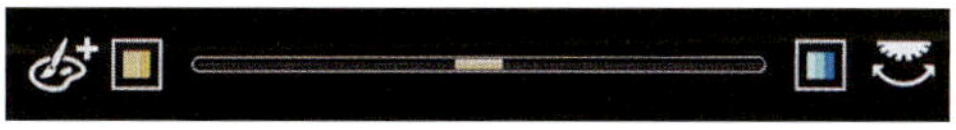

Figure 3.10 Monochrome image effects

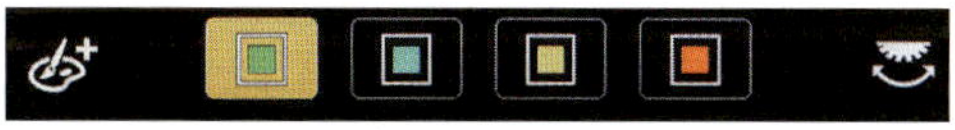

Figure 3.11 Cross Process image effects

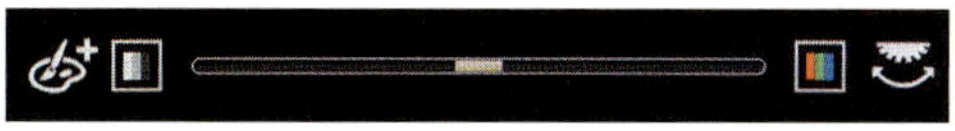

Figure 3.12 Impressive Art image effects

Manual callout

A description of every Creative Control filter and the available image effects starts on page 116 in your GX7 manual, and on page 107 in the GM1 manual.

Custom mode

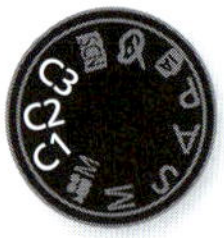

You can save your most-used Creative Control filters to the Custom slots on the Mode dial. Once your filter is adjusted the way you like it, press Menu/Set > Custom > Cust Set Mem. Choose which Custom mode you would like to register the filter to (**Figure 3.13**), and touch Yes to register the settings.

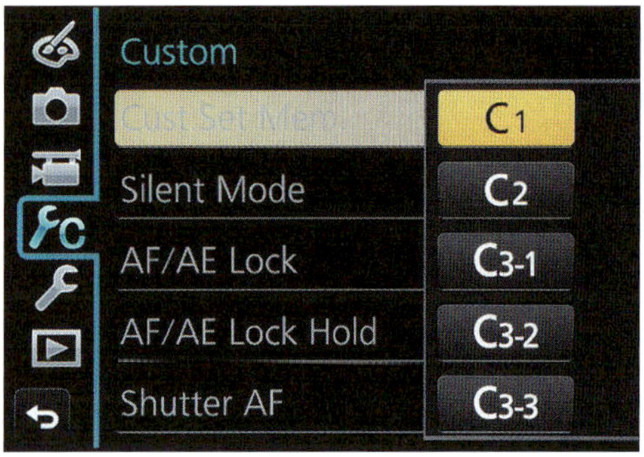

Figure 3.13 You can save your favorite settings in five Custom modes (the GM1 has four Custom modes).

There are three Custom modes on the Mode dial (GM1: two), and the C3 slot actually contains three modes. That gives you five slots in which to store your favorite settings. For example, I have my C3 modes set to three of my favorite black and white looks (**Figure 3.14**). I can access them quickly and easily with a twist of the Mode dial.

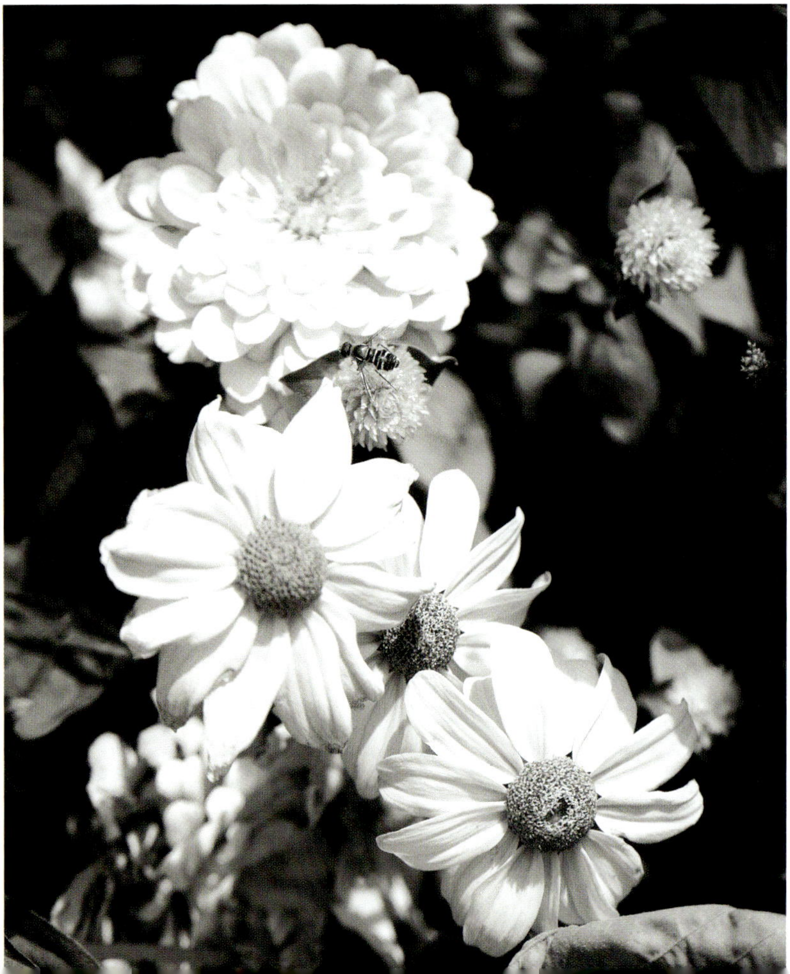

Figure 3.14 I like to use the Dynamic Monochrome filter with the contrast dialed down just a bit.

ISO 200 • 1/2500 sec. • f/2.8 • 35–100mm lens

Why You Shouldn't Overlook Creative Control Mode

A lot of photographers scoff at the creative filters that are included with cameras like the GX7/GM1. I'll admit that I never used in-camera creative filters until I started using Micro Four Thirds cameras. I still use computer software like Adobe Lightroom and Photoshop to edit my images, but making creative decisions in the camera can be a lot of fun. You would probably be surprised to find out how many photos in this book are JPEGs I shot using Creative Control mode. Here are a few reasons I recommend at least trying Creative Control mode.

- **Pre-processing.** If you are just learning the basics of exposure and other camera controls, it can be daunting to try to learn image-editing software at the same time. Creative Control mode allows you to use the camera controls to pre-process your images instead of post-processing them in your computer.
- **Creative control.** With 22 filter effects, you are sure to find a few you like. Unlike the creative filters in many other cameras, you can dial in the look of your images using exposure compensation and Defocus Control.
- **WYSIWYG. This stands for "what you see is what you get."** One advantage of a mirrorless camera is that you can see what your image will look like before you press the shutter button. I think it's more fun to use in-camera filters when you can see the effect in the EVF and on the LCD.
- **Image effect adjustment.** Each filter has its own unique adjustments, and you aren't limited to the default settings. Experiment with the filters and image effect adjustments and come up with your own "digital film."
- **It's fun.** Using the Creative Control filters is just plain fun. In-camera filters may not be considered a "professional" way to use your camera, but sometimes it's nice to make some photos without being too serious.
- **RAW+JPEG.** I recommend using the RAW+JPEG quality setting when you are using Creative Control mode. If you use RAW+JPEG, the filter effect will be applied to the JPEG and you'll have an unfiltered RAW file in case you need it.

Scene Guide Mode

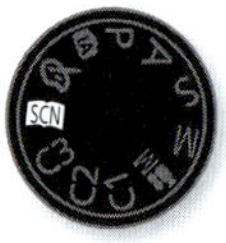

Scene Guide mode works a little bit differently than the Intelligent Auto and Intelligent Auto Plus modes. When using the Scene Guide mode, you select the type of photo you're trying to make and the camera makes the necessary adjustments for you (**Figure 3.15**). In some ways it is more advanced than Intelligent Auto mode, because you are making creative decisions about how you want your photo to look based on your subject, but the camera still adjusts most of the settings for you. You can control the exposure compensation to make the image brighter or darker, just as you would in the other automatic modes, but that's about it.

The GX7 has 24 Scene Guide modes (GM1: 23), which represent many of the shooting situations you are likely to come across. There are options for everything from portraits to landscapes to sports. Come to think of it, all of those subjects are covered later in this book! By the time you finish with this book, you should be well beyond the automatic modes, but there are a few things you can learn from Scene Guide mode.

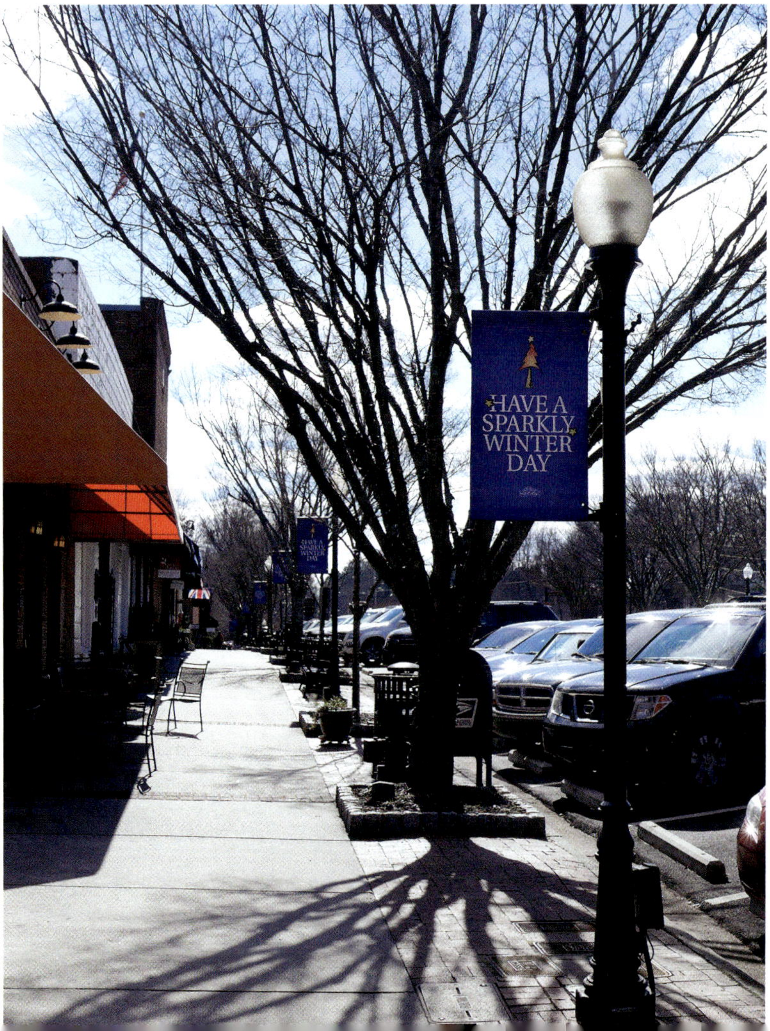

Figure 3.15
I used the Bright Blue Sky scene mode to make the sky more vibrant in this image.

ISO 200 • 1/1250 sec. • f/5 • 25mm lens

Guide display

Scene Guide mode has four different screen displays, and you press the Disp button to cycle through them. If you're going to use Scene Guide mode, be sure to take advantage of the information in the Guide display.

Manual callout

A detailed description of the Scene Guide modes starts on page 101 in your GX7 manual, and on page 95 in the GM1 manual.

Guide display contains four screens for each scene, and you can scroll from screen to screen using the ▲ and ▼ buttons. The first screen tells you how the scene affects your image (**Figure 3.16**), the One Point screen gives you a basic tip for shooting that type of scene (**Figure 3.17**), the Advance screen tells you something about camera settings (**Figure 3.18**), and the Recommended Lens screen tells you what type of lens you should use for the scene (**Figure 3.19**). That's a lot of good info that you can apply to your photography when you start using the professional modes and taking more control of your camera.

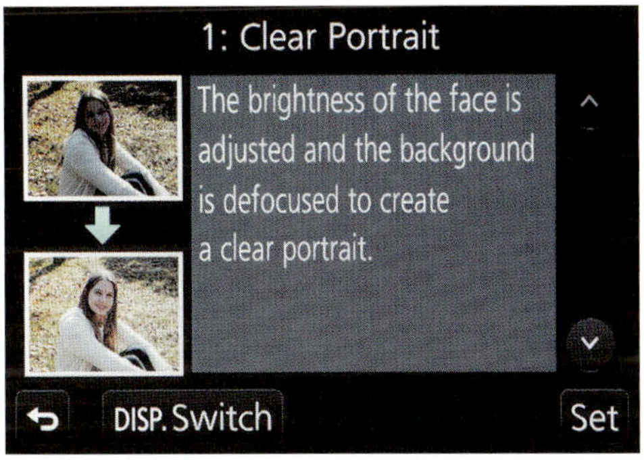

Figure 3.16 **Guide display for the Clear Portrait scene mode**

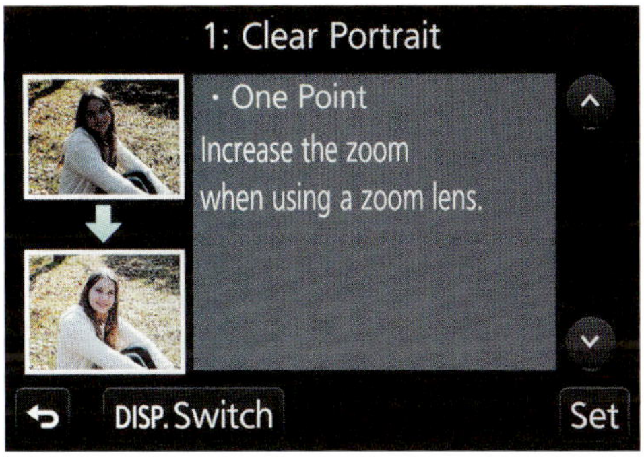

Figure 3.17 **One Point**

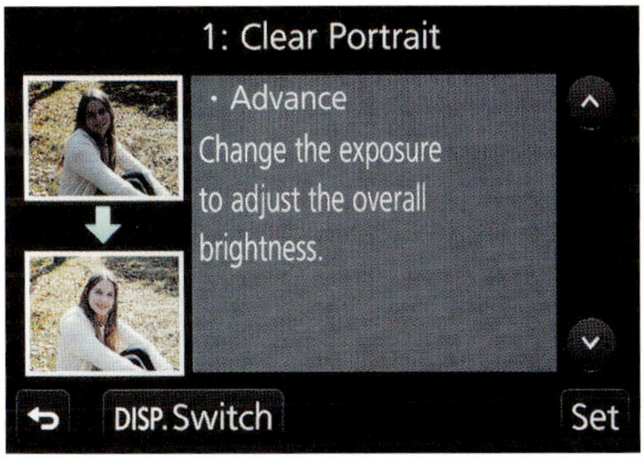

Figure 3.18 **Advance**

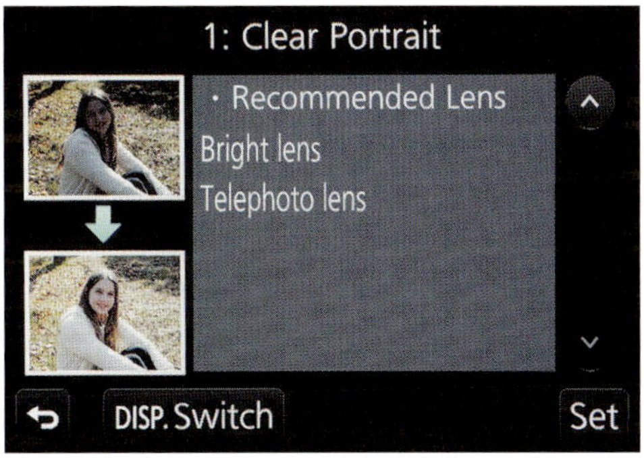

Figure 3.19 **Recommended Lens**

Panorama Shot

Once you finish with this book and get familiar with your camera, you will most likely leave the Scene Guide mode behind—with one exception. The only reason I turn the Mode dial on my GX7 to Scene Guide mode is for shooting panoramas (**Figure 3.20**). Panorama Shot mode (GX7 only) allows you to capture a series of images that the camera stitches together into a seamless panorama. The stitching works better with stationary objects, and it takes a bit of practice to get the speed of the camera movement just right. With a little practice you can create beautiful panoramic images, and even apply creative effects, right inside the camera.

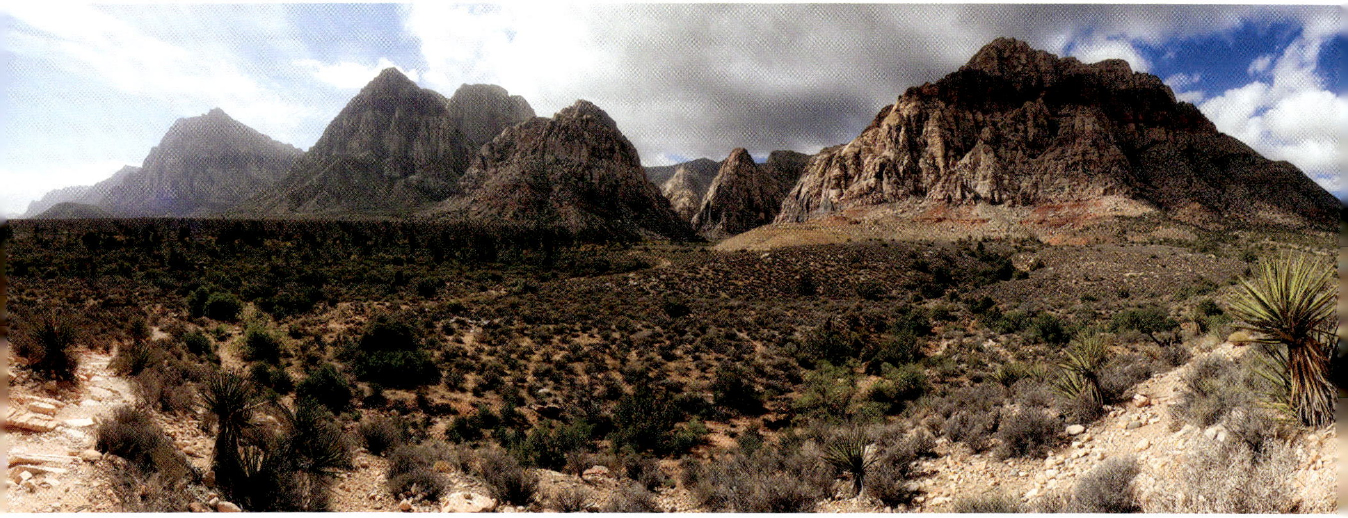

Figure 3.20 Panorama Shot mode does a fantastic job of stitching multiple images together into a seamless panorama.

ISO 200 • 1/640 sec. • f/9 • 12–35mm lens

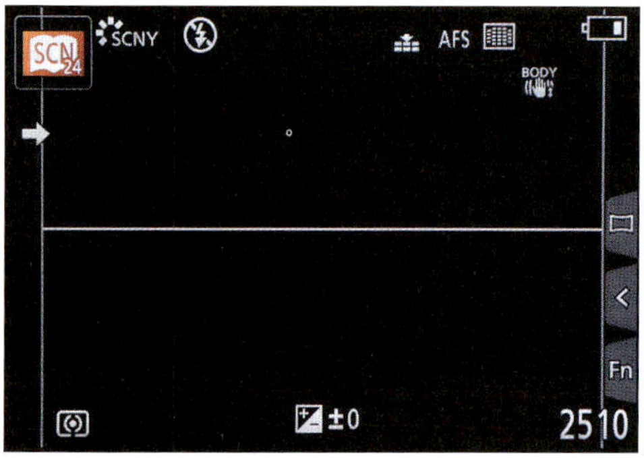

Figure 3.21 The directional arrow and the center line will help keep your panoramas straight.

Turn the Mode dial to Scene Guide mode and select Panorama Shot (it is the last scene on the list) to shoot a panorama. You will see an arrow in the upper-left corner of the LCD that indicates the direction you need to move the camera, and a line in the middle of the LCD to help you keep your panning motion straight (**Figure 3.21**).

The default setting has you move the camera from left to right, so I'll use that as an example. To begin the pano, point the camera toward the left side of your desired shot. Press the shutter button halfway to focus, then press and release the shutter button to begin shooting. It is important that you release the shutter button! Move the camera slowly from left to right (also called panning), and use the line on the LCD to keep the camera as level as possible. Press the shutter button to stop shooting. The camera will process your panorama and show you when it is done.

The photo style for your panoramas will be set to Scenery, but you can adjust the contrast, sharpness, saturation, and noise reduction. To make these adjustments, press Menu/Set > Rec > Photo Style and move the sliders (**Figure 3.22**). You can adjust your white balance with the WB button (▶), your focus area mode with the AF Mode button (◀), and your exposure compensation by pressing and turning the Rear dial.

You can change the direction of your pano and even apply creative filter effects by touching the Panorama icon on the touchscreen (**Figure 3.23**). Touch the direction icon to choose left, right (**A**), up, or down. Touch the Filter effect (**B**) to apply filter effects from the Creative Control mode. Some of the filter effects won't be applied on the screen, but they will be applied to the final panorama. See page 109 in your manual for a list of available filter effects.

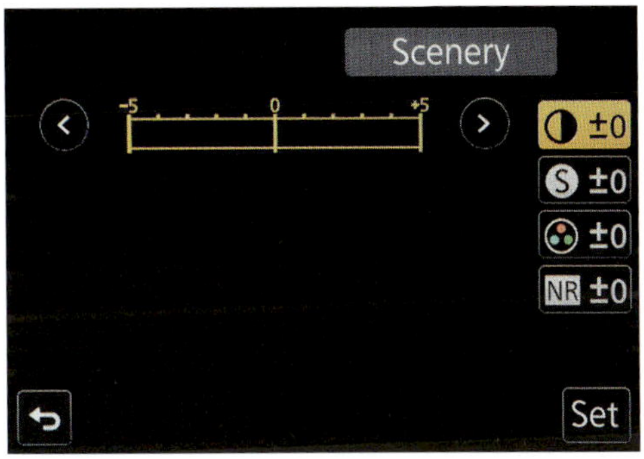

Figure 3.22 You can adjust the Scenery photo style for your panos.

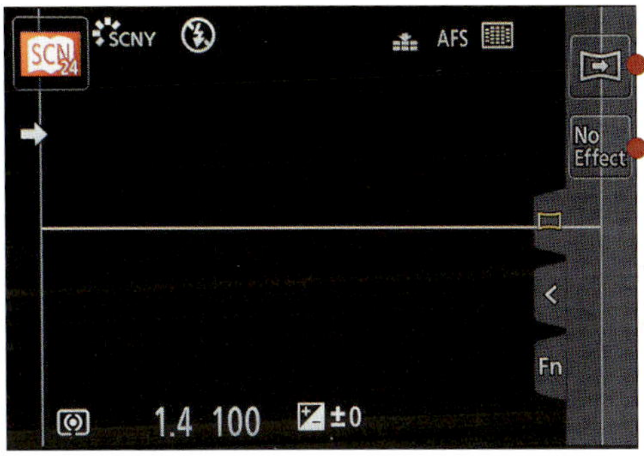

Figure 3.23 Touch the panorama icon to access the panorama settings.

A few tips for Panorama Shot mode

- Shoot past where you want the edges of your pano to be. The camera will not record to the edges of what you see in your viewfinder.
- Stationary subjects make better panoramas. Moving subjects can produce unpredictable and often strange-looking results.
- Pan more slowly if you're using longer lenses. Telephoto lenses require slower panning to produce a good result.
- Try using filter effects with your panos. Adding a creative filter to your panorama can produce really interesting results.

Chapter 3 Assignments

These assignments will have you shooting in the automatic modes so you can experience the advantages and disadvantages of using them in your daily photography.

Shooting in Intelligent Auto mode

It's time to give up complete control and just concentrate on what you see in the viewfinder. Set your camera to Intelligent Auto and practice shooting in a variety of conditions, both indoors and outside. Take notice of the camera settings when you are reviewing your pictures.

Shooting in Intelligent Auto Plus mode

Switch your camera to Intelligent Auto Plus mode to take more control. Use the Brightness control to adjust the exposure compensation and see the results on the LCD. Adjust the Defocus Control function to see its effect on the sharpness of your background. Shoot the same subject with different defocus settings and notice how changing the depth of field affects your images.

Getting creative with Creative Control mode

Now it's time to have a little fun exploring the options that are available to you using the filters in Creative Control mode. Get a feel for navigating through the options. Then, working your way down the list, start making adjustments to each filter, taking a picture with each to see how it affects the final photo. The key here is to select one scene and then use it for each change in your settings. This will give you a reference for how the image is affected by each filter. Use the image effect controls to fine-tune your photos.

Capturing the scenery with Scene Guide mode

Take your camera outside and switch to Scene Guide mode for some landscape and macro work. Find a nice scene, and with your widest available lens, take some pictures using Distinct Scenery mode. Then switch back to Intelligent Auto so you can compare the settings used for each image as well as the changes to colors and sharpness. Now, while you are still outside, find something in the foreground—a leaf or a flower—and switch the camera to Soft Image of a Flower mode. See how close you can get, and take note of the f-stop that the mode uses. Then switch to Intelligent Auto and shoot the same subject.

Stopping the action with Scene Guide mode

This assignment requires that you find a subject that is in motion. That could be the traffic in front of your home or a child at play. The only real requirement is that the subject be moving. This will be your opportunity to test out Clear Sports Shot mode. There isn't a lot to worry about here—just point and shoot. Try shooting a few frames one at a time, and then hold down the shutter button and shoot a burst of about five or six frames. It will help if your subject is in good available light to start with so that the camera won't be forced to use high ISOs.

Get wide with Panorama Shot mode

It's time to use my favorite part of Scene Guide mode. Find a scene that would make a great panorama. Wide landscapes and city skylines make excellent pano subjects. Activate Panorama Shot mode and start practicing. Use the widest lens you have and get a feel for how fast you need to pan the camera to get good results. Switch to a vertical panorama and try shooting a tall subject like a tree or a tall building. Shoot a few panos with different filter effects to stretch your creative muscles.

Share your results with the book's Flickr group!
Join the group here: flickr.com/groups/panasonicGX7_fromsnapshotstogreatshots

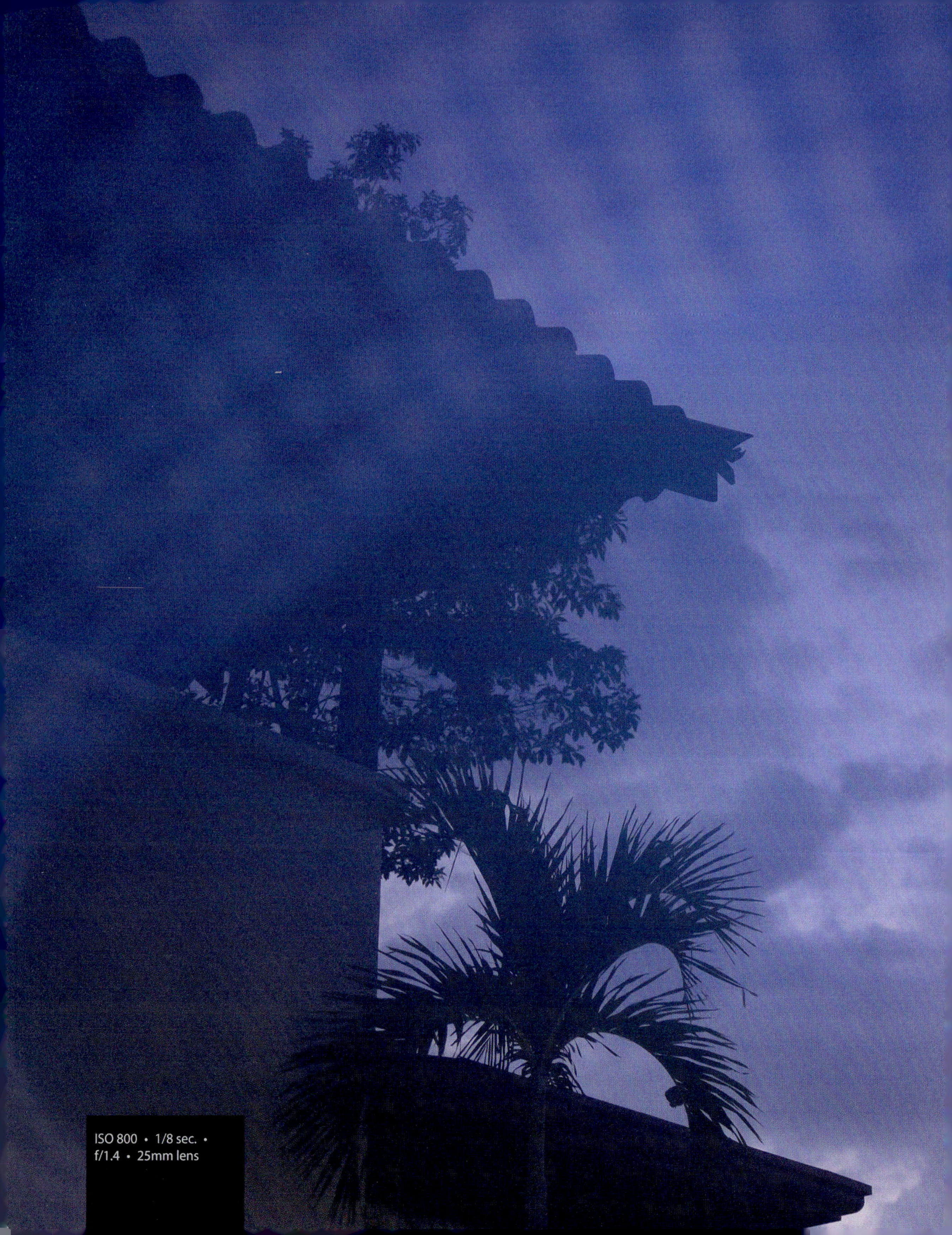

ISO 800 • 1/8 sec. • f/1.4 • 25mm lens

4

The Professional Modes

Taking Your Photography to the Next Level

Your creativity comes through in your images when you can control your camera, and the professional exposure modes allow you such control. With practice, these modes will probably become the backbones of your photography. They allow you to influence the three factors that make exposure: *aperture, shutter speed, and ISO.* Accessing the professional modes is as simple as turning the Mode dial to P, A, S, or M. If you want to take that next step in controlling your photography, it is important to understand not only how to control these modes, but why and when to adjust them so that you make the images you want. So let's move that Mode dial to the first of our professional modes: Program Auto.

Poring Over the Picture

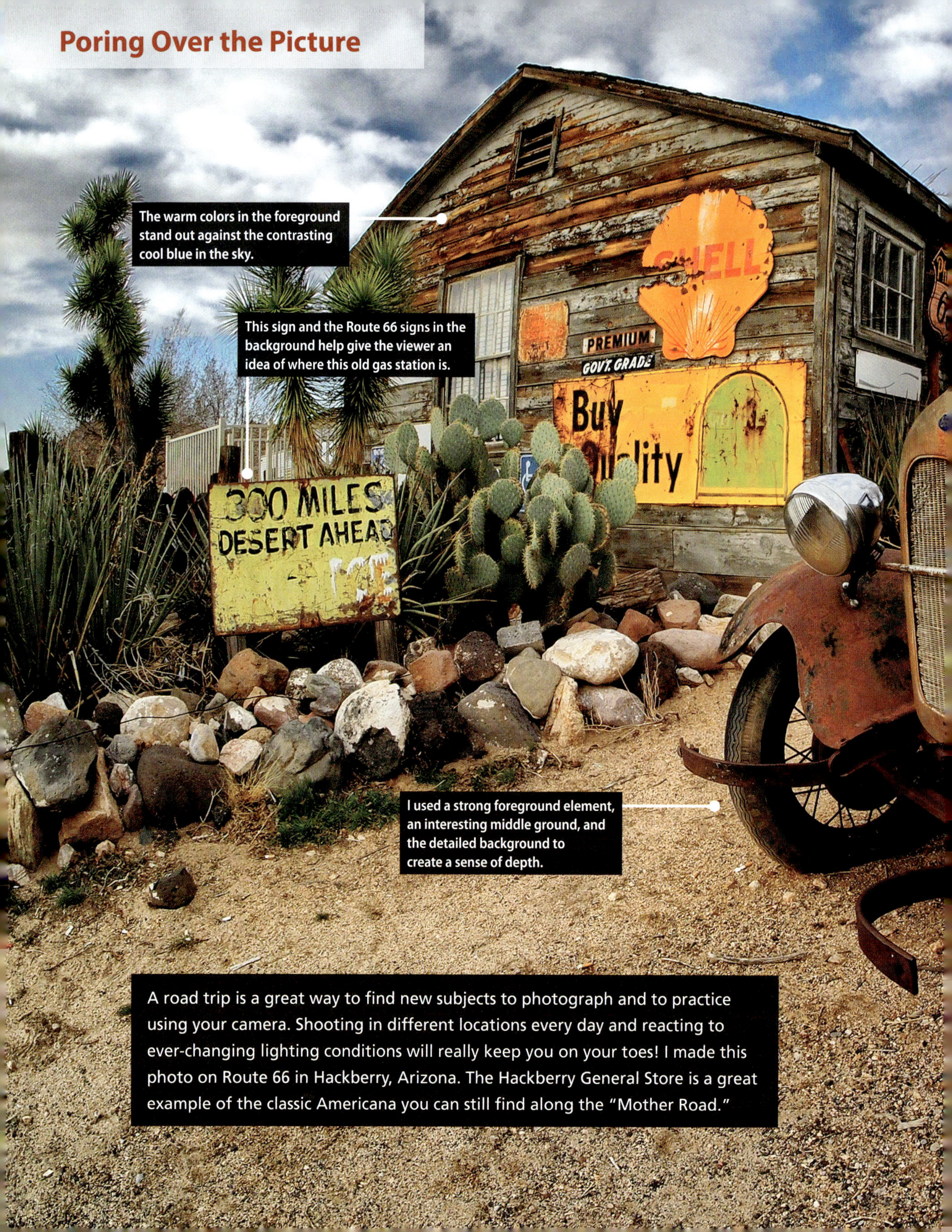

The warm colors in the foreground stand out against the contrasting cool blue in the sky.

This sign and the Route 66 signs in the background help give the viewer an idea of where this old gas station is.

I used a strong foreground element, an interesting middle ground, and the detailed background to create a sense of depth.

A road trip is a great way to find new subjects to photograph and to practice using your camera. Shooting in different locations every day and reacting to ever-changing lighting conditions will really keep you on your toes! I made this photo on Route 66 in Hackberry, Arizona. The Hackberry General Store is a great example of the classic Americana you can still find along the "Mother Road."

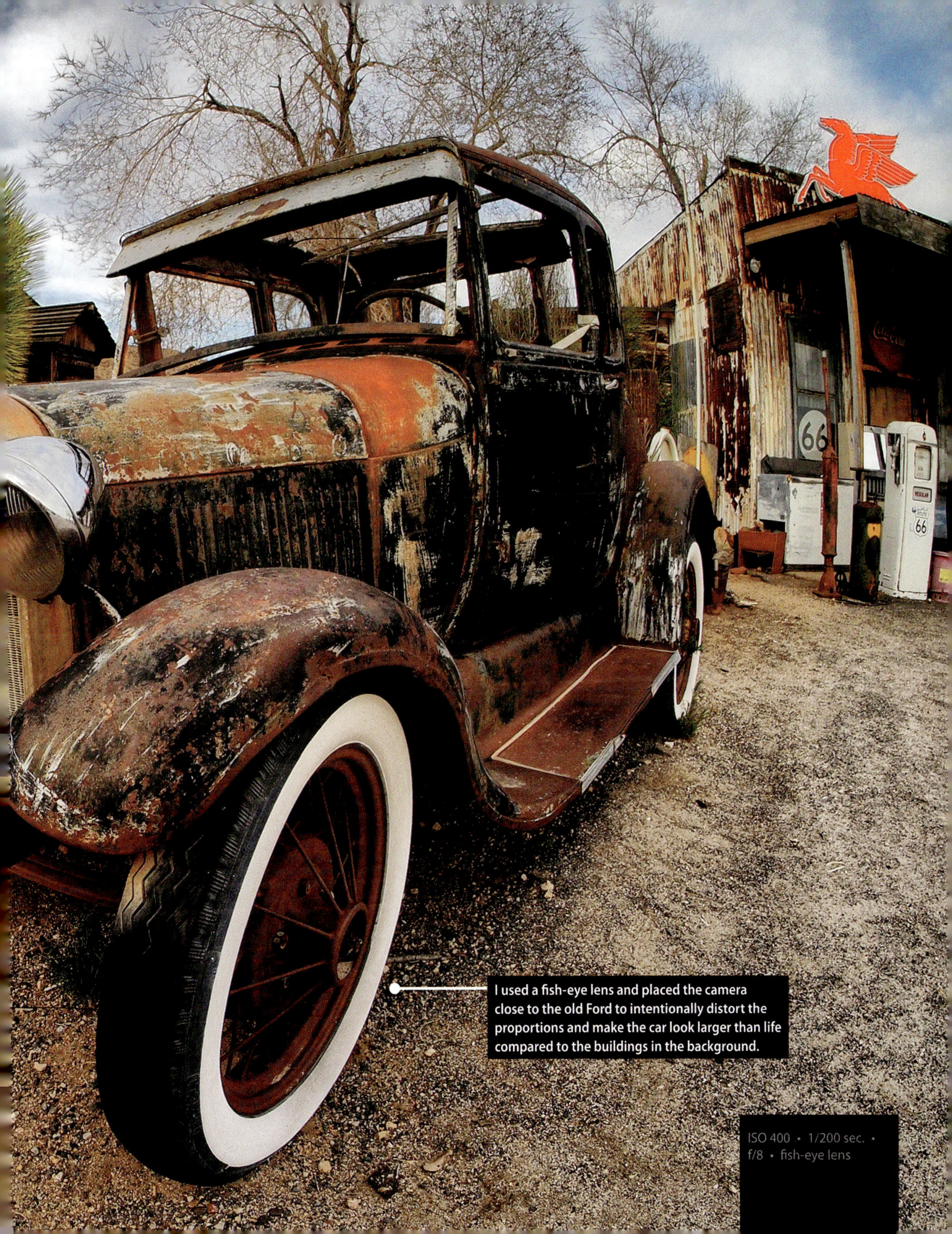

I used a fish-eye lens and placed the camera close to the old Ford to intentionally distort the proportions and make the car look larger than life compared to the buildings in the background.

ISO 400 • 1/200 sec. • f/8 • fish-eye lens

P: Program Auto Mode

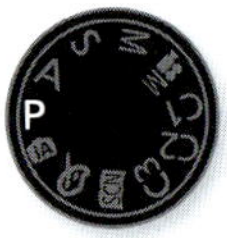

There is a reason that Program Auto (P) mode is only one click away from the Intelligent Auto mode: With respect to aperture and shutter speed, the camera is doing most of the thinking for you. If that is the case, why use Program Auto mode instead? Program Auto mode gives you the ease of use offered by Intelligent Auto Mode, and adds the ability to change settings like ISO and white balance. Think of a family picnic outdoors in a partial shade/sun environment—I want great-looking pictures, but I'm not looking for anything to hang in a gallery. I might use Program Auto mode because it's quick and easy, but it gives me more control than the automatic modes, including Intelligent Auto Plus, can deliver.

Manual Callout

A comparison of the different professional shooting modes begins on page 89 of your GX7 owner's manual, and on page 83 in the GM1 manual.

When to use Program Auto (P) mode instead of the automatic modes

- When shooting in a casual environment where quick adjustments are needed
- When you want control over the ISO
- If you want to make corrections to the white balance

Let's go back to our picnic scenario. As I said, the light is moving from deep shadow to bright sunlight, so the camera is trying to balance our three photo factors (ISO, aperture, and shutter speed) to make a good exposure. Since the idea is to take more control of my images, I'll choose a white balance setting that is appropriate for the conditions. In this case I would probably choose the Daylight setting. Then I would choose an appropriate ISO setting. The lower the ISO number, the better the quality of our photographs, but the less light sensitive the camera becomes. It's a balancing act, with the main goal always being to keep the ISO as low as possible—too low an ISO, and we will get camera shake in our images from a long shutter speed; too high an ISO means we will have an unacceptable amount of digital noise. For our purposes, let's go ahead and select ISO 400 so that we provide enough sensitivity for those shadows while allowing the camera to use shutter speeds that are fast enough to stop motion.

With the ISO selected, we can now make use of the other controls built into Program Auto mode. By rotating the Front dial (the Control dial on the GM1), we have the ability to shift the program settings. Remember, your camera is using the internal light meter to pick what it believes are suitable exposure values, but sometimes it doesn't know what it's looking at and how you want those values applied (**Figures 4.1** and **4.2**). With the program shift, you can influence what the shot will look like. Do you need faster shutter speeds in order to stop the action? Just turn the Front dial (GM1: Control dial) clockwise. Do you want a larger aperture so that you get a narrow depth of field? Then turn the dial counterclockwise until you get the desired f-stop. By clicking and rotating the Rear dial (GM1: ▲, then Control dial), we can adjust the exposure compensation. Turn the dial to the left to make the image darker, and to the right to make the image brighter.

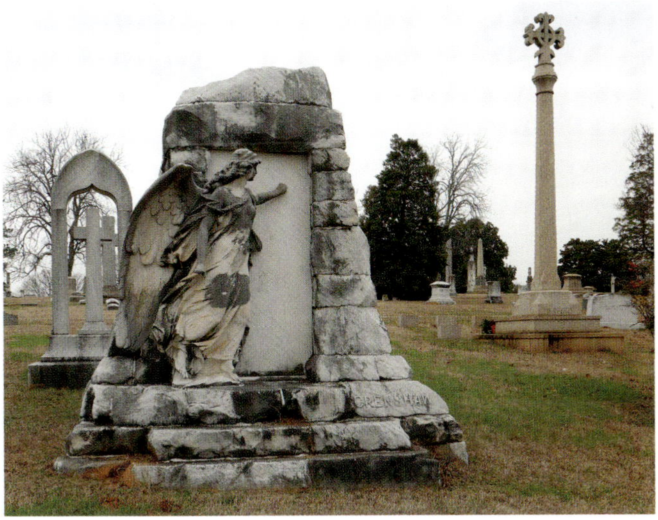

Figure 4.1
This is my first shot, using Program Auto mode. The camera chose f/8, which gives me enough depth of field that the foreground and background are in focus.

ISO 200 • 1/160 sec. • f/8 • 20mm lens

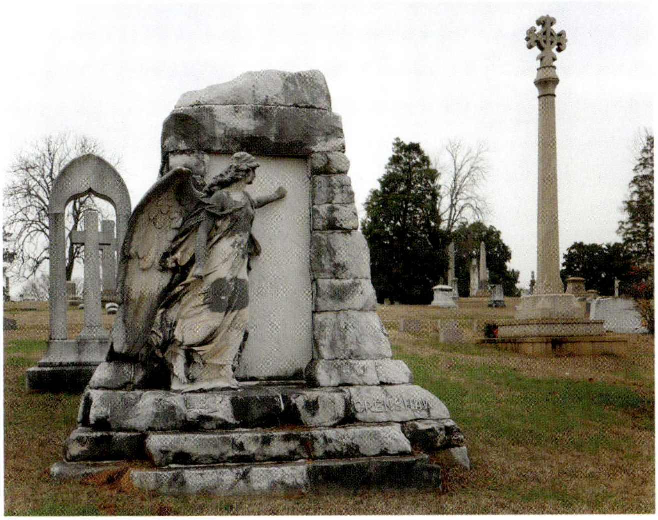

Figure 4.2
I turned the Front dial on my GX7 to "shift the program." I opened up the aperture to blur the background. Notice that the camera kept the exposure the same by changing both the aperture value and the shutter speed.

ISO 200 • 1/3200 sec. • f/1.8 • 20mm lens

Starting points for ISO selection

There is a lot of discussion concerning ISO in this and other chapters, but it might be helpful if you know where your starting points should be for your ISO settings. The first thing you should always try to do is use the lowest possible ISO setting. That being said, here are some good starting points for your ISO settings:

- 200: Bright, sunny day
- 400: Outdoor shade, or when using flash
- 800: Indoor lighting at night or cloudy conditions outside
- 1600: Late night, low-light conditions or sporting arenas at night

These are just suggestions, and your ISO selection will depend on a number of factors that will be discussed later in the book. You might have to push your ISO even higher as needed, but at least now you know where to start.

Let's set up the camera for Program Auto mode and see how we can make all of this come together.

Setting up and shooting in Program Auto mode

1. Turn your camera on, and then turn the Mode dial to align the P with the indicator line.
2. To select your ISO on the GX7, press the ISO button (▲), rotate the Rear dial to the desired setting, and press the Rear dial to select (the ISO selection will appear in the electronic viewfinder and the rear LCD panel).

   On the GM1, press the Fn1 button we assigned to ISO in Chapter 1. Rotate the Control dial to the desired setting and press MENU/SET.
3. Point the camera at your subject, and then activate the camera meter by depressing the shutter button halfway.
4. View the exposure information in the electronic viewfinder or on the display panel on the back of the camera.
5. While the meter is activated, roll the Front dial (GM1: Control dial) left and right to shift the program and use a different aperture and shutter speed combination. Click and turn the Rear dial (GM1: ▲, then Control dial) to adjust the exposure compensation.
6. Select the program and exposure that is right for you and start shooting. (Don't worry if you aren't sure what the right exposure is. We will start working on making the right choices for those great shots beginning with the next chapter.)

A: Aperture Priority Mode

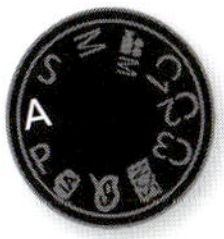

A on the Mode dial refers to Aperture Priority mode. It is one of the most useful and popular of the professional modes. Aperture Priority mode is considered a semiautomatic mode because it allows you to control two factors of exposure while the camera adjusts for the other. You choose the aperture value and the ISO, and the camera chooses the shutter speed.

This is one of my favorite modes because the aperture value largely dictates depth of field. Depth of field, along with composition, is a major factor in how you direct attention to what is important in your image. It is the factor that controls how much of your image is in focus. If you want to isolate a subject from the background, such as when shooting a portrait, you can use a large aperture (low f-stop number) to keep the focus on your subject and make both the foreground and background blurry. If you want to keep the entire scene sharply focused, such as with a landscape, then using a small aperture (high f-stop number) will render the greatest possible depth of field.

When to use Aperture Priority (A) mode

- When shooting portraits or wildlife (**Figure 4.3**)
- When bracketing images for HDR photography (**Figure 4.4**)
- When shooting landscape photography, which often benefits from a large depth of field (**Figure 4.5**)

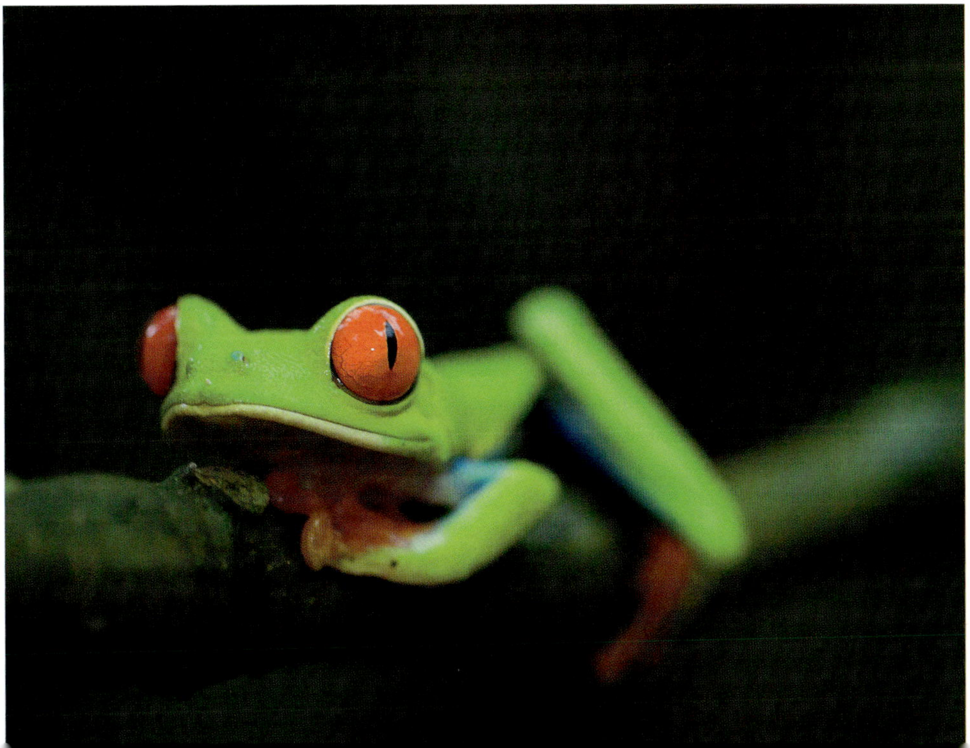

Figure 4.3
A large aperture (low f-stop number) and a longer focal length create a very blurry background to emphasize the subject.

ISO 100 • 1/200 sec. • f/5.6 • 45mm lens

Figure 4.4
I combined three different exposures of the same scene to create this HDR image. Combining multiple exposures can help capture the entire dynamic range of a scene. It is best to keep the aperture value consistent while adjusting the shutter speed for different exposures.

ISO 800 • f/11 • multiple shutter speeds • 16–35mm lens

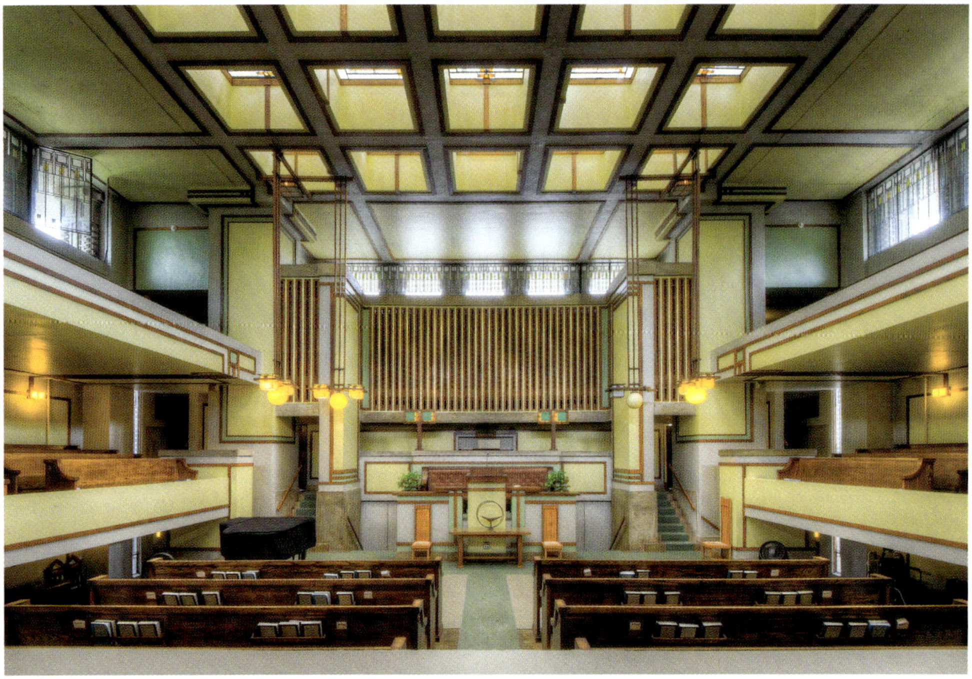

Figure 4.5
The smaller aperture setting (higher f-stop number) brings sharpness to near and far objects.

ISO 200 • 1/400 sec. • f/8 • 35–100mm lens

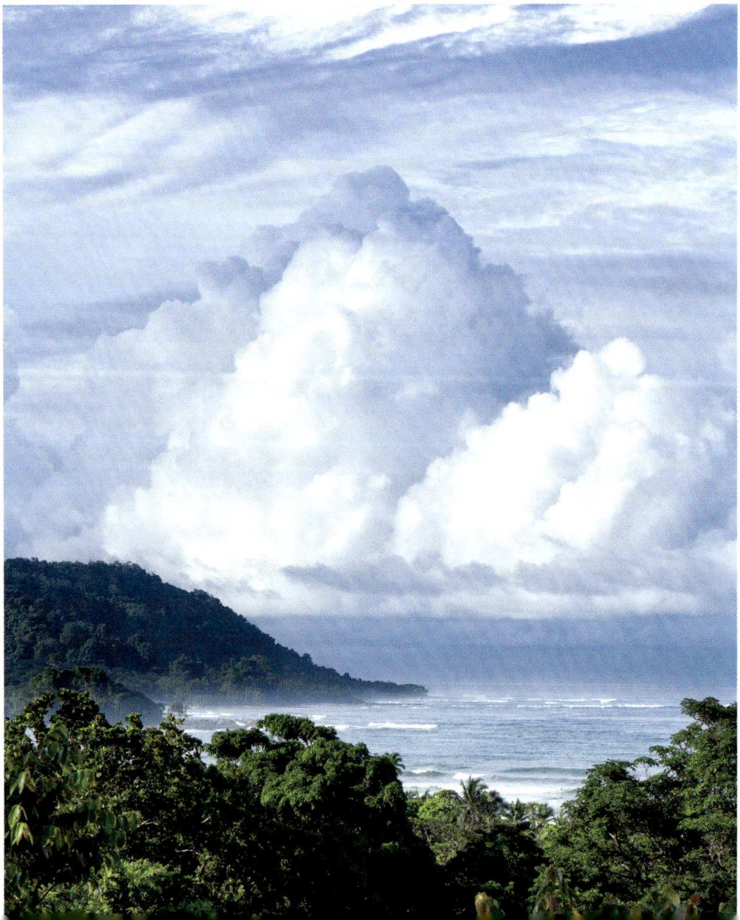

F-stops and aperture

The numeric value of your lens aperture is described as an *f-stop*. The f-stop is a photography term that technically relates to the focal length of the lens (e.g., 200mm) divided by the effective aperture diameter. These measurements are defined as "stops" and work incrementally with your shutter speed and ISO to create proper exposure. Older camera lenses used one-stop increments to assist in exposure adjustments, such as 1.4, 2, 2.8, 4, 5.6, 8, 11, 16, and 22. Each stop represents about half the amount of light entering the lens iris as the larger stop before it. Today, most lenses don't have f-stop markings since all adjustments to this setting are performed via the camera's electronics. The stops are also now typically divided into 1/3-stop increments to allow much finer adjustments to exposures.

We have established that Aperture Priority (A) mode is highly useful in controlling the depth of field in your image. It's also pivotal in determining the limits of available light that you can shoot in. Different lenses have different maximum apertures. The larger the maximum aperture, the less light you need in order to achieve a properly exposed image. If your lens has a larger aperture, you can let in more light all at once, which means that you can use faster shutter speeds to reduce hand shake and blurriness in the final picture. This is why lenses with large maximum apertures, such as f/1.4, are called "fast" lenses.

On the other hand, bright scenes require the use of a small aperture (such as f/16 or f/22), especially if you want to use a slower shutter speed. That small opening reduces the amount of incoming light, and this reduction of light allows the shutter stay open longer.

Setting up and shooting in A mode

1. Turn your camera on and then turn the Mode dial to align the A with the indicator line.
2. To select your ISO on the GX7, press the ISO button (▲), rotate the Rear dial to the desired setting, and press the Rear dial to select (the ISO selection will appear in the electronic viewfinder and the rear LCD panel).

   On the GM1, press the Fn1 button we assigned to ISO in Chapter 1. Rotate the Control dial to the desired setting and press MENU/SET.
3. Turn the Front dial (GM1: Control dial) to select the aperture value (f-stop). Turn the dial to the left for a larger aperture (lower f-stop number) and to the right for a smaller aperture (higher f-stop number).
4. Point the camera at your subject, and then activate the camera meter by depressing the shutter button halfway.
5. View the exposure information in the electronic viewfinder or on the rear LCD panel.
6. Press and turn the Rear dial (GM1: ▲, then Control dial) to change the exposure compensation to make the image brighter or darker.

Zoom lenses and maximum apertures

Some zoom lenses (like the GX7's 14–42mm kit lens) have a variable maximum aperture. This means that the largest opening will change depending on the zoom setting. In the example of the 14–42mm zoom, the lens has a maximum aperture of f/3.5 at 14mm and only f/5.6 when the lens is zoomed out to 42mm. Fixed-aperture zoom lenses maintain the same maximum aperture throughout the zoom range. They are typically much more expensive than their variable maximum aperture counterparts.

S: Shutter Priority Mode

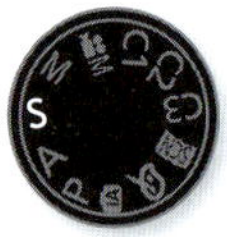

The S on the mode dial stands for Shutter Priority mode. Like the Program Auto and Aperture Priority modes, Shutter Priority mode gives us freedom to control certain aspects of our photography. In this case, you select the shutter speed and ISO, and the camera chooses the aperture value.

The shutter speed determines just how long you expose your camera's sensor to light. The longer the shutter remains open, the more time your sensor has to gather light. Two of the major influences on the sharpness of an image are camera shake and the subject's movement. The shutter speed can affect how sharp your photographs are. This is different from the image being sharply in focus. Because a slower shutter speed means that light from your subject is hitting the sensor for a longer period of time, any movement by you or your subject will show up in your photos as blur.

Shutter speeds

A *slow* shutter speed refers to leaving the shutter open for a long period of time—like 1/30 of a second or longer. A *fast* shutter speed means that the shutter is open for a very short period of time—like 1/250 of a second or less. The camera doesn't display the entire fraction. 1/30 is shown as 30, 1/250 is shown as 250, and so on.

When to use Shutter Priority (S) mode

- When working with fast-moving subjects where you want to freeze the action (**Figure 4.6**); much more on this in Chapter 5
- When you want to emphasize movement in your subject with panning or with motion blur (**Figure 4.7**)
- When you want to create silky-looking water in a waterfall (**Figure 4.8**); more on this in Chapter 7

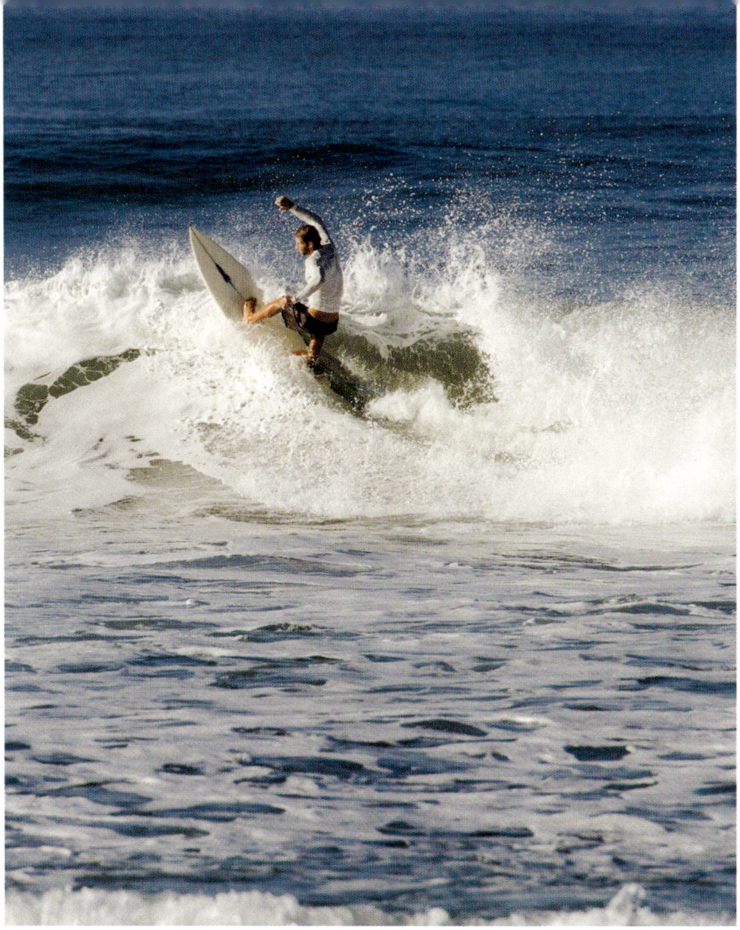

Figure 4.6
Fast-moving subjects can be frozen with the right shutter speed.

ISO 200 • 1/1000 sec. • f/8 • 70–200mm lens

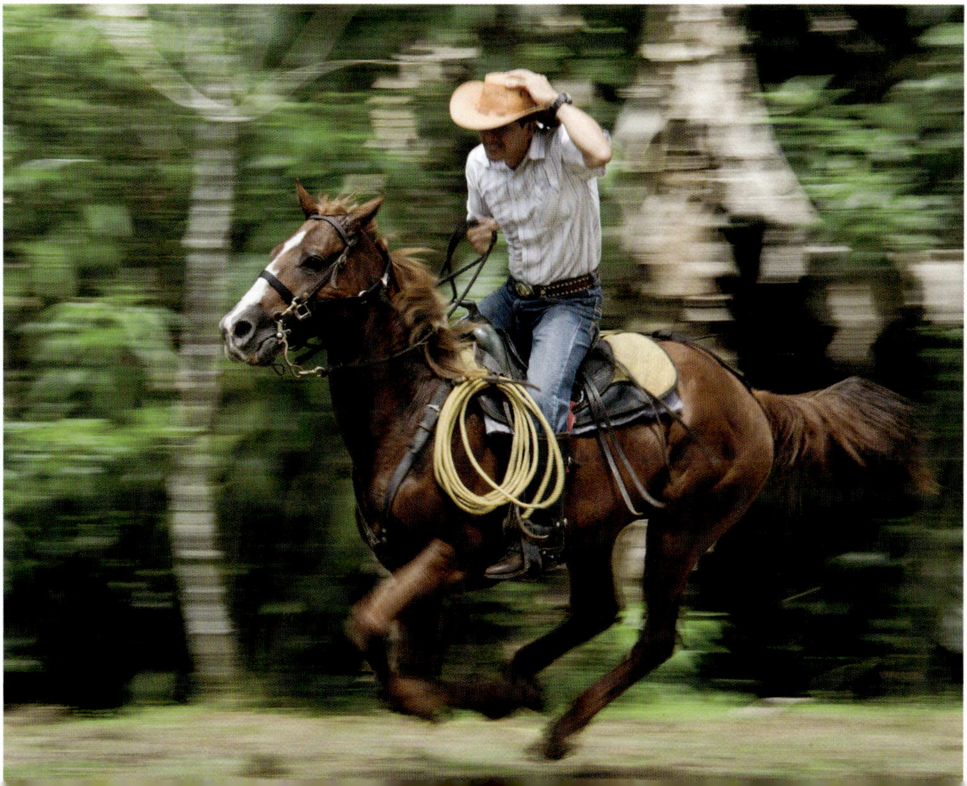

Figure 4.7
I used a relatively slow shutter speed and panned the camera to follow the subject and create this motion blur effect.

ISO 400 • 1/60 sec. • f/20 • 28–300mm lens

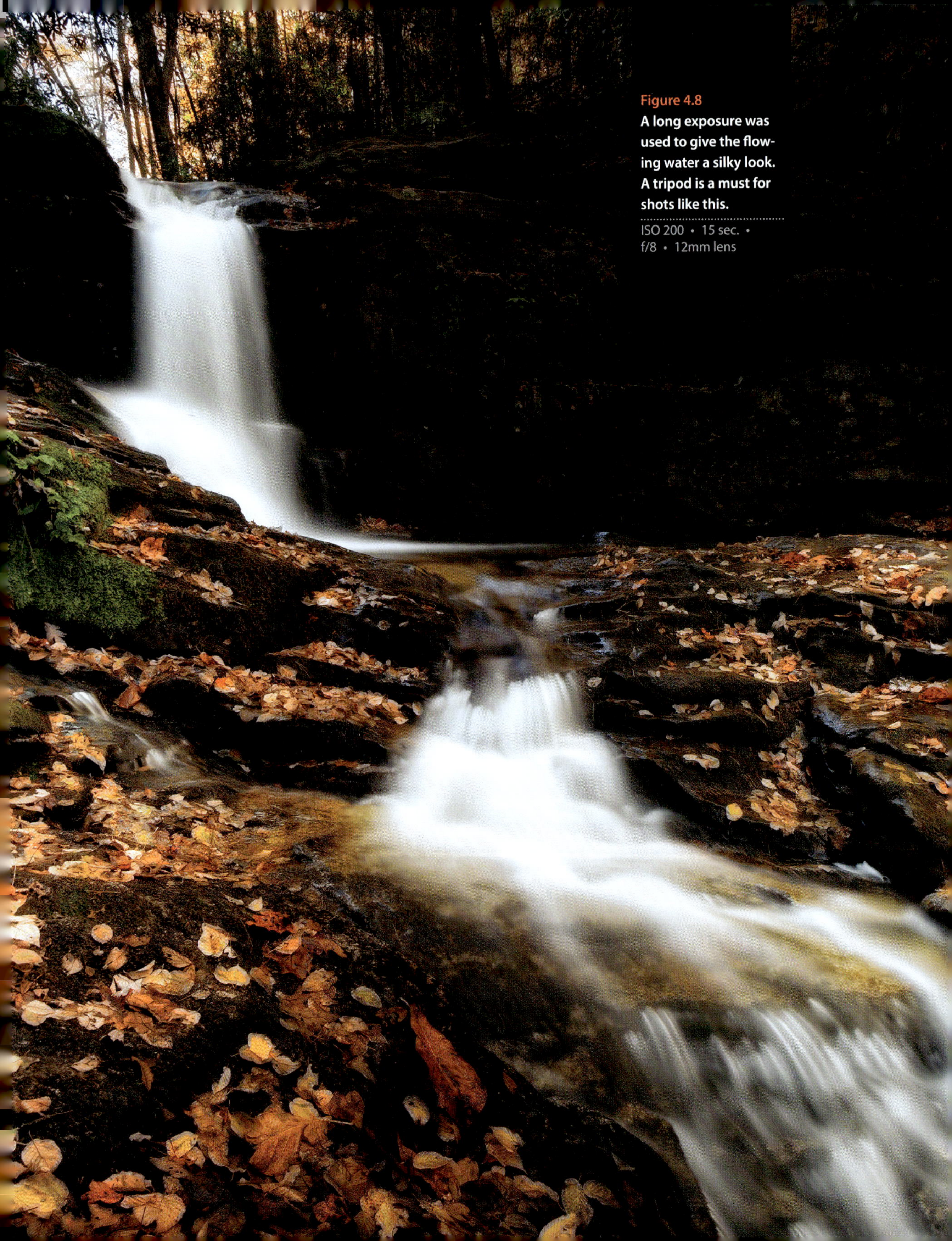

Figure 4.8
A long exposure was used to give the flowing water a silky look. A tripod is a must for shots like this.

ISO 200 • 15 sec. • f/8 • 12mm lens

As you can see, the subject of your photo usually determines when you will use S mode. If freezing action or showing motion is the most important factor in making the photo you want, then Shutter Priority mode might be the way to go. It is important that you are able to visualize the result of using a particular shutter speed. The great thing about shooting with digital cameras is that you get instant feedback by checking your shot on the LCD screen, but you don't always get a second chance to shoot a fast-moving subject. It is important to practice and learn what those speeds represent in terms of their ability to stop the action or show motion blur.

First, let's examine just how much control you have over the shutter speeds. The GX7/ GM1 has a shutter speed range from 1/8000 of a second all the way down to 60 seconds. With that much latitude, you should have enough control to capture almost any subject. The other thing to think about is that S mode is considered a "semiautomatic" mode. This means that you are taking control over two aspects of the total exposure while the camera handles the other. In this instance, you are controlling the shutter speed and ISO, and the camera is controlling the aperture. This is important to know because there will be times that you want to use a particular shutter speed but your lens won't be able to accommodate your request.

For example, you might encounter this problem when shooting in low-light situations: If you are shooting a fast-moving subject that will blur at a shutter speed slower than 1/125 of a second but your lens's largest aperture is f/3.5, you might see your aperture display in the electronic viewfinder and the rear LCD panel begin to blink. This is your warning that there won't be enough light available for the shot—due to the limitations of the lens—so your picture will be underexposed (too dark).

Another case where you might run into this situation is when you are shooting moving water. To get that look of silky, flowing water, it's usually necessary to use a shutter speed of at least 1/15 of a second, if not longer. If your waterfall is in full sunlight, you may get that blinking aperture display once again because the lens you are using only closes down to f/22 at its smallest opening. In this instance, your camera is warning you that you will be overexposing your image (too light). There are workarounds for these problems, which we will discuss later (see Chapter 7), but it is important to know that there can be limitations when using S mode.

Setting up and shooting in S mode

1. Turn your camera on, and then turn the Mode dial to align the S with the indicator line.
2. To select your ISO on the GX7, press the ISO button (▲), rotate the Rear dial to the desired setting, and press the Rear dial to select (the ISO selection will appear in the electronic viewfinder and the rear LCD panel).

   On the GM1, press the Fn1 button we assigned to ISO in Chapter 1. Rotate the Control dial to the desired setting and press MENU/SET.
3. Turn the Front dial (GM1: Control dial) to select the shutter speed. Turn the dial to the right for faster shutter speeds and to the left for slower speeds.
4. Point the camera at your subject, and then activate the camera meter by depressing the shutter button halfway.
5. View the exposure information in the electronic viewfinder or on the rear LCD panel.
6. Press and turn the rear dial (GM1: ▲, then Control dial) to change the exposure compensation to make the image brighter or darker.

M: Manual Mode

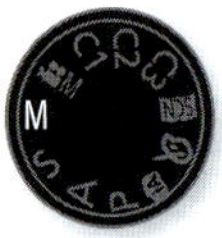

Once upon a time, long before digital cameras and programmed modes, there was manual mode. In those days it wasn't called "manual mode," because there were no other modes. It was just photography. In fact, many photographers cut their teeth on completely manual cameras. If you want to learn the effects of aperture and shutter speed on your photography, there is no better way to learn than by setting these adjustments yourself. With the advancement of camera technology, many new photographers never give this mode a second thought. That's truly a shame, as not only is it an excellent way to learn your photography basics, it's also an essential tool to have in your photographic bag of tricks.

When you have your camera set to Manual (M) mode, the camera meter will give you a reading of the scene you are photographing. It's your job to set the f-stop (aperture), the shutter speed, and the ISO to achieve a correct exposure. If you need a faster shutter speed, you will have to make the reciprocal change to your f-stop or ISO to get the correct exposure. Using any other mode, such as S or A, would mean that you just have to worry about one of these changes, but Manual mode means you have to do it all yourself. This can be a little challenging at first, but after a while you will have a complete understanding of how each change affects your exposure, which will, in turn, improve the way that you use the other modes.

When to use Manual (M) mode

- When your environment is fooling your camera's light meter and you need to maintain a certain exposure setting (**Figure 4.9**)
- When shooting with flash, LEDs, or strobes (**Figure 4.10** on the next page)
- When you need to maintain exposures between different frames for a panorama (**Figure 4.11** on the next page)

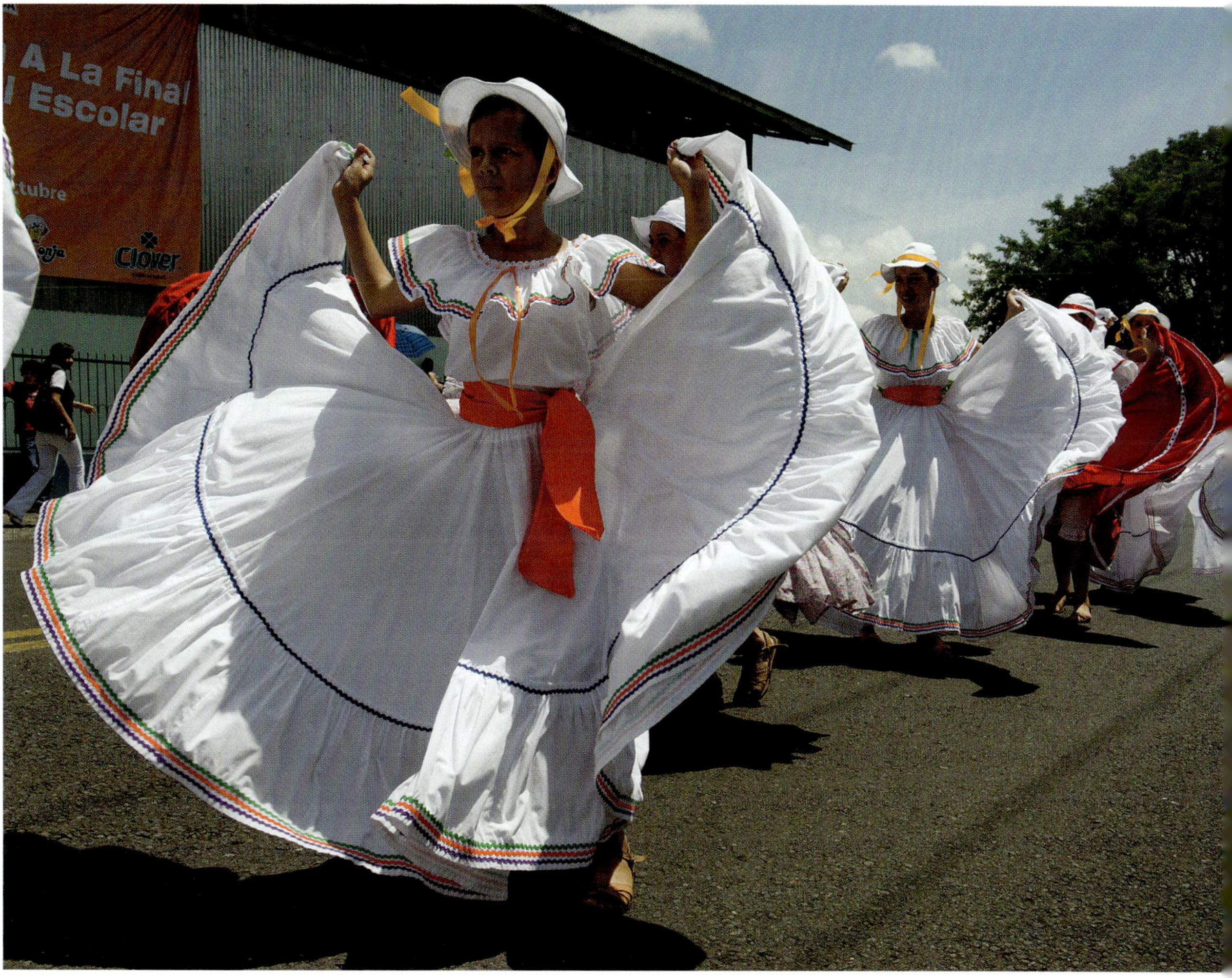

Figure 4.9 **The bright costumes and dark background can fool your camera's meter. Even though the light falling on the dancers isn't changing, the camera might make different exposure decisions based on what is in the frame at the time.**

ISO 200 • 1/500 sec. • f/11 • 24–70mm lens

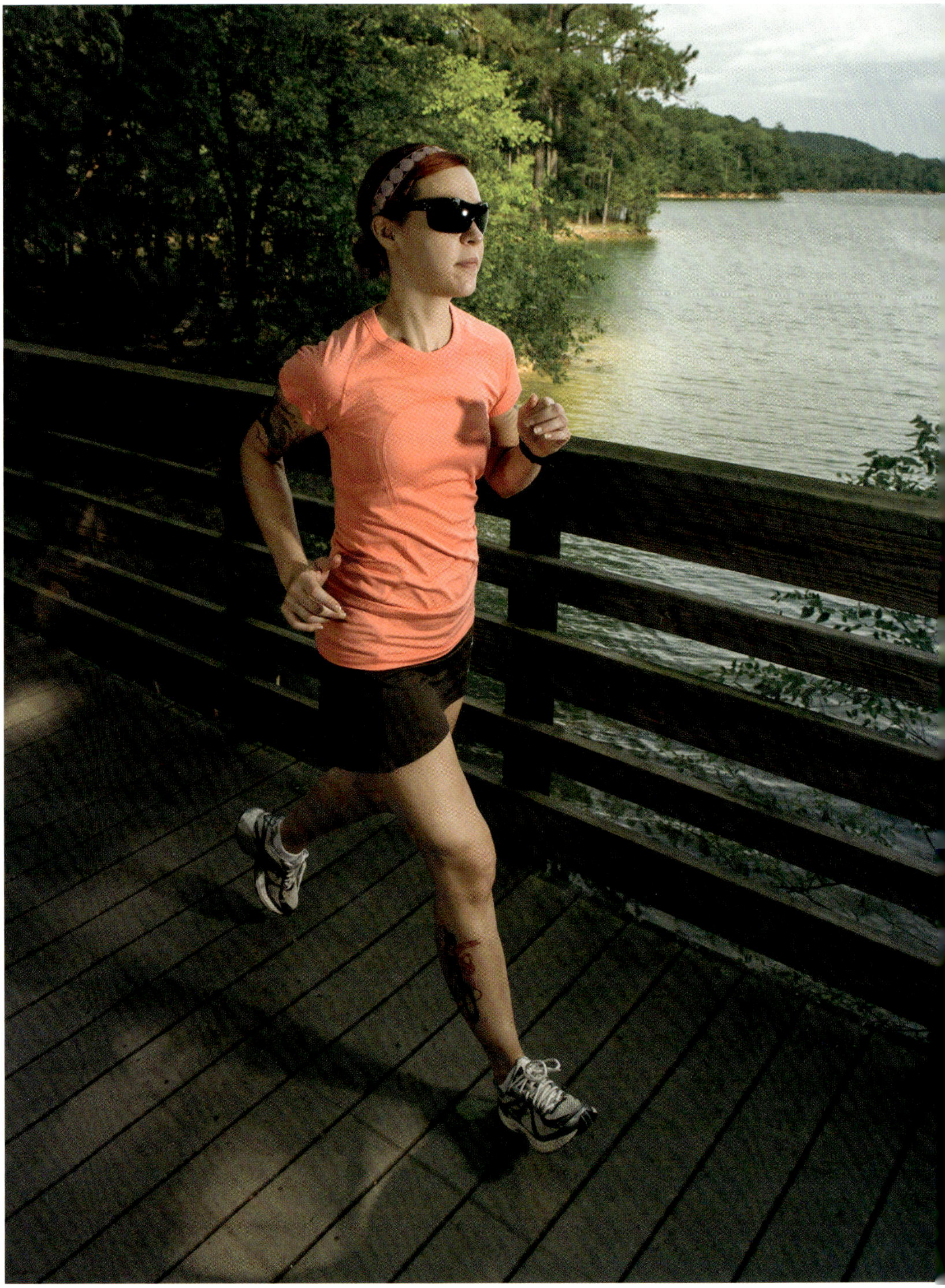

Figure 4.10
Shooting in Manual exposure mode makes it relatively easy to balance ambient light with strobes or (in this case) Speedlights.

ISO 1000 • 1/1000 sec. • f/8 • 24–70mm lens

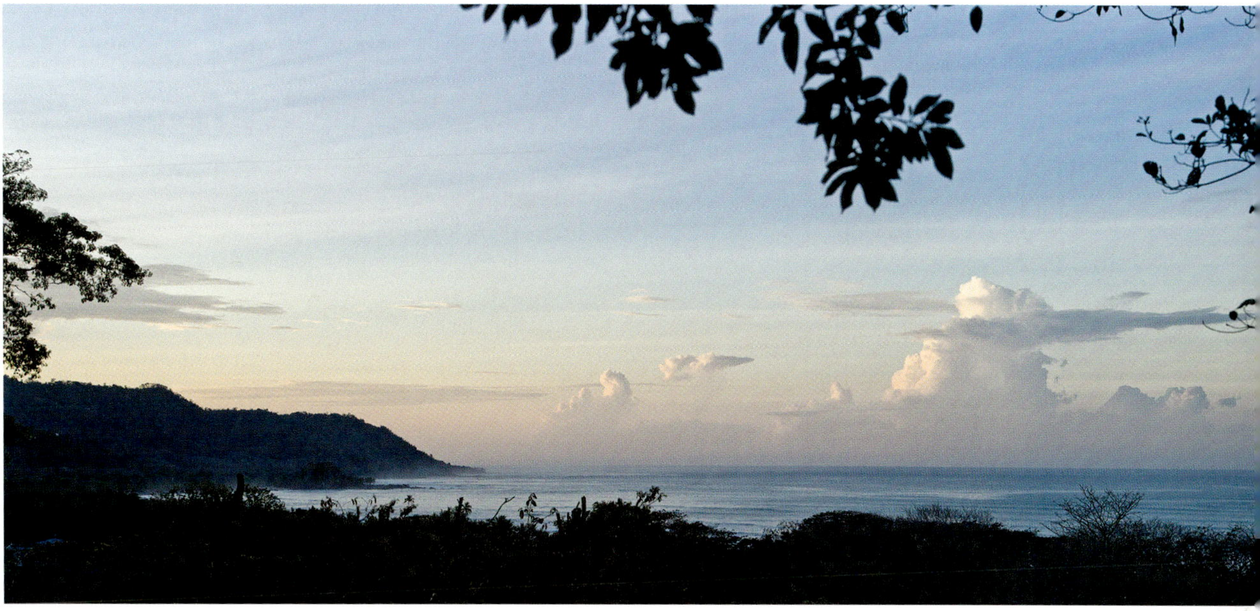

Figure 4.11 I combined six individual images to make this panorama. Manual exposure mode is essential to keep the exposure consistent between frames.

ISO 200 • 1/80 sec. • f/8 • 70–200mm lens

Setting up and shooting in Manual mode

1. Turn the Mode dial to align the M with the indicator line.
2. To select your ISO on the GX7, press the ISO button (▲), rotate the Rear dial to the desired setting, and press the Rear dial to select (the ISO selection will appear in the electronic viewfinder and the rear LCD panel).

   On the GM1, press the Fn1 button we assigned to ISO in Chapter 1. Rotate the Control dial to the desired setting and press MENU/SET.
3. Point the camera at your subject, and then activate the camera meter by depressing the shutter button halfway.
4. View the exposure information in the electronic viewfinder (GX7 only) or on the rear LCD display.
5. The exposure is displayed on a scale with marks that run from –3 to +3 stops, with a 0 mark in the center. Adjust your aperture value, shutter speed, and ISO to move the exposure indicator along the scale. A "proper" exposure will line up the indicator with the 0 mark in the middle of the scale. As the indicator moves to the left, it is a sign that you will be underexposing (there is not enough light hitting the sensor to provide adequate exposure). Move the indicator to the right and you will be overexposing (allowing too much light for a proper exposure).

6. (GX7) Use the Front dial to change the aperture value. Turn the dial left for a larger aperture (small f-stop number), and right for a smaller aperture (large f-stop number).
7. (GX7) Use the Rear dial to change the shutter speed. Turn the Rear dial left for a slower shutter speed, and right for a faster shutter speed.
8. (GM1) Use the Control dial to adjust both the aperture value and shutter speed. Use the ▲ cursor button to switch between the two.

How I Shoot: A Closer Look at the Camera Settings I Use

I shoot mostly travel photography, landscapes and wildlife. For travel and landscape work, the depth of field is usually my first consideration, so I use Aperture Priority mode for the majority of my shooting. I use the aperture value along with my lens selection to get the effects I'm looking for. A narrow aperture (high f-stop number) and a wide-angle lens give me maximum depth of field. A telephoto lens and a wide aperture (low f-stop number) make it easy to defocus the background and isolate my subject.

I try to keep the shutter speed above 1/60 if I am handholding the camera so I get sharp images with no camera shake. The GX7 has in-body image stabilization that allows me to handhold the camera at slower shutter speeds if I need to, and many Lumix lenses have an Optical Image Stabilizer.

I like to keep the ISO as low as possible, but I'm not afraid to raise the ISO to get a shutter speed I can work with. The GX7 and GM1 have such great performance at higher ISOs that I regularly shoot up to ISO 1600 or even 3200 when I need to.

When I'm shooting on a tripod, I set the ISO as low as possible, set my desired aperture value, and let the shutter speed fall where it may. I don't worry if the shutter speed gets too slow, because the tripod will keep the shot steady. It is also a good idea to use a remote or timer when using a tripod so you don't introduce camera shake when you press the shutter release.

When the camera and I don't see eye to eye about what the "correct" exposure is, I use exposure compensation to make the image brighter or darker. I get a live exposure preview on the LCD and EVF so I can see the effect of my adjustments before I take the shot. In Manual mode, you adjust all of the settings yourself based on the camera's meter, so you don't need exposure compensation. You can get a live exposure preview in Manual mode if you turn on Constant Preview in the Custom menu.

Normally I shoot in Manual exposure mode if I'm shooting wildlife. I'm shooting multiple images at a time in Burst mode, and want my exposure to be consistent from shot to shot. For wildlife, you need a fast shutter speed to freeze the motion of fast-moving animals. I like to use a lens with a fast maximum aperture, and I shoot with the lens wide open (at its lowest f-stop). Then I set the shutter speed and adjust the ISO to get a good exposure. A fast shutter speed helps reduce camera shake when you are using longer telephoto lenses. As a rule, you want the shutter speed to be equal to or greater than your focal length. For example, if you are shooting with a 200mm lens, you want your shutter speed to be at least 1/200 of a second.

When reviewing my images on the GX7 or GM1, I use the DISP button to cycle through the different review screens (**Figure 4.12**). Most important to me are the "blinkies" and the histogram. The blinkies show areas of overexposure in the image as blinking black and white. The histogram shows the tones in the image as a graph, with the shadows on the left and the highlights on the right. These tools let me know when I need to adjust my exposure so I'm not losing information in the highlights or shadows.

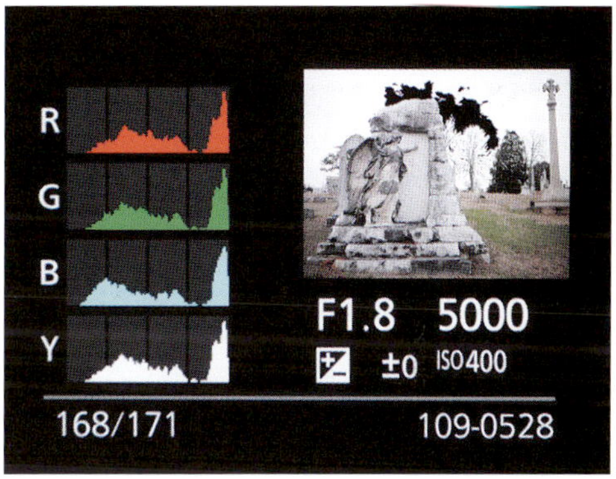

Figure 4.12 **The GX7 and GM1 have several options for reviewing your images. This view shows an RGB histogram, as well as a blinking warning on the image (shown here in black) where highlights are overexposed, or "clipping."**

As you work your way through the coming chapters, you will see other tips and tricks I use in my daily photography, but the most important tip I can give is that you take the time to understand the features of your camera so you can leverage the technology in a knowledgeable way. This will result in better photographs.

Chapter 4 Assignments

The information covered in this chapter will define how you work with your camera from this point on. Granted, there may be times that you just want to grab some quick pictures and will resort to the automatic modes, but to get serious with your photography, you should learn the professional modes.

Starting off with Program Auto mode

Set your camera on Program Auto (P) mode and start shooting. Become familiar with the adjustments you can make to the program and exposure by turning the Control dials. While you're shooting, try different ISO settings and notice how your aperture and shutter speed values change.

Controlling depth of field with A mode

The name of the game with A mode is depth of field. Set up three items at different distances from you. I would use chess pieces or something similar that you can place close to the camera. Now focus on the middle item, and set your camera to the largest aperture that your lens allows (remember that large aperture means a small number, like f/3.5). Now, while still focusing on the middle subject, start shooting with ever-smaller apertures until you are at the smallest f-stop for your lens. If you have a zoom lens, try doing this exercise with the lens at the widest and then the most telephoto settings. Now move up to subjects that are farther away, like telephone poles, and shoot them in the same way. The idea is to get a feel for how each aperture setting affects your depth of field.

Learning to control time with S mode

Find some moving subjects and then set your camera to S mode. Have someone ride a bike back and forth, or even just photograph cars as they go by. Start with a slow shutter speed of around 1/30 of a second and then start shooting with faster and faster shutter speeds. Keep shooting until you can freeze the action. Now find something that isn't moving, like a flower. Start with your shutter speed at something fast, like 1/500 of a second, and then work your way down to about 1/4 of a second. The point is to see how well you can handhold your camera before you start introducing hand shake into the image.

Giving and taking with Manual mode

Go outside on a sunny day, and with the camera in Manual mode (M), set your ISO to 200, your shutter speed to 1/200 of a second, and your aperture to f/16. Now press your shutter release button to get a meter reading. You should be pretty close to that zero mark. If not, make small adjustments to one of your settings until it hits that mark. Now is where the fun begins. Start moving your shutter speed slower, to 1/100, and then set your aperture to f/22. Now go the other way. Set your aperture to f/8 and your shutter speed to 1/400. Now review your images. If all went well, all the exposures should look the same. This is because you balanced the light with reciprocal changes to the aperture and shutter speed. Now go back to our original setting of 1/200 at f/16 and try just moving the shutter speed without changing the aperture. Just make 1/3-stop changes (1/160 to 1/125 to 1/100 to 1/80), and then review your images to see what 1/3 stop of overexposure looks like. Then do the same thing going in the opposite way. It's hard to know if you want to over- or underexpose a scene until you have actually done it and seen the results.

Share your results with the book's Flickr group!
Join the group here: flickr.com/groups/panasonicGX7_fromsnapshotstogreatshots

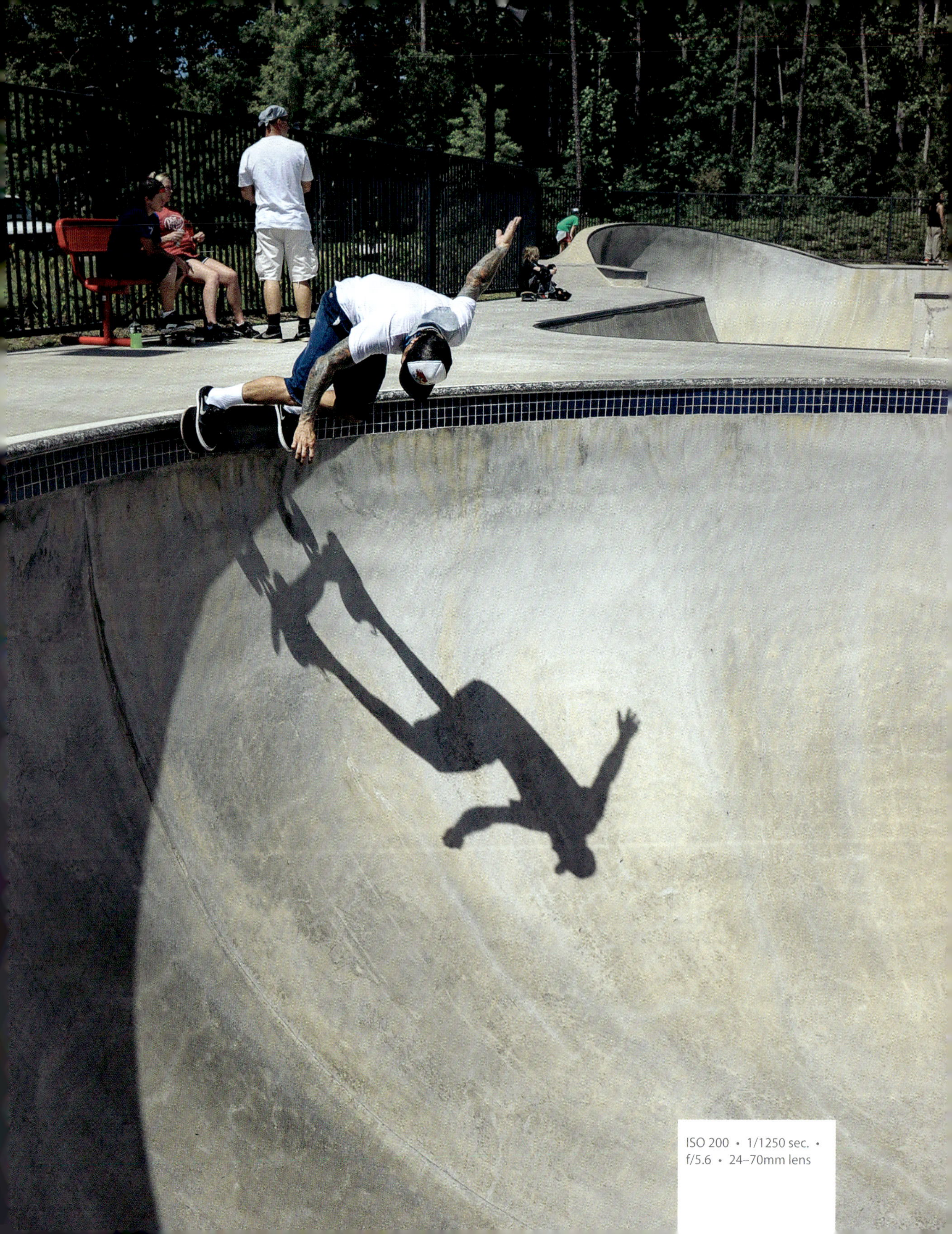

ISO 200 • 1/1250 sec. • f/5.6 • 24–70mm lens

5

Moving Target

The Tricks to Shooting Sports and More

Now that you have learned about the professional modes, it's time to put your newfound knowledge to good use. Whether you are shooting the action at a professional sporting event or a child on a merry-go-round, you'll learn techniques that will help bring out the best in your photography when your subject is in motion.

The number one thing to know when you are trying to capture a moving target is that speed is king! I'm not talking about how fast your subject is moving, but rather how fast your shutter is opening and closing. Shutter speed is the key to freezing a moment in time—but also to conveying movement. It's all in how you turn the dial. There are also some other considerations for taking your shot to the next level: composition, lens selection, and a few more items that we will explore in this chapter. So strap on your seatbelt and hit the gas, because here we go!

Poring Over the Picture

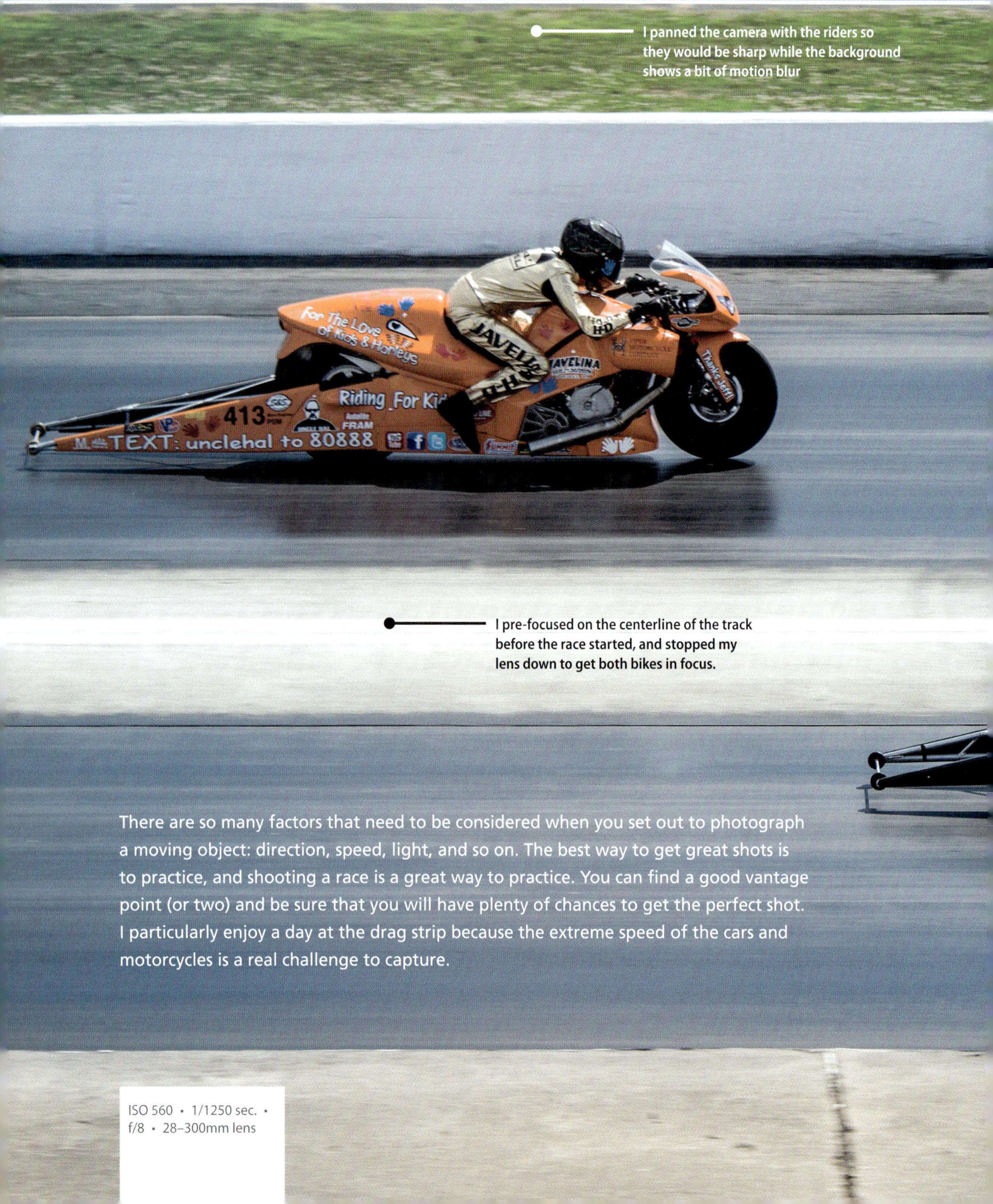

I panned the camera with the riders so they would be sharp while the background shows a bit of motion blur

I pre-focused on the centerline of the track before the race started, and stopped my lens down to get both bikes in focus.

There are so many factors that need to be considered when you set out to photograph a moving object: direction, speed, light, and so on. The best way to get great shots is to practice, and shooting a race is a great way to practice. You can find a good vantage point (or two) and be sure that you will have plenty of chances to get the perfect shot. I particularly enjoy a day at the drag strip because the extreme speed of the cars and motorcycles is a real challenge to capture.

ISO 560 • 1/1250 sec. • f/8 • 28–300mm lens

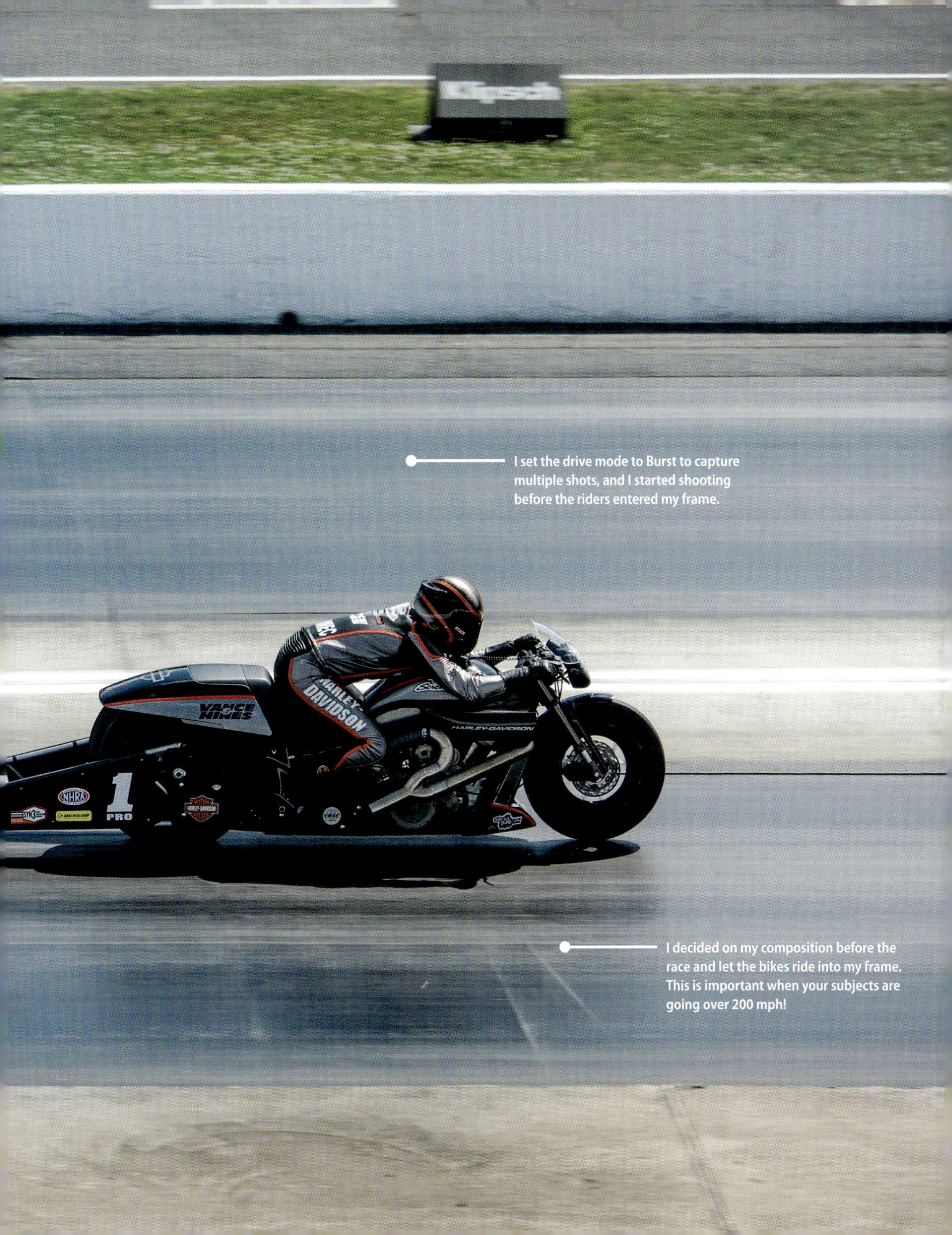

I set the drive mode to Burst to capture multiple shots, and I started shooting before the riders entered my frame.

I decided on my composition before the race and let the bikes ride into my frame. This is important when your subjects are going over 200 mph!

Stop Right There!

Shutter speed is the main tool in the photographer's arsenal for capturing great action shots. The ability to freeze a moment in time often makes the difference between a good shot and a great one. To take advantage of this concept, you should have a good grasp of the relationship between shutter speed and movement. When you press the shutter release button, your camera goes into action by opening the shutter curtain and then closing it after a predetermined length of time. The longer you leave your shutter open, the more your subject will move across the frame, so common sense dictates that the first thing to consider is just how fast your subject is moving.

Typically, you will be working in fractions of a second. How many fractions depends on several factors. Subject movement, while simple in concept, is actually based on three factors. The first is the direction of travel. Is the subject moving across your field of view (left to right) or traveling toward or away from you? The second consideration is the actual speed at which the subject is moving. There is a big difference between a moving sports car and a child on a bicycle. Finally, the distance from you to the subject has a direct bearing on how fast the action seems to be taking place. Let's take a brief look at each of these factors to see how they might affect your shooting.

Direction of travel

Typically, the first thing that people think about when taking an action shot is how fast the subject is moving, but in reality the first consideration should be the direction of travel. Where you are positioned in relation to the subject's direction of travel is critically important in selecting the proper shutter speed. When you open your shutter, the lens gathers light from your subject and records it on the camera sensor. If the subject is moving across your viewfinder, you need a faster shutter speed to keep that lateral movement from being recorded as a streak across your image. Subjects that are moving in line with your shooting location do not move across your viewfinder and appear to be more stationary. This allows you to use a slightly slower shutter speed (**Figure 5.1**). A subject that is moving in a diagonal direction—both across the frame and toward or away from you—requires a shutter speed in between the two.

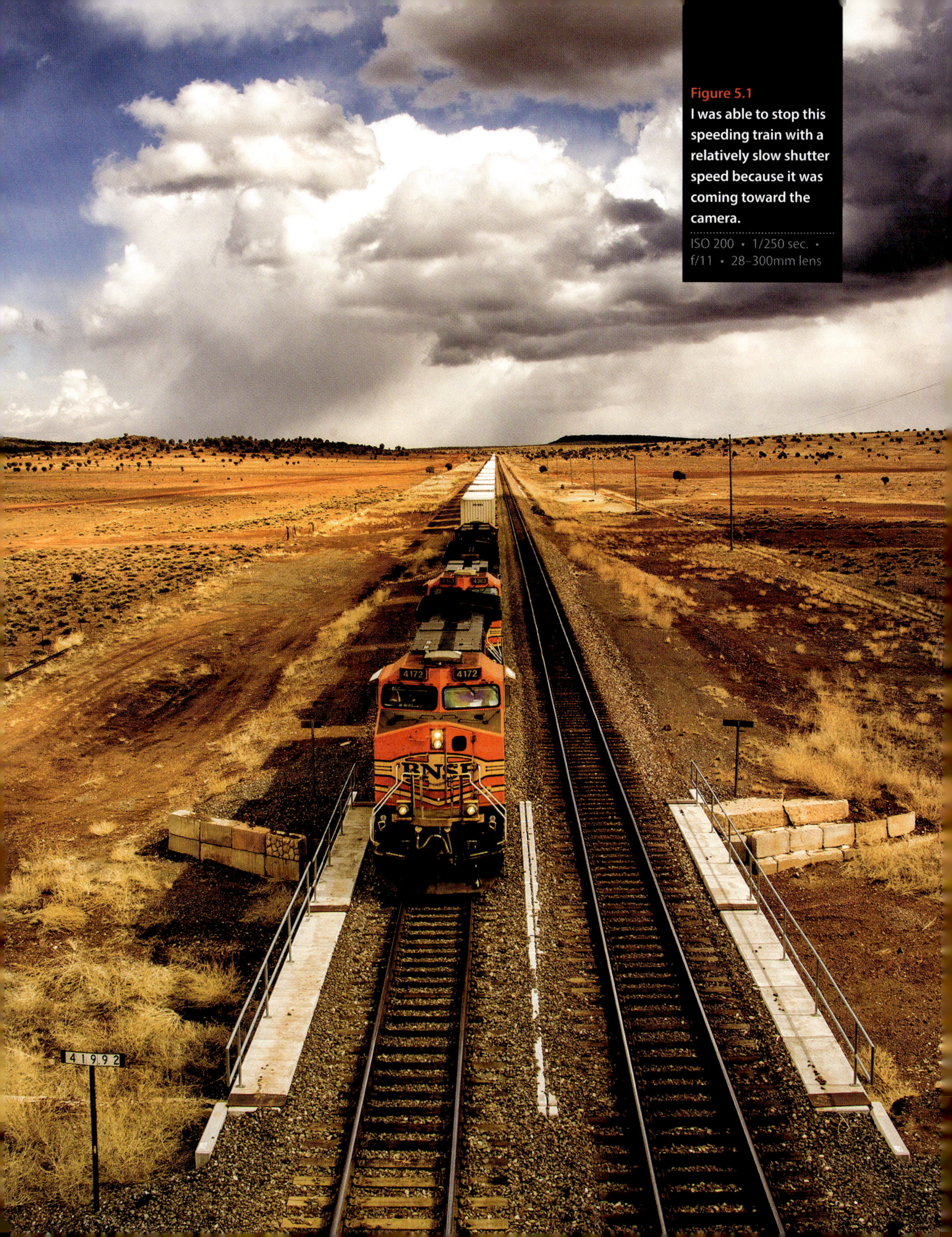

Figure 5.1
I was able to stop this speeding train with a relatively slow shutter speed because it was coming toward the camera.

ISO 200 • 1/250 sec. • f/11 • 28–300mm lens

Subject speed

Once the angle of motion has been determined, you can then assess the speed at which the subject is traveling. The faster your subject moves, the faster your shutter speed needs to be in order to "freeze" that subject. A person walking across your frame might only require a shutter speed of 1/80 of a second (**Figure 5.2**), whereas a cyclist traveling in the same direction would call for 1/500 of a second. That same cyclist traveling at the same rate of speed toward you, rather than across the frame, might only require a shutter speed of 1/125 of a second. You can start to see how the relationship of speed and direction comes into play in your decision-making process.

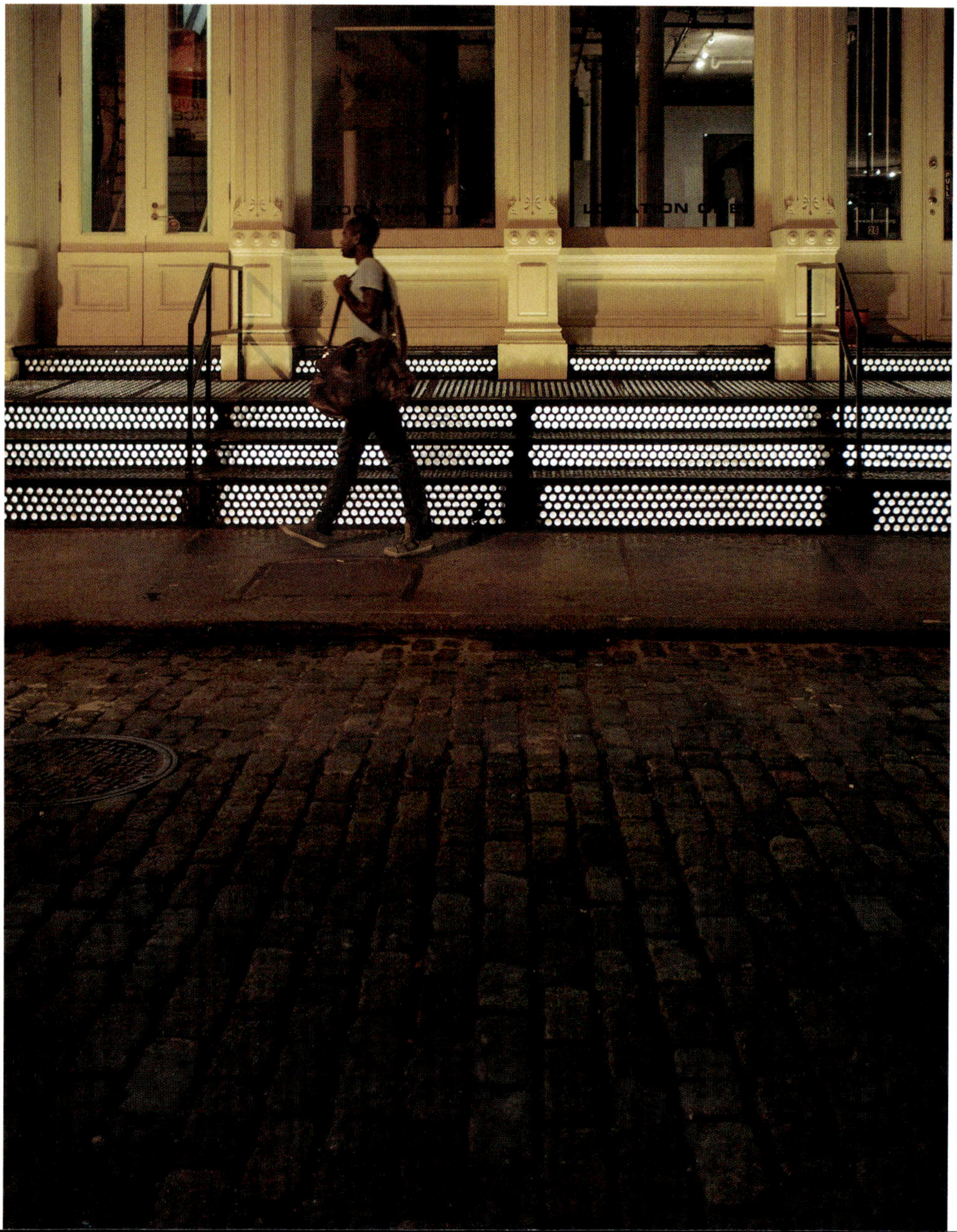

Figure 5.2

A person walking can be captured with a much slower shutter speed than a faster subject. Use as fast a shutter speed as possible if your goal is to freeze the action.

ISO 1600 • 1/80 sec. • f/2 • 17mm lens

Subject-to-camera distance

So now we know both the direction and the speed of your subject. The final factor to address is the distance between you and the action. Picture yourself looking at a highway full of cars from up in a tall building a quarter of a mile from the road. As you stare down at the traffic moving along at 55 miles per hour, the cars and trucks seem to be slowly moving along the roadway. Now picture yourself standing in the median of that same road as the same traffic flies by at the same rate of speed.

Although the traffic is moving at the same speed, the shorter distance between you and the traffic makes the cars look like they are moving much faster. This is because your field of view is much narrower; therefore, the subjects are not going to present themselves within the frame for the same length of time. The concept of distance applies to the length of your lens as well (**Figure 5.3**). If you are using a wide-angle lens, you can probably get away with a slower shutter speed than if you were using a telephoto, which puts you in the heart of the action. It all has to do with your field of view. That telephoto gets you "closer" to the action—and the closer you are, the faster your subject will be moving across your viewfinder.

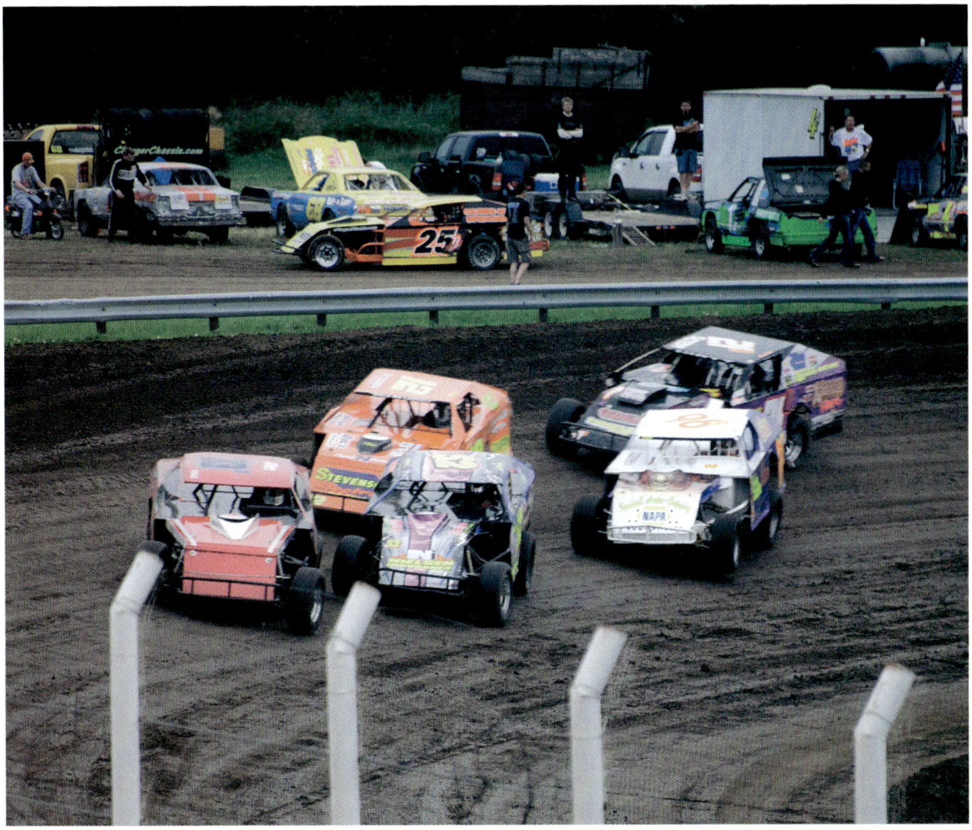

Figure 5.3
Due to the action's distance from the camera, a slower shutter speed could be used to capture it.

ISO 3200 • 1/250 sec. • f/5.6 • 70–300mm lens

Zoom in to be sure

When reviewing your shots on the LCD, don't be fooled by the display. The smaller your image is, the sharper it will look. To ensure that you are getting sharp, blur-free images, make sure that you zoom in on your LCD display.

To zoom in on your images, press the Playback button and then turn the Rear dial (GM1: Control dial) to the right to zoom in. A 4.0x zoom is roughly equivalent to 100% view (**Figure 5.4**).

To zoom out, simply turn the dial to the left.

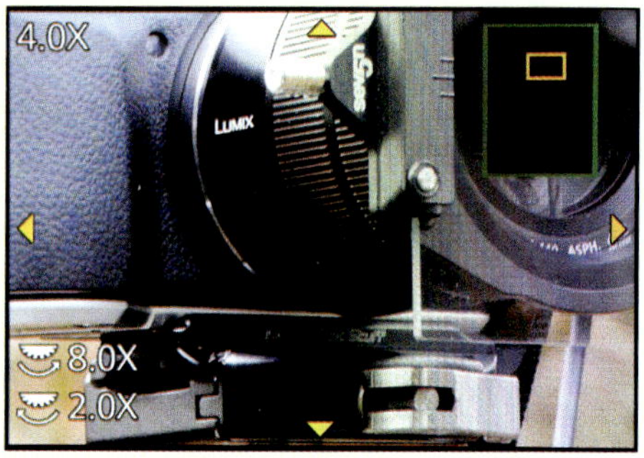

Figure 5.4 Zooming in on your image helps you confirm that the image is really sharp.

Using Shutter Priority (S) Mode to Stop Motion

In Chapter 4, you were introduced to the professional shooting modes. You'll remember that the mode that gives you ultimate control over shutter speed is S mode, where you are responsible for selecting the shutter speed while handing over the aperture selection to the camera. The ability to concentrate on just one exposure factor helps you quickly make changes on the fly while staying glued to your viewfinder and your subject.

There are a couple of things to consider when using S mode, both of which have to do with the amount of light that is available when shooting. Although you have control over which shutter speed you select in S mode, the range of shutter speeds that is available to you depends largely on how well your subject is lit.

When shooting fast-paced action, you will typically be working with very fast shutter speeds. This means that your lens will probably be set to its largest aperture. If the light is not sufficient for the shutter speed selected, you will need to do one of two things: select a lens that offers a larger working aperture, or raise the ISO of the camera. Working off the assumption that you have only one lens available, let's concentrate on balancing your exposure using the ISO.

Let's say that you are shooting a baseball game at night and want to get some great action shots. You set your camera to S mode and, after testing out some shutter speeds, determine that you need to shoot at 1/500 of a second to freeze the action on the field. When you place the viewfinder to your eye and press the shutter button halfway, you notice that the f-stop readout is blinking at f/4.5. This is your camera's way of telling you that the lens has now reached its maximum aperture and that you will be underexposed if you shoot your pictures at the currently selected shutter speed. You could slow your shutter speed down until the aperture reading stops blinking, but then you would get images with too much motion blur.

The alternative is to raise your ISO to a level that is high enough for a proper exposure. The key here is to always use the lowest ISO that you can get away with. That might mean ISO 200 in bright, sunny conditions, or ISO 1600 (or higher) for an indoor or low-light situation (**Figure 5.5**). Just remember that the higher the ISO, the greater the amount of noise in your image. This is the reason that you see professional sports photographers using those mammoth lenses perched atop monopods: They could use a smaller lens, but to get those very large apertures they need a huge piece of glass on the front of the lens. The larger the glass on the front of the lens, the more light it gathers, and the larger the aperture for shooting. For the working pro, the large aperture translates into low ISO (and thus low noise), fast shutter speeds, and razor-sharp action.

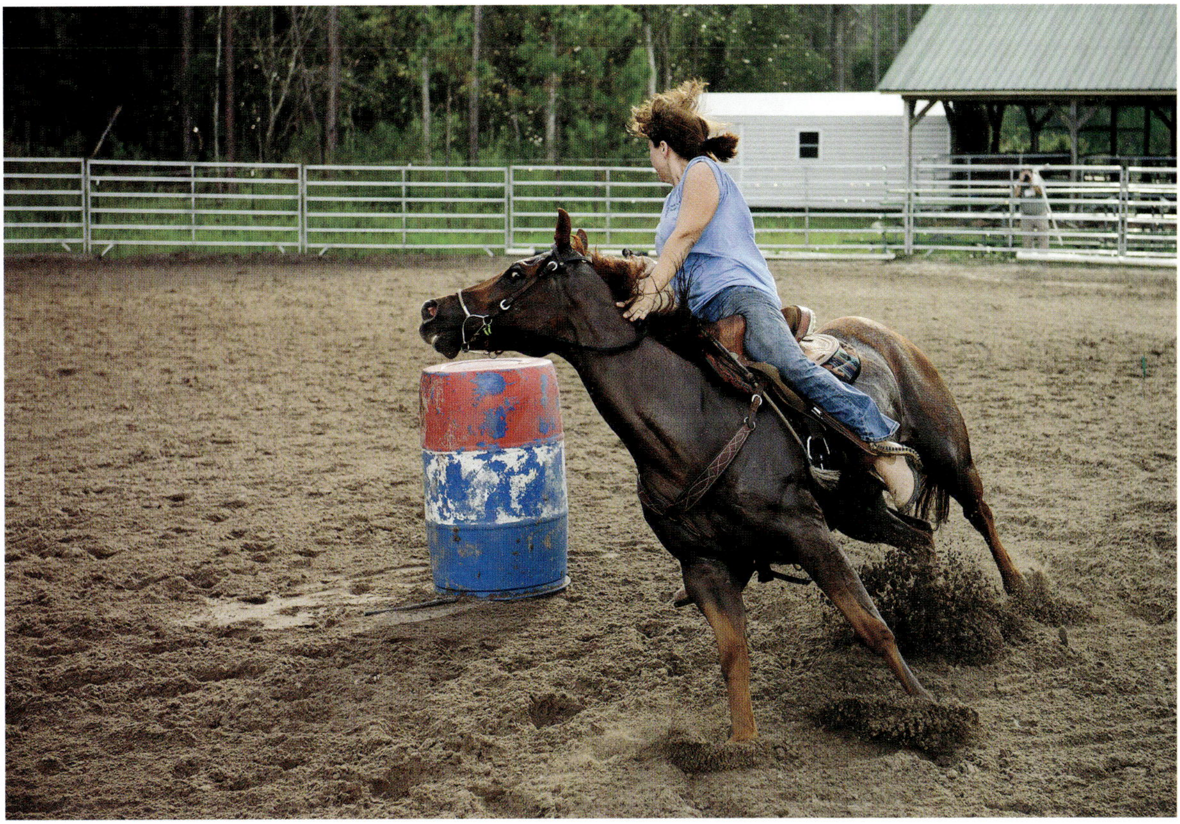

Figure 5.5 I had to crank the ISO up to 800 to freeze this barrel racer in the late afternoon light. I wanted to capture the intensity in the horse's face, so I needed the image to be tack sharp.

ISO 800 • 1/1250 sec. • f/4 • 24–70mm lens

Adjusting your ISO on the fly

1. Check for the blinking aperture readout in the lower-left portion of your electronic viewfinder.
2. If it is blinking, use your thumb to press the ISO button (▲) (GM1: Fn1 button), and the ISO options appear in the viewfinder.
3. Turn the Rear dial (GM1: Control dial) to the right to raise the ISO to the next highest level.
4. Lightly press the shutter button and check to see if the aperture is still blinking.
5. If it's not blinking, shoot away. If it is, repeat steps 2–4 until it is set correctly.

Using Aperture Priority (A) Mode to Isolate Your Subject

One of the benefits of working in S mode with fast shutter speeds is that, more often than not, you will be shooting with the largest aperture available on your lens. Shooting with a large aperture allows you to use faster shutter speeds, but it also narrows your depth of field.

To isolate your subject in order to focus your viewer's attention on it, a larger aperture is required. The larger aperture reduces the foreground and background sharpness: The larger the aperture, the more blurred everything except your subject will be.

When you are shooting wildlife or sporting events, the idea is to isolate your main subject by having it in focus while the rest of the image has some amount of blur. This sharp focus draws your viewer right to the subject. Studies have shown that the eye is drawn to sharp areas before moving on to the blurry areas. Also, depending on what your subject matter is, there can be a tendency to get distracted by a busy background if everything in the photo is equally sharp. Without a shallow depth of field, it might be difficult for the viewer to identify exactly what the main subject is in your picture.

Let's look at how to use depth of field to bring focus to your subject. In the previous section, I told you that you should use S mode for getting those really fast shutter speeds to stop action. Generally speaking, S mode will be the mode you most often use for shooting sports and other action, but there will be times when you want to ensure that you are getting the shallowest depth of field possible in your image. The way to do this is by using Aperture Priority (A) mode **(Figure 5.6)**.

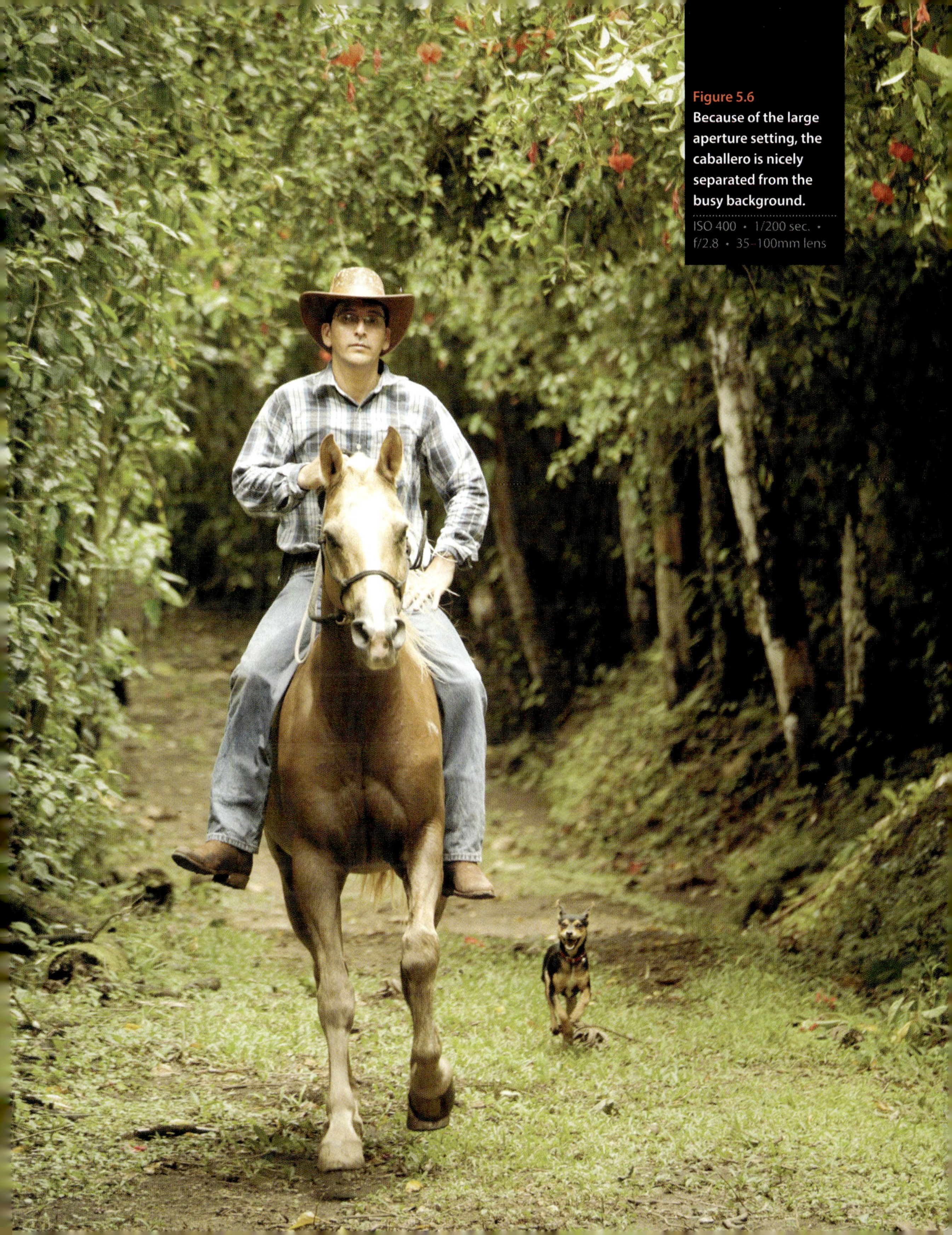

Figure 5.6
Because of the large aperture setting, the caballero is nicely separated from the busy background.
ISO 400 • 1/200 sec. • f/2.8 • 35–100mm lens

So how do you know when you should use A mode as opposed to S mode? It's not a simple answer, but your LCD screen can help you make this determination. The best scenario for using A mode is a brightly lit scene where maximum apertures will still give you plenty of shutter speed to stop the action.

Let's say that you are shooting a soccer game in the midday sun. If you have determined that you need something between 1/500 and 1/1250 of a second for stopping the action, you could just set your camera to a high shutter speed in S mode and start shooting. But you also want to be using an aperture of, say, f/4.5 to get that narrow depth of field. Here's the problem: If you set your camera to S and select 1/1000 of a second as a nice compromise, you might get that desired f/stop—but you might not. As the meter is trained on your moving subject, the light levels could rise or fall, which might actually change that desired f-stop to something higher, like f/5.6 or even f/8. Now the depth of field is extended, and you will no longer get that nice isolation and separation that you wanted.

To rectify this, switch the camera to A mode and select f/4.5 as your aperture. Now, as you begin shooting, the camera holds that aperture and makes exposure adjustments with the shutter speed. As I said before, this works well when you have lots of light—enough light so that you can have a high enough shutter speed without introducing motion blur.

Keep Them in Focus with Continuous AF and Autofocus Tracking

With the exposure issue handled for the moment, let's move on to a subject of equal importance: focusing. If you have browsed your manual, you know that there are three autofocus modes to choose from in the GX7/GM1. The first is AFS, or Single-shot AF, which works best for stationary subjects (such as portraits or macro work). Once focus is achieved, it is locked at that particular distance until the shutter is fully depressed or released and pressed again.

For the most part, AFS is not a popular mode for photographing movement. For this type of photography, AFC, or Continuous AF, is ideal. AFC continuously tries to focus on the focus point selected in the camera as long as you press the shutter button halfway. AFC can help keep your subject in focus as long as you can keep the focus point on target.

The third focus mode is AFF, or Flexible AF. This mode locks focus like AFS unless the camera detects movement. If it thinks the subject is moving, it behaves like AFC. I prefer to choose AFS or AFC, depending on the situation, instead of letting the camera choose in AFF.

Selecting and shooting in AFC

1. Press the Menu/Set button, then select the Custom menu.
2. On the GX7, navigate to AFS/AFF/AFC and choose AFC (**A**).

   On the GM1, switch the Focus Mode lever to AFC.
3. Locate your subject within a focus point in the EVF (GX7 only) or LCD, then press and hold the shutter button halfway to activate the focus mechanism.

   The camera will maintain focus on your subject as long as it remains within the focus point in the viewfinder or until you take a picture.

A

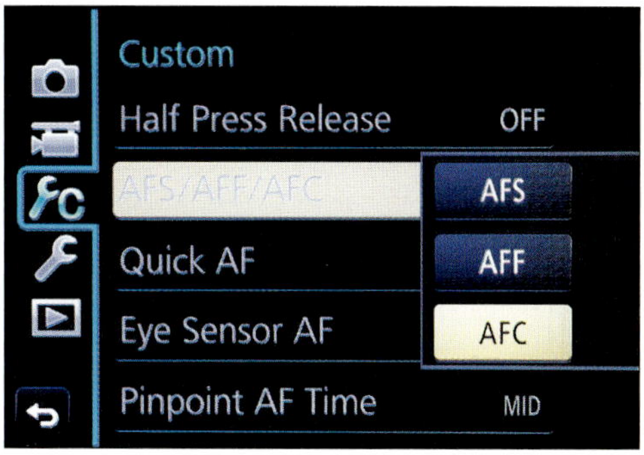

When using AFS, AFF, or AFC, you may select from four AF modes: Face Detection, AF Tracking, 23-Area, and 1-Area. AFS mode has an additional option, called Pinpoint. Face Detection looks for faces to lock onto. AF Tracking tracks a moving subject through the frame after you lock focus. Choosing 23-Area puts most of the control in the hands of the camera; the camera determines what to focus on based on the prominent subject matter in the frame. 1-Area allows you to manually select the point in the frame on which autofocus will engage. Pinpoint allows for precise focus on a point that is smaller than is possible in other AF modes.

Selecting and using an autofocus mode

1. Press the AF mode button (◀).
2. Turn the Rear dial (GM1: Control dial) to select the desired AF mode, or simply touch your choice on the LCD (**B**).
3. Press the Menu/Set button or press the shutter button halfway to return to shooting mode.
4. Touch the LCD screen where you want to focus.

B

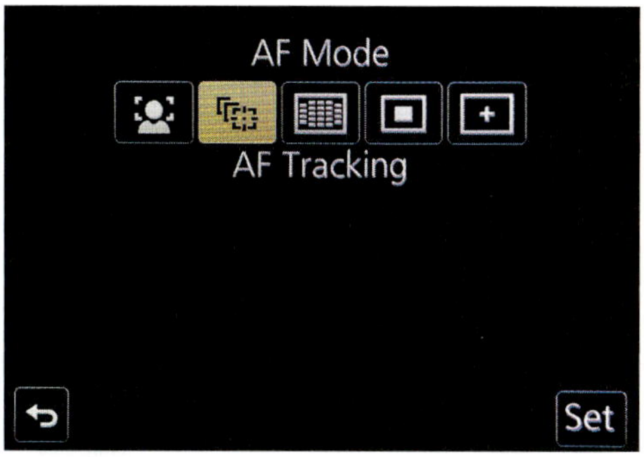

Choosing a focus mode

Selecting the proper focus mode depends largely on what type of subject you are photographing. Typically 1-Area is best for stationary subjects. It allows you to touch exactly where you want to focus and adjust the size of the focus point. If you are taking pictures of an active subject that is moving quickly, try locking on to your subject with AF Tracking. In AF Tracking mode, simply touch the subject you want to track. The AF area turns yellow when the focus is locked and tracking.

Manual Focus for Anticipated Action

I usually use the automatic focus modes, but there are times when I like to focus manually. This is usually when I know when and where the action will occur and I want to capture the subject as it crosses a certain plane of focus. This is useful in sports like skateboarding or auto racing, where the subjects are on a defined track. By pre-focusing the camera, all I have to do is wait for the subject to approach my point of focus and then start firing the camera. The GX7 and GM1 easily switch to manual focus with a flick of the Focus Mode lever.

It is relatively easy to figure out where a skateboarder will be doing tricks in (or *out* of) a pool or bowl **(Figure 5.7)**. There are usually only one or two places in a bowl that offer the right combination of angle and speed to perform a particular move, and a skater usually attempts the same move several times in a row. They are moving so fast that it is hard for autofocus to lock on, so this is a perfect time to switch to manual focus. This skater was attempting this aerial trick in the same place every run, so when he got started I manually focused where I knew he would clear the edge of the bowl. I decided on my composition ahead of time and waited for him to fly into it.

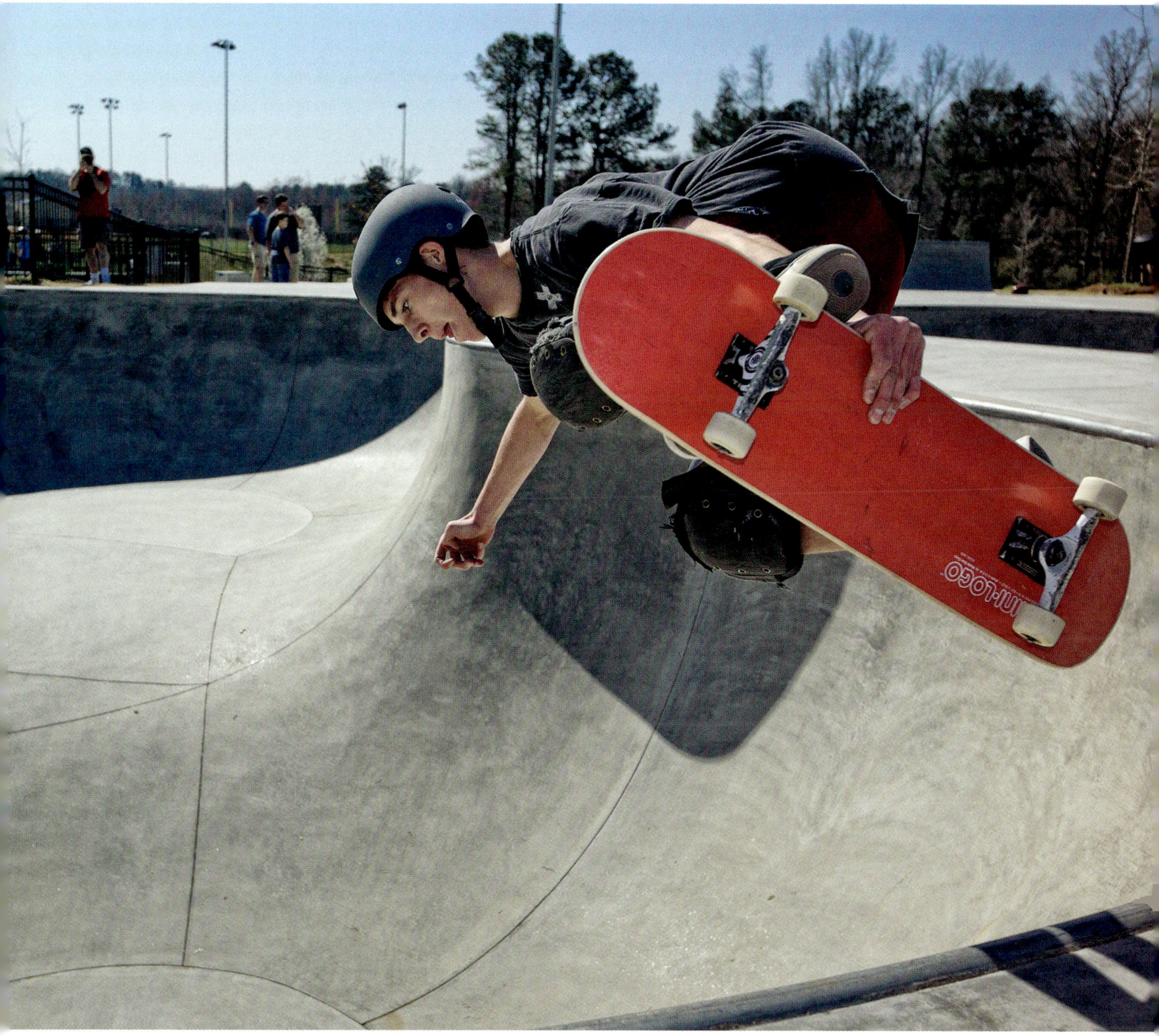

Figure 5.7 Pre-focus the camera to a point where you know the subject will be, and start shooting right before they get there.

ISO 400 • 1/3200 sec. • f/5.6 • 16–35mm lens

Keeping Up with Burst Mode

The drive mode determines how fast your camera will take pictures. Single shooting mode is for taking one photograph at a time; with every full press of the shutter, the camera will take a single image. Getting great focus is one thing, but capturing the moment can be difficult if you are shooting just one frame at a time.

In the worlds of sports and wildlife—and in life in general—things move pretty fast. Burst mode allows for continuous capture at Low, Medium, and High speeds. If you're shooting JPEGs with the electronic shutter enabled, you can shoot in Super High speed at 40 frames per second! When you are using one of the Burst modes, the camera continues to take pictures as long as the shutter release button is held down (or until the memory buffer fills up) (**Figure 5.8**).

Setting up and shooting in Burst mode

A

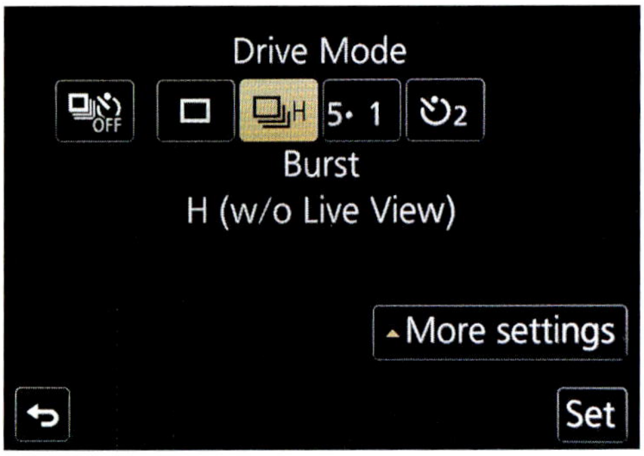

1. Press the Drive Mode button (▼).
2. Rotate the Rear dial (GM1: Control dial) to select Burst mode, or simply touch your choice on the LCD. The icon that looks like stacked-up little rectangles is Burst mode.
3. Press the ▲ button to choose between Low, Medium, High, and Super High speed (**A**). SH, or Super High speed, will not be available if you are capturing RAW images.
4. Press the Menu/Set button, or press the shutter release halfway, to return to Shooting mode.
5. To shoot, just depress the shutter button and hold until the desired number of frames has been captured.

Your camera has an internal memory, called a "buffer," where images are stored while they are being processed prior to being moved to your memory card. If the buffer fills up (this is more likely when you are shooting in the RAW or RAW+JPEG format), the burst rate will slow until space is made in the buffer for new images.

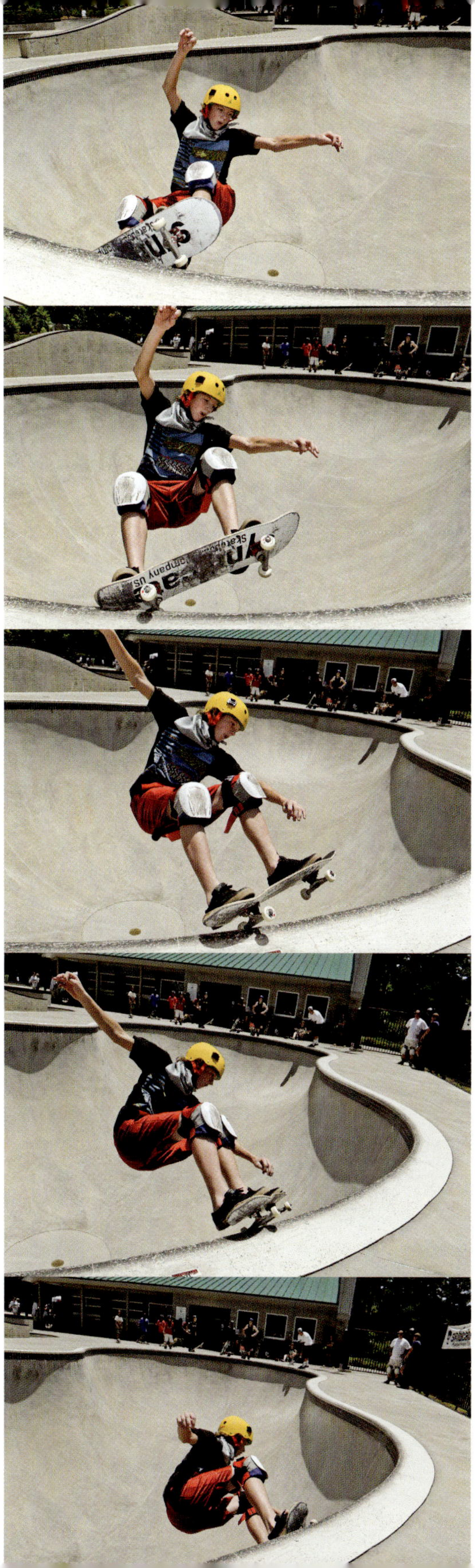

Figure 5.8

Using the Burst drive mode means that you are sure to capture the peak of the action.

ISO 200 • 1/1250 sec. • f/8 • 24–70mm lens

A Sense of Motion

Shooting action isn't always about freezing the action. There are times when you want to convey a sense of motion so the viewer can get a feel for the movement and flow of an event. Two techniques you can use to achieve this effect are panning and motion blur.

Panning

Panning has been used for decades to capture the speed of an object as it moves across the frame. It doesn't work well for subjects that are moving toward or away from you. Panning is achieved by following your subject across your frame, moving your camera along with the subject, and using a slower-than-normal shutter speed so that the background (and sometimes even a bit of the subject) has a sideways blur but the main portion of your subject is sharp and blur-free. The key to a great panning shot is selecting the right shutter speed: Too fast and you won't get the desired blurring of the background; too slow and the subject will have too much blur and will not be recognizable. Practice the technique until you can achieve a smooth camera motion that follows along with your subject. The other thing to remember when panning is to follow through even after the shutter has closed. This will keep the motion smooth and give you better images.

In **Figure 5.9**, I used the panning technique to follow this New York City taxi as it drove past me. I set the camera drive mode to Burst, and I used S mode to select a shutter speed of 1/15 of a second. I used AFC to help keep the cab in focus.

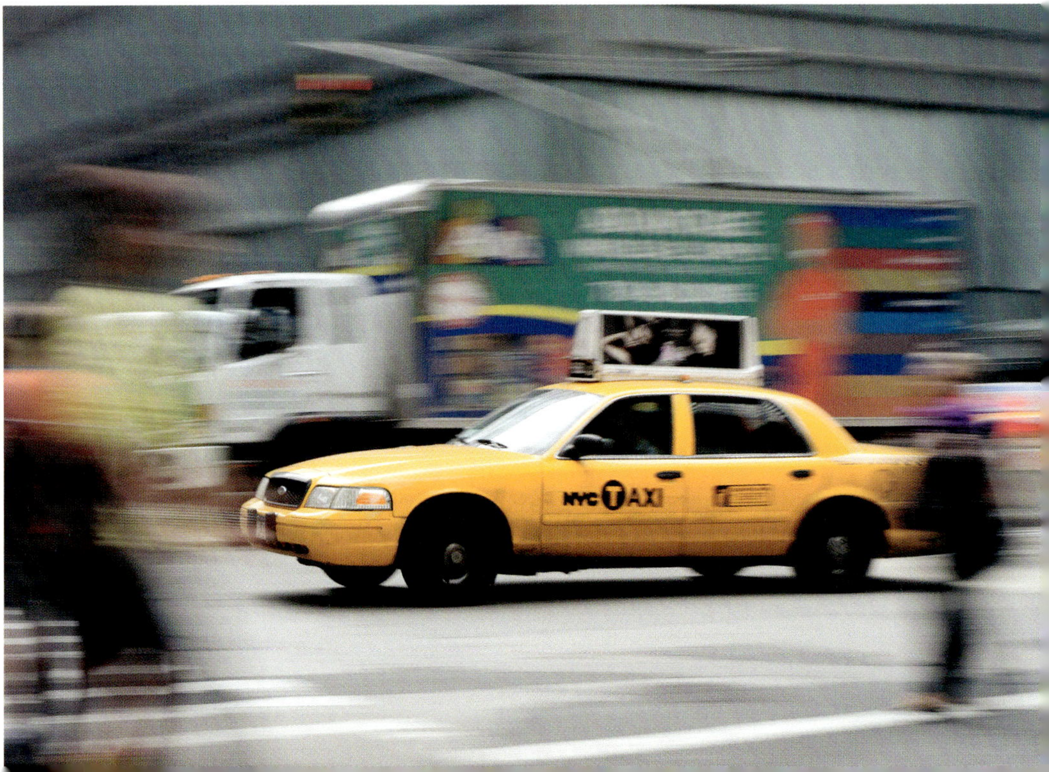

Figure 5.9
Following the subject as it moves across the field of view allows for a slower shutter speed and adds a sense of motion to the shot. I think the blurred background and foreground convey the kinetic energy of downtown NYC.

ISO 200 • 1/15 sec. • f/20 • 24–70mm lens

Motion blur

Another way to let the viewer in on the feel of the action is to include some blur in the image. This isn't accidental blur from choosing the wrong shutter speed. This blur is more exaggerated, and it tells a story. In **Figure 5.10**, I wanted to show the raceway sign with the cars speeding by to provide a little context. A fast shutter speed would have frozen the cars, but then the shot would have looked like the Boone County parking lot. I used a slow shutter speed to show the motion of the cars and depict the energy of a race.

Just as in panning, there is no preordained shutter speed to use for this effect. It is simply a matter of trial and error until you have a look that conveys the action. The key to this technique is the correct shutter speed combined with keeping the camera still during the exposure. You are trying to capture the motion of the subject, not the photographer or the camera, so use a good shooting stance or even a tripod.

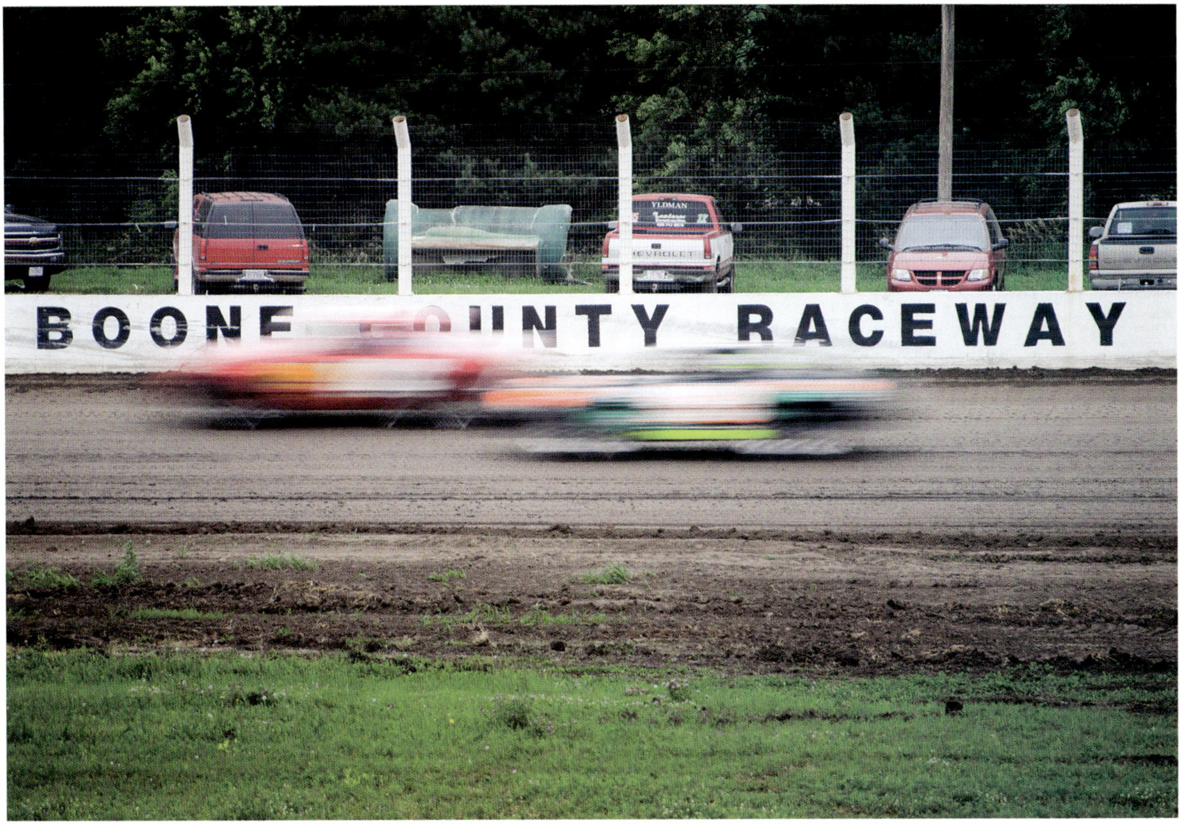

Figure 5.10 **I framed the raceway sign the way I wanted and waited for the cars to speed into the frame. The slow shutter speed blurred the cars to convey the action.**

ISO 400 • 1/25 sec. • f/5.6 • 70–300mm lens

Tips for Shooting Action

Give them somewhere to go

How you frame a moving subject is just as important as how well you expose the image. A poorly composed shot can completely ruin a great moment by not holding the viewer's attention.

The one mistake I see many times in action photography is that the photographer doesn't use the frame properly. If you are dealing with a subject that is moving horizontally across your field of view, give the subject somewhere to go by placing them to the side of the frame, with their motion leading toward the middle of the frame (**Figure 5.11**). This offsetting of the subject will introduce a sense of direction and anticipation for the viewer. Unless you are going to completely fill the image with the action, try to avoid placing your subject in the middle of the frame.

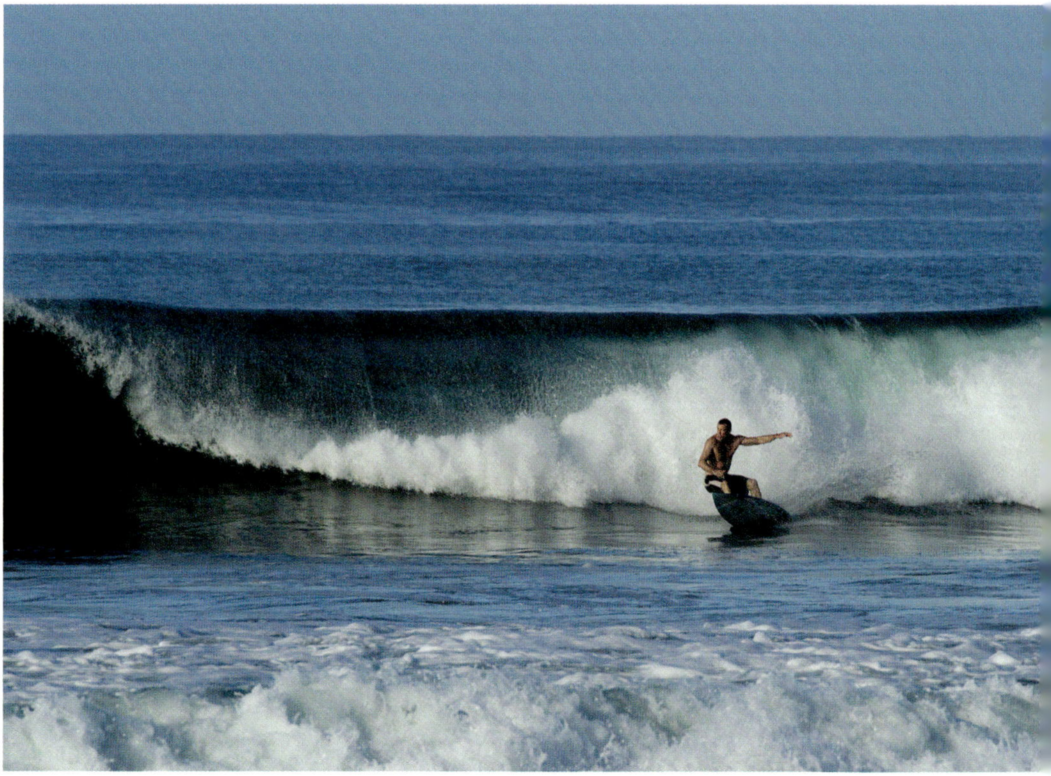

Figure 5.11
The surfer has plenty of room to ride into this shot from Santa Teresa, Costa Rica. The board, the wave, and even his sightline convey a sense of motion from right to left.

ISO 200 • 1/1000 sec. • f/9 • 70–200mm lens

Get in front of the action

Here's another one. When shooting action, show the action coming toward you (**Figure 5.12**). Don't shoot the action going away from you. People want to see faces.

Faces convey the action, the drive, the sense of urgency, and the emotion of the moment. So if you are shooting action involving people, try to position yourself so that the action is coming at you or is at least facing your shooting position.

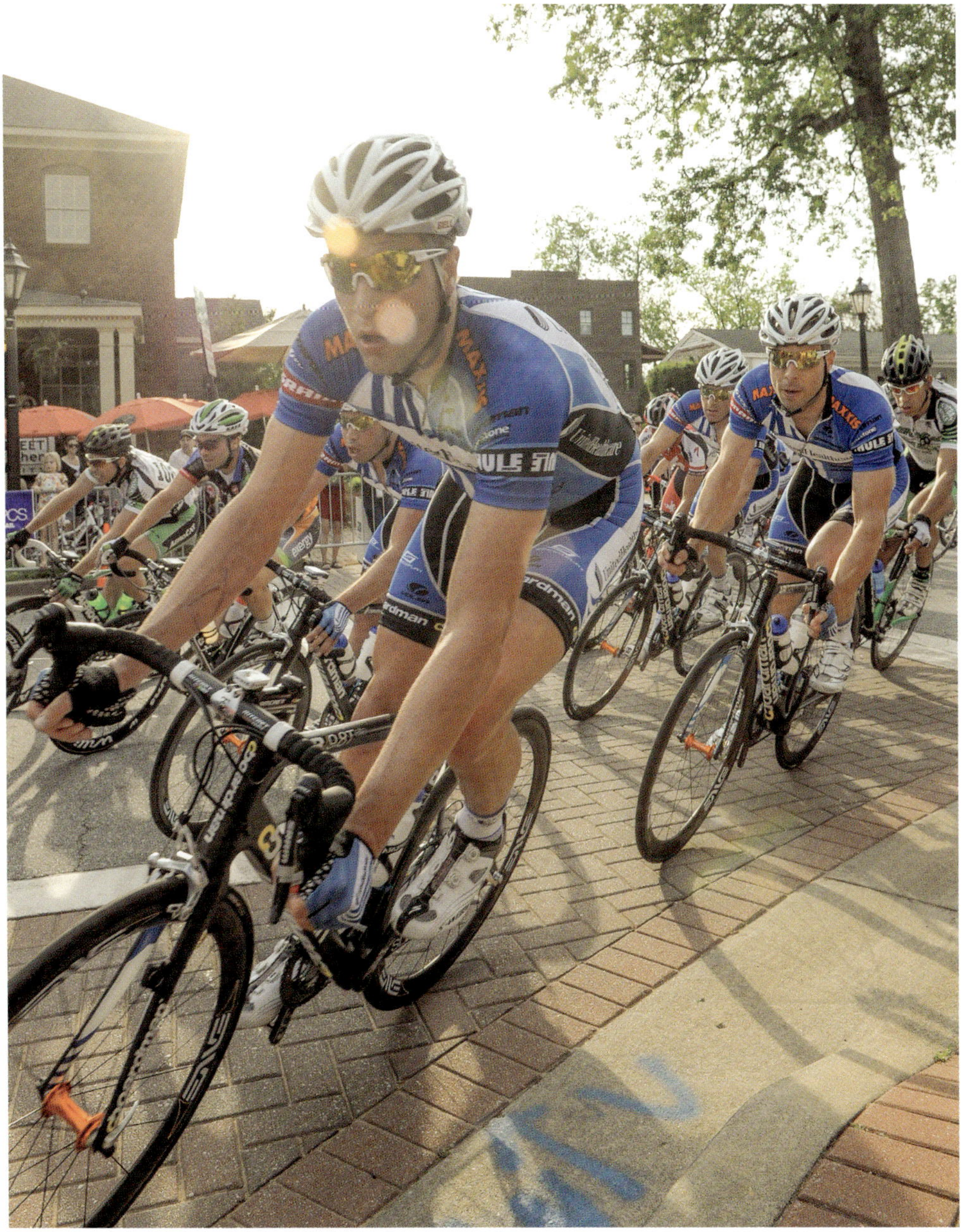

Figure 5.12
Shooting the cyclists coming toward me with a wide-angle lens puts the viewer right in the action.

ISO 1600 • 1/1600 sec. • f/8 • 24–70mm lens

Chapter 5 Assignments

The mechanics of motion

For this first assignment, you need to find some action. Explore the relationship between the speed of an object and its direction of travel. Use the same shutter speed to record your subject moving toward you and across your view. Notice the difference made by the direction of travel.

Wide vs. telephoto

Just as with the first assignment, photograph a subject moving in different directions, but this time, use a wide-angle lens and then a telephoto (or at least a standard zoom lens that zooms from a relatively wide angle to a more telephoto position). Check out how the telephoto setting on the zoom lens requires faster shutter speeds than the lens at its wide-angle setting.

Getting a feel for Continuous AF

We discussed the use of the GX7/GM1's primary autofocus mode for action: AFC. Find a moving subject and get familiar with the way the mode works. Use the 1-Area and AF Tracking modes, and note the differences between them.

The point of the exercise is to become familiar enough with the AF modes to decide which one to use for the situation you are photographing.

Anticipating the spot using manual focus

For this assignment, you will need to find a subject that you know will cross a specific line that you can pre-focus on. A street with moderate traffic works well for this. Focus on a spot on the street that the cars will travel across (don't forget to turn manual focus on). To do this right, you need to set the drive mode on the camera to Medium or High Speed Burst mode. Now, when a car approaches the spot, start shooting. Try shooting in three- or four-frame bursts.

Following the action

Panning is a great way to show motion. To begin, find a subject that will move across your path at a steady speed, and practice following it in your viewfinder from side to side. Now, with the camera in S mode, set the shutter speed to 1/30 of a second and the focus mode to Continuous AF. Pan along with the subject and shoot as it moves across your view. Experiment with different shutter speeds and focal lengths. Panning takes some time to get a feel for, so try it with different types of subjects moving at different speeds. Be sure to "follow through" and keep the camera moving after you take your shots. This will help to give you nice blurred backgrounds.

Feeling the movement

Instead of panning with the motion, use a stationary camera position and adjust the shutter speed until you get a blurred effect that gives the sense of motion but still allows the subject to be identified. There is a big difference between a slightly blurred photo that looks like you picked the wrong shutter speed and one that looks intentional for the purpose of showing motion. As with panning, it will take some experimentation to find just the right shutter speed to achieve the desired effect.

Share your results with the book's Flickr group!
Join the group here: flickr.com/groups/panasonicGX7_fromsnapshotstogreatshots

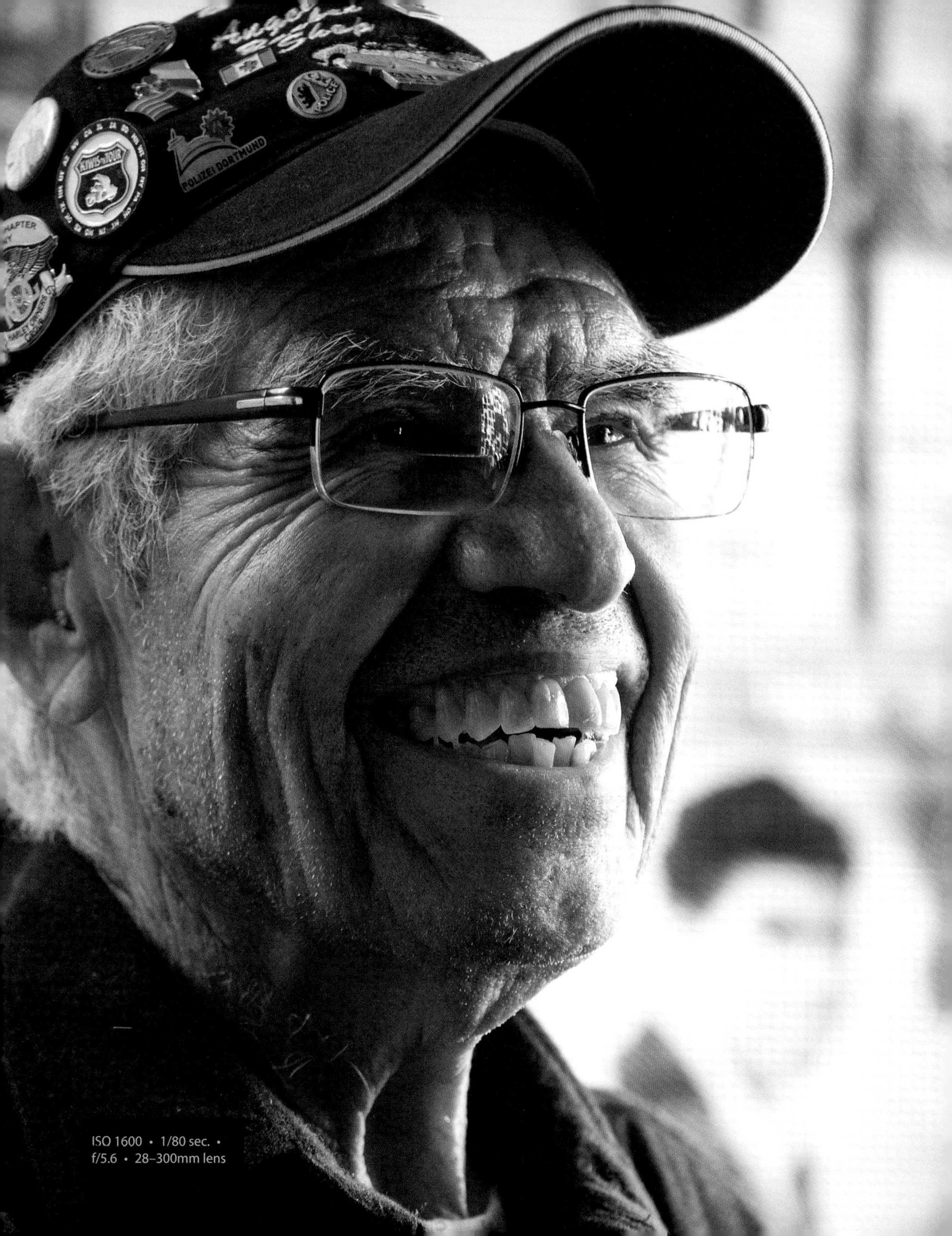

ISO 1600 • 1/80 sec. •
f/5.6 • 28–300mm lens

6

Say Cheese!

Settings and Features to Make Great Portraits

Taking pictures of people is one of the great joys of photography. You will experience a great sense of accomplishment when you capture the spirit and personality of someone in a photograph. At the same time, you have a great responsibility because the person in front of the camera is depending on you to make them look good. You can't always change how someone looks, but you can control the way you photograph that individual. In this chapter, we will explore some camera features and techniques that can help you create great portraits.

Poring Over the Picture

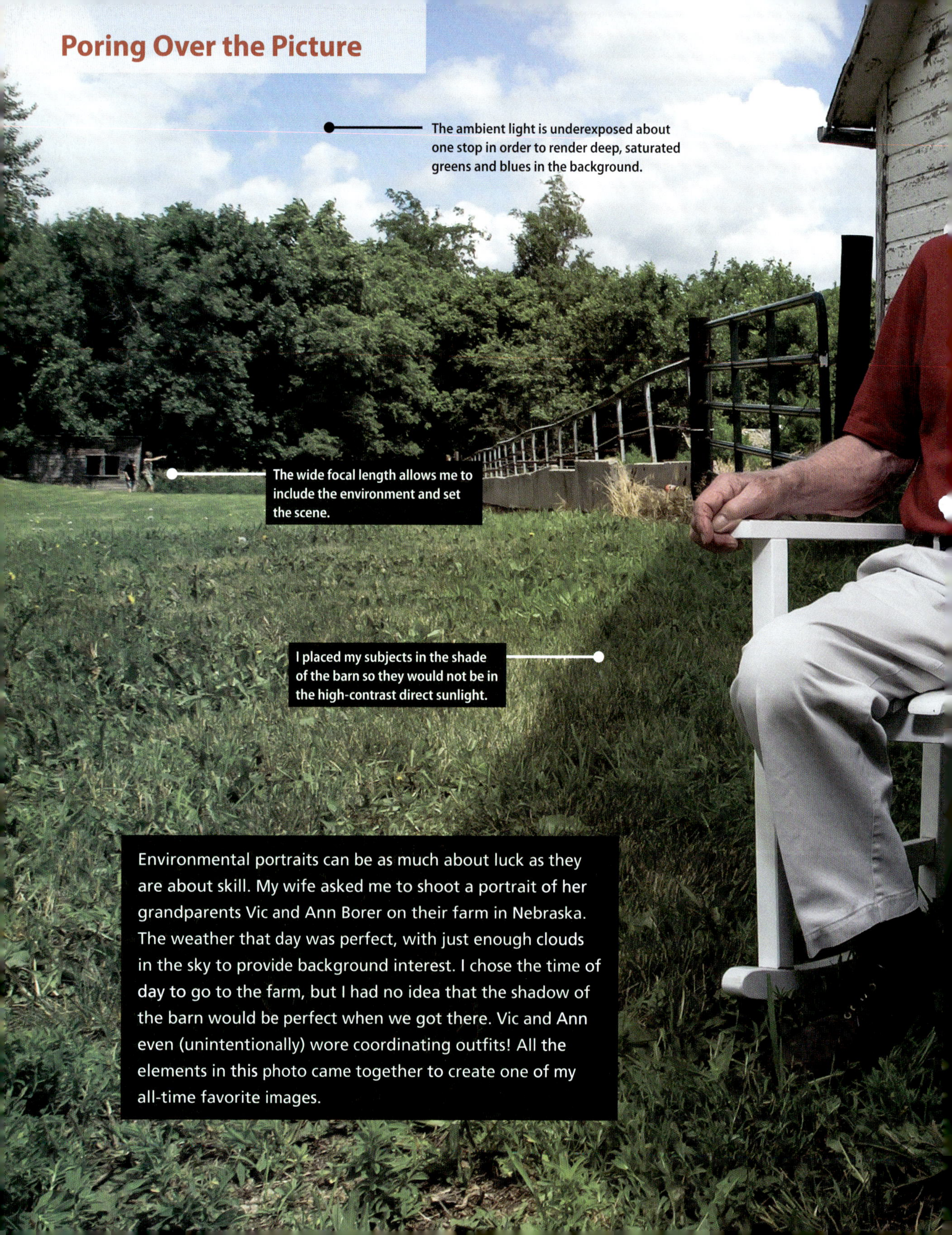

Environmental portraits can be as much about luck as they are about skill. My wife asked me to shoot a portrait of her grandparents Vic and Ann Borer on their farm in Nebraska. The weather that day was perfect, with just enough clouds in the sky to provide background interest. I chose the time of day to go to the farm, but I had no idea that the shadow of the barn would be perfect when we got there. Vic and Ann even (unintentionally) wore coordinating outfits! All the elements in this photo came together to create one of my all-time favorite images.

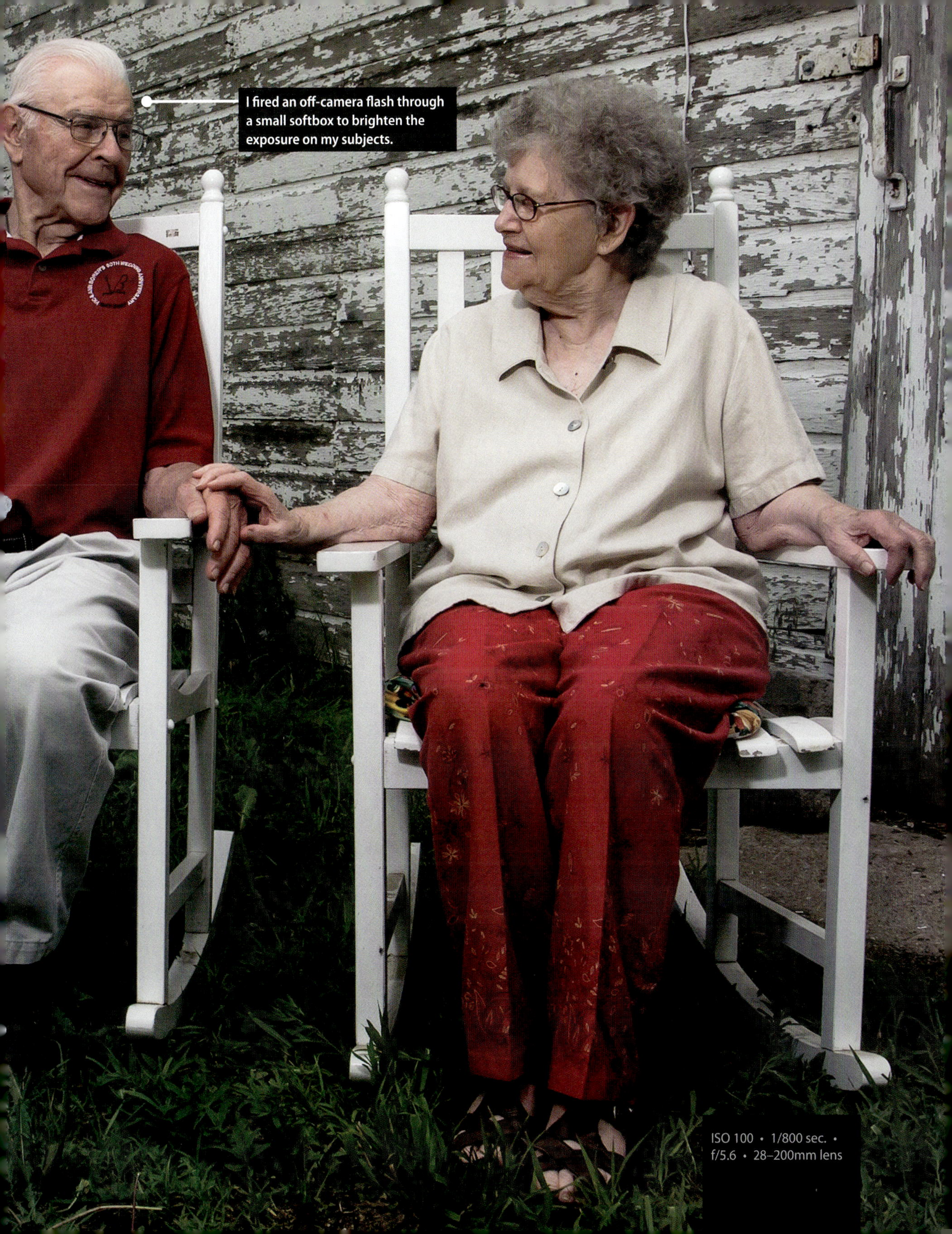

ISO 100 • 1/800 sec. • f/5.6 • 28–200mm lens

Automatic Portrait Mode

In Chapter 3, we reviewed the automatic modes. The first six modes (GM1: the first five) are dedicated to shooting portraits. They are a great jumping-off point for those who are just starting out. When selecting a scene mode, press the Disp button to bring up tips on camera settings and lens choice for the chosen mode. Use these tips to understand what is going on with the camera so that when you venture further into portrait photography, you can expand on the settings and get the most from your camera and, more importantly, your subject.

Whether you are photographing an individual or a group, the emphasis should always be on the subject. The portrait scene modes utilize a larger aperture setting to keep the depth of field very shallow, which means that the background will appear slightly blurred or out of focus. To take full advantage of this effect, use a medium- to telephoto-length lens (**Figure 6.1**). Also, keep a pretty close distance to your subject. If you shoot from too far away, the shallow depth of field will not be as effective.

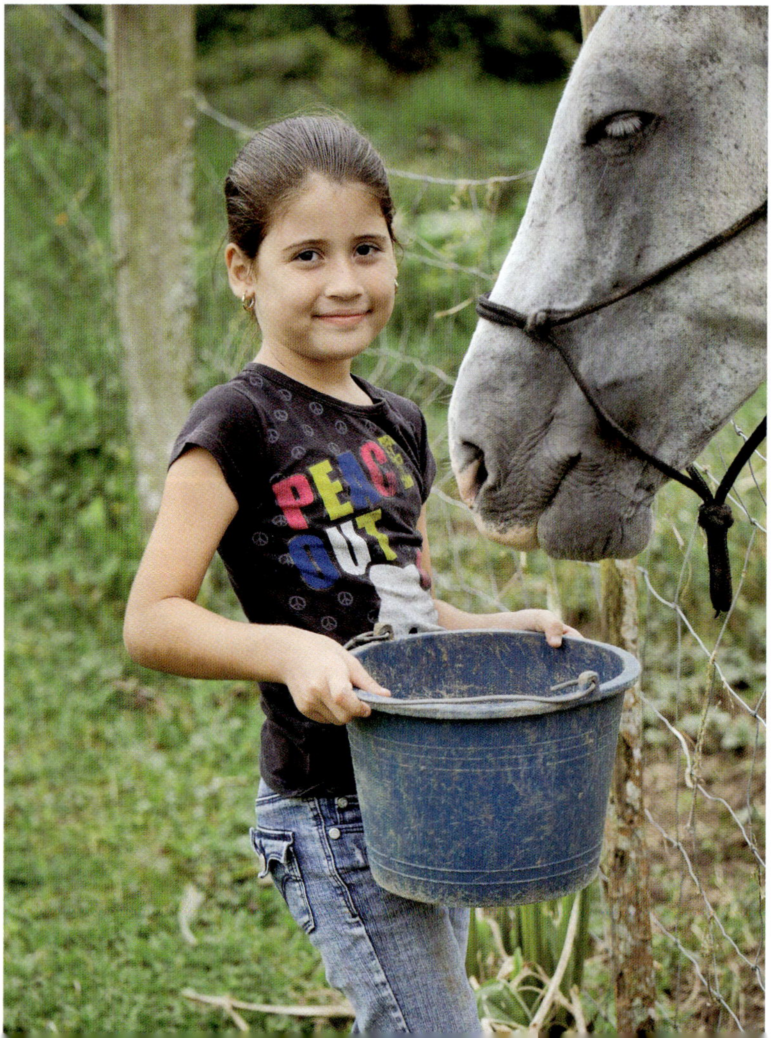

Figure 6.1
The automatic portrait modes work best when combined with a medium or long lens.

ISO 200 • 1/320 sec. • f/2.8 • 35–100mm lens

Using Aperture Priority Mode

If you took a poll of portrait photographers to see which shooting mode was most often used for portraits, the answer would certainly be Aperture Priority (A) mode. Selecting the right aperture is important for placing the most critically sharp area of the photo on your subject, while simultaneously blurring all of the distracting background clutter (**Figure 6.2**). Not only will a large aperture give the shallowest depth of field, it will also allow you to shoot in lower light levels at lower ISO settings. There are several good options for fast medium-telephoto portrait lenses for your GX7 and GM1. Your Lumix camera is compatible with any Micro Four Thirds lens, as well as with Leica and Four Thirds lenses with adapters.

You don't always have to use the largest aperture on your lens. A good place to begin is f/5.6. This will give you enough depth of field to keep the entire face in focus, while providing enough blur to eliminate distractions in the background. This isn't a hard-and-fast setting; it's just a good all-around number to start with. Your aperture might change depending on the focal length of the lens you are using and on the amount of blur that you want for your foreground and background elements.

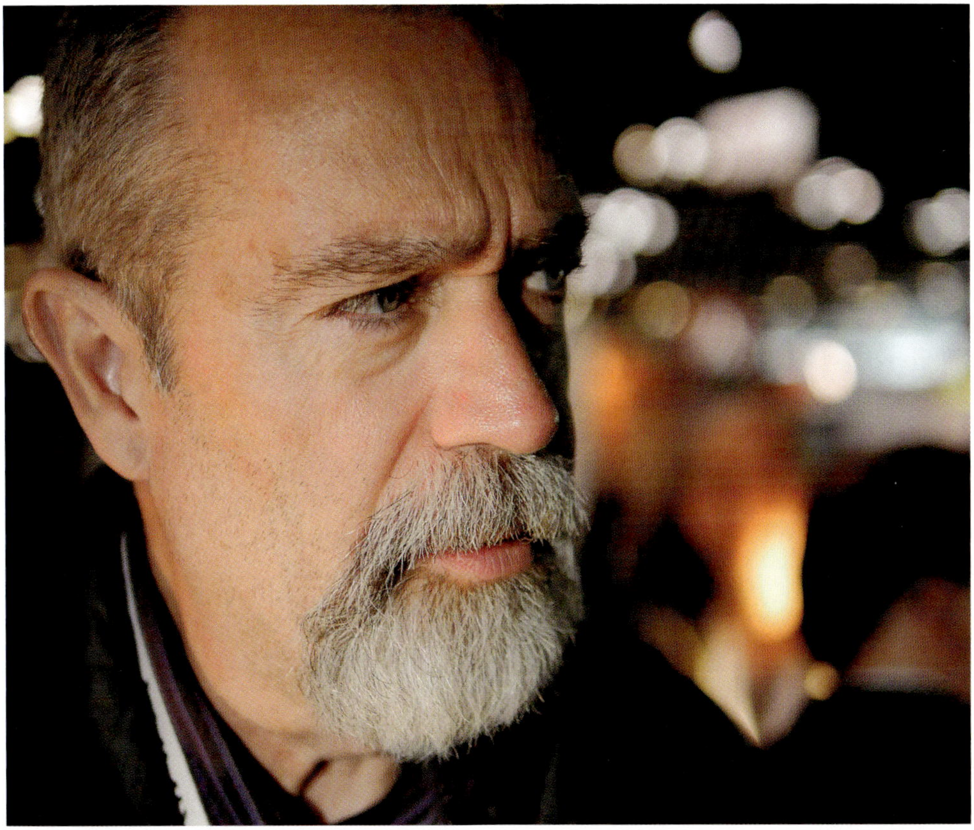

Figure 6.2

Using a wide aperture, especially with a longer lens, blurs distracting background details.

ISO 1600 • 1/800 sec. • f/1.4 • 25mm lens

Go wide for environmental portraits

There will be times when your subject's environment is of great significance to the story you want to tell. This might mean using a smaller aperture to get more detail in the background or foreground. Once again, by using A mode you can set your aperture to a higher f-stop, such as f/8 or f/11, and include the important details of the scene that surrounds your subject.

Using a wider-than-normal lens can also assist in getting more depth of field, as well as showing the surrounding area. A wide-angle lens requires less stopping down of the aperture to achieve an acceptable depth of field. A wider lens might also be necessary to relay more information about the subject's environment (**Figure 6.3**). Select a lens length that is wide enough to tell the story but not so wide that you distort the subject. There's nothing quite as unflattering as giving someone a big, distorted nose (unless you are going for that sort of look). When shooting a portrait with a wide-angle lens, keep the subject away from the edge of the frame. This will reduce the distortion, especially in very wide focal lengths. As the lens length increases, distortion will be reduced. I generally don't like to go wider than about 12mm for portraits. For standard portraits, I prefer focal lengths of anywhere from 25mm to 75mm.

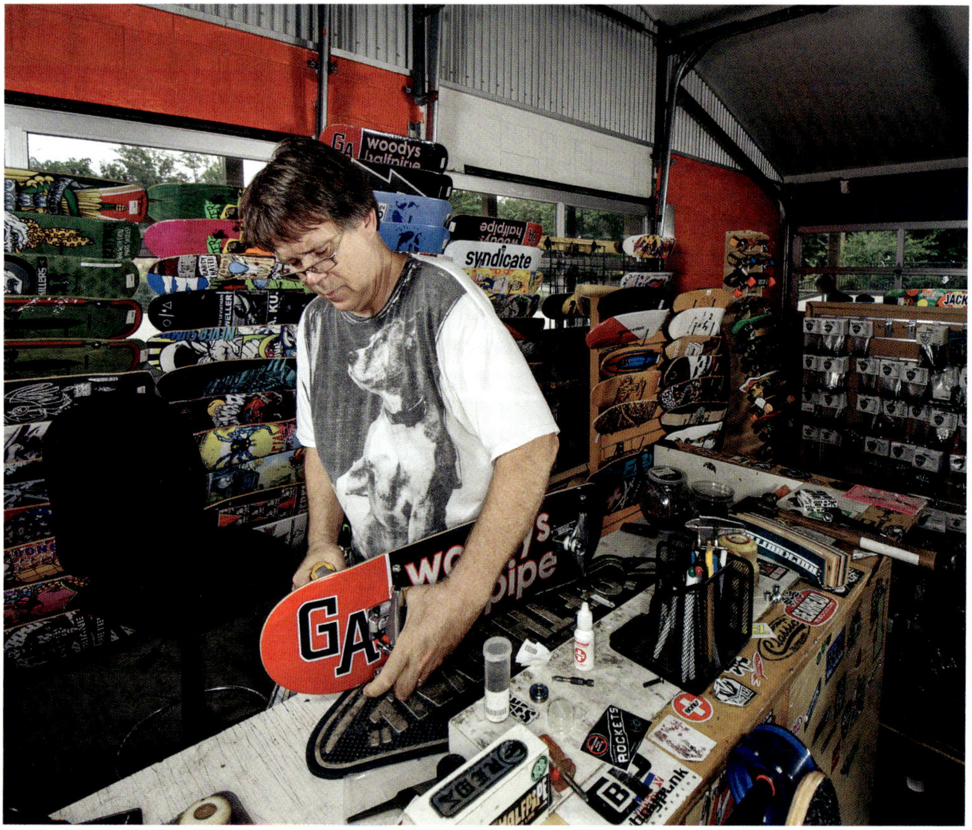

Figure 6.3
A wide-angle lens allows you to capture more of the environment along with your subject. The wide-angle lens and the high f-stop help keep both the subject and the background in focus.

ISO 200 • 1/250 sec. • f/8 • 16–35mm lens

Metering Basics

There are multiple metering modes in your camera, but the way they all work is very similar. A light meter measures the amount of light being reflected off your subject and then renders a suggested exposure value based on the brightness of the subject and the ISO setting of the sensor. To establish this value, the meter averages all of the brightness values to come up with a middle tone, sometimes referred to as 18 percent gray. The exposure value is then rendered based on this middle gray value. This means that a white wall would be underexposed and a black wall would be overexposed in an effort to make each one appear gray. To assist with special lighting situations, the GX7 and GM1 have three metering modes: Multi (**Figure 6.4**), which evaluates the entire frame in different segments before establishing an exposure; Center Weighted (**Figure 6.5**), which looks at the entire frame but places most of the exposure emphasis on the center of the frame; and Spot (**Figure 6.6**), which takes specific readings from a small area outlined in the center of the frame (often used with a gray card).

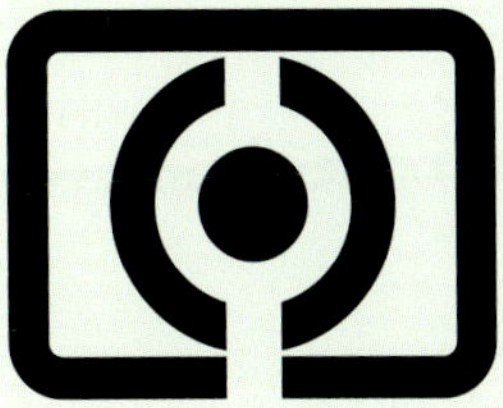

Figure 6.4 The Multi metering mode uses the entire frame.

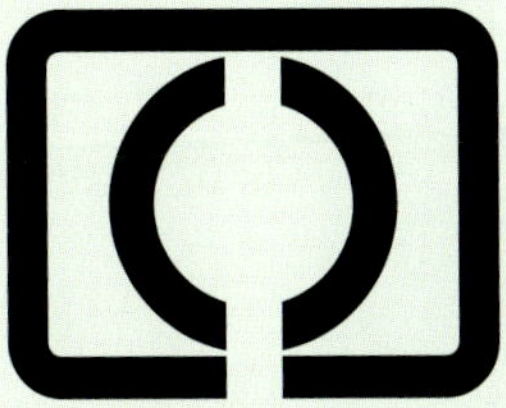

Figure 6.5 The Center Weighted metering mode emphasizes the middle of the frame.

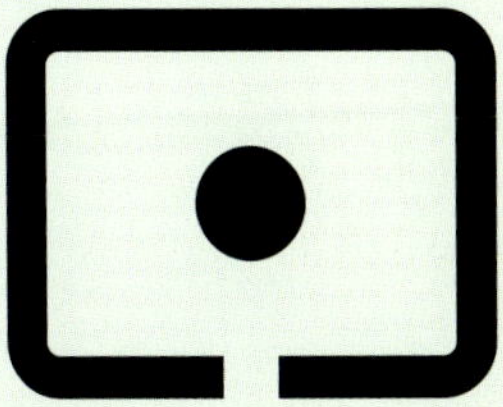

Figure 6.6 The Spot metering mode uses a very small area in the center of the frame.

Metering Modes for Portraits

For most portrait situations, the Multi metering mode is ideal. (For more on how metering works, see the "Metering Basics" sidebar.) This mode measures light values from all portions of the viewfinder and then establishes a proper exposure for the scene. The only time you might encounter a problem when using this metering mode is when you have very light or very dark backgrounds in your portrait shots.

In these instances, the meter might be fooled into using the wrong exposure information because it will be trying to lighten or darken the entire scene based on the prominence of dark or light areas (**Figure 6.7**). In the semiautomatic modes you can deal with this in one of two ways. You can use exposure compensation to lighten or darken the image, or you can change the metering mode from Multi to Center Weighted. The Center Weighted metering mode assesses the entire frame, but it places more emphasis on the center of the frame. This is the best way to achieve proper exposure for many portraits; metering off of skin tones, averaged with hair and clothing, will often give a more accurate exposure (**Figure 6.8**). This metering mode is also great to use when the subject is strongly backlit.

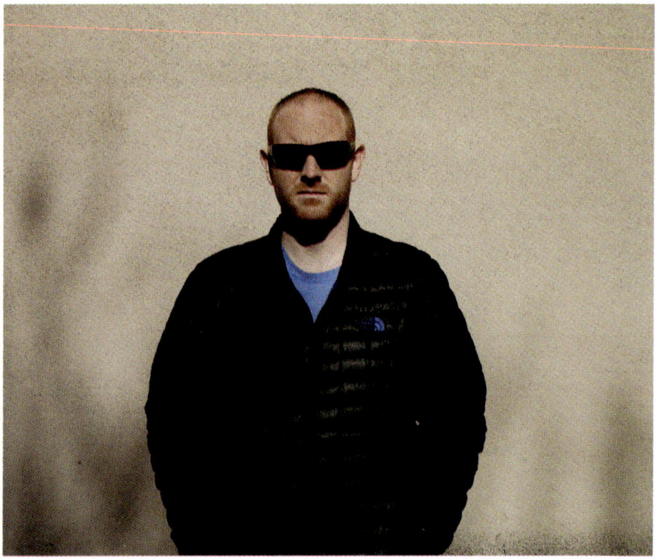

Figure 6.7
The bright background fooled the Multi metering mode into choosing a slightly underexposed setting.

ISO 200 • 1/1000 sec. • f/8 • 20mm lens

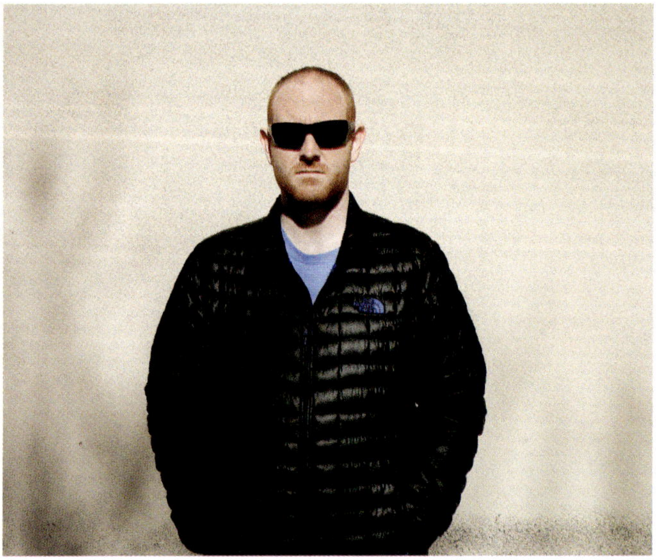

Figure 6.8
With the Center Weighted metering mode, the camera increases the exposure time so that the subject is exposed properly.

ISO 200 • 1/500 sec. • f/8 • 20mm lens

Setting your metering mode to Center Weighted

1. Press Menu/Set, then select Rec and navigate to Metering Mode.
2. Select the icon for Center-Weighted metering (**A**).
3. You can also press the Q.Menu button to navigate to the metering mode (**B**).
4. Press the shutter button halfway or press the Menu/Set button to return to shooting mode.

A

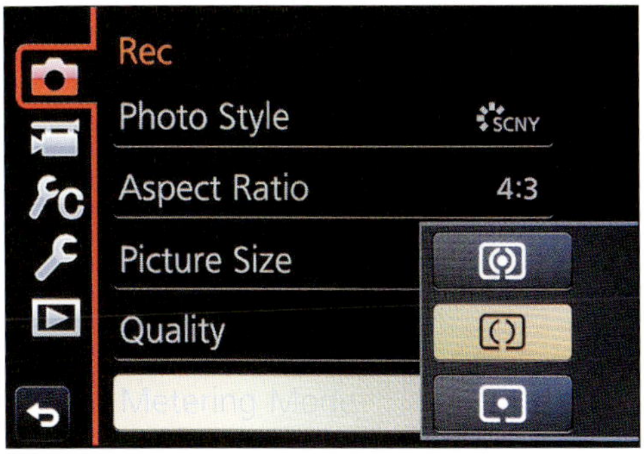

B

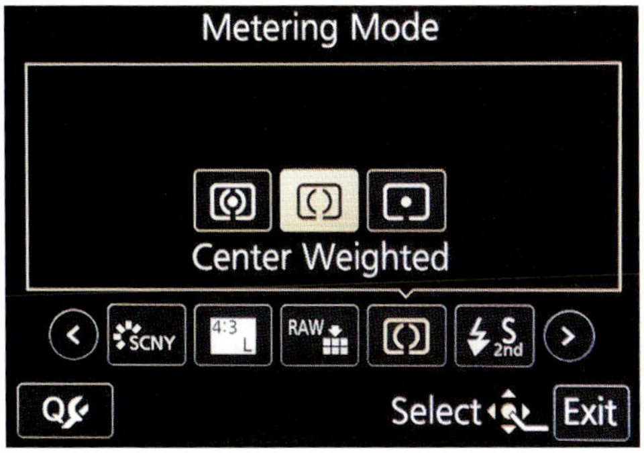

Using the AE Lock Feature

There will often be times when your subject is not in the center of the frame but you still want to use the Center or Spot metering modes. So how can you get an accurate reading if the subject isn't in the center? Try using the AE (Auto Exposure) Lock feature to hold the exposure setting while you recompose.

AE Lock lets you use the exposure setting from any portion of the scene that you think is appropriate, and then lock that setting in regardless of how the scene looks when you recompose. An example of this would be when you're shooting a photograph of someone and a large amount of blue sky appears in the picture. Normally, the meter might be fooled by all that bright sky and try to reduce the exposure. Using AE Lock, you can establish the correct metering by zooming in on the subject (or even pointing the camera toward the ground), taking the meter reading and locking it in with AE Lock, and then recomposing and taking your photo with the locked-in exposure.

Shooting with the AE Lock feature

1. On the GX7, find the AF/AE Lock button on the back of the camera.

   In order to use this technique on the GM1, you must first assign AF/AE Lock to the Fn1 button.

2. While looking through the viewfinder, fill the frame with your subject and press the shutter button halfway to get a meter reading.
3. Press and hold the AF/AE Lock button. AEL will appear in the bottom left of your viewfinder or LCD, letting you know that the exposure has been locked. Continue to hold the AF/AE Lock button.

   On the GM1, press and release the Fn1 button to lock the exposure.

4. Recompose your shot, and then take the photo.
5. To take more than one photo without having to take another meter reading, just hold down the AF/AE Lock button until you are done using the meter setting.

   On the GM1, the exposure will remained locked until you press the Fn1 button again.

Focusing: The Eyes Have It

It has been said that the eyes are the windows to the soul, and nothing could be truer when you are taking a photograph of someone (**Figure 6.9**). You could have the perfect composition and exposure, but if the eyes aren't sharp the entire image suffers. Although there are three different focusing modes to choose from on your GX7/GM1, as well as five different autofocus modes, for portrait work you can't beat AFS and 1-Area mode. AFS, or AF Single, will establish a single focus for the lens and then hold it until you take the photograph. Using 1-Area focus lets you place the focusing point right on your subject's eye and set that spot as the critical focus point. The touchscreen makes it easy to focus wherever your subject is in the frame.

Setting up for AFS focusing mode

1. Press Menu/Set, then select Custom and navigate to the AFS/AFF/AFC menu.
2. Select AFS (**A**).

   You can also press the Q.Menu button to navigate to the AFS/AFF/AFC menu.

A

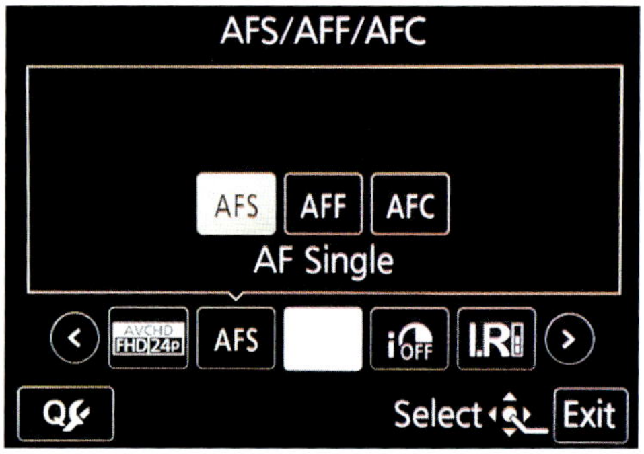

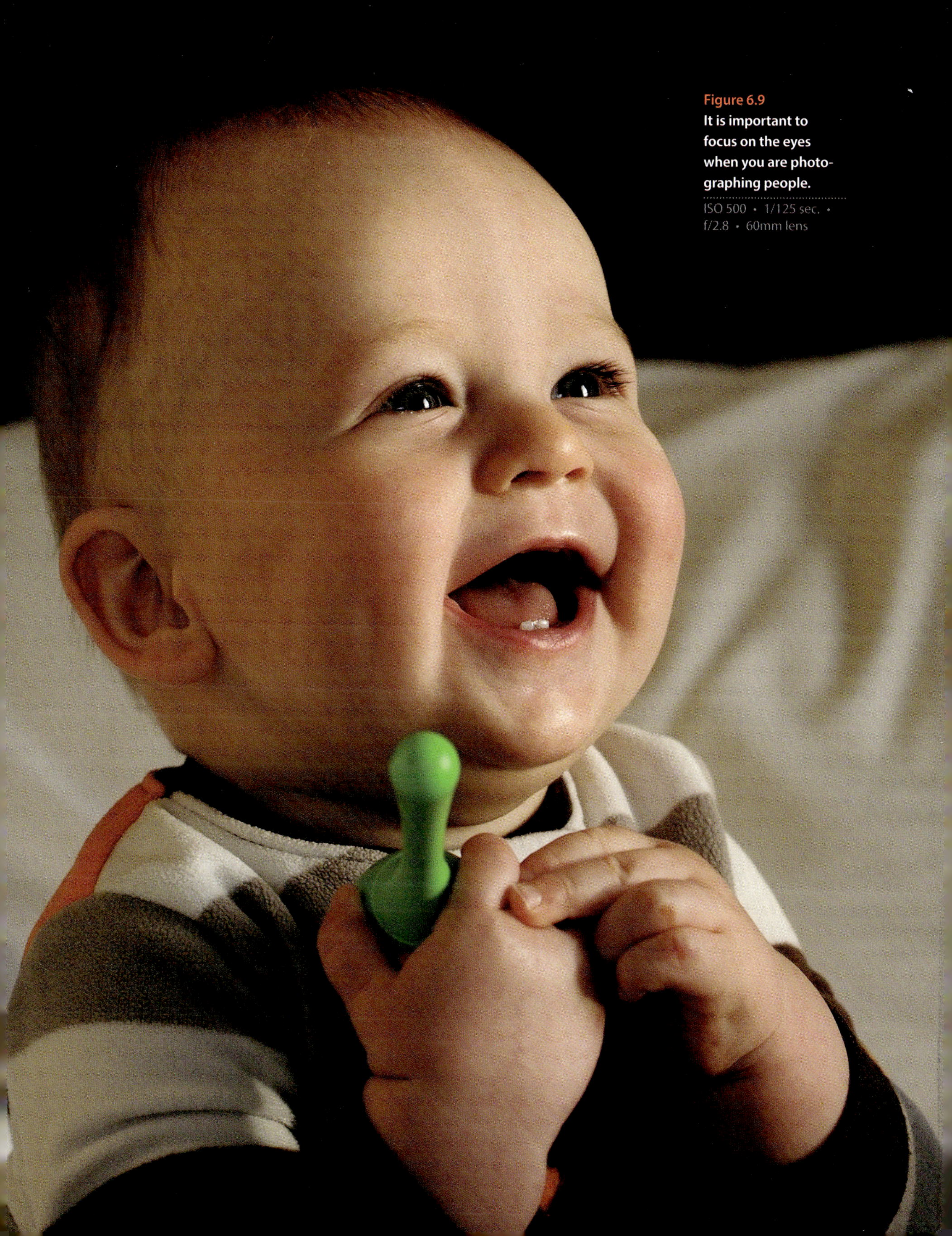

Figure 6.9
It is important to focus on the eyes when you are photographing people.
ISO 500 • 1/125 sec. • f/2.8 • 60mm lens

Setting your focus to 1-Area

1. Press the AF mode button (◀).
2. Use the cursor buttons to scroll to 1-Area focus, or simply touch the icon on the LCD.
3. Press the shutter button halfway or press the Menu/Set button to return to shooting mode.

Touch the LCD screen wherever you want to focus (your subject's eye in this case) and press the shutter button halfway to focus. You can change the size of the focus point by turning the Rear dial (GM1: Command dial) while the yellow focus point is highlighted.

Using Face Detection and Registration

Face detection in digital cameras has been around for a few years, and the face detection AF in the GX7/GM1 does a remarkable job. Face detection AF adjusts both the focus and exposure for the detected faces in your photo. When you turn on face detection focusing, the camera zeroes in on any face appearing on the LCD and places a box around it (**Figure 6.10**). It will even detect multiple faces, but the green box is where the focus is set. Another great thing about face detection is that it doesn't slow down the autofocus function.

In addition to face detection AF you can use face recognition to register up to six faces in the GX7/GM1. The camera will then give priority to your registered faces when it detects multiple faces in a scene. You can find out how to register faces on page 197 of your GX7 owner's manual, and on page 185 in the GM1 manual.

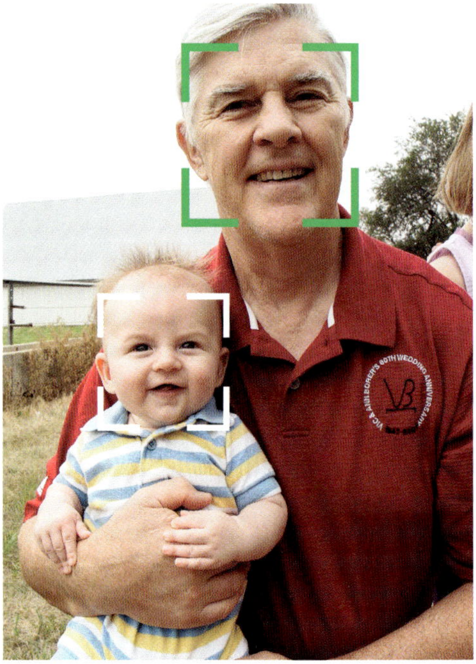

Figure 6.10 Face detection can lock in on your subject's face for easy focusing. The green box indicates the face where the focus is set, and the white box indicates other detected faces.

ISO 200 • 1/125 sec. • f/8 • 17mm lens

Setting up and shooting with face detection focusing

1. Press the AF mode button (◀).
2. Use the cursor buttons to scroll to Face Detection, or simply touch the icon on the LCD (**A**).
3. Press the shutter button halfway or press the Menu/Set button to return to shooting mode.

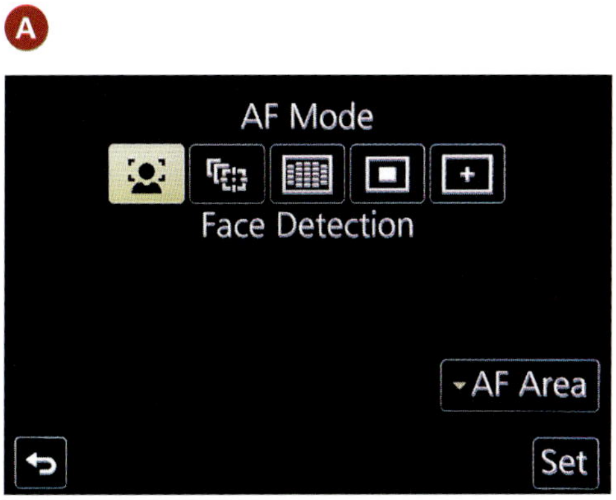

Point your camera at a person, and watch as a frame appears over the face in the LCD or in the electronic viewfinder. Press and hold the shutter release button halfway to focus on the face. Press the shutter button fully to take the photograph.

Classic Black-and-White Portraits

There is something timeless about a black-and-white portrait. It eliminates the distraction of color and puts all the emphasis on the subject. To get great black and whites without having to resort to any image-processing software, set your photo style to Monochrome (**Figure 6.11** on the following page). You should know that the photo styles are only applied when shooting with the JPEG file format. If you are shooting in RAW, the picture that shows up on your rear LCD display will look black and white, but it will appear as a color image when you open it in any RAW processing software. For example, if you are using Adobe Photoshop Lightroom to edit and process your images, the RAW image will appear as an unaltered, color image and you will have to convert it to black-and-white using the software. Set the Quality setting to RAW+ Fine JPEG to get the great Monochrome JPEG out of the camera and still have the RAW file to play with in the computer.

The real key to using the Monochrome photo style is to customize it for your portrait subject. The style can be changed by adjusting the contrast, sharpness, saturation (which makes your black-and-white image warm- or cool-toned), noise reduction, and filter effect. The filter effect simulates using a yellow, orange, red, or green filter in front of your lens. For women, children, puppies, and anyone else who should look somewhat soft, set the Sharpness setting to –1 or 0 and the Contrast to –1 or –2. For old cowboys, longshoremen, and anyone else you want to look really detailed, try a Sharpness setting of 2 or 3 and crank up the Contrast a couple of points. I like to leave the noise reduction at –5 because I think a little grain looks good in a black-and-white image.

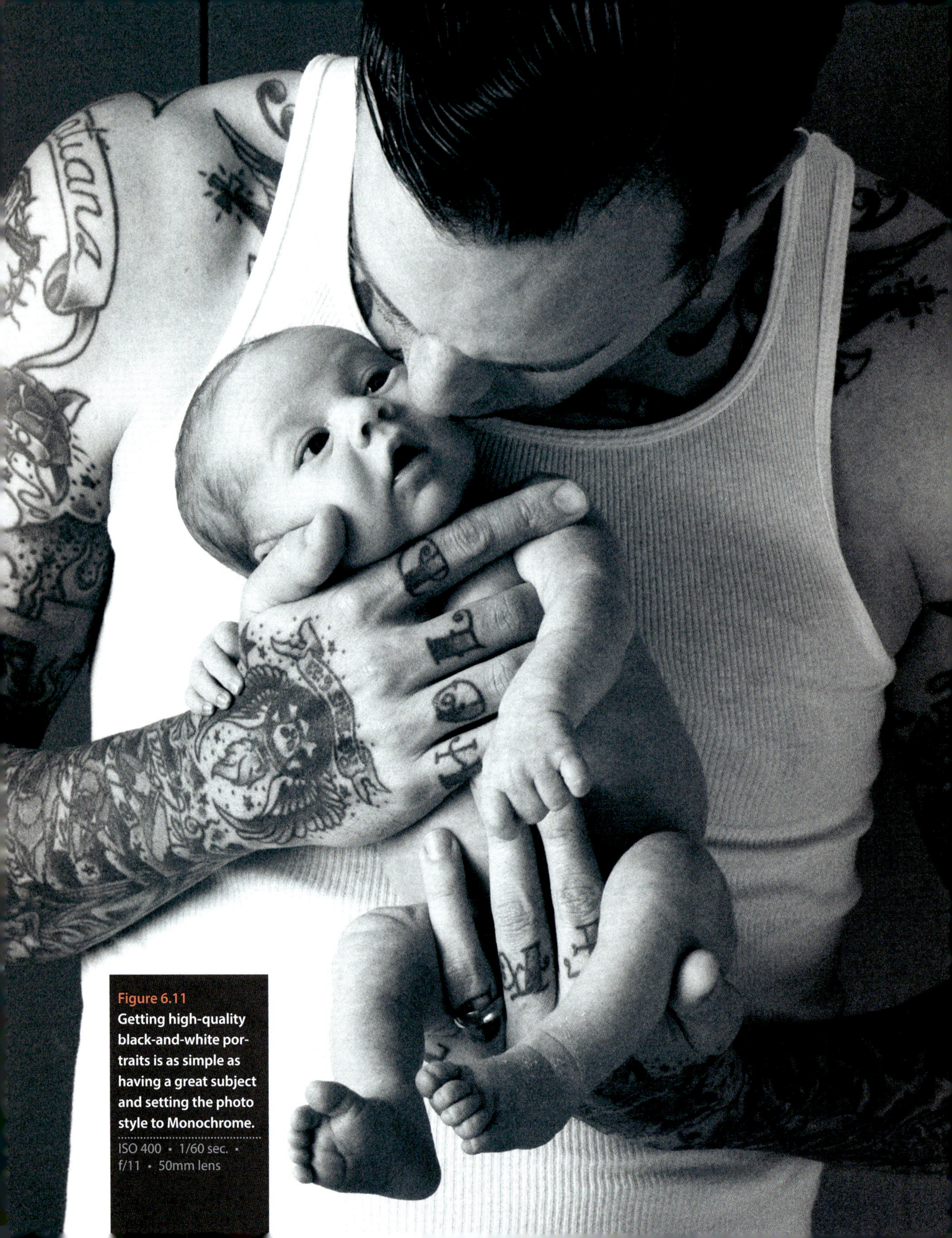

Figure 6.11
Getting high-quality black-and-white portraits is as simple as having a great subject and setting the photo style to Monochrome.

ISO 400 • 1/60 sec. • f/11 • 50mm lens

Setting and customizing the Monochrome photo style

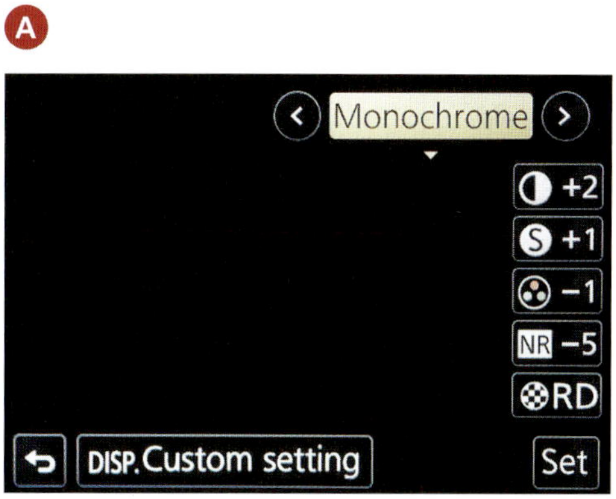

1. Press the Menu/Set button, then select the Rec menu.
2. Select Photo Style and press Menu/Set.
3. Use the left and right cursor buttons to select the Monochrome photo style.
4. Use the up and down cursor buttons to move from one adjustment to the other, and use the left and right cursor buttons to move the sliders (**A**).

   You can also touch the adjustment you want to make on the LCD and drag the sliders with your finger.

Your camera will continue to shoot with the Monochrome photo style until you change it to another setting.

The Portrait Photo Style for Better Skin Tones

The Portrait photo style on your GX7/GM1 is designed specifically to make skin tones look great. To set this style on your camera, simply follow the same directions as earlier, but select the Portrait style instead of Monochrome. You have the same adjustments available for the Portrait style that you had for the Monochrome style, minus the black-and-white filter effect. I like saturated colors, and the Portrait photo style does a nice job with the skin tones, even when the Saturation slider is bumped up a few points. You won't be able to use the same adjustments for every situation, so do some experimenting to see what works best.

Use Fill Flash for Reducing Shadows

A common problem when taking pictures of people outside, especially during the midday hours, is that the overhead sun can create dark shadows under the eyes and chin. You could have your subject turn his or her face to the sun, but that is usually considered cruel and unusual punishment. So how can you have your subject's back to the sun and still get a decent exposure of the face? Try turning on your flash to fill in the shadows. This also works well when you are photographing someone who's wearing a ball cap or someone who has a bright scene behind them (**Figure 6.12**). The fill flash helps lighten the subject so they don't appear in shadow, while providing a really nice catchlight in the eyes.

The key to using the flash as a fill is to not use it on full power. If you do, the camera will try to balance the flash with the daylight, and you will get a very flat and featureless face.

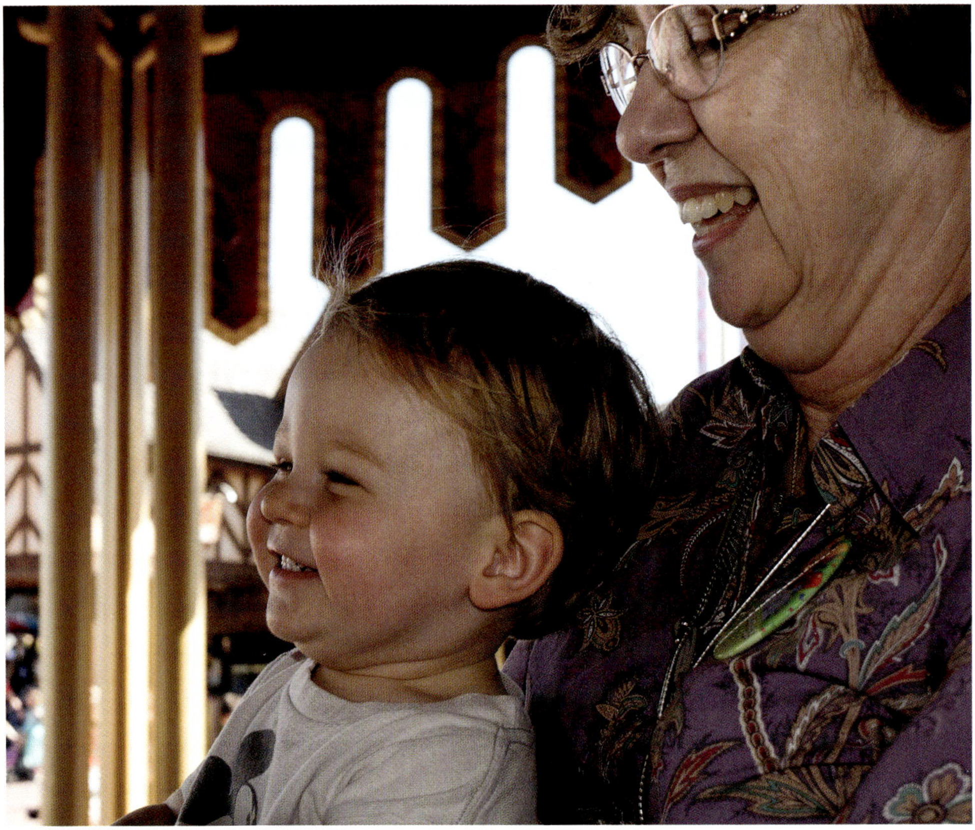

Figure 6.12
My subjects were in the shade with a bright background, so I used the built-in flash on my GX7 to fill in the shadows.

ISO 200 • 1/250 sec. • f/4.5 • 12–35mm lens

Catchlight

A *catchlight* is that little sparkle that adds life to the eyes. When you are photographing a person with a light source in front of them, you will usually get a reflection of that light in the eye, be it your flash, the sun, or something else brightly reflecting in the eye. The light is reflected off the surface of the eyes as bright highlights, which brings attention to the eyes.

Setting up and shooting with fill flash

1. Press Menu/Set, then select the Rec menu.
2. Select Flash and press Menu/Set (**A**).
3. Select Flash Mode and choose Forced Flash On (the lightning bolt) (**B**).
4. Select Flash Adjust and try a setting of –1 to start (**C**).
5. Press Menu/Set to confirm the setting, and press the shutter button halfway to return to shooting mode.

A

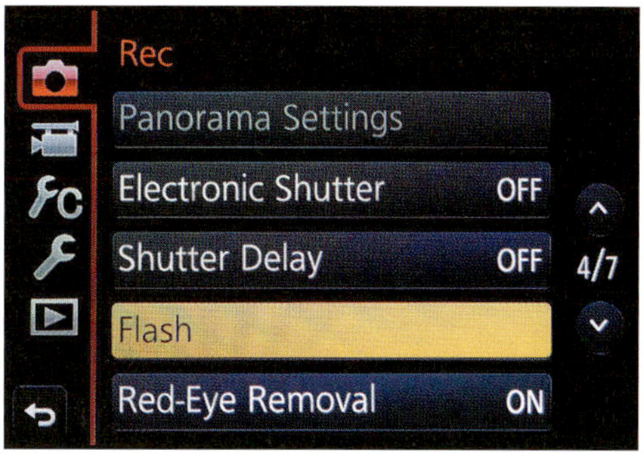

B

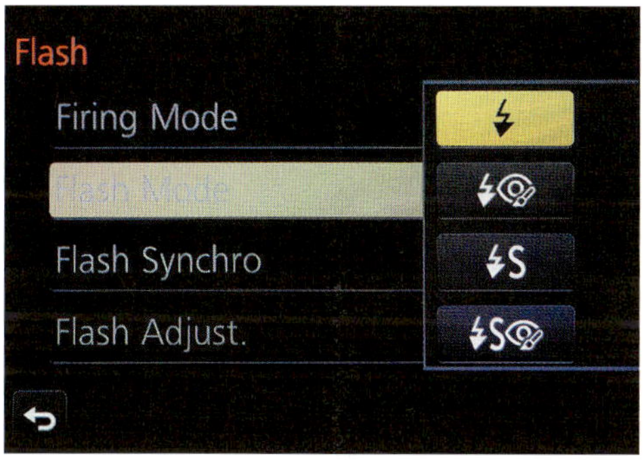

C

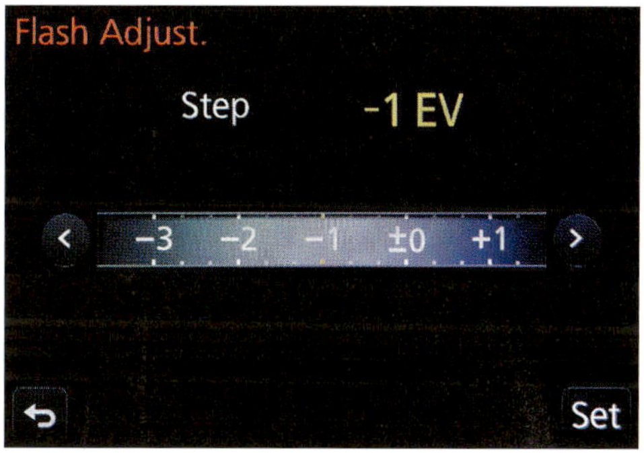

If you need more or less fill light, simply return to the Flash Adjust menu and adjust the power.

Tips for Shooting Better Portraits

Before we get to the assignments for this chapter, I thought it might be a good idea to leave you with a few extra portrait pointers that don't necessarily have anything specific to do with your camera. There are entire books that cover things like portrait lighting, posing, and so on, but here are a few pointers that will make your people photos look a lot better.

Avoid the center of the frame

This falls under the category of composition. Place your subject to the side of the frame (**Figure 6.13**)—it just looks more interesting than plunking them smack dab in the middle (**Figure 6.14**). As my friend Rick Sammon says, "The dead center is deadly!"

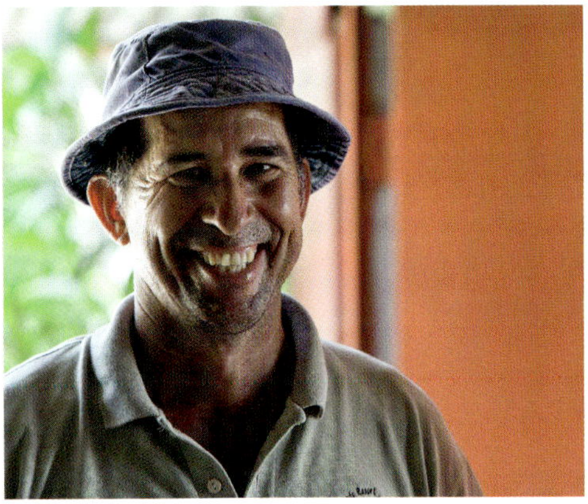

Figure 6.13 **Place the subject off to one side. Dynamic composition can make the difference between a photograph and a snapshot.**

ISO 800 • 1/640 sec. • f/4 • 70–200mm lens

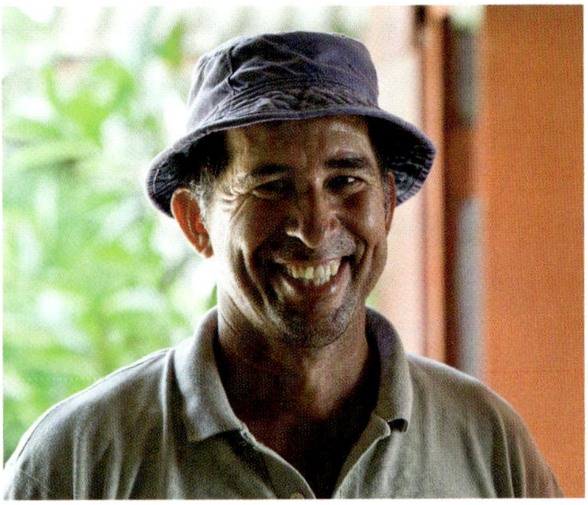

Figure 6.14 **Having the subject in the middle of the frame usually makes the shot much less interesting.**

ISO 800 • 1/640 sec. • f/4 • 70–200mm lens

Choose the right lens

Choosing the correct lens can make a huge impact on your portraits. A wide-angle lens can distort the features of your subject, which can lead to an unflattering portrait (**Figure 6.15**). Select a longer focal length to make a more flattering portrait (**Figure 6.16**).

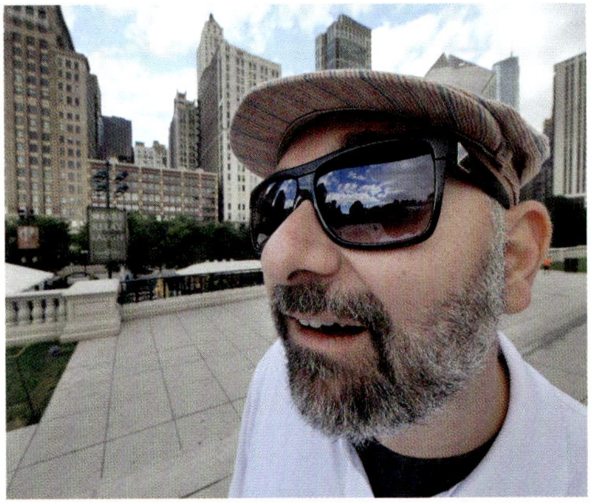

Figure 6.15 **At this close distance and angle, the ultra-wide lens exaggerates my subject's features.**

ISO 200 • 1/80 sec. • f/8 • 7–14mm lens

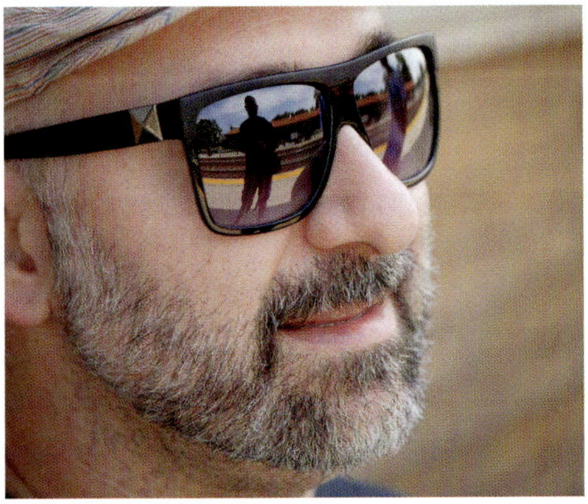

Figure 6.16 **I use a telephoto lens to get the tight shot I want without distorting his features.**

ISO 200 • 1/640 sec. • f/2.8 • 35–100mm lens

Don't cut them off at the knees

There is an old rule about photographing people: Never crop the picture at a joint. This means no cropping at the ankles or the knees. If you need to crop at the legs, the proper place to crop is mid-shin or mid-thigh (**Figure 6.17**).

Use the frame

Have you ever noticed that most people are taller than they are wide? Turn your camera vertically for a more pleasing composition (**Figure 6.18**).

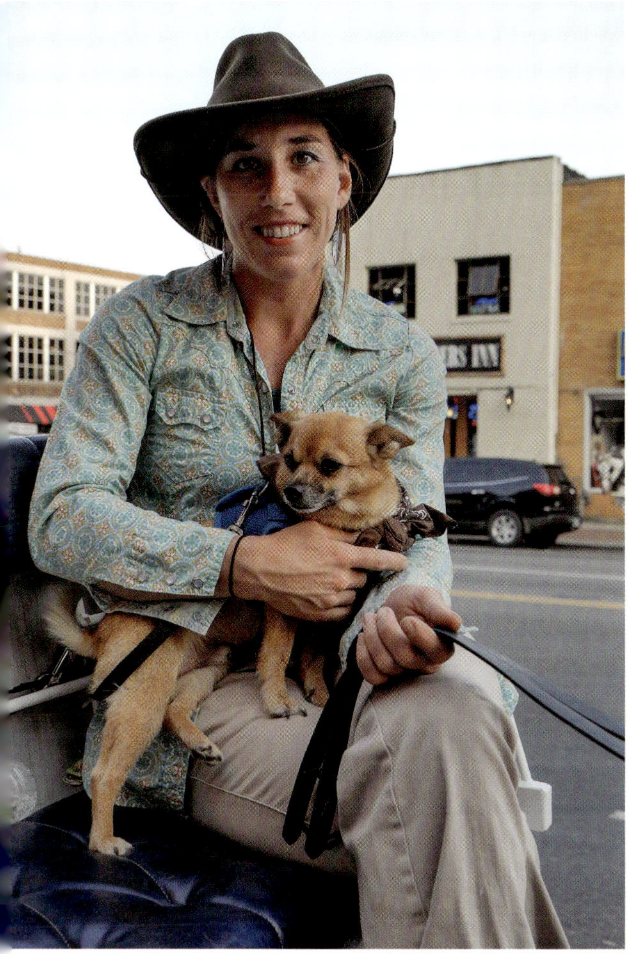

Figure 6.17 A good crop for people is at mid-thigh or mid-shin, even when they are sitting down.

ISO 200 • 1/320 sec. • f/4 • 12–35mm lens

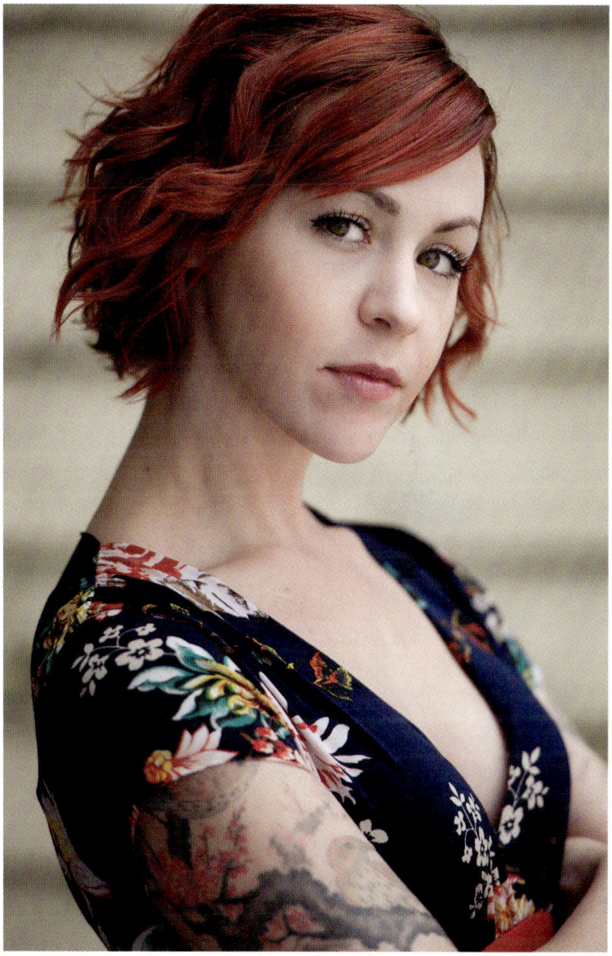

Figure 6.18 Get in the habit of turning your camera to a vertical position when shooting portraits. This is also referred to as portrait orientation.

ISO 200 • 1/800 sec. • f/2.8 • 70–200mm lens

Sunblock for portraits

The midday sun can be harsh and do unflattering things to people's faces (**Figure 6.19**). If you can, find a shady spot out of the direct sunlight (**Figure 6.20**), or block the sunlight with a diffuse material such as a white bedsheet. You will get softer shadows, smoother skin tones, and better detail. This holds true for overcast skies as well. Just be sure to adjust your white balance accordingly.

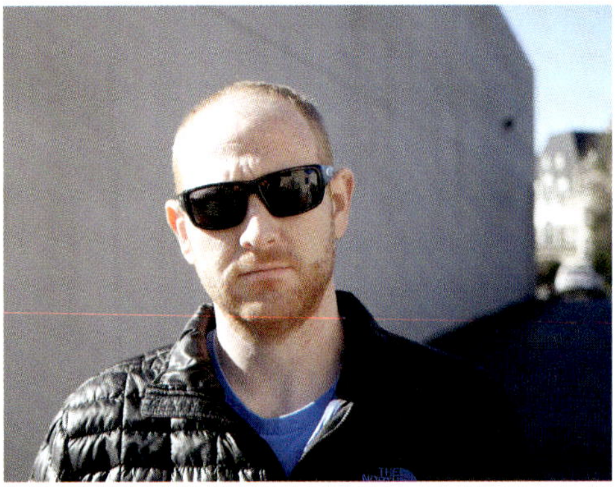

Figure 6.19 **The bright, direct sunlight looks too harsh on the subject's face.**

ISO 200 • 1/4000 sec. • f/1.7 • 20mm lens

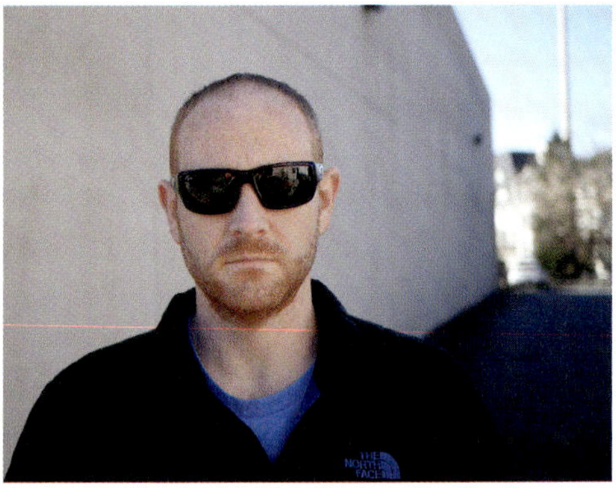

Figure 6.20 **I had my subject take two steps backward into the shade of the building. The result is much more flattering light, with lower contrast and softer shadows.**

ISO 200 • 1/3200 sec. • f/1.7 • 20mm lens

Frame the scene

Using elements in the scene to create a frame around your subject is a great way to draw the viewer's eye to what is most important: your subject! You don't have to use a window frame to do this. Just look for elements in the environment's foreground and background that could be used to force the viewer's eye toward your subject (**Figure 6.21**).

Get down on their level

If you want better pictures of children, don't shoot from an adult's eye level. Getting the camera down to the child's level will make your images look more personal (**Figure 6.22**).

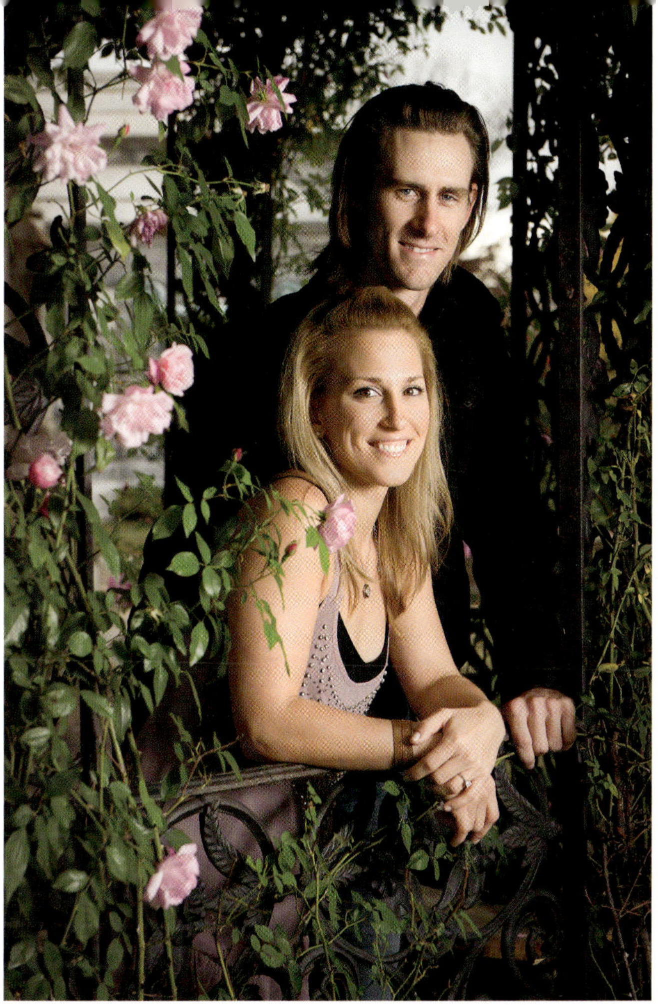

Figure 6.21

The trellis and flowers make a perfect frame for this couple.

ISO 200 • 1/160 sec. • f/6.3 • 24–70mm lens

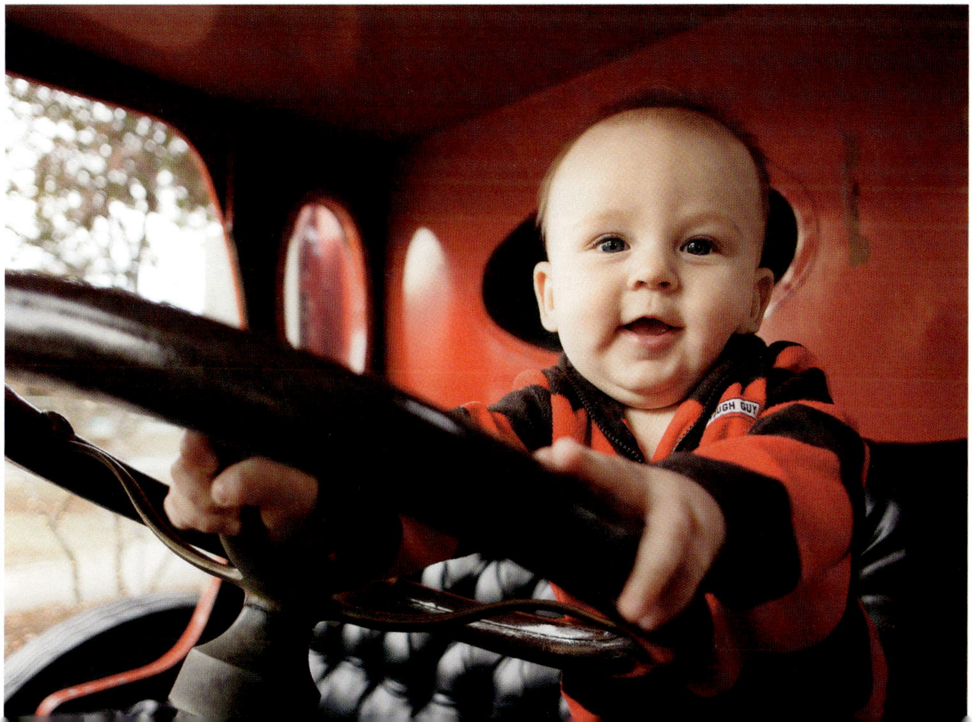

Figure 6.22

When you are taking photographs of children, try to shoot from their eye level for a less imposing view.

ISO 400 • 1/60 sec. • f/2 • 12mm lens

Don't be afraid to get close

When you are taking someone's picture, don't be afraid of getting close and filling the frame (**Figure 6.23**). This can eliminate distractions and help your viewer connect with your subject.

Try a long lens for candid shots

Putting a camera in someone's face can elicit unnatural results. People just feel a need to pose, or they get nervous and stiff. If you really want to capture some nice portraits with a more candid feel, try shooting with a long lens (**Figure 6.24**). The distance will remove you and your camera from the equation, and people will tend to react more normally. If you are looking to be a street photographer, a long lens will be one of your best tools.

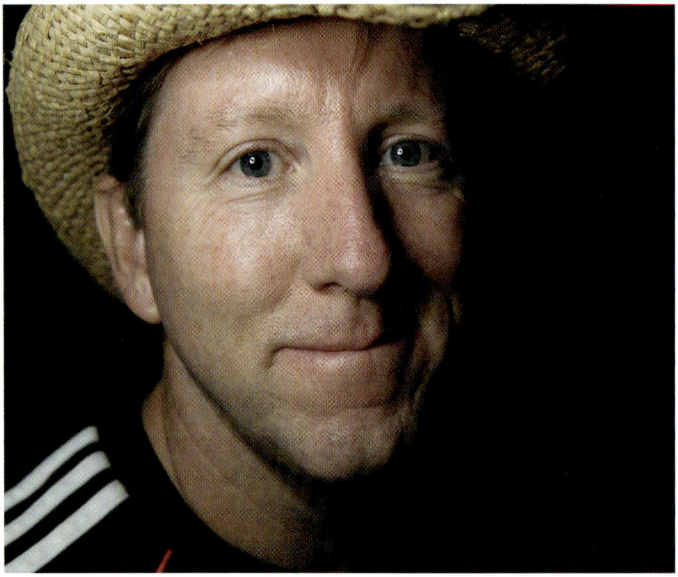

Figure 6.23
Filling the frame with the subject's face can lead to a much more intimate portrait.

ISO 400 • 1/2500 sec. • f/5.6 • 24–70mm lens

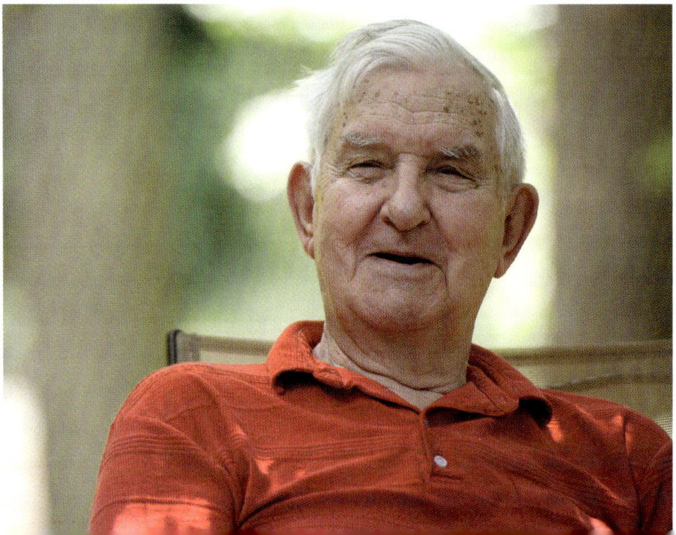

Figure 6.24
Using a long lens can help you get more candid portraits.

ISO 200 • 1/250 sec. • f/2.8 • 70–200mm lens

Chapter 6 Assignments

Depth of field in portraits

Let's start with something simple. Grab your favorite person and start experimenting with using different aperture settings. Shoot wide open (the widest your lens goes, such as f/2.8 or f/3.5) and then really stopped down (like f/22). Look at the difference in the depth of field and how it plays an important role in placing the attention on your subject. (Make sure you don't have your subject standing against the background. Give some distance so that there is a good blurring effect of the background at the wide f-stop setting.)

Discovering the qualities of natural light

Pick a nice sunny day and try shooting some portraits in the midday sun. If your subject is willing, have them turn so the sun is in their face. If they are still speaking to you after you've blinded them, have them turn their back to the sun. Try this with and without the fill flash so you can see the difference. Finally, move them into a completely shaded spot and take a few more.

Picking the right metering method

Find a very dark or very light background and place your subject in front of it. Now take a couple of shots, giving a lot of space around your subject for the background to show. Now switch metering modes and use the AE Lock feature to get a more accurate reading of your subject. Notice the differences in exposure between the metering methods.

Photo styles for portraits

Have some fun playing with the different photo styles. Try the Portrait style as compared to the Standard style. Then try out Monochrome and play with the different style options and filter effects to see how they affect skin tones.

Share your results with the book's Flickr group!
Join the group here: flickr.com/groups/panasonicGX7_fromsnapshotstogreatshots

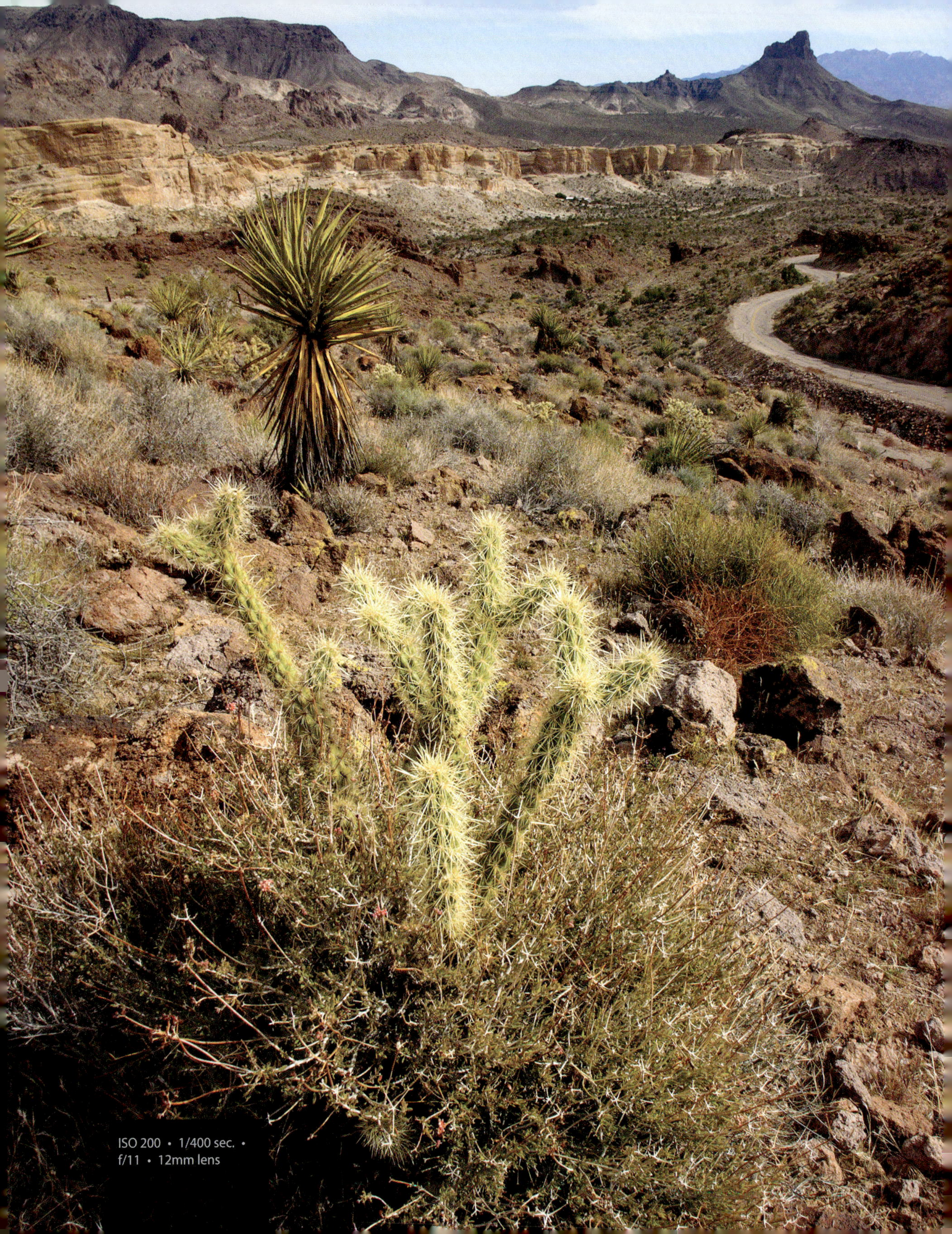

ISO 200 • 1/400 sec. •
f/11 • 12mm lens

7

Landscape Photography

Tips, Tools, and Techniques to Get the Most out of Your Landscape Photography

I think Landscape photography introduces a lot of people to making pictures. I was first inspired to pick up a camera because I wanted to capture the beautiful landscapes I would see on my travels. Landscapes are a great learning ground for photographers, particularly in the areas of light and composition. For those of us who enjoy spending time outdoors, there are few better ways to do so.

This chapter explores the functions of the GX7/GM1 that make landscape photography not only a possibility, but also an exciting and enjoyable venture. It also covers techniques that will improve your landscape photography.

Poring Over the Picture

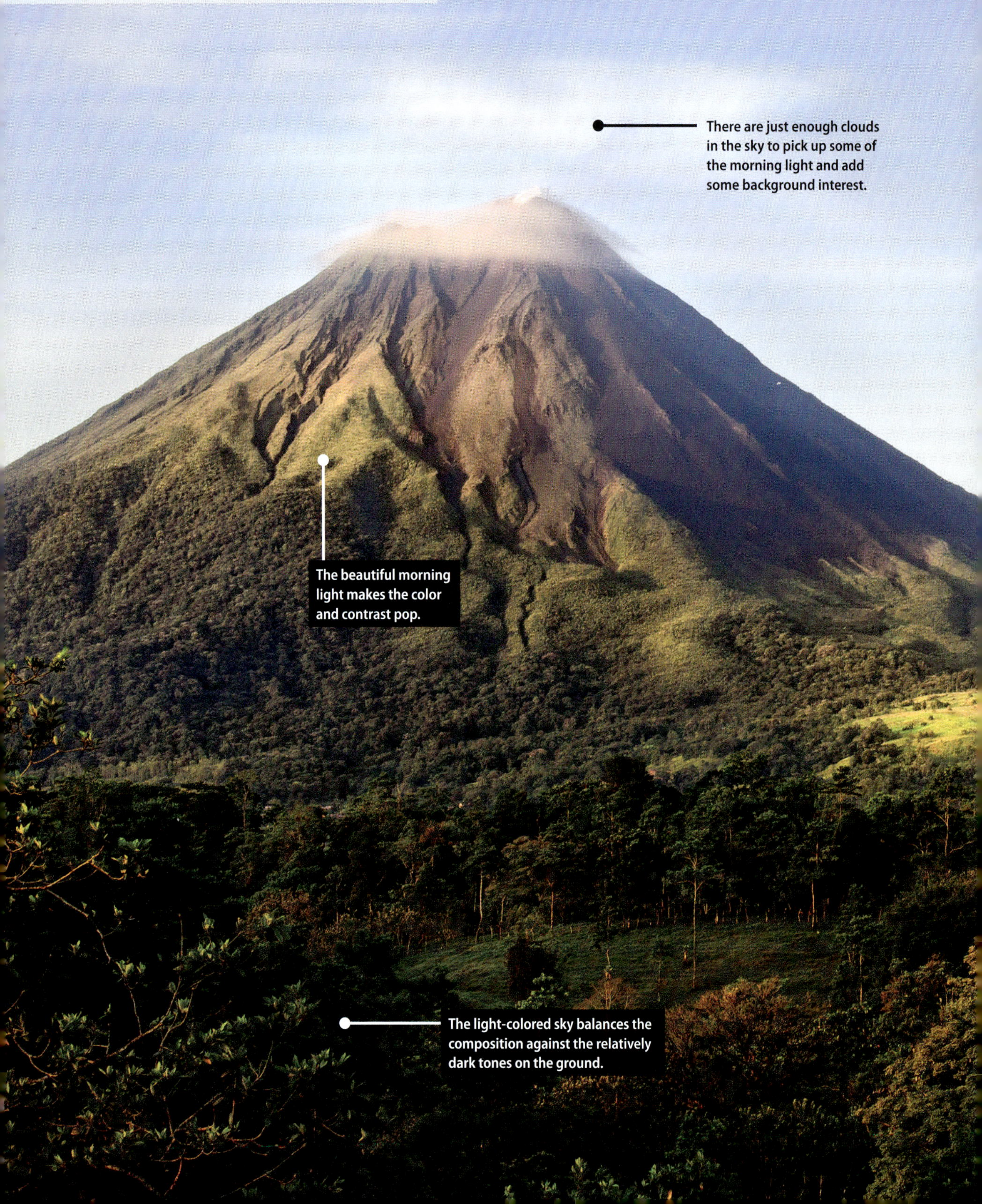

I always enjoy the chance to shoot Arenal Volcano in Costa Rica. The light on the volcano always seems to be just a bit different than the last time I saw it, and every part of the day offers a different range of color and contrast. I made this shot in the early morning, and there were just a few wispy clouds in the sky. The sun was already up, but the light still warm and golden.

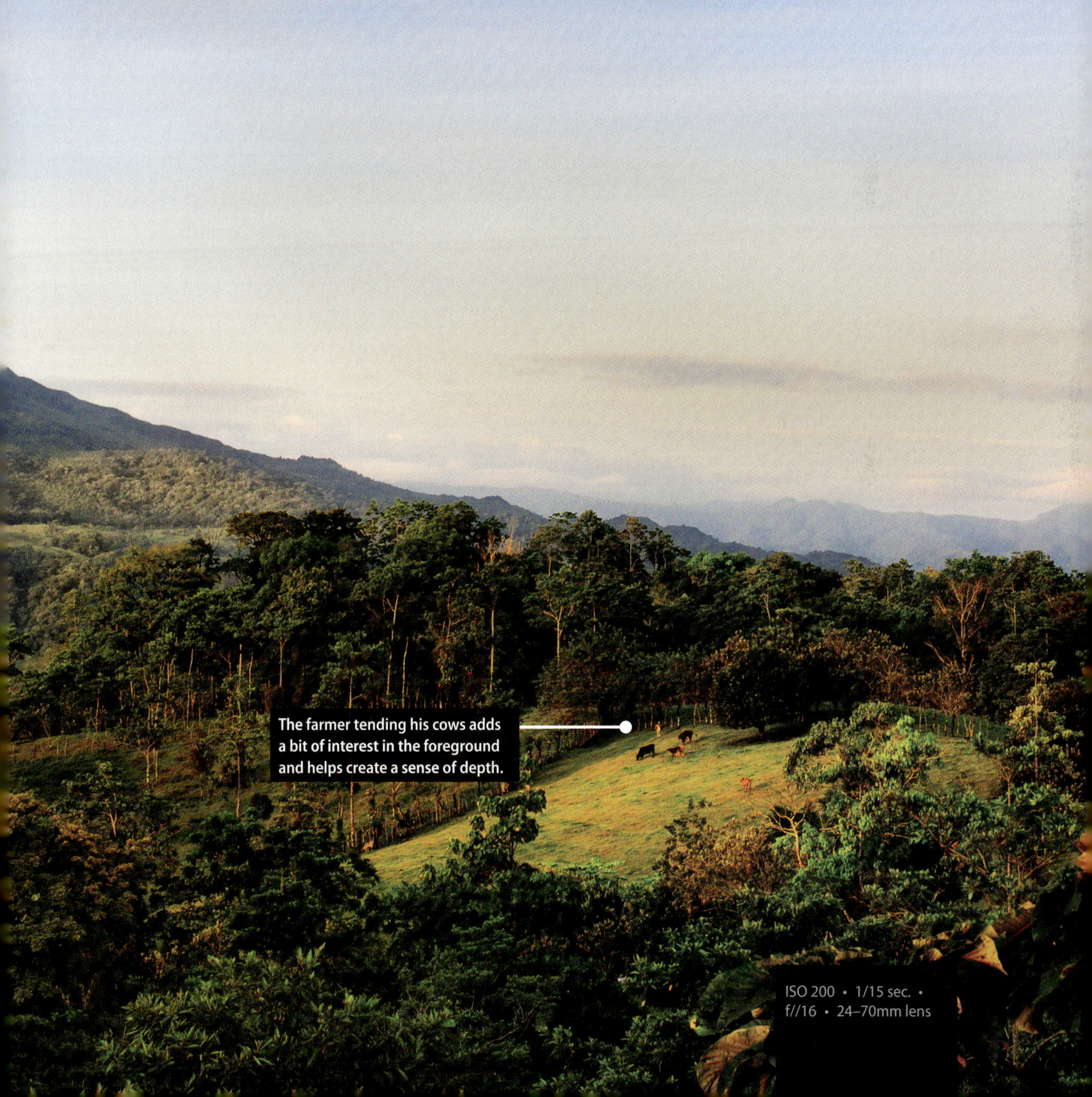

The farmer tending his cows adds a bit of interest in the foreground and helps create a sense of depth.

ISO 200 • 1/15 sec. • f//16 • 24–70mm lens

Sharp and In Focus: Using Tripods

I'll admit that tripods can be kind of a pain to deal with. Large tripods are more stable, but they are often cumbersome and heavy. The ultra-light travel models are tiny, but they are much less stable. Even so, I suggest you get used to the idea of carrying one. A good tripod is one of the best investments you can make for your photography, particularly if you are interested in landscapes.

The number one reason we use tripods is in order to use relatively slow shutter speeds. Landscape photography is often done at the beginning and end of the day and into the night. At these times, the light values, although extremely attractive, are very low. This forces you to shoot with a slower shutter speed. At the same time, landscape photographers often employ small apertures for greater depth of field, which also necessitates slower shutter speeds for proper exposures. A tripod is the best tool to have at hand in these situations (**Figure 7.1**).

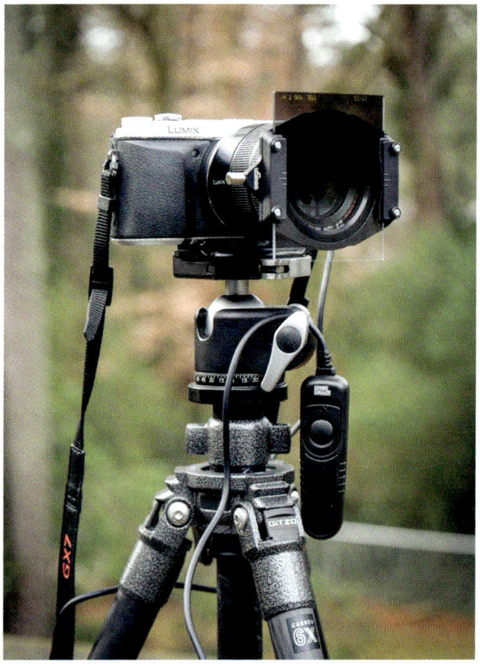

Figure 7.1 Here is my GX7 decked out for landscape photography. It's attached to a ball head atop a sturdy tripod. I've also got my remote shutter release and filter holder (For more on filters, see "Making Water Fluid," later in this chapter.)

ISO 800 • 1/50 sec. • f/4 • 45mm lens

Minimum sustaining shutter speed

The rule of thumb known as *minimum sustaining shutter speed* gives a photographer an idea of when to place the camera on a tripod. It suggests that when your shutter speed numerically lines up with your focal length, it might be a good time to place the camera on a tripod instead of risking the camera shake that results from hand-holding. For example, if you are zoomed to 42mm on the GX7's kit lens and are shooting at or close to 1/50 of a second, place the camera on a tripod to ensure sharp imagery. Of course, the more you shoot and the more comfortable you become with handling the camera, the slower you might be able to shoot at any given focal length.

Choosing a tripod

A tripod can potentially last you for years, so it behooves you to do some shopping before settling on one. One characteristic to consider is the tripod's overall sturdiness. The bigger the sticks, the sturdier they are. Bigger is usually heavier, but I find a larger tripod made of carbon fiber has a nice balance of sturdiness and weight. Wind and water, two elements one often encounters when shooting landscapes, can be hazardous to the lighter (and sometimes cheaper) tripods. Also, consider a tripod that can extend to and beyond your eye level. This will save you from bending over all the time to compose and view your images, and it will allow you to shoot from a higher level with maximum stability. Finally, consider a tripod with a ball head. Ball heads are quickly and easily adjusted into just the right position. Look for a ball head with a quick-release plate that attaches to the bottom of your GX7/GM1. A quick-release plate will let you easily remove the camera from the tripod if you need to quickly grab a handheld shot.

Tripod stability

Most tripods have a center column that allows the user to extend the height of the camera above the point where the tripod legs join together. This might seem like a great idea, but the reality is that the farther you raise that column, the less stable your tripod becomes. Think of a tall building that sways near the top. To get the most solid base for your camera, always try to use it with the center column at its lowest point so that your camera is right at the apex of the tripod legs.

OIS and tripods don't mix

If you are using Optical Image Stabilizer (OIS) lenses on your camera, remember to turn this feature off when you use a tripod (**Figure 7.2**). This is because the stabilization technology can, while trying to minimize camera movement, actually create movement when the camera is already stable. To turn off the OIS feature, use the switch on the lens.

Be sure to turn off the in-body OIS when shooting on a tripod with non-OIS lenses on the GX7. Press Menu/Set and navigate to the Stabilizer menu in the Rec menu. Set the Operation mode to Off.

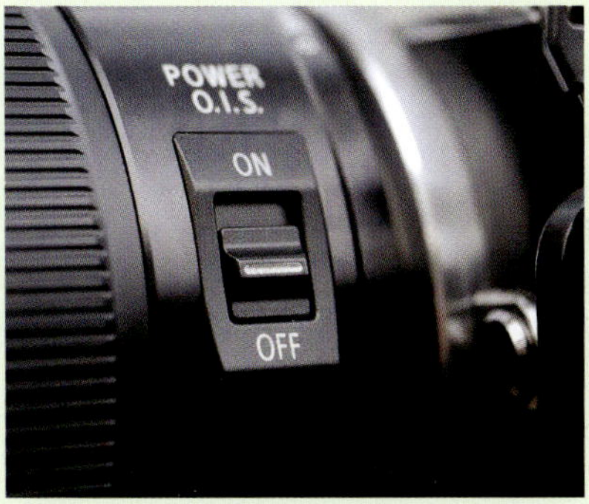

Figure 7.2 Turn off the OIS feature when using a tripod.

Selecting the Proper ISO and White Balance

One of the most important things you'll learn about landscape photography is to shoot with the lowest ISO possible. The lower the ISO, the better the quality of the image from a pixel point of view. And the higher the ISO, the more noise there will be in your image. Noise can detract from the dynamic range, color quality, and finer details of an image (**Figures 7.3** and **7.4**). In landscape photography, you'll want to preserve these details as

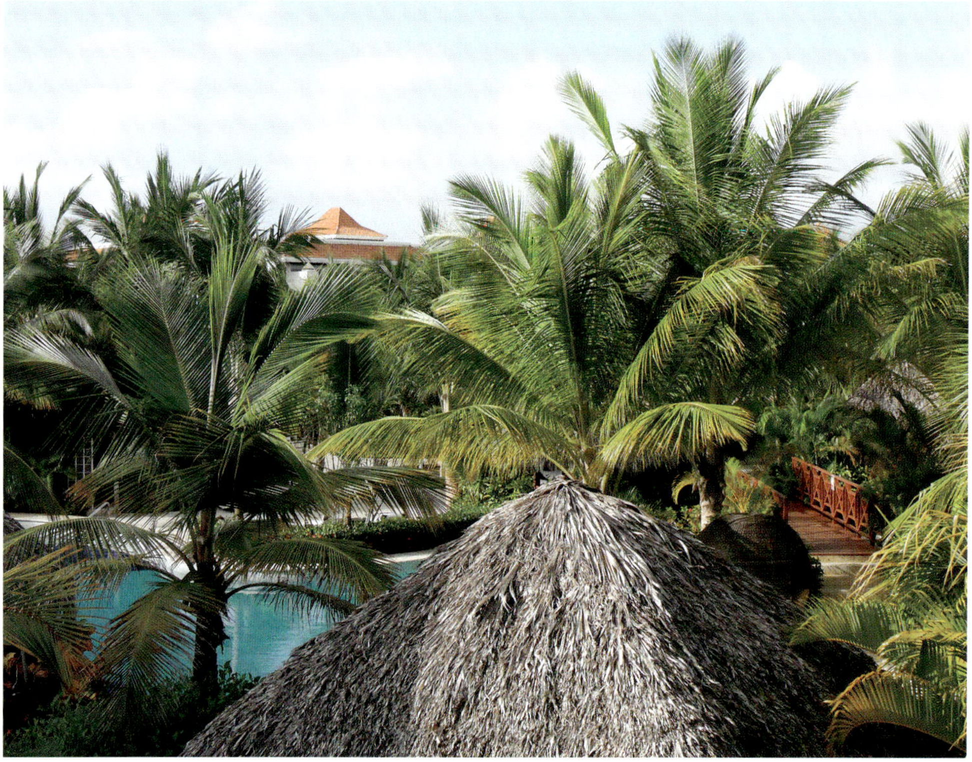

Figure 7.3
The GX7 handles noise fairly well at ISO 3200, but the image looks flat and washed out.

ISO 3200 • 1/4000 sec. • f/8 • 14–140mm lens

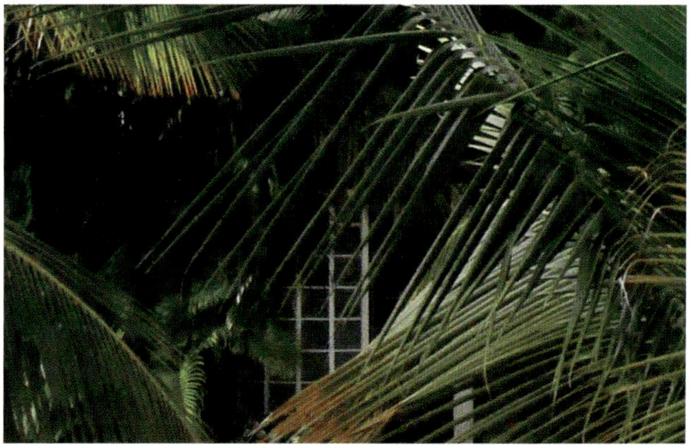

Figure 7.4
Even in the shadows there is not much noise, but the dynamic range is compressed.

much as possible. Shooting with lower ISOs forces you to shoot at slower shutter speeds, particularly when you stop your aperture down for maximum depth of field, but the better dynamic range and finer quality of the images is the payoff (**Figures 7.5** and **7.6**).

Even with continual improvements to in-camera noise reduction, using the lowest ISO possible for landscape photography is ideal. With a good tripod in tow, you'll find little need to shoot above an ISO of 200 or 400. The majority of my landscape work is shot at no more than ISO 200.

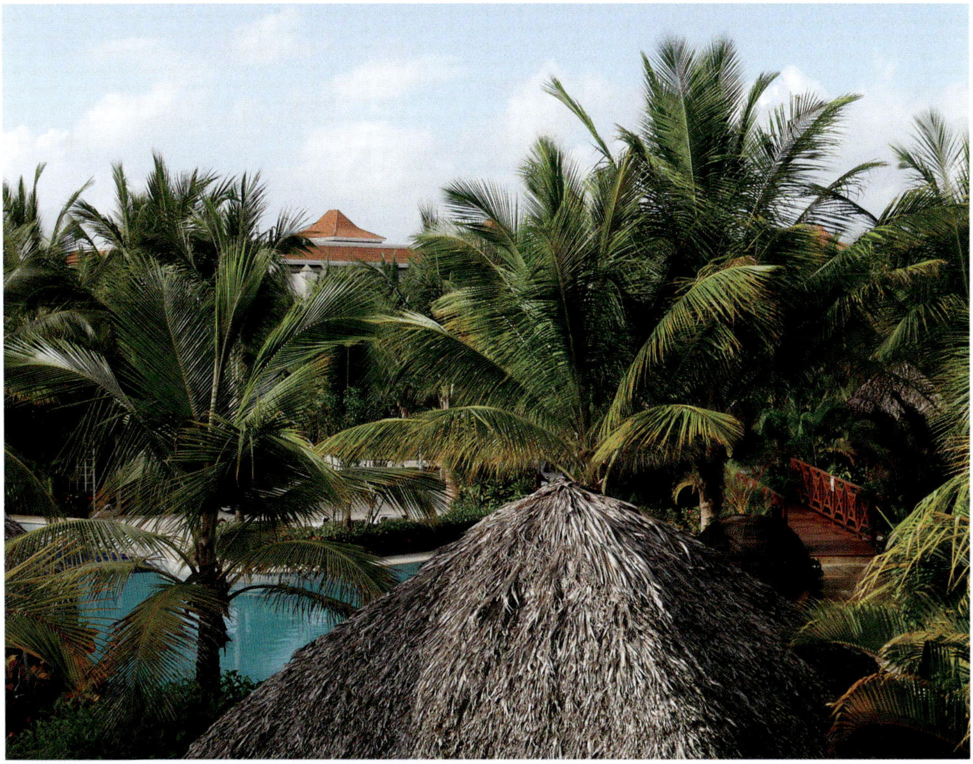

Figure 7.5
The dynamic range is much better after lowering the ISO to 200.

ISO 200 • 1/200 sec. • f/8 • 14–140mm lens

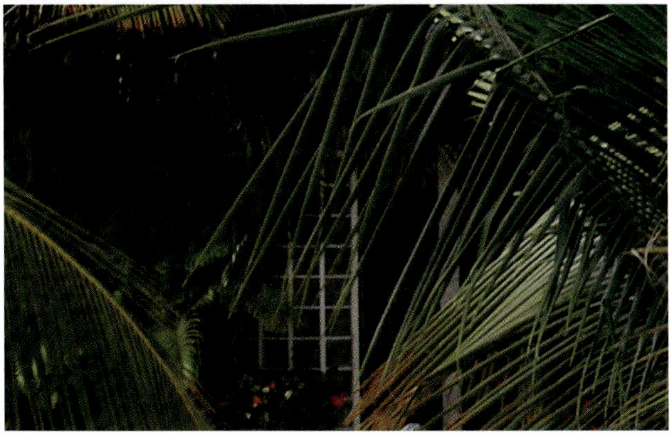

Figure 7.6
Zooming in shows that the noise levels for this image are almost nonexistent.

Selecting a white balance

White balance can be used in two distinct ways: to obtain as close to correct color as possible, or in a more interpretive manner. The GX7/GM1's preset white balances can be used in corresponding light conditions without any problem. If it's sunny outside, Daylight WB will work well, as will Cloudy WB if it is overcast. At the same time, there are no real rules about the use of white balance, and it's worth experimenting with how different iterations affect an image's personality.

I made this shot a few minutes after the sun had dipped below the trees after a fairly boring sunset (**Figure 7.7**). I liked the composition, but the "correct" white balance didn't have the cool tones I was seeing across the lake. I switched the WB to the Kelvin setting and I was able to dial in exactly the color I was looking for (**Figure 7.8**). The final image has more blue than I actually saw, but I made a creative decision in order to make a more interesting photo.

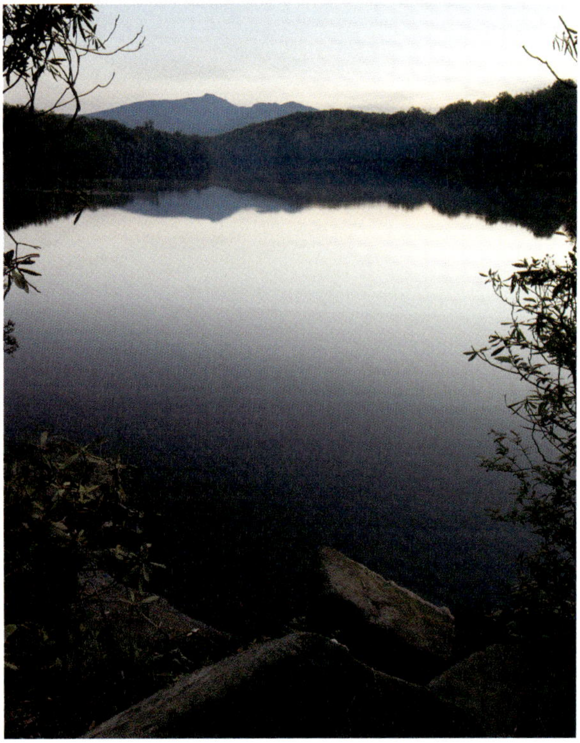

Figure 7.7 **The "correct" white balance looks OK, but there is not enough color in the sunset to be particularly interesting.**

ISO 200 • 3 sec. • f/16 • 16–35mm lens

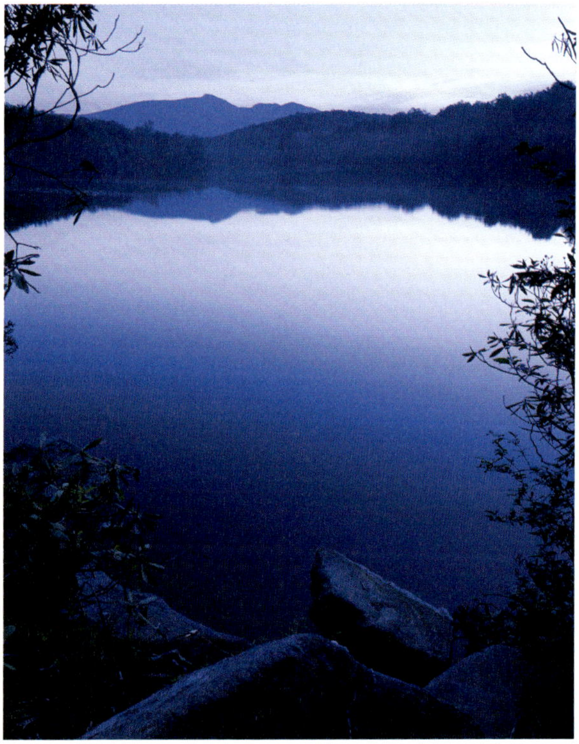

Figure 7.8 **I changed the white balance to dial in more blue and give a different feel to the final image.**

ISO 200 • 3 sec. • f/16 • 16–35mm lens

Thanks to the live view on the EVF (GX7 only) and LCD, there is no need to make test shots to get the perfect white balance with your camera. As you scroll through the white balance settings, they are displayed for you on the LCD or the EVF. If you want to be even more precise, you can choose a custom setting that will let you dial in exactly the right look for your image.

Using the LCD or EVF to preview white balance settings

1. Press the WB button (▶).
2. Use the ◀ and ▶ buttons or the Rear dial (GM1: Command dial) to cycle through the white balance settings.
3. The image on the LCD or in the EVF will change to reflect the chosen white balance.
4. Select the white balance setting that looks most appropriate for your scene, then press the Menu/Set button or press the shutter button halfway to return to shooting mode.

Using Noise Reduction

The temptation to use higher ISOs should be avoided when possible, as the end result will be more image noise and less detail. I also like to turn the noise reduction all the way down, even at low ISOs. I would rather have all the detail I can get, even if that means I might see a little grain in the shadows.

Turning down the noise reduction

1. Press the Menu/Set button, then select the Rec menu.
2. Select Photo Style and press Menu/Set.
3. Choose a photo style, then scroll down to the NR setting (**A**).
4. Turn the NR all the way down to –5.

A

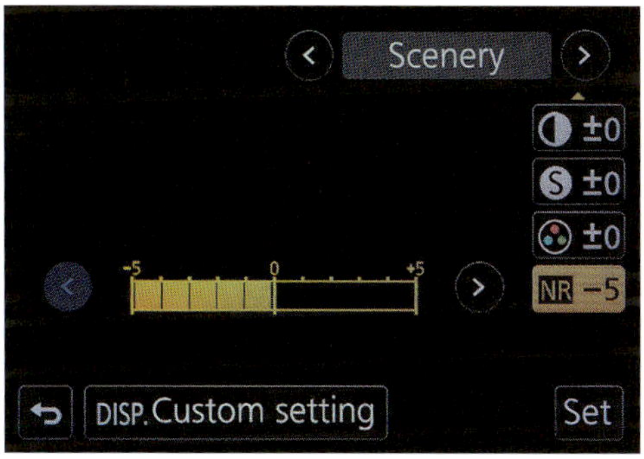

Setting up Long Shutter noise reduction

When shooting at shutter speeds over 1 second, even low ISOs can accumulate noise because of the extended length of time the sensor is activated. This type of noise, sometimes referred to as dark noise, is the result of the camera's sensor heating up during exposure. The GX7/GM1 can compensate for such noise using its Long Shutter noise reduction.

1. Press the Menu/Set button, then select the Rec menu.
2. Navigate to Long Shtr NR and turn it On (**B**).

   The default setting is On. If you know you are going to be making extremely long exposures, ensure that it is set before shooting.

B

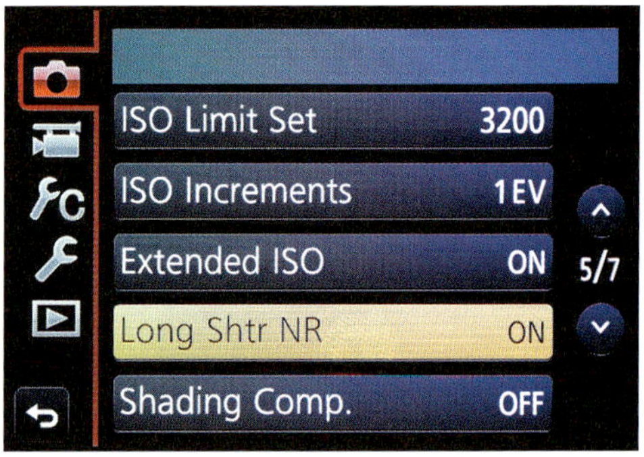

Photo Styles for Landscapes

When photographers shoot landscapes on film, they use the types of film that accentuate those elements—such as color and structure—that are indicative of nature. Films that provide a bit of saturation and contrast help bring out the colors that are enhanced by beautiful early-morning and late-evening light. Fortunately, we're able to achieve this type of effect with the Scenery photo style (**Figures 7.9** and **7.10**).

This photo style increases the contrast of the image, and it provides a saturation increase to the colors relevant to landscape photography, such as greens and blues. I like to lower the Contrast setting to –2 in the Scenery photo style, as well as setting the NR to –5. Using the Scenery photo style not only gives you that added boost for your images, but also saves you time in postproduction because you don't have to make some of those enhancements on the computer.

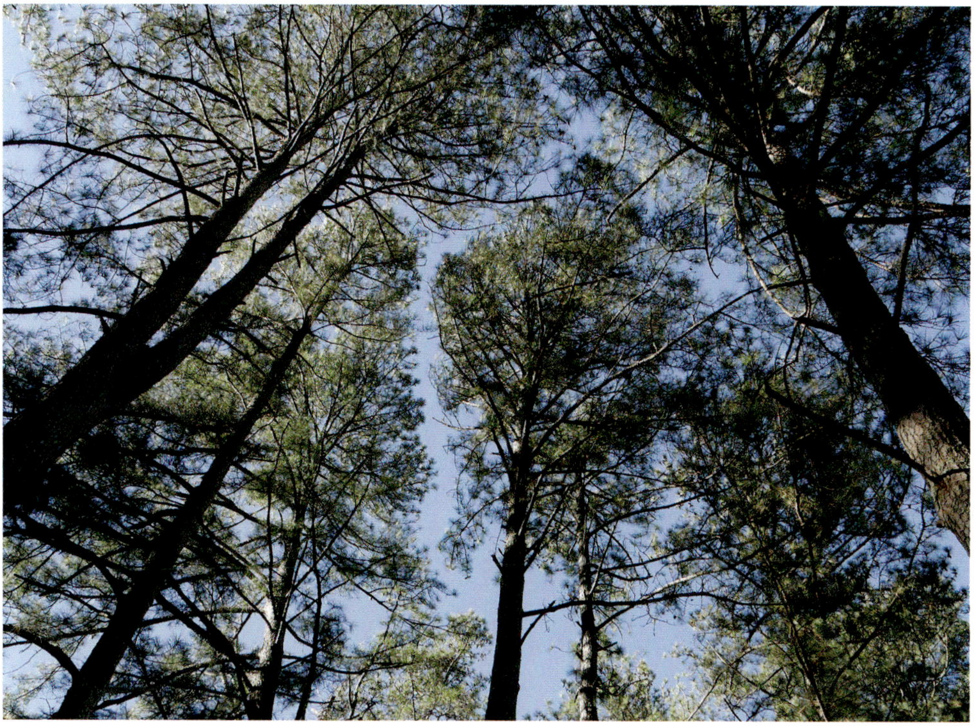

Figure 7.9

Using the Standard photo style, the colors are OK but don't really pop.

ISO 100 • 1/100 sec. • f/9 • 16mm lens

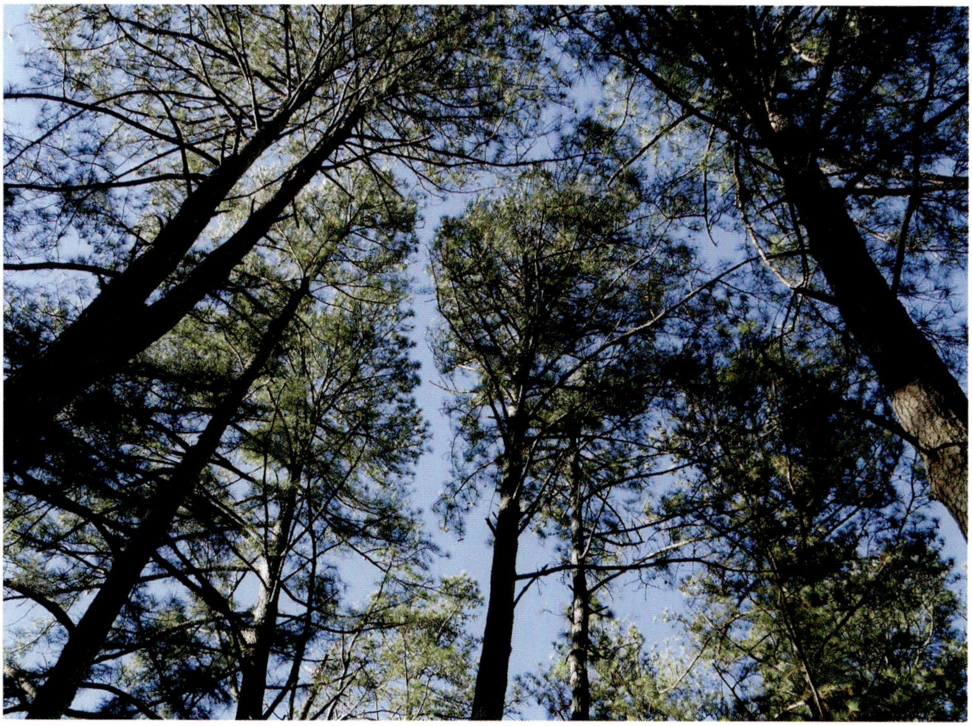

Figure 7.10

The Scenery photo style adds contrast and more vivid color to skies and vegetation.

ISO 100 • 1/100 sec. • f/9 • 16mm lens

Setting up the Scenery photo style

1. Press the Menu/Set button, then select the Rec menu.
2. Select Photo Style and press Menu/Set.
3. Use the ◀ and ▶ buttons to select the Scenery photo style.
4. Use the ▲ and ▼ buttons to move from one adjustment to the other, and use the ◀ and ▶ buttons to move the sliders (**A**). You can also touch the adjustment you want to make on the LCD and drag the sliders with your finger.

A

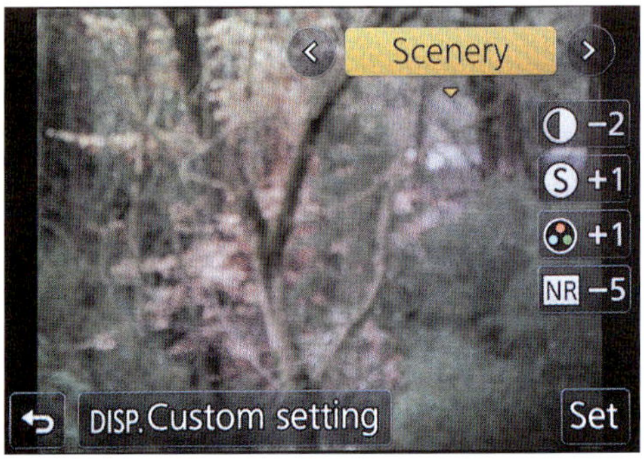

Don't stop with the Scenery photo style. Try using the Vivid and Natural photo styles for shooting landscapes as well. Each one has its own look. Use the Contrast and Saturation adjustments to dial in each style just the way you like it.

Photo styles and RAW

If you are shooting RAW, your images will look like they have the photo style applied when you view them on the back of the camera, but the style will go away once you open the images in postprocessing software. Only JPEGs have the photo style applied as part of the final in-camera image processing.

Fine-Tuning Exposure with the Highlight/Shadow Curve

Many landscape photographs are made in conditions that pit high-contrast highlights and darker tones against each other. Often, skies are intensely brighter than shadow areas in the foreground. Other times, specific areas below the horizon might receive light while others lie in the shadows. For the most part, it is to your advantage to keep from overexposing any of these parts of the frame, especially clouds and running water. If this happens, all detail is lost in those "hot" areas and cannot be resurrected. The same goes for dark areas. Shadows that are underexposed too much, or "clipped," cannot be recovered (**Figure 7.11**).

The GX7/GM1 can tell you when you are overexposing your highlights or underexposing your shadows. Using the Highlight Warning feature, or "blinkies," the LCD display will indicate which areas of the image are overexposed by blinking at you during image playback. You can also watch the histogram to see if you are clipping the shadows or highlights (see the "How I Shoot" section of Chapter 4). If you find there is no detail in those areas, you must decide whether those areas are important enough to the image to try to maintain. First, try adjusting the exposure compensation to bring back the details, and then use the GX7's Highlight/Shadow curve to refine the look of the image.

The GX7's Highlight/Shadow curve function allows you to adjust the highlights and shadows in your image independently. You can see the effects of your adjustments on the EVF and LCD as you make them. This allows you to compensate for the contrast range of a scene and truly fine-tune the look of your images (**Figure 7.12**).

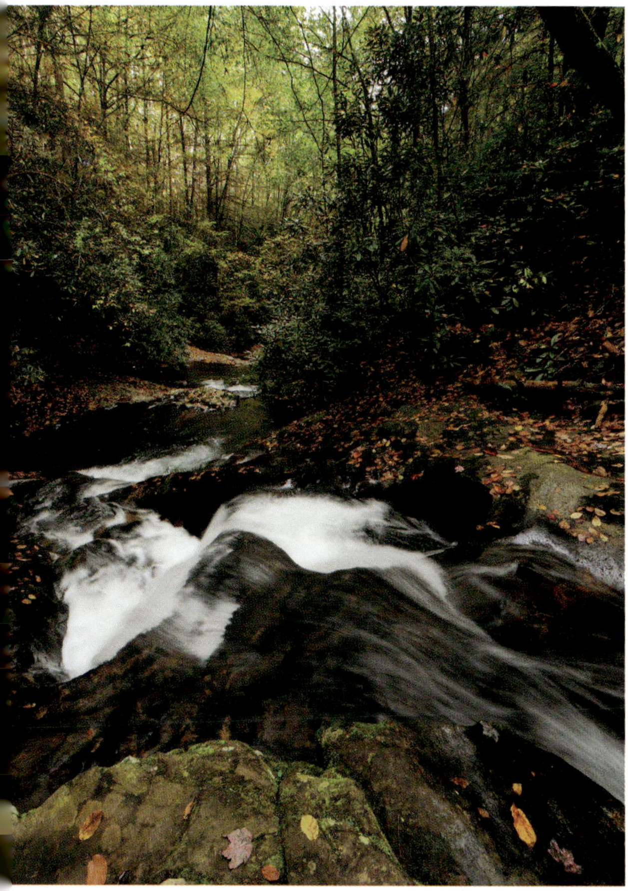

Figure 7.11 **The camera has done a good job of averaging the exposure, but the highlights are hot and the shadows are clipping.**

ISO 200 • 1/5 sec. • f/13 • 7–14mm lens

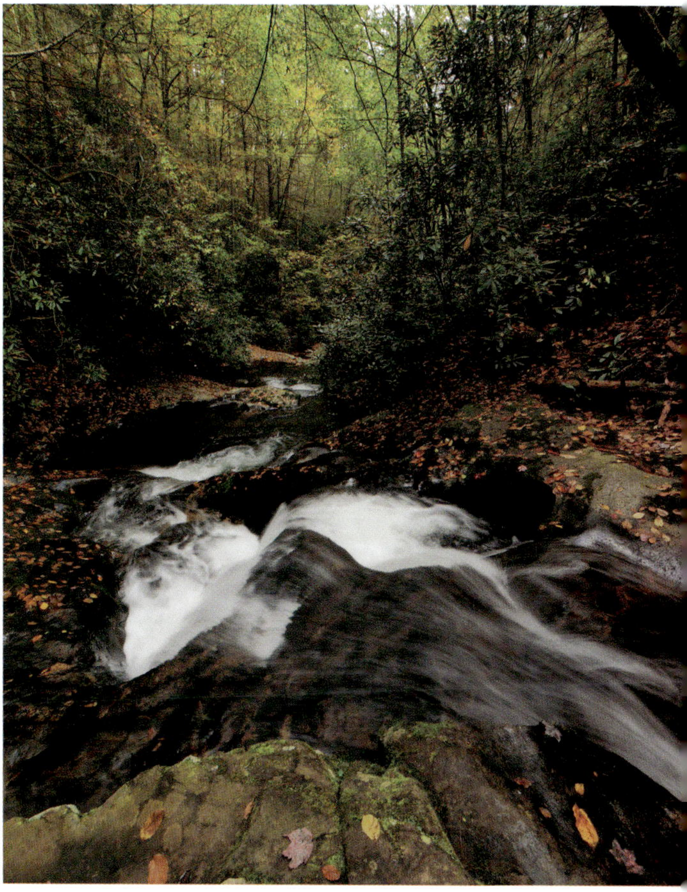

Figure 7.12 **I used the Highlight/Shadow curve to bring the highlights down two points, bring the shadows up two points, and control the contrast range in the image.**

ISO 200 • 1/5 sec. • f/13 • 7–14mm lens

i.Dynamic

The GX7 and GM1 have a tool for tackling high-contrast scenes: i.Dynamic, or Intelligent Dynamic Range (**Figures 7.13** and **7.14**). To activate this feature, press Menu/Set > Rec > i.Dynamic. The settings Low, Standard, and High control how much the shadows and highlights are adjusted. The Auto setting sets the effect based on the shooting conditions.

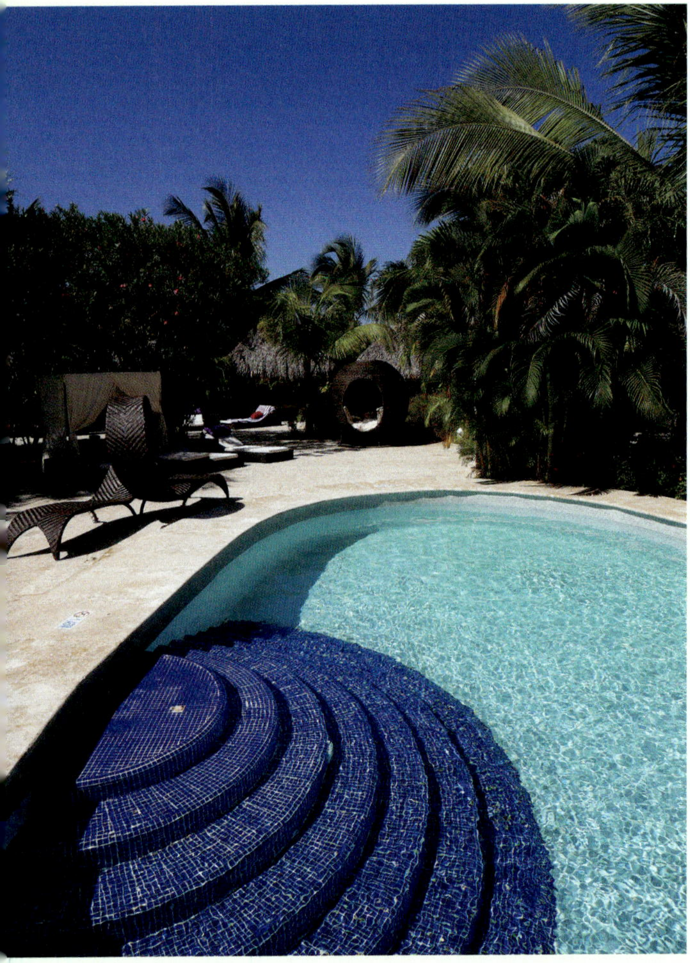

Figure 7.13 With i.Dynamic off, this high-contrast scene has bright highlights and deep shadows.

ISO 200 • 1/800 sec. • f/8 • 12–32mm lens

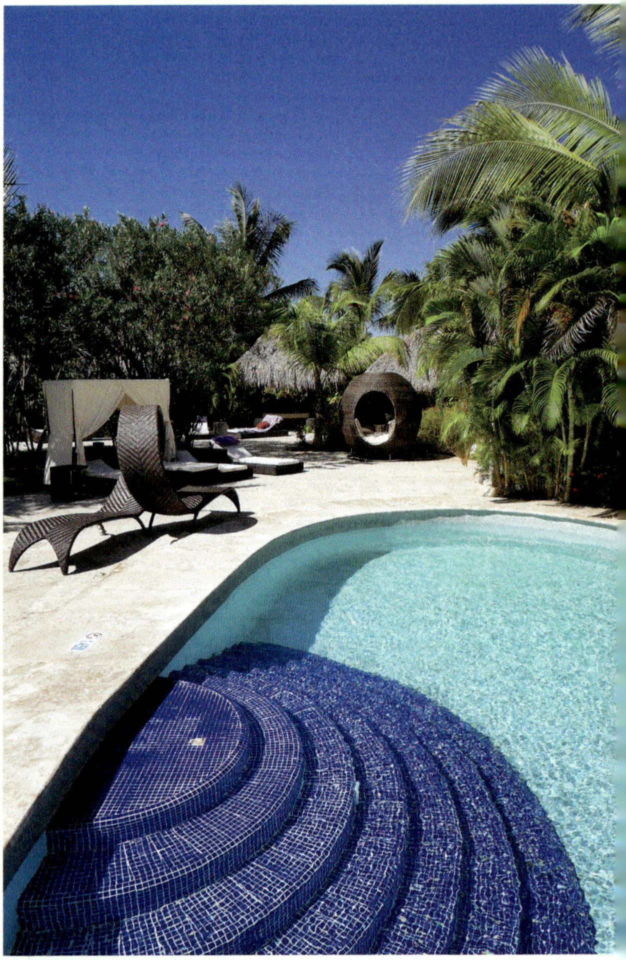

Figure 7.14 The i.Dynamic control adjusts the shadows and highlights to capture the full dynamic range of the scene.

ISO 200 • 1/800 sec. • f/8 • 12–32mm lens

Using the Highlight/Shadow curve

1. Press Menu/Set, then select the Rec menu.
2. Navigate to Highlight Shadow and press Menu/Set.
3. Rotate the Front dial to adjust the highlights and the Rear dial to adjust the shadows. You will see the effects of your adjustments on the LCD.
4. Use the ◀ and ▶ buttons to scroll through the Highlight/Shadow presets. Press the ▲ button to save your own preset in one of three custom slots: C1, C2, and C3.
5. Touch Set on the screen, or press the Menu/Set button, to save your changes.

Easier Focusing with the Touchscreen

One benefit the GX7 and GM1 have over traditional DSLRs is their lack of conventional focus points. Instead of selecting from a grid of set AF points in the viewfinder, we can simply touch the LCD screen to choose any focus point (**Figure 7.15**). For landscape photography this means you can set up your camera on your tripod, compose the shot you want, and then touch the screen wherever you want to focus. You don't have to deal with the focus-and-recompose or manual focus techniques you might need when using other cameras.

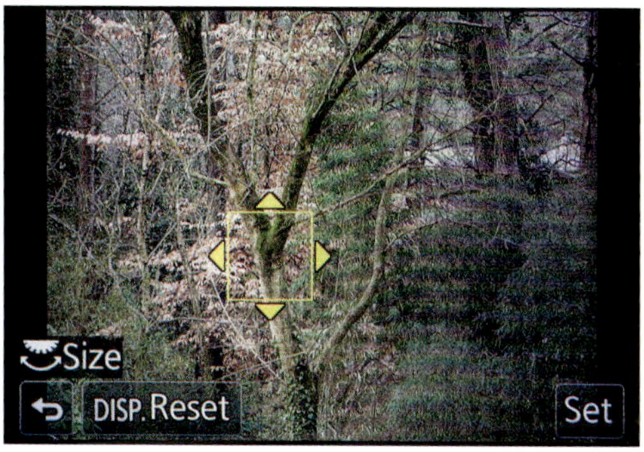

Figure 7.15 The touchscreen on the GX7/GM1 makes focusing simple. You can touch the screen anywhere you want to focus, and change the size of the focus point with the turn of a dial.

Getting focused while using a tripod

1. Make sure your camera is in the 1-Area focus mode by pressing the AF Mode button (◀) and choosing 1-Area.
2. Set up your shot and decide where you want to focus. The tilting LCD and EVF on the GX7 make it easy to compose images from different angles (**A**).
3. Touch the LCD where you want the camera to focus.

A

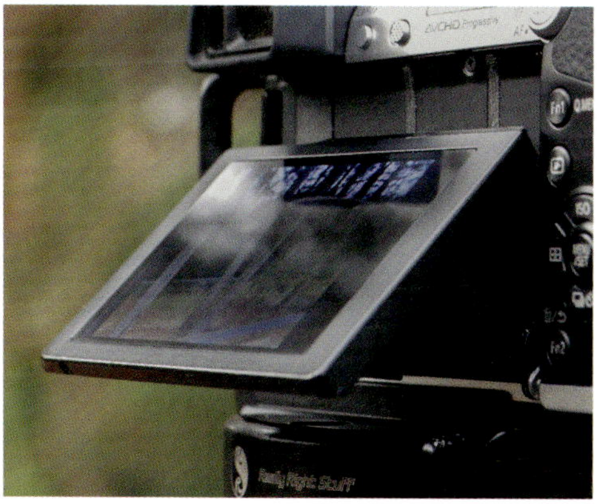

4. You can change the size of the focus point by turning the Rear dial (GM1: Command dial) while the yellow focusing square is highlighted.
5. Press the shutter button to focus and shoot.

Using Manual Focus Assist

If you choose to manually focus, the GX7/GM1 has a built-in feature that helps you achieve exact focus. Whether you have your eye to the electronic viewfinder (GX7 only) or are using the LCD display to compose your scene, the MF Assist (Manual Focus Assist) function will digitally "zoom in" to the area on which you are placing focus so you can have greater control over where the plane of critical focus actually lands. While you are zoomed in, you can still see the handy focus-peaking highlight.

To turn on the MF Assist function, press Menu/Set and then navigate to MF Assist in the Custom menu. The GX7/GM1 has four ways to operate the MF Assist. You can activate the zoom effect by rotating the focus ring on the lens, by pressing the AF Mode button (◀), or by using a combination of the two. Only pressing the AF Mode button (◀) operates the MF Assist on the GM1 if you're using the 12–32mm kit lens. You can touch anywhere on the LCD to set the MF Assist point. Be sure to turn your camera's focus mode lever to MF to manually focus.

Where to focus

As with any type of photography, you can use various depths of field to shoot landscapes. But if you are interested in those big, encompassing shots (as most landscape shooters are), you more than likely want everything in your shot to be in focus. Ideally you want the foreground, middle ground, and background all tack sharp. But where do you focus in order to achieve this?

First you need to make sure you are set up to shoot the large landscape. To gain maximum depth of field and focus, it is typical to use your smallest aperture that affords you a sharp image. Most Micro Four Thirds lenses are sharpest from f/8 to f/11. Stopping down the lens to more than f/16 introduces diffraction effects and actually reduces sharpness. Since a smaller aperture forces you to shoot with a slower shutter speed, you'll need to be set up on a sturdy tripod. The tripod allows you to concentrate on the other part of the formula: where to focus to achieve maximum depth of field. Traditionally you would use the "hyper focal distance" of your lens, but most M4/3 lenses do not have a distance scale.

Hyper focal distance, also referred to as HFD, is the point of focus that will give you the greatest acceptable sharpness from a point near your camera all the way out to infinity. Since the HFD isn't marked on our lenses, it is good practice to focus on an object that is about one-third of the distance into your frame (**Figure 7.16**). You can either manually focus or use 1-Area AF and simply touch where you want to focus on the LCD.

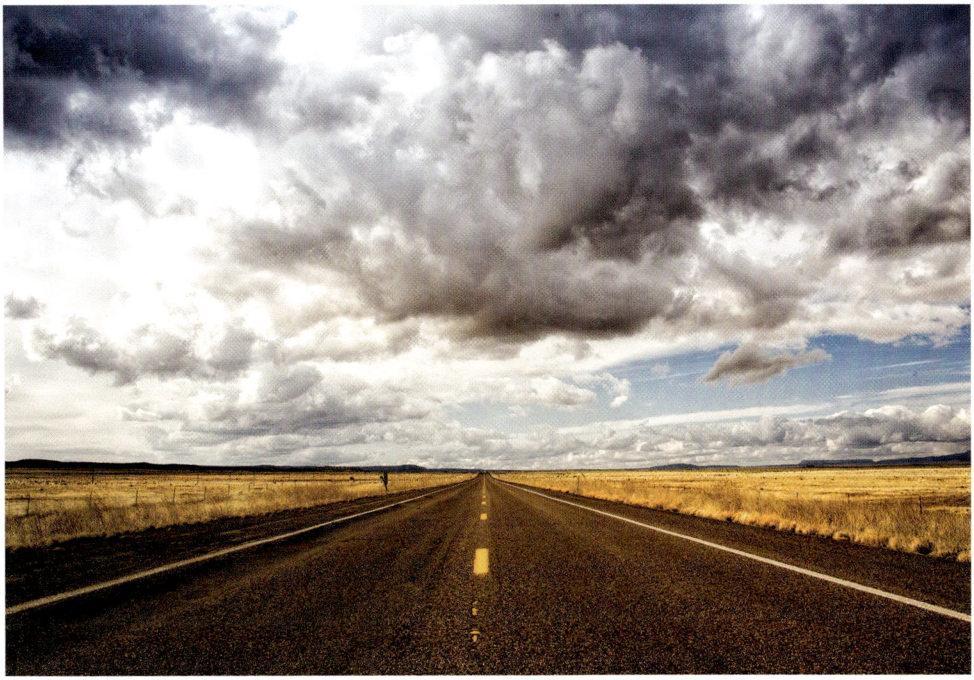

Figure 7.16
To get maximum focus from near to far, the focus was set one-third of the way into this image along Route 66. Lucky for me there was a small sign on the left side of the road right where I wanted to focus!

ISO 400 • 1/800 sec. • f/11 • 28–300mm lens

Tack sharp

Here's one of those terms that photographers like to throw around. Tack sharp refers to the overall sharpness of the image. This term is often used to describe a nice lens, as in "The Lumix 12–35mm f/2.8 lens is tack sharp." It also has a lot to do with the photographer. A tack sharp image has no sign of camera shake, which can give soft edges to subjects that should look nice and crisp. To get your images tack sharp, stop down your aperture, don't forget your tripod, and use a cable release or the self-timer to activate the shutter.

Both the GX7 and GM1 allow you to see your depth of field in real time as you adjust your aperture by using Preview mode. This is a handy feature when you want to preview the amount of depth of field you will achieve. By default, Preview mode is assigned to Fn5 on the GX7 and to Fn2 on the GM1.

Additionally, depth of field is inherently different for different types of lenses. Practically speaking, wider-angle lenses achieve greater depth of field compared to longer lenses. This, among other reasons, is why a wide-angle lens tends to be the go-to lens in the landscape photographer's kit.

Shooting Beautiful Black-and-White Landscapes

There is nothing as timeless as a beautiful black-and-white landscape photo (**Figure 7.17**). For many, it is the purest form of photography. The genre conjures up thoughts of Ansel Adams out in Yosemite Valley, capturing stunning monoliths with his 8x10 view camera. You can create your own stunning black-and-white photos using the power of the Monochrome photo style. (See the "Classic Black-and-White Portraits" section of Chapter 6 for instructions on setting up this feature.)

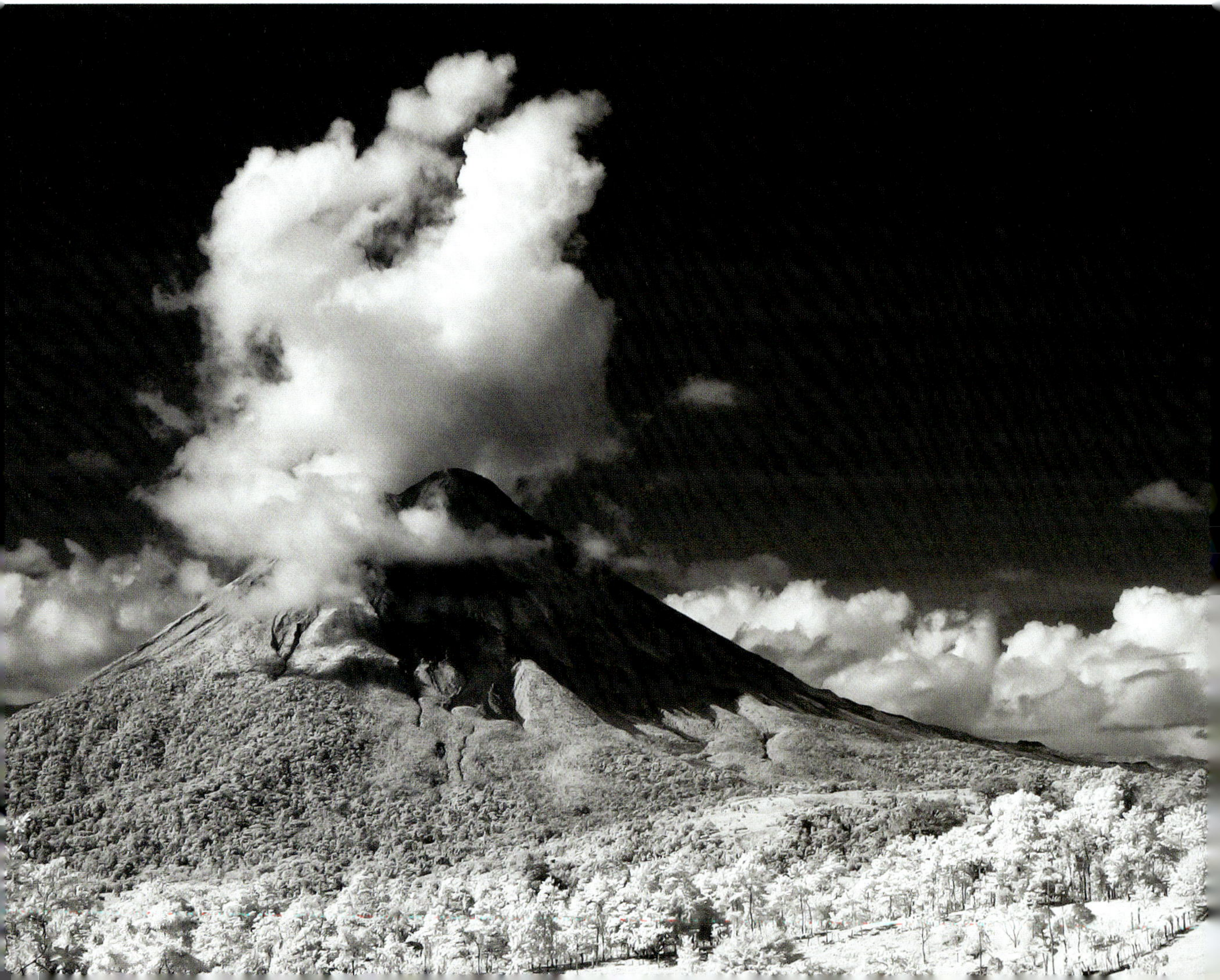

Figure 7.17
A black-and-white landscape photo removes the distraction of color and becomes more about light, contrast, and composition.
ISO 200 • 1/100 sec. • f/8 • 35–100mm lens

Options in the Monochrome photo style enable you to adjust contrast, sharpness, saturation (warm- or cool-toned), noise reduction, and filter effect. I like to have Contrast set to +2, Sharpness set to +1, and NR set to –5 for my landscape images. I often shoot landscapes with the Red filter effect to darken blue skies. This gives an overall look to the image that is reminiscent of the classic black-and-white films. Experiment with the various settings and filter effects to find the combination that is most pleasing to you.

The Golden Light

The best times to shoot landscapes are early in the morning and late in the evening. The light from sunrise to about an hour afterward, as well as from an hour before sunset until the sun dips below the horizon, is the most used light in landscape photography. At these times, the sun is at an extreme angle to the earth, casting long, texture-creating shadows, and because of all the atmospheric debris it must pass through at these angles, the light is warm and it enhances existing color. At no other time of day does the light act in such a way. It is compelling, dramatic, and, well, painterly (**Figures 7.18** and **7.19**).

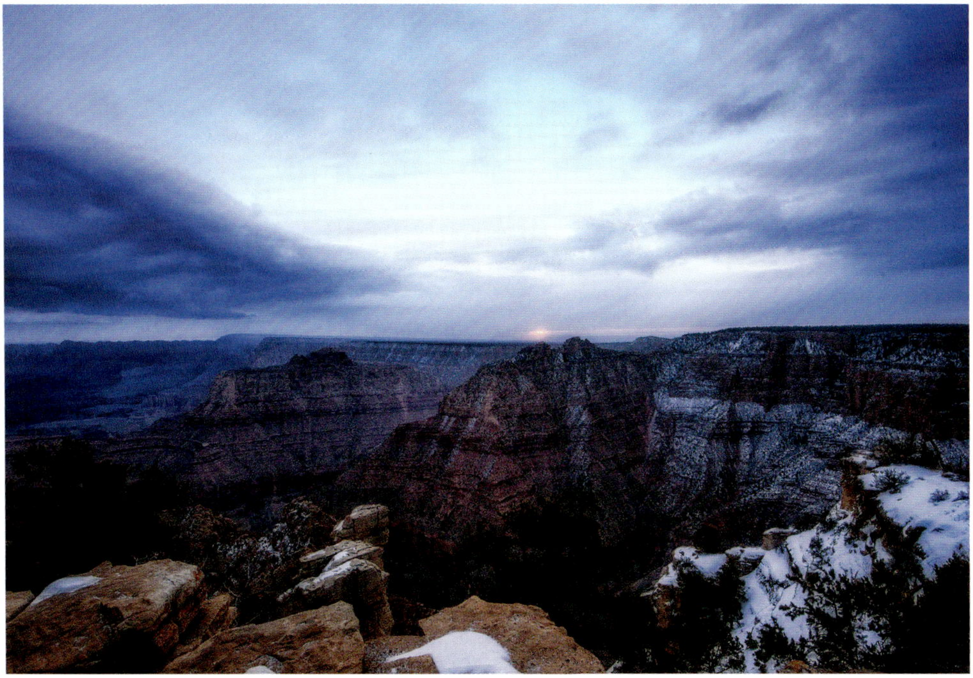

Figure 7.18
Even the Grand Canyon benefits from cool, soft light at dawn. I was lucky to catch this sunrise beneath the snow clouds on a cold February morning.

ISO 400 • 1/5 sec. • f/11 • 16–35mm lens

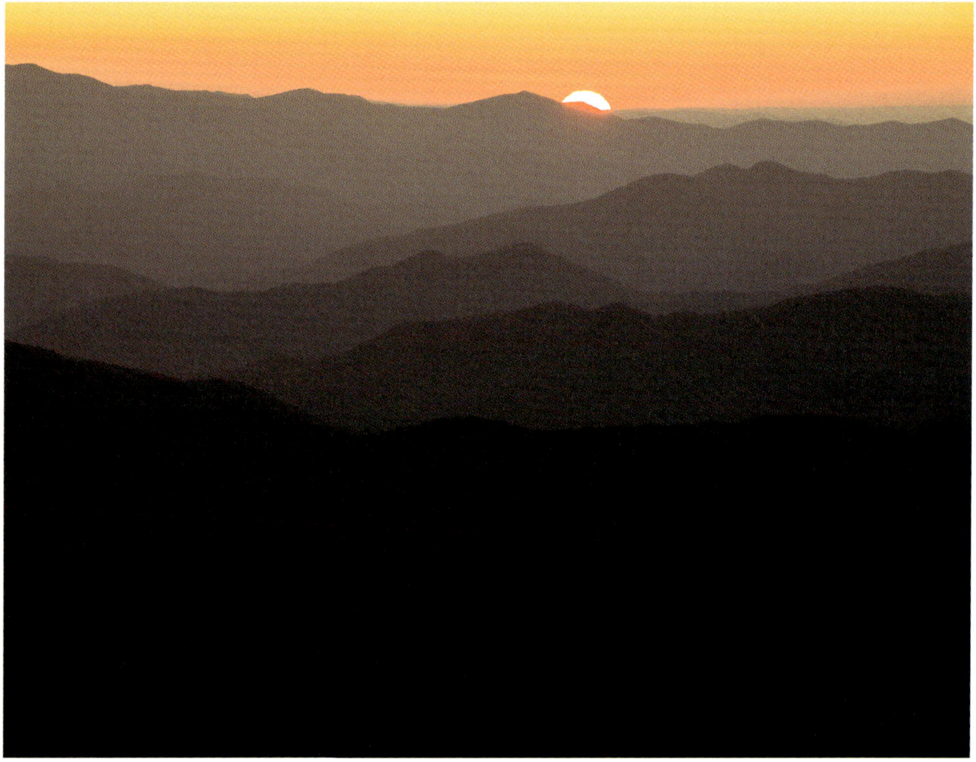

Figure 7.19
The late evening sun adds drama and warmth to this Smokey Mountain sunset.

ISO 200 • 1/50 sec. • f/8 • 35–100mm lens

Interesting clouds in the sky also enhance landscapes at these times of day. Clear skies are OK when shooting with golden light, but clouds add structure to skies that sometimes have no appeal.

Warm and cool color temperatures

These two terms are used to describe the overall color cast of an image. Reds and yellows are said to be warm, which is usually the look that you get from the late afternoon sun. Blue is usually the predominant color when talking about a cool cast.

Shooting Compelling Sunrises and Sunsets

Whether you're shooting a golden sunset on top of a flat horizon or the reflections of the sky in a large body of water before the sun comes up over the horizon, there are a few things to keep in mind to make your sunrise and sunset photography even more exciting.

First, consider putting something in front of the sky, silhouetting it against the color. A tree, an iconic rock formation, or a tall cactus might serve the image well, bringing to the viewer one more area of visual interest (**Figure 7.20**). Be careful not to crowd the scene with too many silhouettes. The idea here is simplicity in the foreground and an explosion of color in the background. With this in mind, it is also useful to keep the horizon line low in the frame to avoid including a large area of black space.

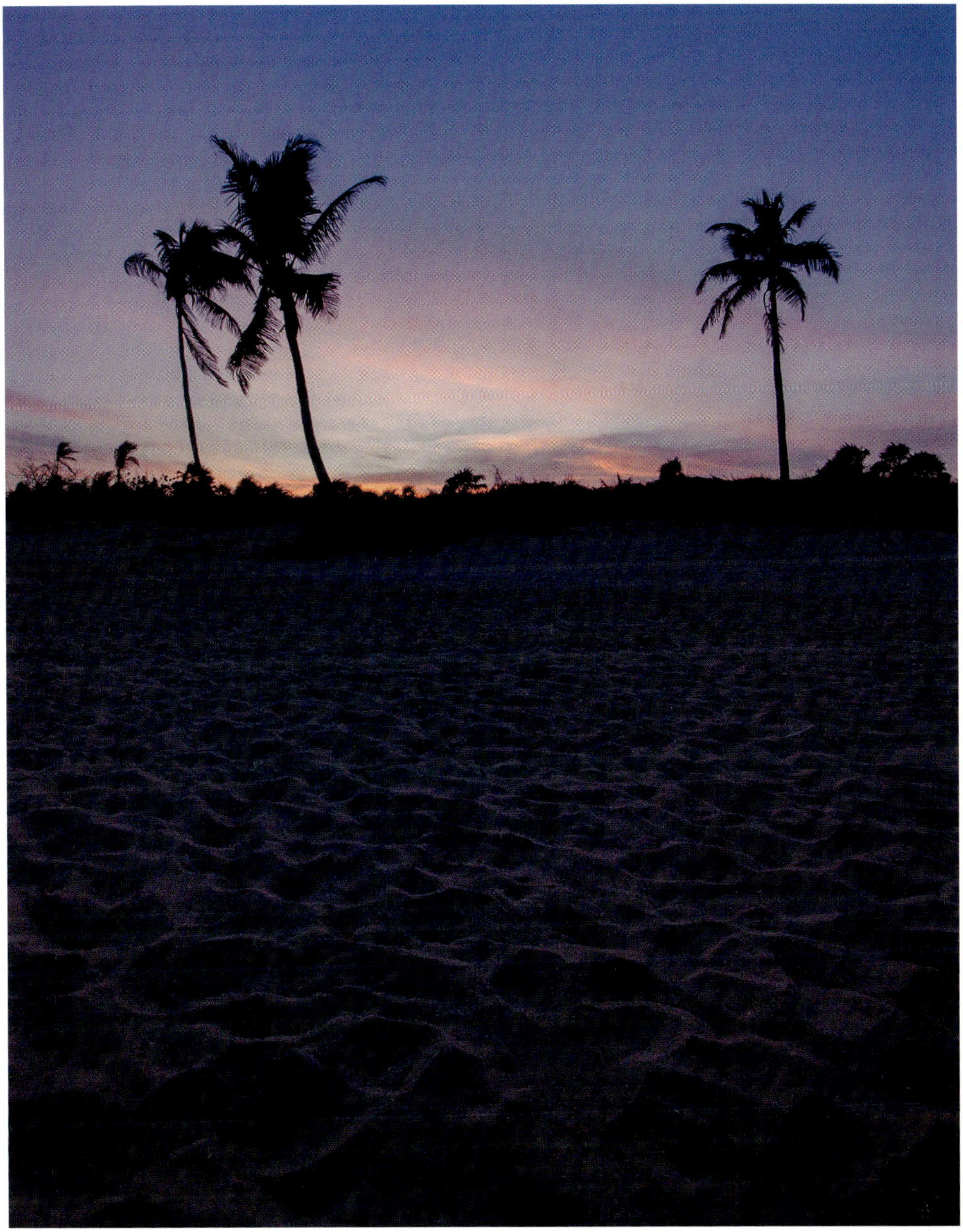

Figure 7.20
The last light falling on the sand in the foreground leads your eye toward the palm trees silhouetted against the sun setting over Tulum, Mexico.

ISO 400 • 1/8 sec. • f/8 • 10–22mm lens

Figure 7.21
When the clouds are just right, the end of the sunset often provides the most drama and color. The clouds steal the show in this shot of Arenal Volcano.

ISO 1000 • 1/30 sec. • f/8 • 18–55mm lens

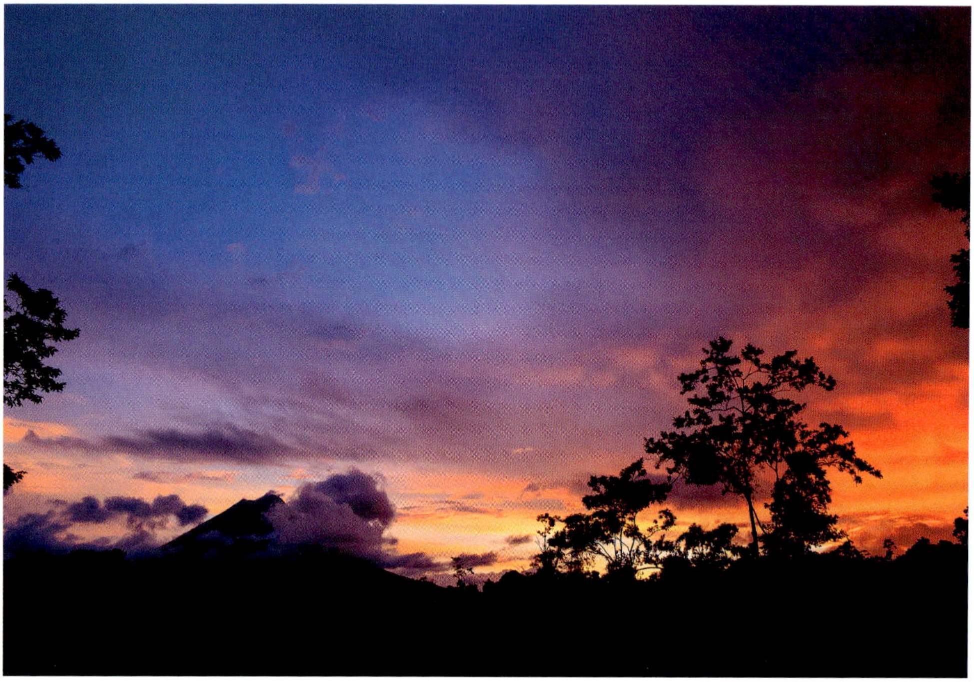

Sometimes we are treated to an amazing show after the sun goes down. When the sun dips below the horizon enough to light the underside of nearby clouds, these wanderers of the sky often light up with color all their own. Clouds can break up the monotony of a clear sky and are frequently featured in exciting sunrise or sunset images (**Figure 7.21**).

Lastly, stay with the sky until the color is absolutely gone. Many an intriguing image is lost because the photographer lacks the patience to see the sky all the way through to nightfall. You never know when a wisp of clouds will suddenly appear in vibrant color against a deep blue sky. Don't get fatigued—stay with the sky and the light, and you might just come away with the next shot you hang up in your living room.

Making Water Fluid

There's nothing quite as satisfying for the landscape shooter as capturing a silky waterfall shot. Creating the smooth-flowing effect is as simple as adjusting your shutter speed to allow the water to be in motion while the shutter is open. The key is to have your camera on a stable tripod so that you can use a shutter speed that's long enough to blur the water (**Figure 7.22**). The "best" shutter speed will depend on the volume and speed of the flowing water, as well as how silky you want the water to look in your photo. You can count on at least 1/15 of a second or longer.

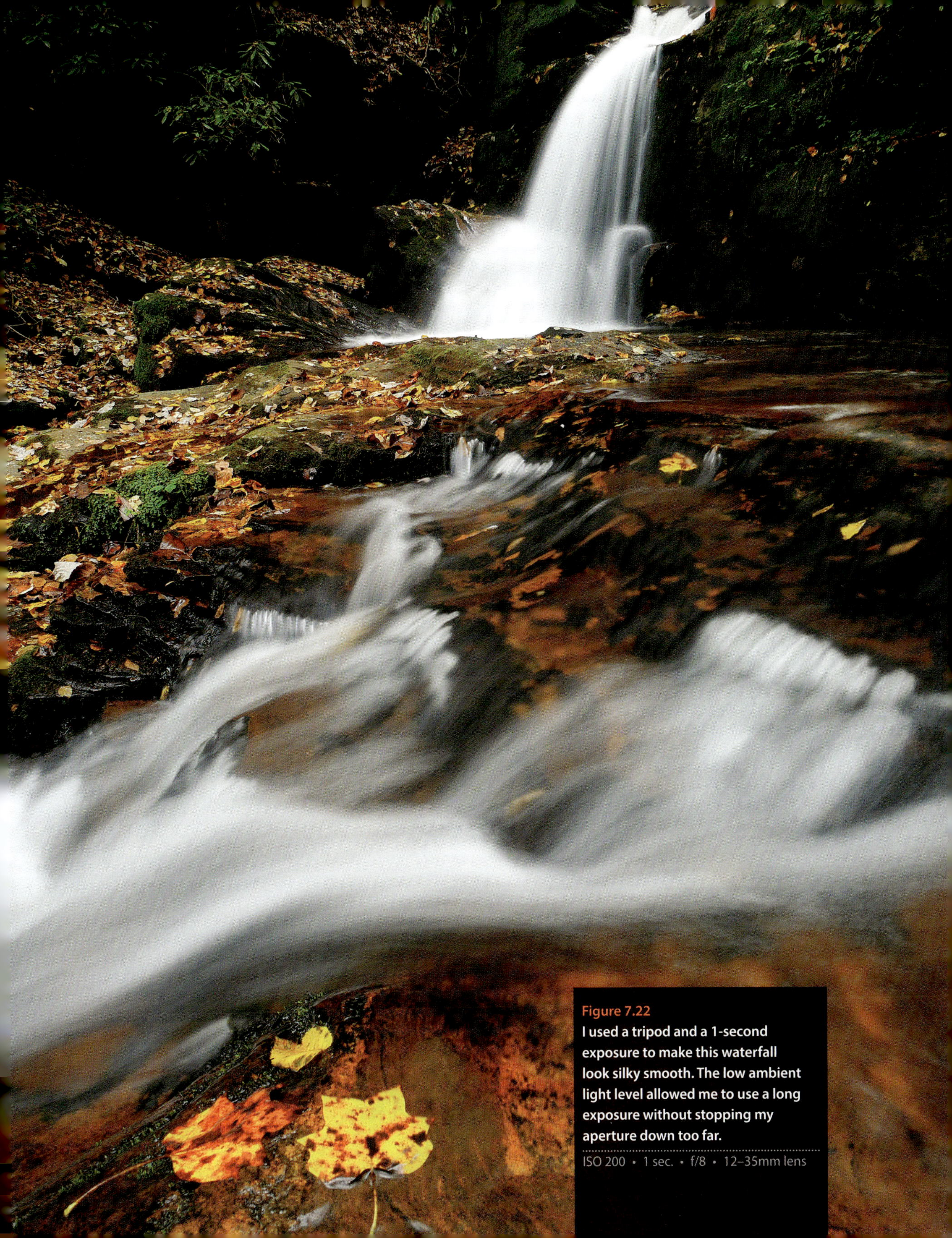

Figure 7.22

I used a tripod and a 1-second exposure to make this waterfall look silky smooth. The low ambient light level allowed me to use a long exposure without stopping my aperture down too far.

ISO 200 • 1 sec. • f/8 • 12–35mm lens

Setting up for a waterfall or river shot

1. Attach the camera to your tripod, then compose and focus your shot.
2. For the best quality, make sure the ISO is set to 200.
3. Using Aperture Priority (A) mode, set your aperture to a small opening (such as f/11 or f/16).
4. Press the shutter button halfway so the camera takes a meter reading.
5. Check to see if the shutter speed is 1/15 of a second or slower.
6. Take a photo and then check the image on the LCD.

If the water is blinking on the LCD during playback, indicating a loss of detail in the highlights, then use exposure compensation to bring details back into the waterfall (see "How I Shoot," in Chapter 4). You can also try the Highlight/Shadow curve (GX7 only) or i.Dynamic settings to tame the bright highlights.

There is a possibility that you will not be able to use a shutter speed that is long enough to capture a smooth, silky effect, especially if you are shooting in bright daylight conditions. To overcome this obstacle, you need a filter for your lens—either a polarizing filter or a neutral density filter. The polarizing filter redirects wavelengths of light to create more vibrant and accurate colors, reduce reflections, and darken blue skies. It also reduces the light hitting your sensor by one or two stops so you can use a slower shutter speed. It is a handy filter for landscape work. The neutral density filter is typically just a dark piece of glass that serves to darken the scene by one, two, three, or even ten stops. This allows you to use slower shutter speeds during bright conditions. Think of it as sunglasses for your camera lens.

Directing the Viewer: A Word About Composition

As a photographer, it's your job to lead the viewer through your image. You accomplish this by utilizing the principles of composition, which is the arrangement of elements in the scene that draws the viewer's eye through your image and holds their attention. As the director of this viewing, you need to understand how people see, and then use that information to focus their attention on the most important elements in your image.

There is a general order in which we look at elements in a photograph. The first is brightness. The eye wants to travel to the brightest object within a scene. So if you have a bright sky, it's probably the first place the eye will travel to. The second order of attention is sharpness. Sharp, detailed elements will get more attention than soft, blurry areas. Finally, the eye will move to vivid colors while leaving the dull, flat colors for last. It is important to know these essentials in order to grab—and keep—the viewer's attention and then direct them through the frame.

In **Figure 7.23**, the eye is drawn to the brightest white at the top of the waterfall. It is then drawn down the cascade of the flowing water, and then up the left side of the frame toward the brighter leaves in the top left of the frame. The detailed leaves lead the eye back to the top of the falls to begin the journey again. The elements within the image all help to keep the eye moving without leaving the frame.

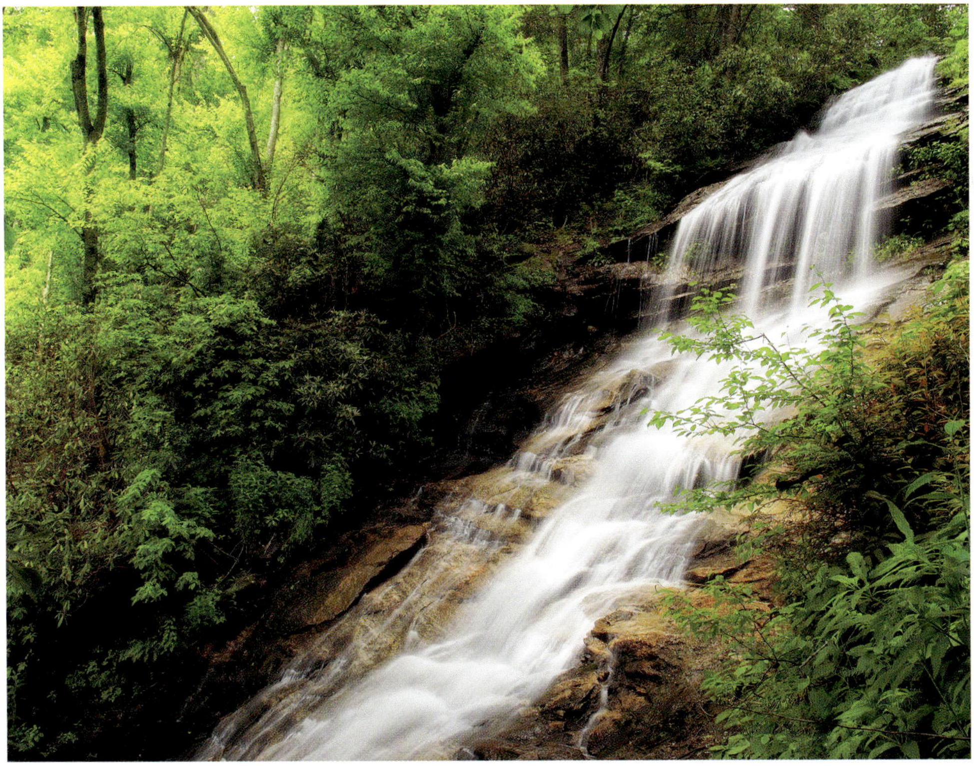

Figure 7.23
The composition of the elements pulls the viewer's eyes around the image, leading from one element to the next in a clockwise motion.

ISO 200 • .6 sec. • f/8 • 12mm lens

Rule of thirds

There are, in fact, quite a few philosophies concerning composition. The easiest one to begin with is known as the "rule of thirds." Using this principle, you simply divide your viewfinder into thirds by imagining two horizontal and two vertical lines that divide the frame equally.

The key to using this method of composition is to have your main subject located at or near one of the intersecting points (**Figure 7.24**).

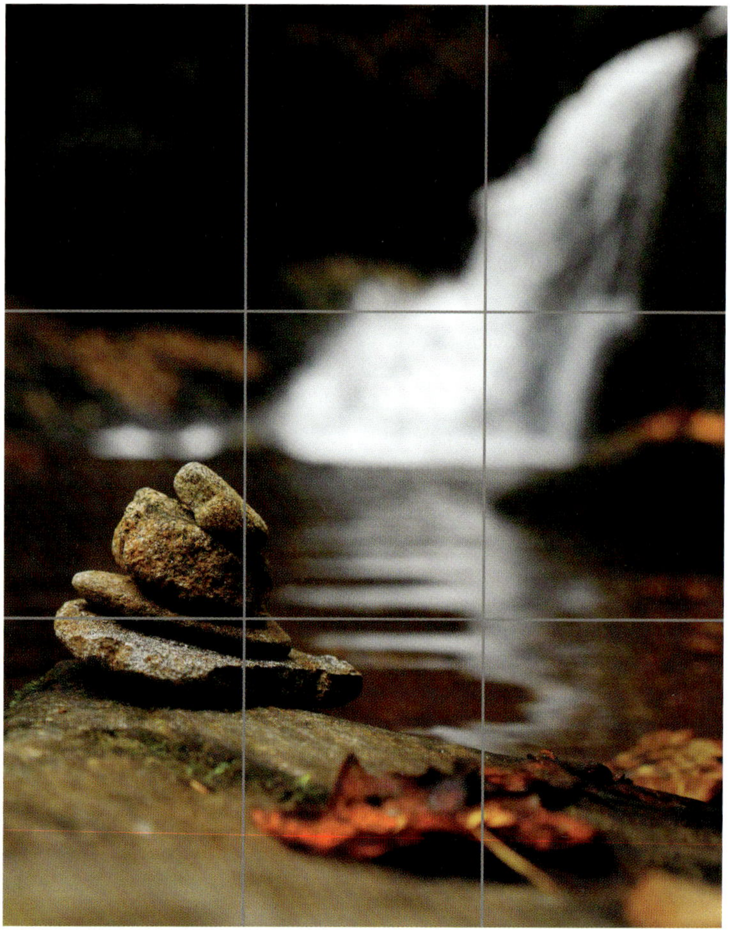

Figure 7.24
With the rule-of-thirds grid atop this image, you can see that I composed the shot so that the rocks are near the lower-left intersection and that the waterfall is near the upper-right intersection.

ISO 1600 • 1/25 sec. • f/2.8 • 12–35mm lens

By placing your subject near these intersecting lines, you are giving the viewer space to move within the frame. The one thing you don't want to do is place your subject smack dab in the middle of the frame. This is sometimes referred to as "bull's eye" composition, and it requires the right subject matter for it to work. It's not always wrong, but it will usually be less appealing and may not hold the viewer's focus.

Speaking of the middle of the frame: The other general rule of thirds deals with horizon lines. Generally speaking, you should position the horizon one-third of the way up or down in the frame. Splitting the frame in half by placing your horizon in the middle of the picture is akin to placing the subject in the middle of the frame—it doesn't lend a sense of importance to either the sky or the ground, creating two equally competing areas of the image.

In **Figure 7.25,** I incorporated the rule of thirds by placing my horizon on the bottom third of the frame. I thought the clouds were more interesting than the large field of snow in front of me, so I decided to feature them more prominently. With this composition I was able to emphasize the clouds and use the hills in the foreground to anchor the frame.

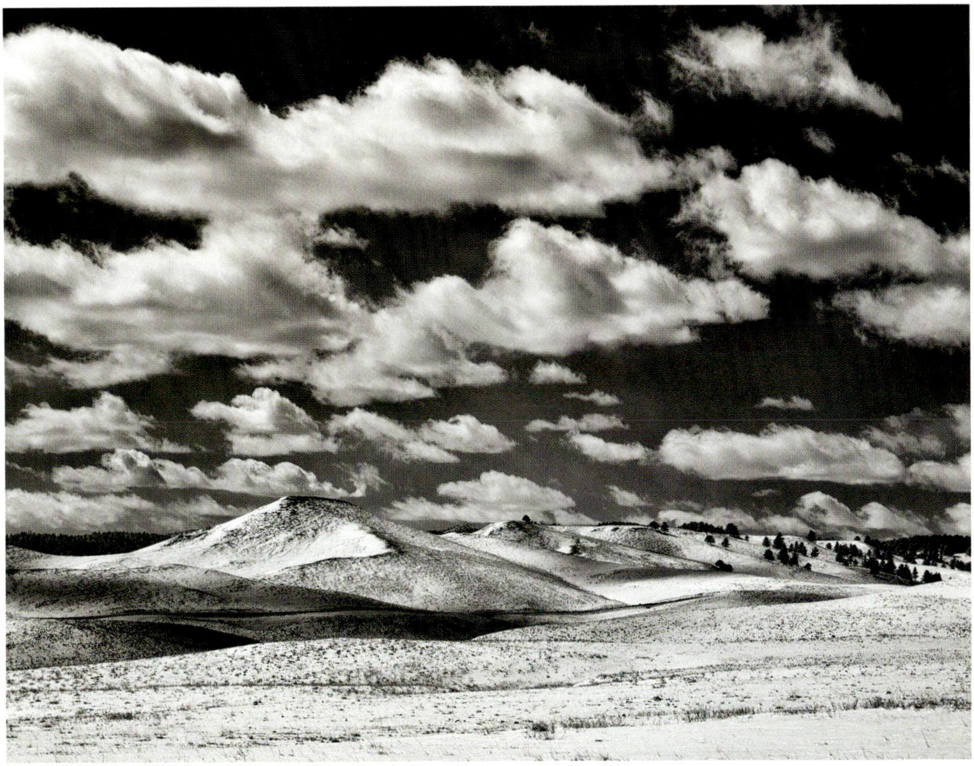

Figure 7.25
Placing the horizon of this image in the bottom third of the frame puts emphasis on the clouds.

ISO 200 • 1/800 sec. • f/8 • 12–35mm lens

Using the rule-of-thirds grid

If you want additional help with composing along the rule of thirds, the GX7/GM1 has a built-in grid overlay function that divides the image into equal vertical and horizontal thirds. You can use it guide the placement of subject matter and horizons or simply to check your already composed image.

Setting up the rule-of-thirds grid

1. Press the Menu/Set button, then select the Custom menu.
2. Select Guide Line and choose the Rule of 3rds Grid option (the top icon).
3. Feel free to experiment using the other grid guides for more compositional exploration.

Poring Over the Picture

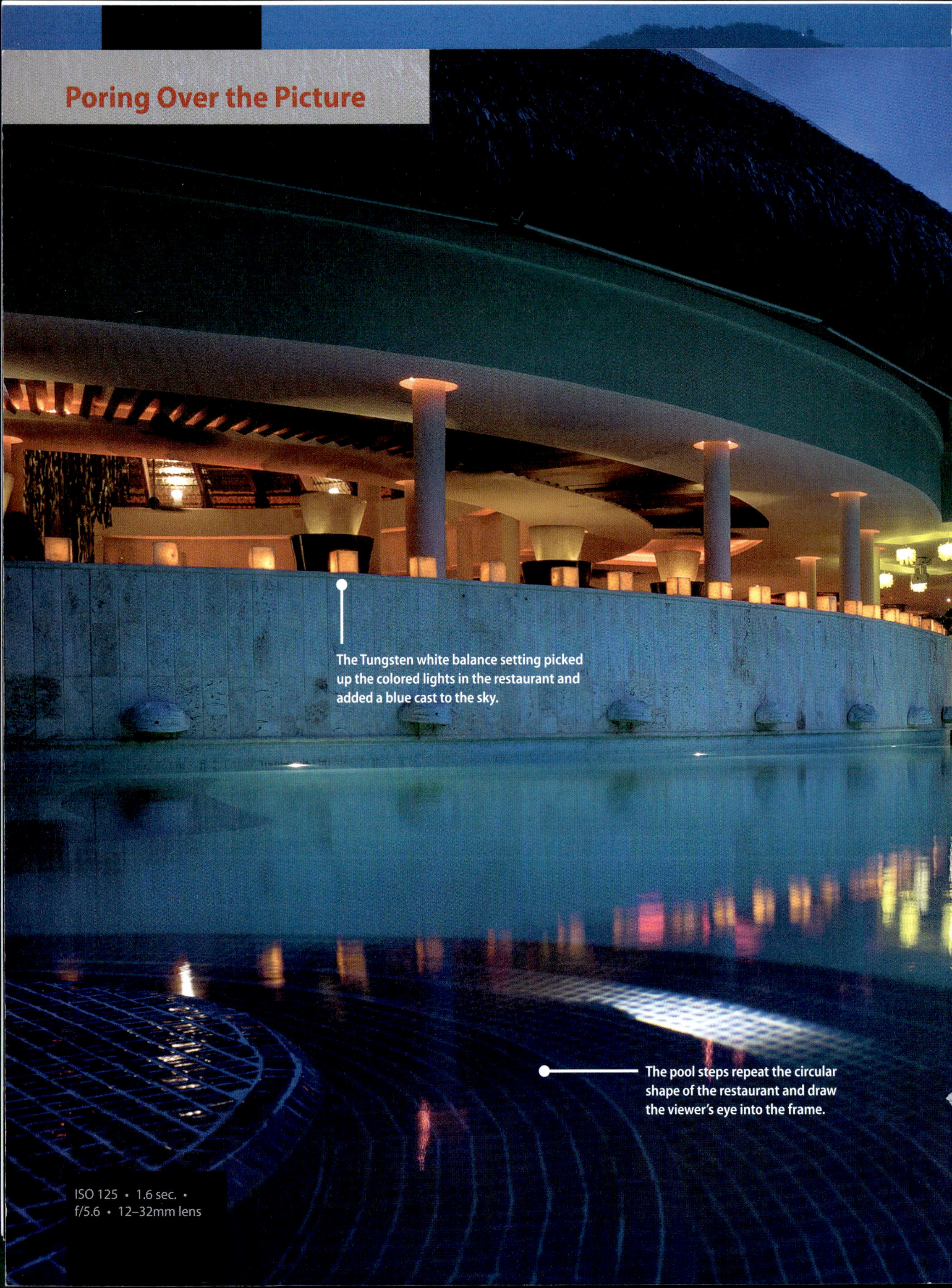

The Tungsten white balance setting picked up the colored lights in the restaurant and added a blue cast to the sky.

The pool steps repeat the circular shape of the restaurant and draw the viewer's eye into the frame.

ISO 125 • 1.6 sec. • f/5.6 • 12–32mm lens

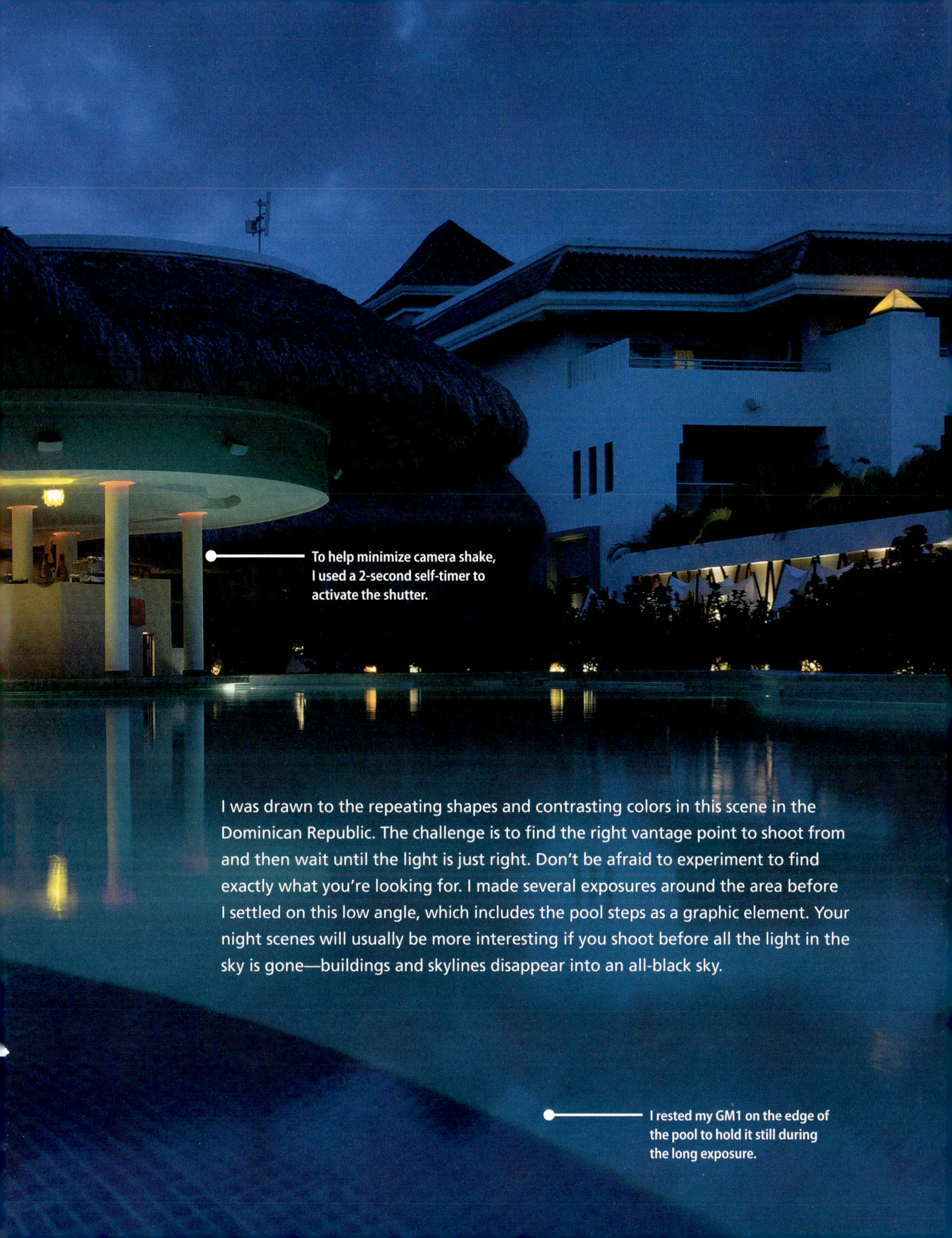

I was drawn to the repeating shapes and contrasting colors in this scene in the Dominican Republic. The challenge is to find the right vantage point to shoot from and then wait until the light is just right. Don't be afraid to experiment to find exactly what you're looking for. I made several exposures around the area before I settled on this low angle, which includes the pool steps as a graphic element. Your night scenes will usually be more interesting if you shoot before all the light in the sky is gone—buildings and skylines disappear into an all-black sky.

Raising the ISO: The Simple Solution

Let's begin with the obvious way to keep shooting when the lights get low: raising the ISO (**Figure 8.1**). By now you know how to change the ISO: Press the ISO button (▲) and rotate the Rear dial to adjust (GM1: press Fn1 and rotate the Control dial). In typical shooting situations, you should keep the ISO in the 200 to 1600 range. This will keep your pictures nice and clean by keeping the digital noise to a minimum. As the available light gets low, however, you might find yourself working in the higher ranges of the ISO scale, which could lead to more noise in your image.

You could use the flash, but that has a limited range (15 to 20 feet at higher ISOs; much shorter at lower ISOs). Also, you could be in a situation where flash is prohibited or at least frowned upon, like at a wedding or in a museum.

And what about a tripod in combination with a long shutter speed? That is also an option, and we'll cover it a little further into the chapter. Using a tripod and a slow shutter speed in low-light photography can be a good option when subjects aren't moving, but sometimes setting up a tripod is not an option.

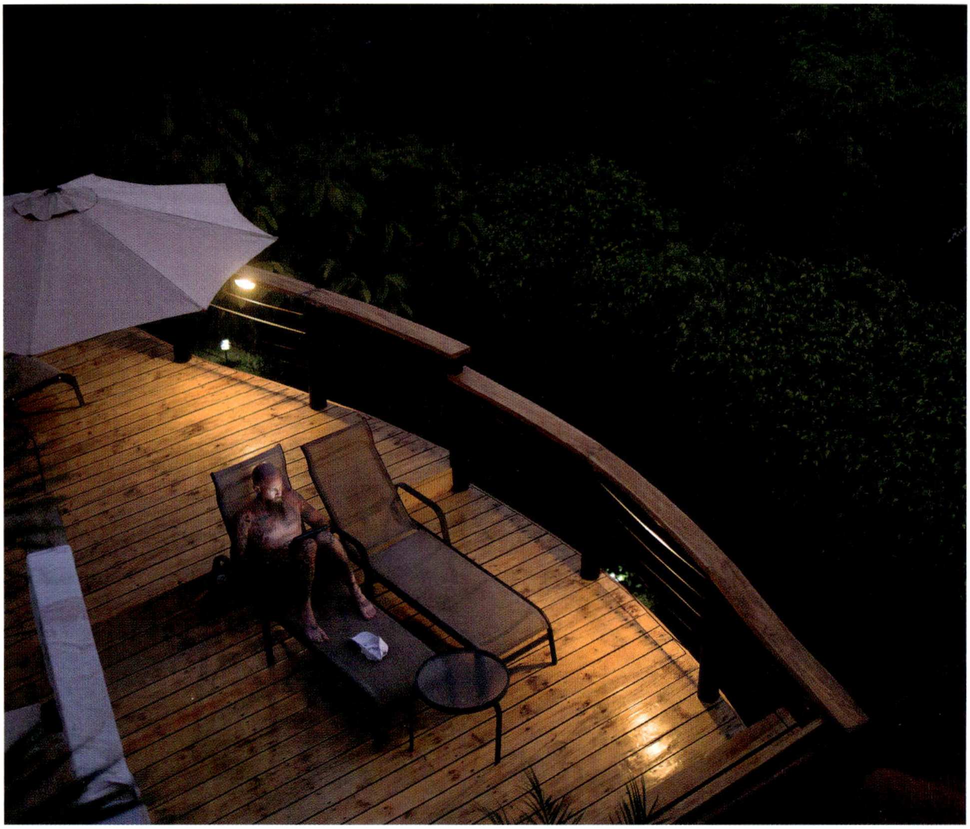

Figure 8.1
I didn't have my tripod with me when I captured this shot in the late evening. Using a wide aperture and raising the ISO to 800 allowed me to use a shutter speed that was fast enough for me to handhold the camera and get a sharp shot.

ISO 800 • 1/80 sec. • f/1.4 • 25mm lens

If the only choice to get the shot is to raise the ISO to 1600 or higher, you may want to use the in-camera noise reduction (NR). You can adjust the NR by pressing Menu > Rec > Photo Style. You can adjust the amount of NR for each photo style from –5 to +5, with 0 being the default. The more NR you apply, the more you lose detail in your images. I usually set the NR to –5 because I would rather have more resolution, even if there is a bit more grain.

To see the effect of noise reduction, you need to zoom in and take a closer look (**Figures 8.2** and **8.3**).

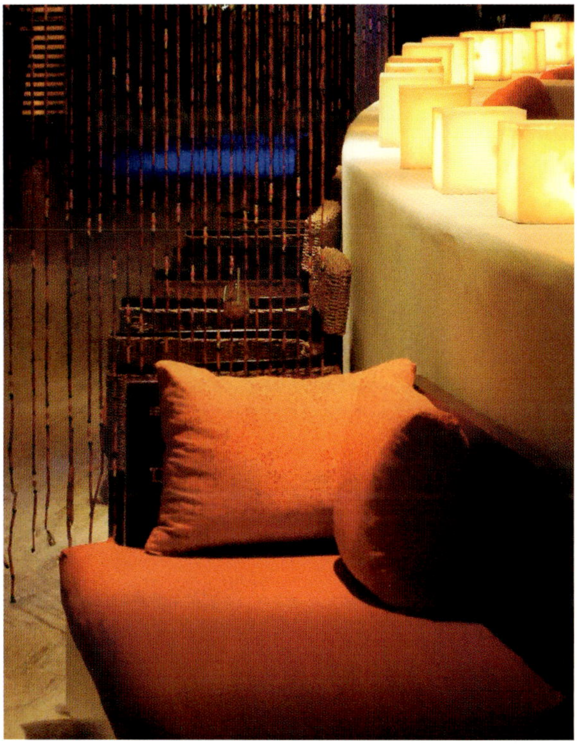

Figure 8.2 Here is an enlargement of a shot with the noise reduction turned all the way down to –5. The GM1 does a remarkable job at ISO 12800!

ISO 12800 • 1/40 sec. • f/5.6 • 12–32mm lens

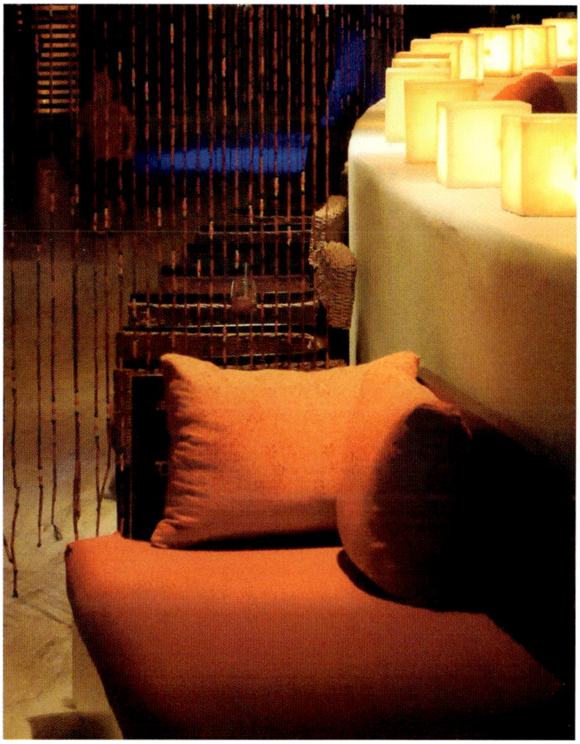

Figure 8.3 Here is the same shot with noise reduction set to 0. The noise has been reduced, but the fine details are not as clear.

ISO 12800 • 1/40 sec. • f/5.6 • 12–32mm lens

Using Very High ISOs

With Extended ISO turned on, the GX7/GM1 is capable of reaching ISO 25600, in one-stop increments from ISO 125. Photographers often joke that ISOs above 6400 help you see in the dark. This isn't too far from the truth!

A note about using extremely high ISOs: Although it is great to have high ISO settings available during low-light shooting, the amount of visible noise will be extremely high, even with the NR turned on. I generally try not to use ISO 25600, but you might find yourself in a dark environment that would require an ISO of 6400 or higher to capture the available light. If you have a choice between getting the shot with high ISO noise or missing the shot, I say crank up the ISO and get the shot (**Figure 8.4**)!

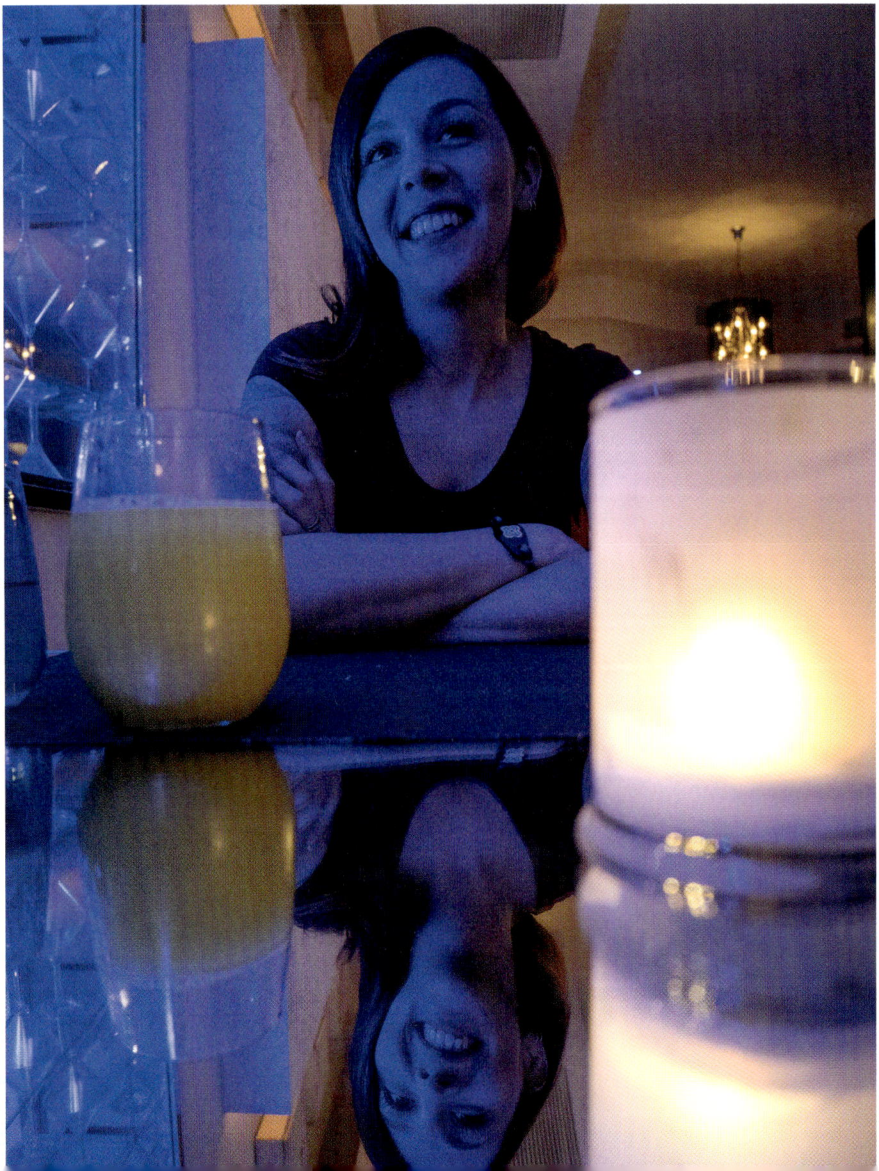

Figure 8.4
I wanted to capture my wife and her reflection in this mirrored table, and using a flash would have done away with the crazy blue ambient light.

ISO 3200 • 1/50 sec. • f/3.5 • 12–32mm lens

Stabilizing the Situation

If you purchased your camera with a lens that uses Optical Image Stabilizer (OIS) technology, you already own a great tool to squeeze two to four stops of exposure out of your camera when shooting without a tripod (**Figure 8.5**). The GX7 also has Optical Image Stabilization built into the body. The in-body stabilizer works by default when using a non-OIS lens. Typically, the average person can handhold their camera down to about 1/60 of a second before blurriness results due to hand shake. As the focal length of the lens is increased (or zoomed), the ability to handhold at slow shutter speeds (1/60 and slower) and still get sharp images is further reduced.

Manual Callout

See page 203 of your GX7 owner's manual for a complete description of the Optical Image Stabilizer settings.

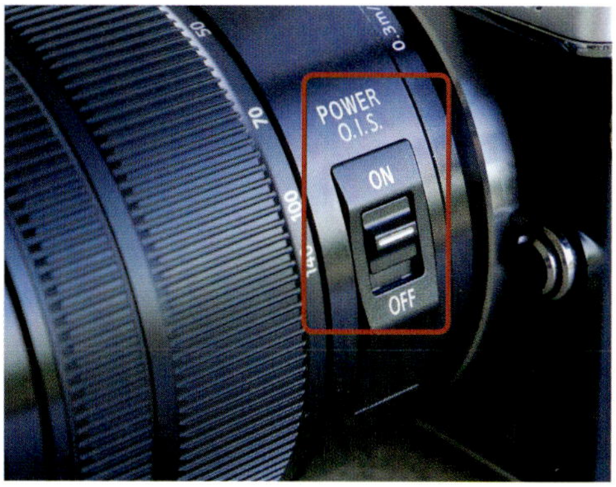

Figure 8.5 Turn the OIS feature on when using longer shutter speeds while handholding your camera.

The OIS technology corrects for camera shake and stabilizes the image. It is so good that it is possible to improve your handheld photography by two, three, or four stops, meaning that if you are pretty solid at a shutter speed of 1/60, OIS lets you shoot at 1/15 and possibly even 1/8 or 1/4 of a second (**Figures 8.6** and **8.7**). But know that shooting any lens, even extremely wide-angle lenses, at slower than 1/15 of a second can be hazardous to the image's focus. OIS is great for hand held shooting, but it is generally a good idea to turn the OIS off when shooting on a tripod.

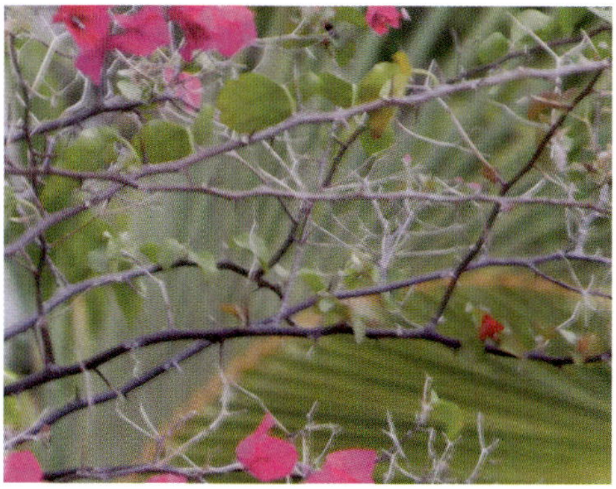

Figure 8.6 This image was shot handheld with OIS turned off.

ISO 1600 • 1/8 sec. • f/5.6 • 14–140mm lens

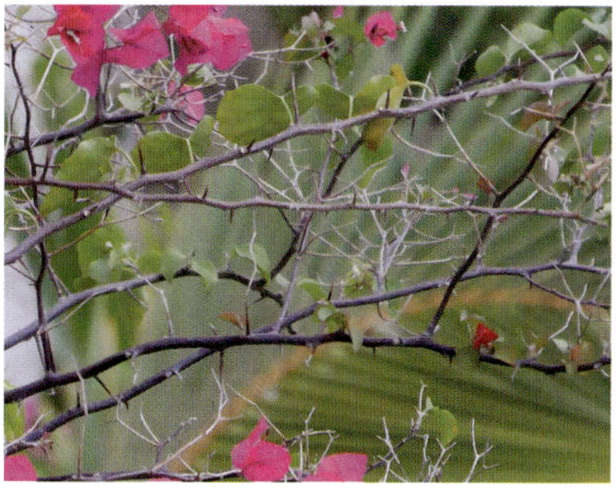

Figure 8.7 Here is the same subject shot with the same settings, but this time with OIS turned on.

Even though image-stabilizing technology like OIS is extremely helpful for shooting in low-light situations, it is still important to continually apply proper shooting technique to bolster your own stability (see Chapter 1 for a more specific look at camera- and lens-stabilizing posture).

Self-timer

Whether you are shooting with a tripod or even resting your camera on a wall, you can increase the sharpness of your pictures by taking your hands out of the equation. Whenever you use your finger to depress the shutter release button, you are increasing the chance that there will be a little bit of shake in your image. To eliminate this possibility, try setting your camera up to use the self-timer. To turn on the self-timer, press the Drive Mode button (▼) to view the drive modes. Rotate the wheel to select the 2-second self-timer. If you need a longer self-timer, press the ▲ button and rotate the Rear dial (GM1: Control wheel) to the 10-second self-timer. An additional self-timer option is available that allows you to shoot three images in succession.

Focusing in Low Light

The GX7/GM1 has a great focusing system, but occasionally the light levels might be too low for the camera to achieve an accurate focus. There are a few things that you can do to overcome this obstacle.

First, you should know that the camera utilizes contrast to establish a point of focus. This is why your camera will not be able to focus when you point it at a white wall or a cloudless sky; it simply can't find any contrast in the scene to work with. Knowing this, you might be able to use 1-Area focus or Pinpoint focus to find an area of contrast that is at the same distance as your subject. Simply touch the screen where you want to focus. You can then hold that focus by holding down the shutter button halfway and recomposing your image if necessary.

Then there are times when there isn't anything for your autofocus to lock on to. A perfect example of this would be a fireworks display. If you point your lens to the night sky in any automatic focus (AF) mode, it will just keep searching for—and not finding—a focus point. On these occasions, you can turn off the autofocus feature and manually focus the lens (**Figure 8.8**). Simply turn the focus mode lever to MF.

Don't forget to put the camera back in AF mode at the end of your shoot.

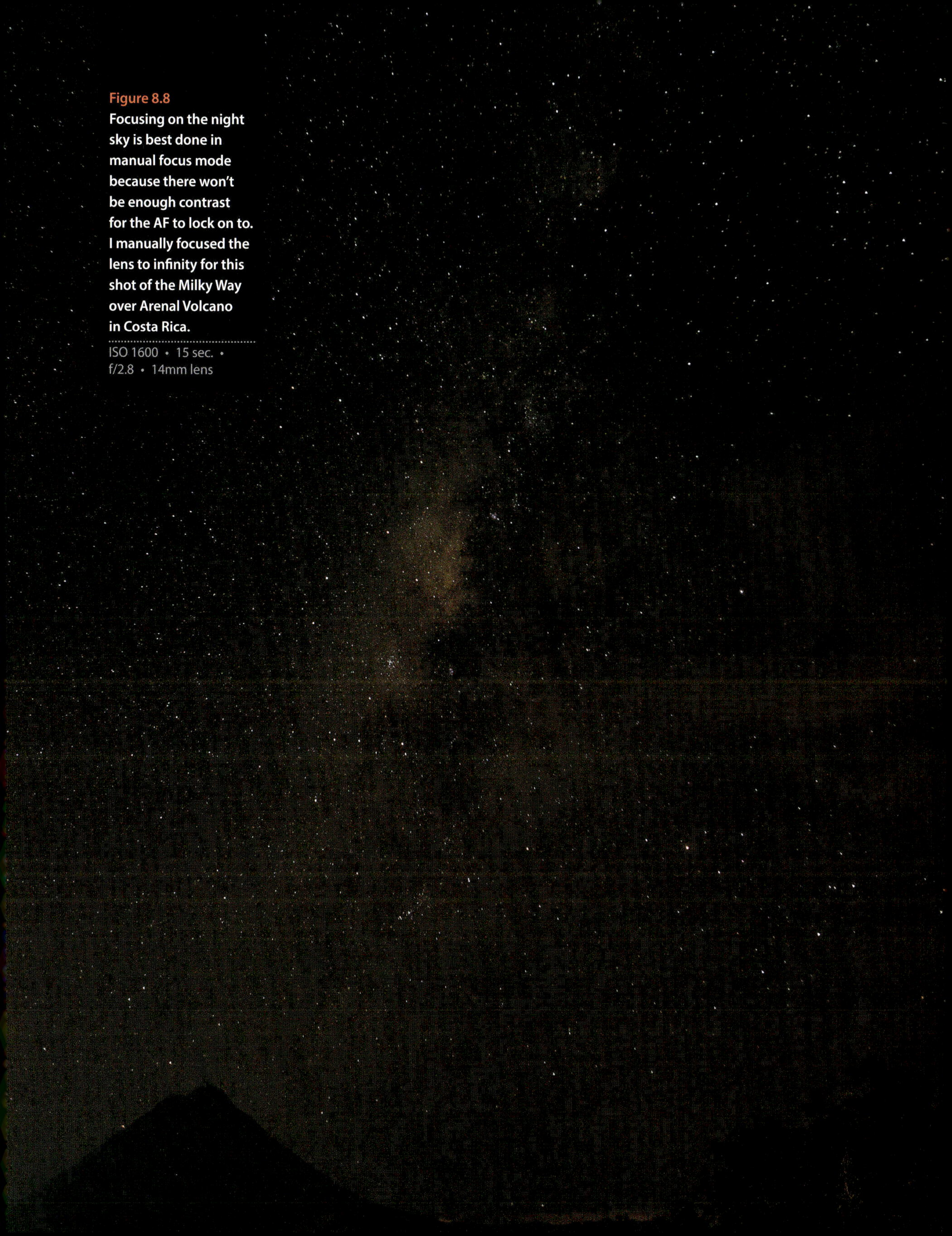

Figure 8.8

Focusing on the night sky is best done in manual focus mode because there won't be enough contrast for the AF to lock on to. I manually focused the lens to infinity for this shot of the Milky Way over Arenal Volcano in Costa Rica.

ISO 1600 • 15 sec. • f/2.8 • 14mm lens

Autofocus Assist Lamp

Another way to ensure good focus is to enable the GX7/GM1's AF Assist Lamp. The AF Assist Lamp uses a small reddish-orange LED light near the shutter button to shine some light on the scene, which assists the autofocus system in locating more detail. The AF Assist Lamp has a limited range, but it can come in handy for things like portraits in low light. The AF Assist Lamp should be enabled by default, but you can check the menu just to make sure.

Activating the AF Assist Lamp

1. Press the Menu/Set button, then select the Custom menu.
2. Select AF Assist Lamp.
3. Select On if it is not already enabled. Depress the shutter button halfway to exit the menu once you've made your selection. Now whenever the lighting is too low for the camera to grab focus, it will use the AF Assist Lamp.

Shooting Long Exposures

We have covered some of the techniques for shooting in low light, so let's go through the process of capturing a night or low-light scene for maximum image quality. The first thing to consider is that in order to shoot in low light with a low ISO, you will need to use shutter speeds that are longer than you could possibly handhold (longer than 1/15 of a second). This will require the use of a tripod or stable surface for you to place your camera on. For maximum quality, the ISO should be low—somewhere at or below 400. The Long Shutter noise reduction should be turned on to minimize the effects of exposing for longer durations. Long Shutter NR is on by default, but you can turn it off in the Rec menu under Long Shtr NR.

Set your camera to Aperture Priority (A) mode. Set an appropriate aperture value for your desired depth of field, and let the camera determine the best shutter speed (**Figure 8.9**). If it is too dark for the autofocus to function properly, try manually focusing. Finally, consider using a remote control to activate the shutter. If you don't have one, use the self-timer. Once you shoot the image, you may notice some lag time before it is displayed on the rear LCD. This is due to the noise reduction process, which takes the same amount of time as the exposure.

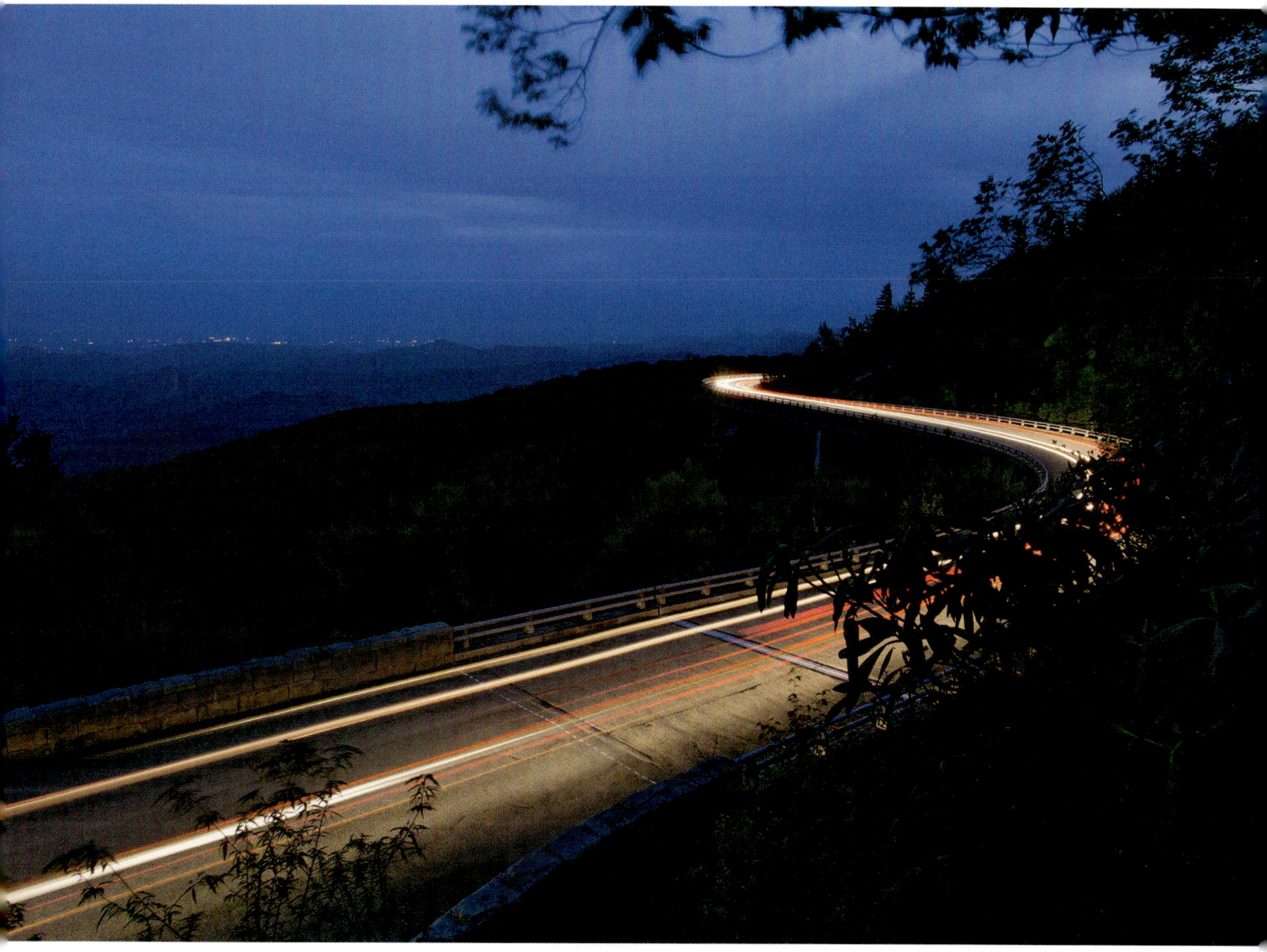

Figure 8.9 A long exposure and a tripod were necessary to capture this twilight photo of two cars on the Linn Cove Viaduct along the Blue Ridge Parkway in North Carolina.

ISO 200 • 30 sec. • f/8 • 12mm lens

Using the Built-In Flash

There are going to be times when you have to turn to your camera's built-in flash to get the shot. The pop-up flash on the GX7/GM1 is not extremely powerful, but with the camera's advanced metering system it does a pretty good job of lighting up the night... or just filling in the shadows.

If you are working in any of the professional modes, you will have to turn the flash on for yourself. To do this, just slide the pop-up flash button located on the back of the camera (**Figure 8.10**). Once the flash is up, it is ready to go (**Figure 8.11**). It's that simple.

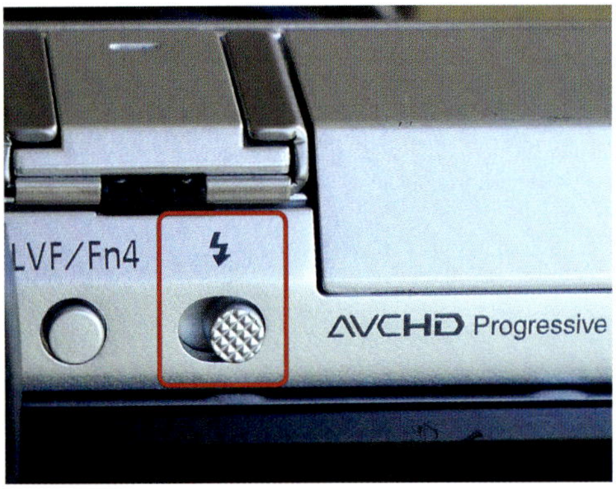

Figure 8.10 A quick press of the pop-up flash button on the GX7 will release the built-in flash to its ready position.

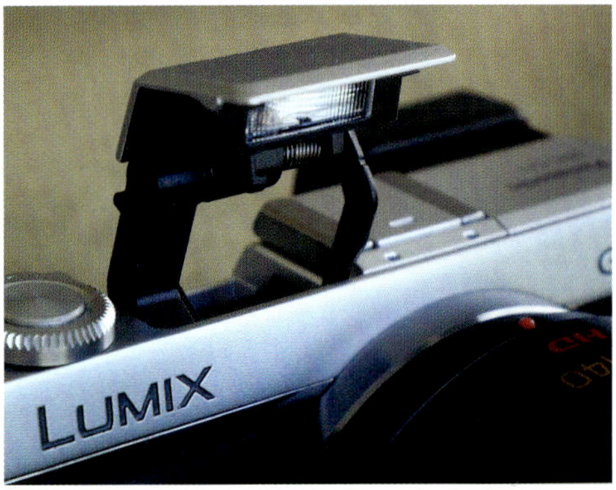

Figure 8.11 The pop-up flash on the GX7 in its ready position.

Bounce the built-in flash

Like many built-in flash units, the GX7/GM1's is spring-loaded and pops up quickly, making the camera look a bit like a Transformer. But you can do something with this flash that you can't do with many built-in flashes without breaking them: bounce it. Bouncing the flash takes some of the bite out of the harsh light that small flashes like this cast on your subjects. Essentially, bouncing the flash against a ceiling or wall increases the size of the light source, softening the light somewhat. You cannot rotate or swivel the built-in flash, but because the spring-loaded mechanism forces you to push it backwards to seat it after you are finished with it, it makes sense that with a little repositioning of your fingers, you can tilt the flash back when you are shooting. I rarely like to fire a flash straight onto my subject, especially a person. This not-so-intentional feature offers an alternative to doing so.

Shutter speeds

The real key to using the flash to get great pictures is to control the shutter speed. The goal is to balance the light from the flash with the existing light so that everything in the picture has an even illumination. Let's take a look at the shutter speeds for the professional modes.

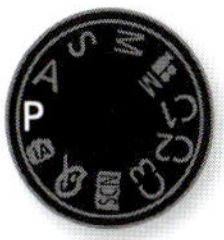

Program Auto (P): The shutter speed stays at from 1/60 to 1/320 of a second (GM1: 1/50 of a second only). With the flash up, you can shift the program and adjust the exposure compensation as usual.

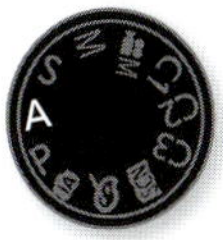

Aperture Priority (A): Like Program Auto, Aperture Priority sets the shutter to from 1/60 to 1/320 of a second (GM1: 1/50 of a second only). When the flash mode is changed to either Slow Sync or Rear Sync, the shutter speed is allowed to go slower and will change according to any change you make to the aperture.

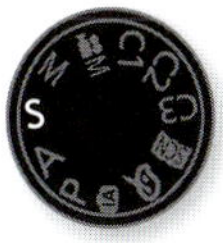

Shutter Priority (S): You can adjust the shutter speed from as fast as 1/320 of a second all the way down to 60 seconds (GM1:1/50 of a second to 60 seconds). The lens aperture will adjust accordingly, but at long exposures the lens will typically be set to its smallest aperture.

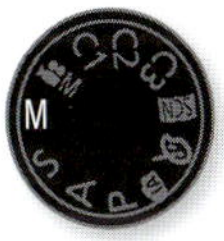

Manual (M): Manual mode works with shutter speeds from 1/320 of a second down to 60 seconds (GM1: 1/50 of a second to 60 seconds). Bulb is accessible as well. You must manually set the f-stop and shutter speed.

Flash range

The pop-up flash does not have enough power to illuminate a large space, but it can be a handy tool when you're working close to your subject (**Figure 8.12**). The effective distance varies depending on the ISO setting and aperture value. This range can be extended to as far as 38 feet depending on the shooting conditions. Use a wide f-stop and raise the ISO for maximum effective range.

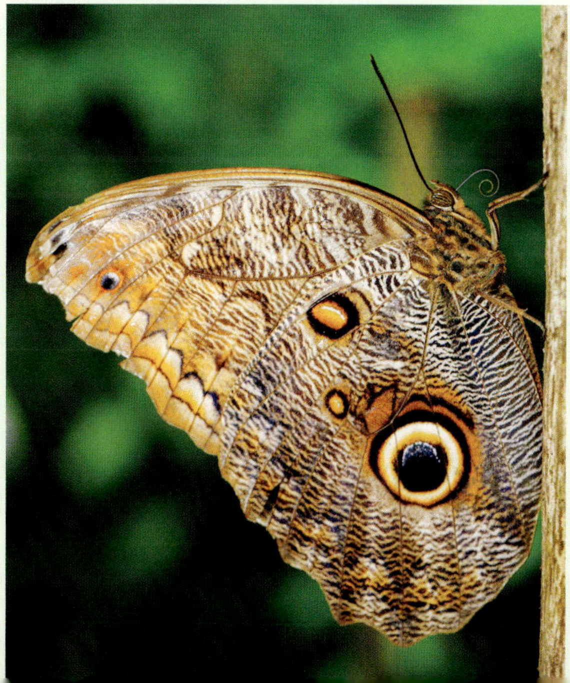

Figure 8.12 The built-in flash does a better job when you're close to your subject. A little pop of light brings out the detail and color in the wings of this butterfly in Costa Rica.

ISO 800 • 1/60 sec. • f/4 • 45mm lens

Compensating for the Flash Exposure

The flash metering system will usually do an excellent job of balancing the flash and ambient light for your exposure, but it does have the limitation of not knowing what effect you want in your image. You may want more or less flash in a particular shot. You can achieve this by using the flash compensation feature.

Just as with exposure compensation, flash compensation allows you to dial in a change in the flash output in increments of 1/3 of a stop. You will probably use this most often to tone down the effects of your flash, especially when you are using the flash as a subtle fill light (**Figures 8.13** and **8.14**).

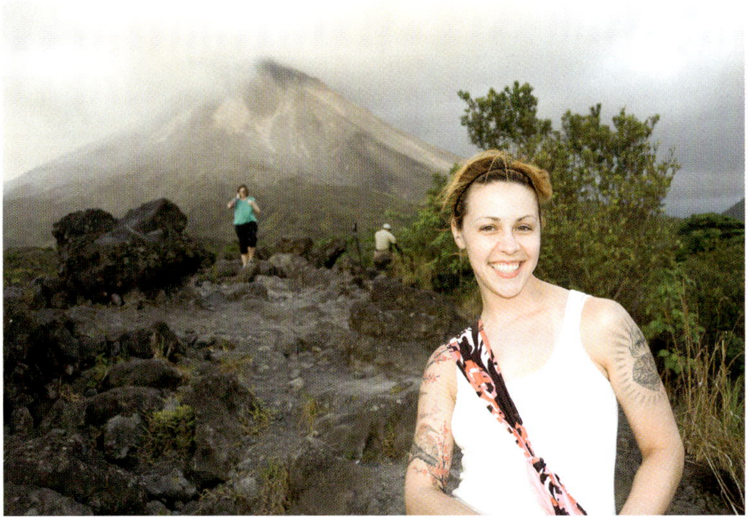

Figure 8.13
At the default flash setting, my foreground subject is too bright and doesn't look natural.

ISO 800 • 1/320 sec. • f/5.6 • 18–35mm lens

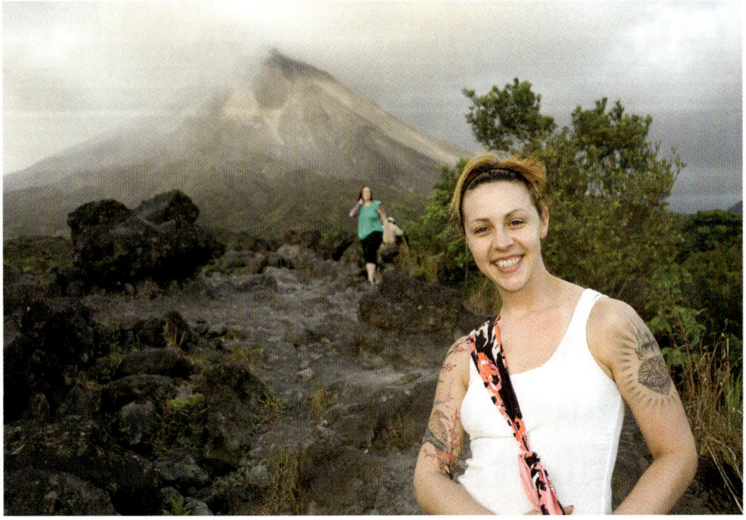

Figure 8.14
This image was made with the same camera settings. The difference is that the flash compensation was set to –1 stop. For daylight fill-in flash, I usually start with the flash output dialed down to –1.

ISO 800 • 1/320 sec. • f/5.6 • 18–35mm lens

Using the flash compensation feature to change the flash output

1. Press Menu/Set, select the Rec menu, select Flash, and then select Flash Adjust.
2. As you rotate the Rear dial (GM1: Control wheel), you are increasing or decreasing the power output of the flash in 1/3-stop increments (**A**).
3. Press the shutter button halfway to return to shooting mode, and then take the picture.
4. Review your image to see if more or less flash compensation is required, and repeat these steps as necessary.

A

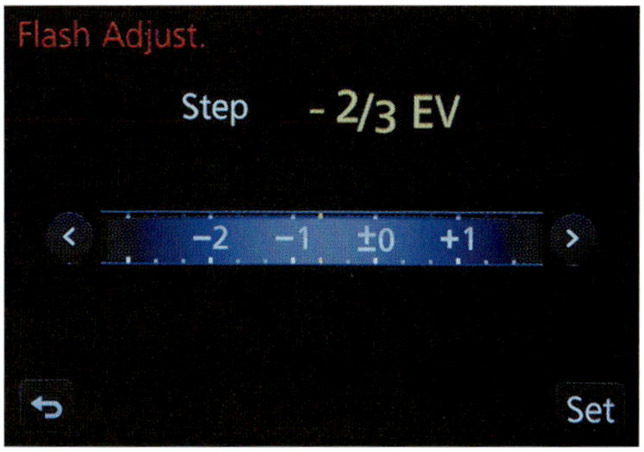

There is an easier way to adjust the flash compensation in the GX7. Navigate to the Flash menu and turn on Auto Exposure Comp. Now when you press and turn the Rear dial to adjust the exposure compensation, the Front dial will adjust the flash exposure compensation. This is a much quicker and easier way to adjust your flash output.

Keep in mind that the flash compensation feature does not reset itself when the camera is turned off, so whatever compensation you have set will remain in effect until you change it.

Reducing Red-Eye

We've all seen the result of using on-camera flashes when shooting people: the dreaded red-eye! This demonic effect is the result of the light from the flash entering the pupil and then reflecting back as an eerie red glow. The closer the flash is to the lens, the greater the chance that you will get red-eye. This is especially true when it is dark and the subject's pupils are dilated. There are two ways to combat this problem. The first is to get the flash away from the lens. That's not really an option, though, if you are using the built-in flash. Therefore, you will need to turn to the Red-Eye Reduction feature.

Turn on the lights!

When shooting indoors, another way to reduce red-eye is to turn on a lot of lights. The brighter the ambient light levels, the smaller the subject's pupils will be. Although this might not completely rid you of the need for red-eye reduction, it will provide your image with ambiance and a sense of place.

This is a simple feature that emits a pre-flash burst from the camera toward the subject, causing his or her pupils to shrink, thus eliminating or reducing the effects of red-eye (**Figure 8.15**).

The feature is set to Off by default and needs to be turned on in the Flash menu.

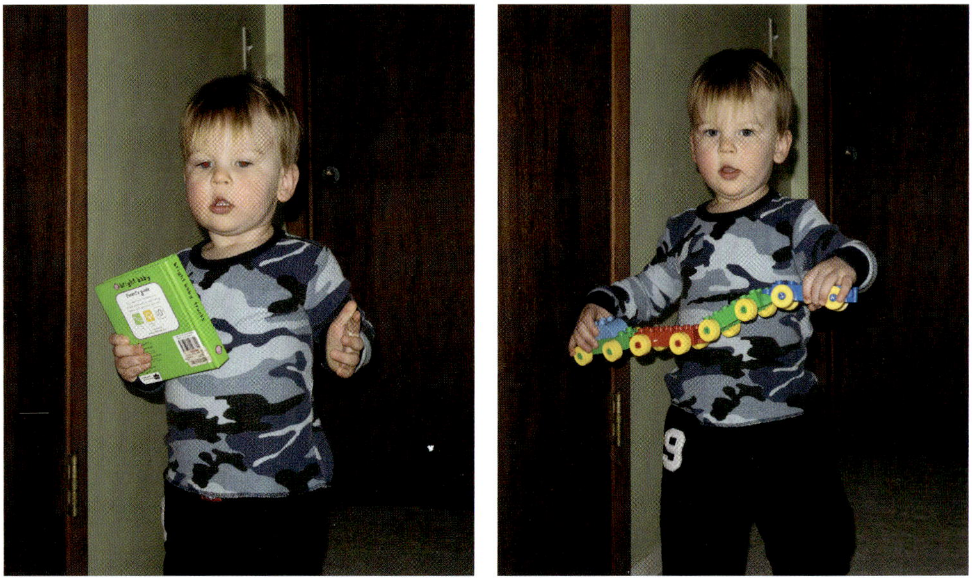

Figure 8.15
The picture on the left did not utilize Red-Eye Reduction, thus the glowing red eyes. Notice that the pupils in the image on the right, without red-eye, are smaller as a result of using the red-eye reduction pre-flash burst. (For the record, it is a real challenge to make example photos like this with a 2-year-old!)

ISO 200 • 1/50 sec. • f/4 • 12–32mm lens

Turning on the Red-Eye Reduction feature

1. Press the Menu/Set button, select the Rec menu, and then select Flash.
2. Select Flash Mode, then select Red-Eye Reduction mode (the lightning bolt with the eye).

   The fourth mode is Slow-Sync Red-Eye Reduction mode. This mode provides red-eye reduction along with slower shutter speeds for more balanced exposures in low light.
3. Press the Menu button or the shutter release button to return to shooting.

I rarely shoot with Red Eye Reduction turned on because of the time it takes before being able to take a picture. If I am after candid shots and have to use the flash, I will take my chances on red-eye and try to fix the problem in my image-processing software.

2nd Curtain Sync Flash

There are two flash synchronization modes in the GX7 and GM1: 1st Curtain and 2nd Curtain. You may be asking, "What in the world does synchronization do, and what's with these 'curtains'?" Good questions.

When a traditional digital SLR camera fires, there are two curtains that open and close to make up the shutter. The first curtain moves out of the way, exposing the camera sensor to the light. At the end of the exposure, the second curtain moves in front of the sensor, ending that picture cycle. The GX7 and GM1 have both mechanical-shutter and electronic-shutter options, but they operate the same way. In flash photography, timing is extremely important because the flash fires in milliseconds and the shutter is usually opening in tenths or hundredths of a second. To make sure these two functions happen in order, the camera usually fires the flash just as the first "curtain" is enabled.

In 2nd Curtain Sync mode, the flash fires at the end of the exposure, just before the second shutter curtain closes. 2nd Curtain Sync is great when you want to have a longer exposure to balance the ambient light with the subject needing the flash. Say you make a flash picture of a moving subject. In 1st Curtain Sync mode, the flash will freeze the subject, but any motion blur will be recorded over your frozen subject. In 2nd Curtain Sync mode, the flash freezes your moving subject after any motion blur is recorded and makes a more natural-looking image.

There is no right or wrong to it. It's just a decision on what type of effect you would like to create. Many times, 2nd Curtain Sync is used for artistic purposes or to record movement in the scene without it overlapping the flash-exposed subject (**Figure 8.16** on the following page). To make sure that the main subject is always getting the final pop of the flash, I leave my camera set to 2nd Curtain Sync.

Using Slow Sync mode with 2nd Curtain Sync (**Figure 8.17** on the following page) will give a more balanced exposure in low light. Even though the flash will help freeze your subject, it is best to use a tripod to stabilize the camera and avoid a blurry background.

Flash sync

The basic idea behind the term *flash synchronization* (*flash sync* for short) is that when you take a photograph using the flash, the camera needs to ensure that the shutter is fully open at the time that the flash goes off. This is not an issue if you are using a long shutter speed such as 1/15 of a second but does become more critical for fast shutter speeds. To ensure that the flash and shutter are synchronized so that the flash is going off while the shutter is open, the GX7 implements a top sync speed of 1/320 of a second (GM1: 1/50). This means that when you are using the built-in flash, you will not be able to have your shutter speed set any faster than 1/320. If you did use a faster shutter speed, the shutter would actually start closing before the flash fired, which would cause a black, underexposed area to appear in the frame where the light from the flash was blocked.

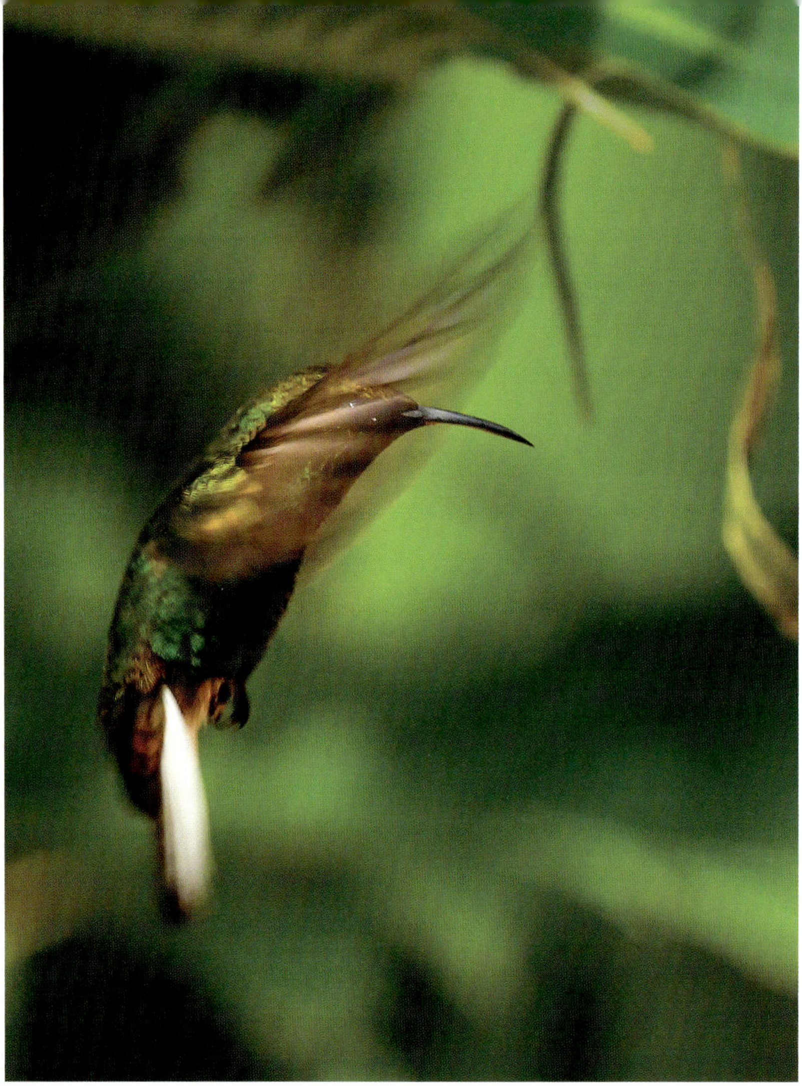

Figure 8.16
2nd Curtain Sync allows the flash to freeze the hummingbird's body after the ambient light shows the blur of its wings.

ISO 400 • 1/250 sec. • f/5.6 • 100–300mm lens

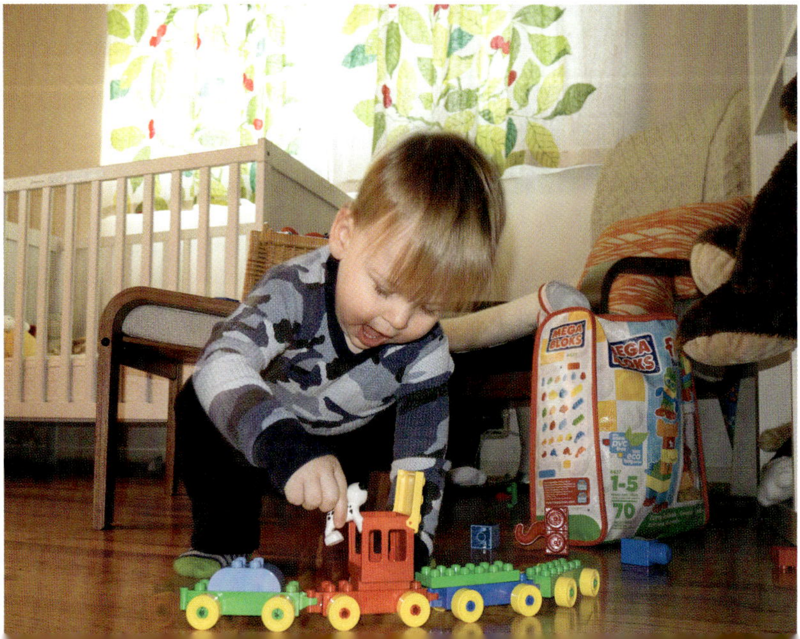

Figure 8.17
Slow Sync flash allows the ambient light to be exposed properly, and 2nd Curtain Sync freezes my subject after the motion blur.

ISO 200 • 1 sec. • f/3.7 • 12–32mm lens

Setting your flash sync mode

1. Press Menu/Set, select the Rec menu, select Flash, and then select Flash Synchro.
2. Select either 1st or 2nd Curtain Sync.
3. Press the shutter button halfway to return to shooting mode.

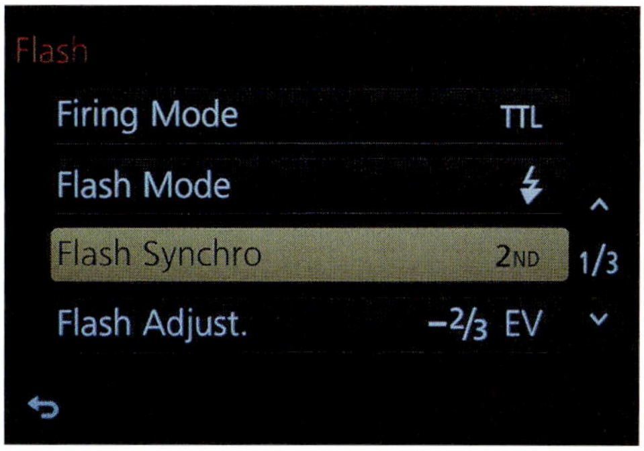

Using an External Flash

An exciting and useful feature of the GX7 is its ability to control an off-camera flash using the built-in flash. The biggest benefit to doing this is that you can move the flash to the side of the camera, which gives you more natural-looking light and shadows. You can also do things like fire the external flash through umbrellas, softboxes, or simple diffusion panels to make the quality of light much softer and more complimentary to your subject (**Figure 8.18**).

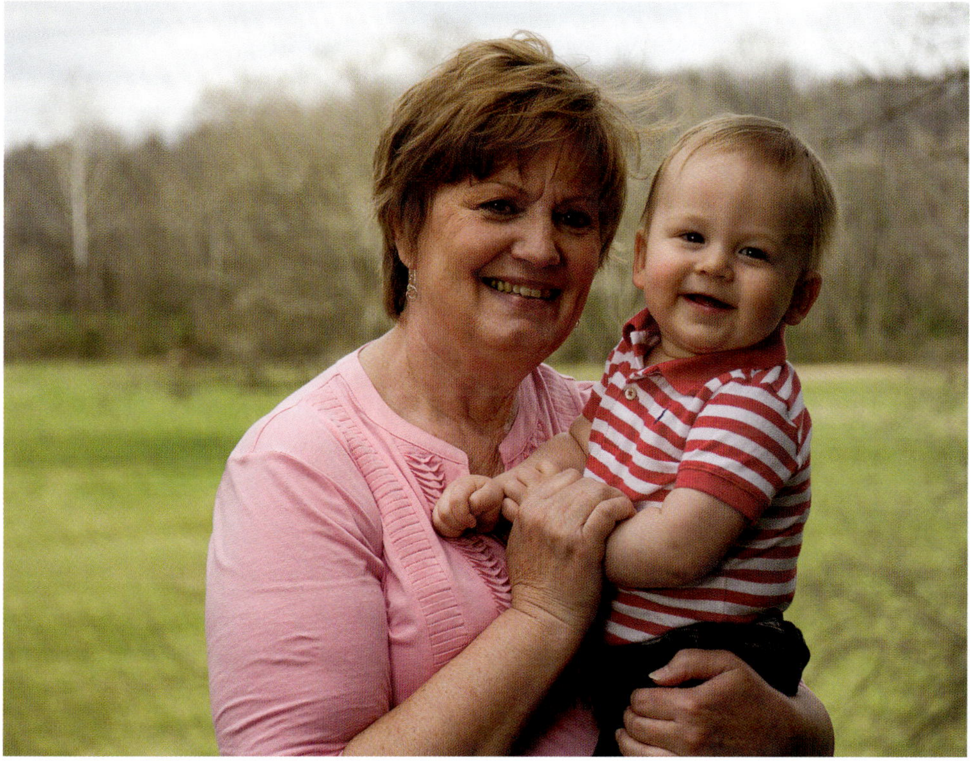

Figure 8.18
I used an FL360L flash remotely in a shoot-through umbrella to fill in the shadows for this outdoor portrait. The flash was in FP mode, so I could use a shutter speed faster than the 1/320 of a second sync speed.

ISO 200 • 1/2500 sec. • f/2.8 • 35–100mm lens

Using off-camera flash (GX7 only)

In order to control an off-camera flash, you can use either the built in flash or a hot-shoe-mounted flash as a wireless commander. I love the convenience of using the built-in flash as a commander, but there are a few advantages of using an additional flash as a commander. A hot-shoe flash can be rotated and bounced to direct the commander signal. This allows for more flexible positioning of remote flashes. A hot-shoe flash like the Panasonic DMW-FL360L (**Figure 8.19**) also has a zoom feature that allows you to extend the range of the commander signal a bit.

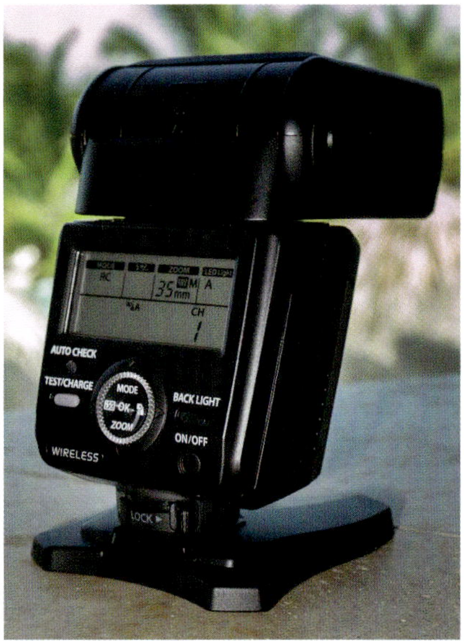

Figure 8.19 **The DMW-FL360L is a great external flash to use with your GX7.**

Setting up your camera for wireless operation

1. Press Menu, select the Rec menu, and then select Flash.
2. Scroll down to Wireless in the Flash menu, and set it to On (**A**).
3. Select a wireless channel, and make sure your off-camera flashes are on the same channel.

   Wireless FP enables high-speed flash sync with your off-camera flashes.

   You will use the Wireless Setup menu to control the flash mode and flash exposure compensation for the commander flash and up to three groups of remote flashes (**B**).

A

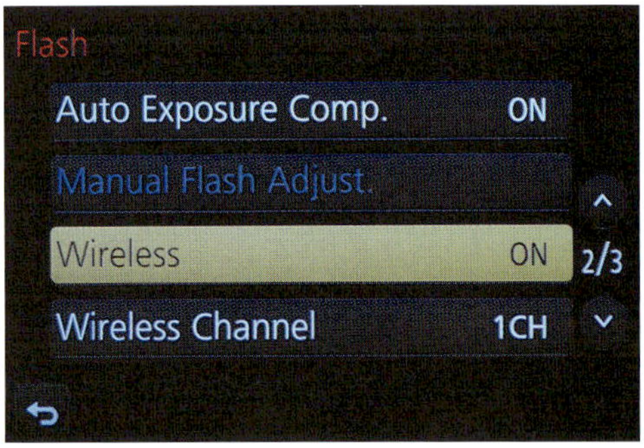

B

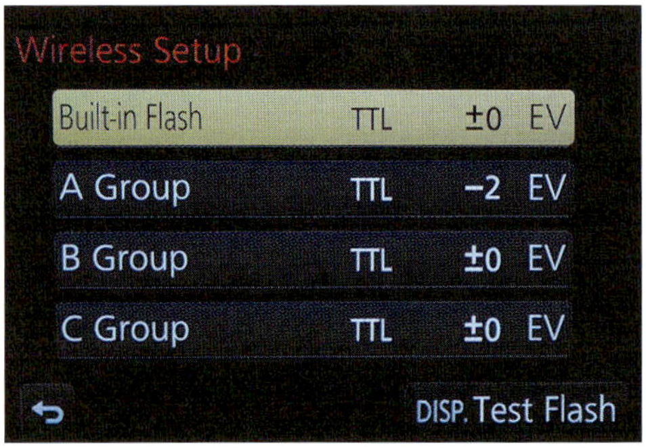

Setting up the hot-shoed and off-camera flash units for wireless control

1. Turn on the off-camera flash unit, press the MODE button, and set the mode to RC. This stands for radio control, but it is not a radio system.
2. Press the Mode button again and select the same channel that you set in the Wireless Channel menu in the camera.
3. While the channel is blinking, press the left cursor button on the flash (marked with the LED icon) to select the flash group (A, B, or C). This corresponds to the groups in the Wireless Setup menu in the camera.

Make sure the front of the base of the flash (use the LED for reference) points toward the commander flash on the camera. The flashes talk to each other via TTL and can determine how much power is needed to light your subject. Use the Wireless Setup menu in the camera to adjust the flash mode and exposure value for each group of off-camera flashes.

A note about wireless flash

Wireless (off-camera) flash allows you to take your photography, especially your portraits, to another level. I use it all the time, from assignment work to family functions. This chapter only scratches the surface of how to get the most out of your camera's ability to interface with off-camera flash units. The automatic TTL flash works very well in the GX7, but I want to challenge you to learn how to control your off-camera flash's power level manually. In the Wireless Setup menu, set the flash group's Firing mode to Manual. Now you can manually adjust the flash's power output by 1/3-stop increments, from full power down to 1/128 power.

Chapter 8 Assignments

Now that we have looked at the possibilities of shooting after dark, it's time to put it all to the test. These assignments cover the full range of shooting possibilities, both with flash and without. Let's get started.

How steady are your hands?

It's important to know just what your limits are in terms of handholding your camera and still getting sharp pictures. This will change depending on the focal length of the lens you are working with. Wider-angle lenses are more forgiving than telephoto lenses, so check this out for your longest and shortest lenses. Using a 14–42mm zoom as an example (GM1: 12–32mm), set your lens to 42mm (GM1: 32mm) and then, with the camera set to ISO 200 and the mode set to S, start taking pictures with lower and lower shutter speeds. Review each image on the LCD at a zoomed-in magnification to take note of when you start seeing visible camera shake in your images. It will probably be around 1/30 of a second for a 42mm lens.

Now do the same for the wide-angle setting on the lens. My limit is about 1/15 of a second. These shutter speeds are with the OIS feature turned off. Try it with and without OIS enabled to see just how slow you can set your shutter while getting sharp results.

Pushing your ISO to the extreme

Find a place to shoot where the ambient light level is low. This could be at night or indoors in a darkened room. Adjust the noise reduction in your preferred photo style to –5. Using the mode of your choice, start increasing the ISO from 100 until you get to 25600. Make sure you evaluate the level of noise in your image, especially in the shadow areas. Only you can decide how much noise is acceptable in your pictures. I don't mind a little grain in my images, and I regularly shoot the GX7 and GM1 at ISOs of from 1600 to 3200.

Getting rid of the noise

Set the noise reduction back to 0 and repeat the previous assignment. Find your acceptable limits with the noise reduction turned on. Also pay attention to how much detail is lost in your shadows with this function enabled.

Long exposures in the dark

If you don't have a tripod, find a stable place to set your camera outside and try some long exposures. Turn off the Long Shutter NR in the Rec menu. Set your camera to A mode, and then use the self-timer to activate the camera (this will keep you from shaking the camera while pressing the shutter button).

Shoot in an area that has some level of ambient light, be it a streetlight, traffic lights, or even a full moon. The idea is to get some late-night, low-light exposures.

Reducing the noise in your long exposures

Now repeat the last assignment with the Long Shutter NR set to On. Look at the difference in the images that were taken before and after the noise reduction was enabled. For best results, perform this assignment and the previous assignment in the same shooting session using the same subject.

Testing the limits of the pop-up flash

Wait for the lights to get low and then press that pop-up flash button to start using the built-in flash. Try using the different shooting modes to see how they affect your exposures. Use the flash compensation feature to take a series of pictures while adjusting from –2 stops all the way to +2 stops so that you become familiar with how much latitude you will get from this feature.

Getting the red out

Find a friend with some patience and a tolerance for bright lights. Have them sit in a darkened room or outside at night and then take their picture with the flash. Now turn on Red-Eye Reduction to see if you get better results. Try Slow-Sync Red-Eye Reduction mode to see the difference.

Getting creative with 2nd Curtain Sync

Now it's time for a little creative fun. Set your camera up for 2nd Curtain Sync and start shooting. Moving targets are best. Experiment with S and A modes to lower the shutter speeds and exaggerate the effect. Try using a low ISO so the camera is forced to use longer shutter speeds. Be creative and have some fun!

Share your results with the book's Flickr group!
Join the group here: flickr.com/groups/panasonicGX7_fromsnapshotstogreatshots

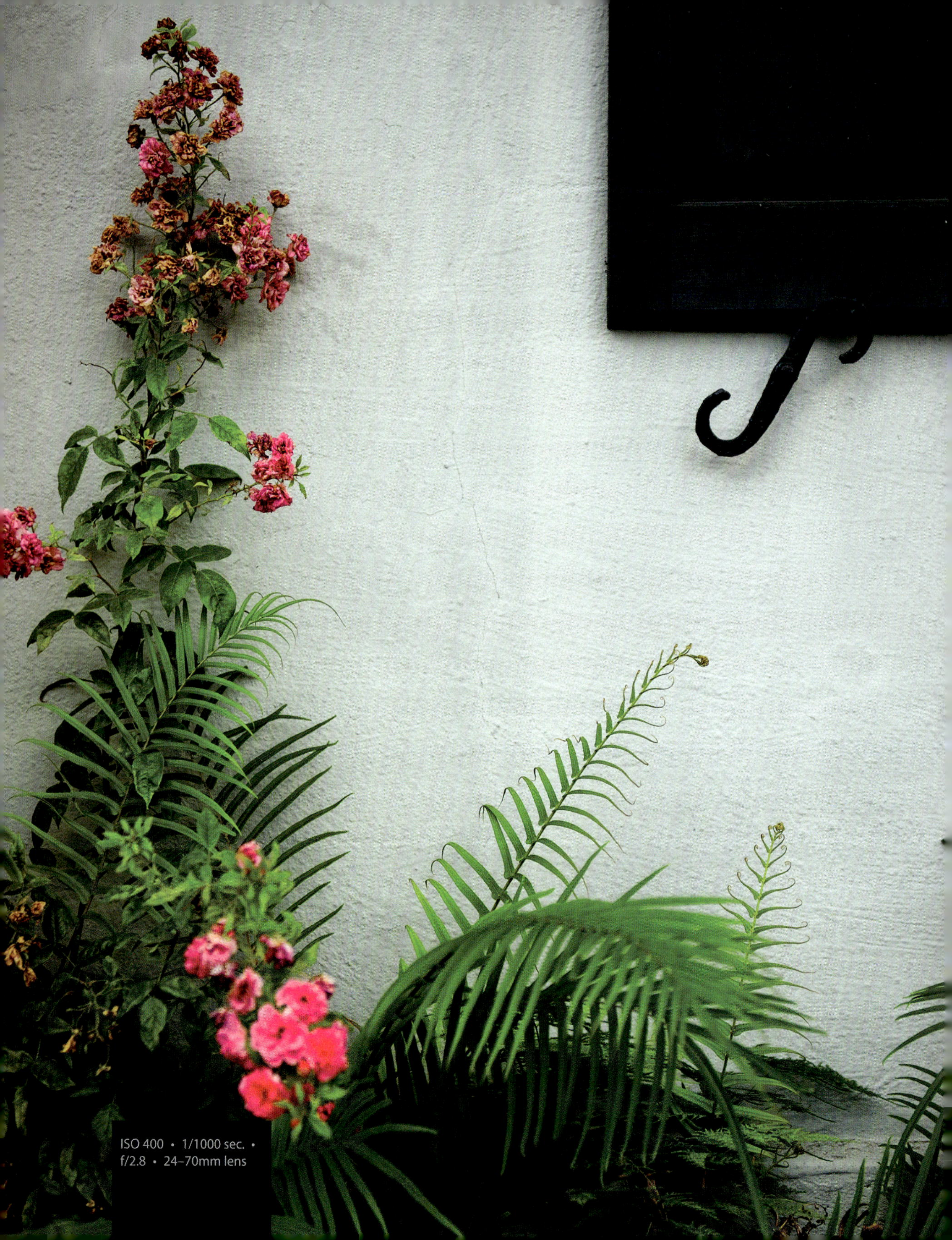

ISO 400 • 1/1000 sec. • f/2.8 • 24–70mm lens

9

Creative Compositions

Improve Your Pictures with Sound Compositional Elements

Creating a great photograph takes more than just using the right settings on your camera. To take your photography to the next level, you need to gain an understanding of how the elements within the frame come together to create a compositionally pleasing image. Composition is the culmination of light, shape, and, to borrow a word from iconic photographer Jay Maisel, gesture. Composition is a way for you to pull your viewing audience into your image and guide them through the scene. Let's examine some common compositional elements you can use to add interest to your photos.

Poring Over the Picture

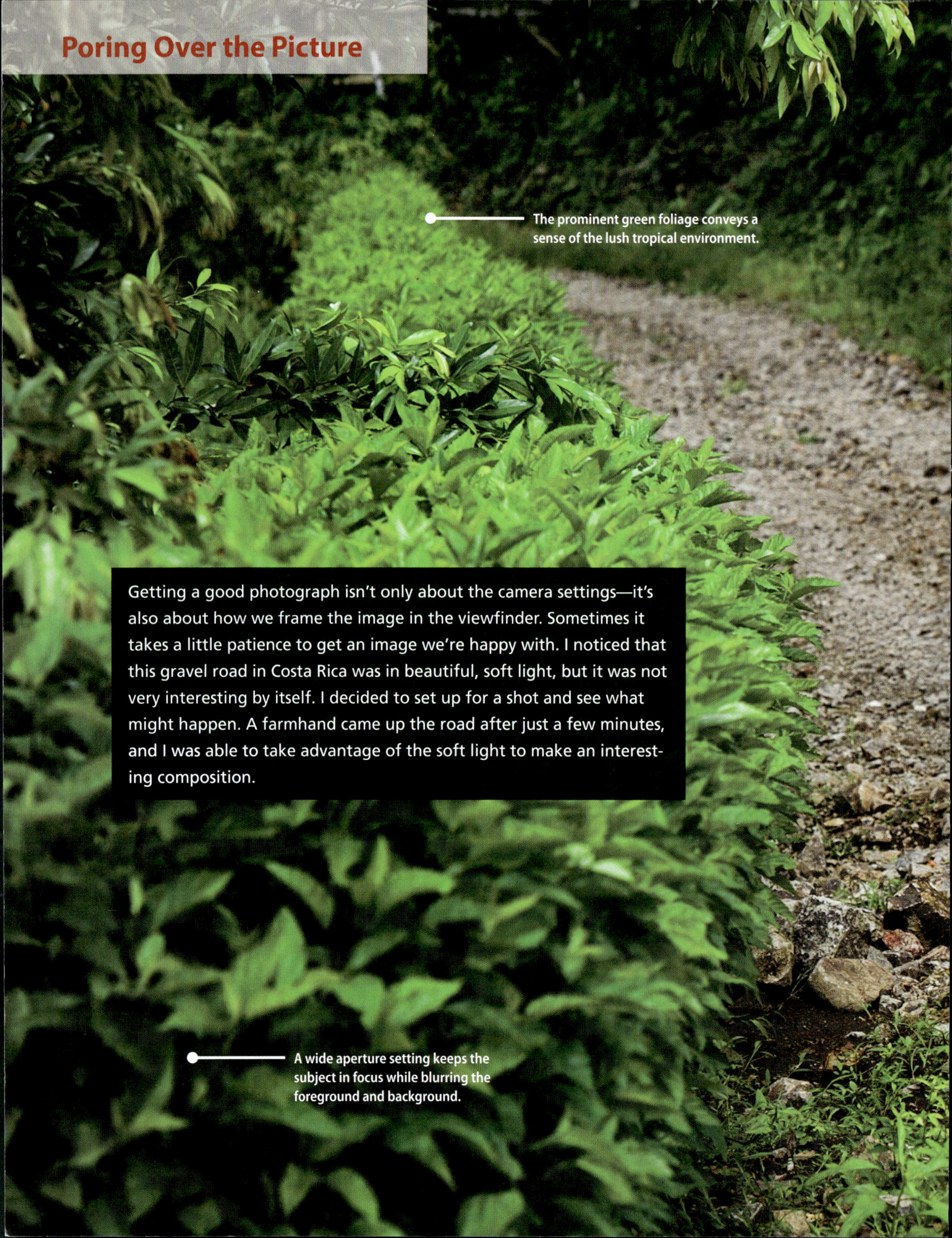

The prominent green foliage conveys a sense of the lush tropical environment.

Getting a good photograph isn't only about the camera settings—it's also about how we frame the image in the viewfinder. Sometimes it takes a little patience to get an image we're happy with. I noticed that this gravel road in Costa Rica was in beautiful, soft light, but it was not very interesting by itself. I decided to set up for a shot and see what might happen. A farmhand came up the road after just a few minutes, and I was able to take advantage of the soft light to make an interesting composition.

A wide aperture setting keeps the subject in focus while blurring the foreground and background.

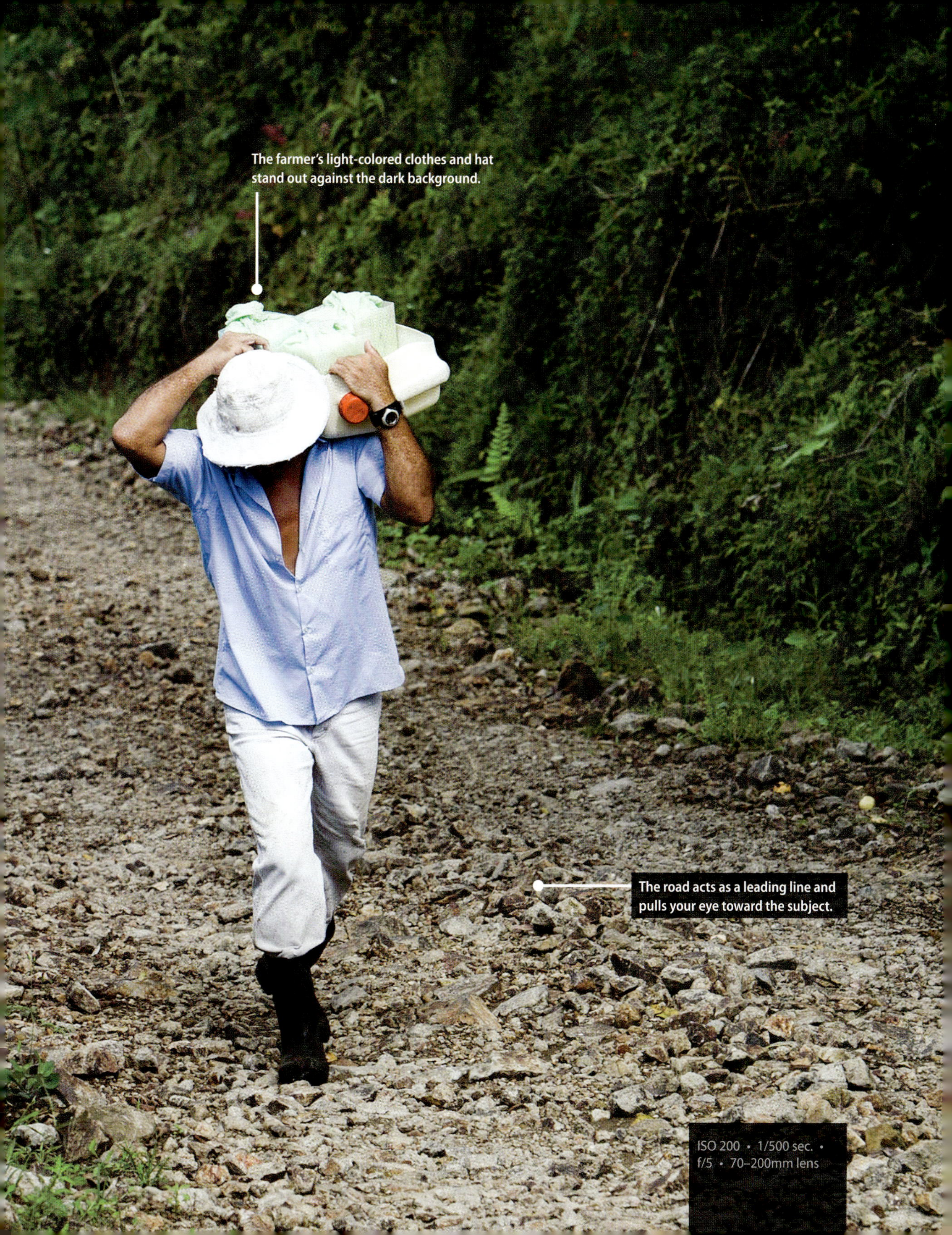
The farmer's light-colored clothes and hat stand out against the dark background.
The road acts as a leading line and pulls your eye toward the subject.
ISO 200 • 1/500 sec. • f/5 • 70–200mm lens

Depth of Field

Long focal lengths and large apertures allow you to isolate your subject from a busy background. I use Aperture Priority (A) mode for the majority of my shooting so I can easily control the depth of field in my images. A telephoto lens helps to shrink the depth of field to a very narrow area (**Figure 9.1**).

The blurred background directs the viewer's eye toward the sharper, in-focus areas, which gives greater emphasis to the subject.

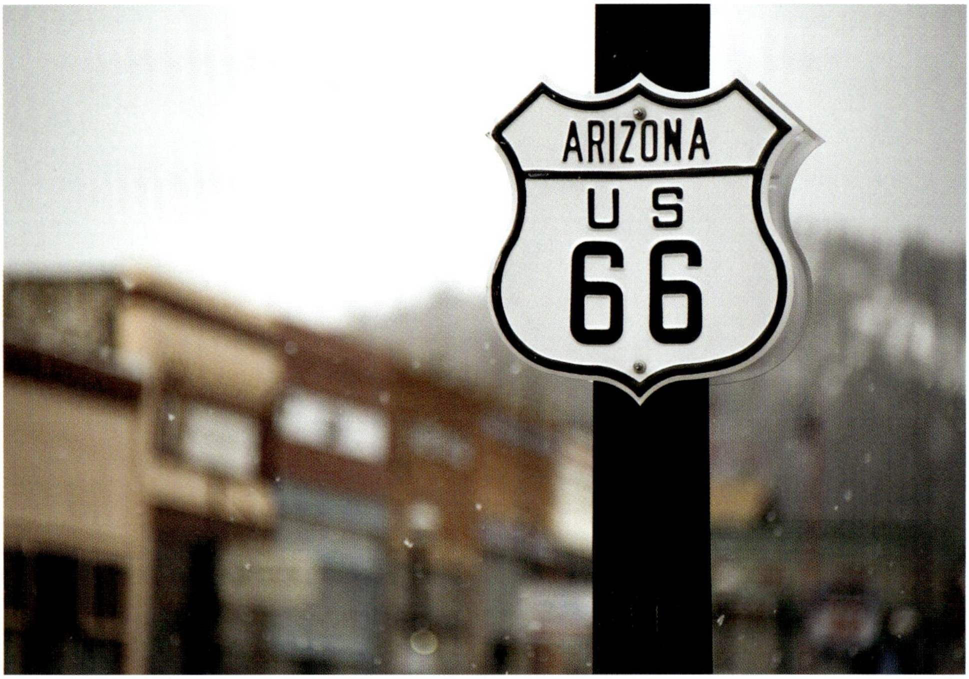

Figure 9.1
A large aperture can create a shallow depth of field to isolate the subject.
ISO 400 • 1/800 sec. • f/5.6 • 28–300mm lens

Sometimes a greater depth of field is required to maintain sharp focus across a greater distance. This might be due to the sheer depth of your subject, where you have objects that are near the camera but sharpness is desired at a greater distance as well (**Figure 9.2**).

Or perhaps you are photographing a reflection in a puddle or another smooth, calm water surface. With a narrow depth of field, you will only be able to get either the reflected object or the surface in focus. By making the aperture smaller, you will be able to maintain acceptable sharpness in both areas (**Figure 9.3**).

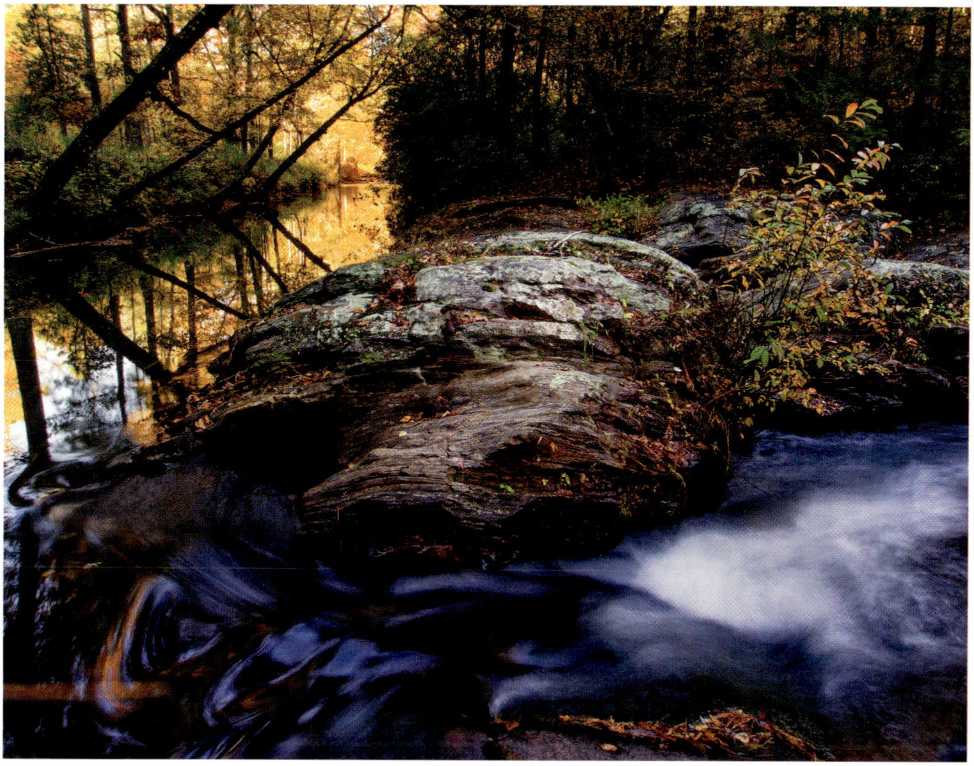

Figure 9.2
Using a smaller aperture allowed me to focus on the foreground elements and keep the background sharp as well. Wide-angle lenses are also useful in achieving greater depth of field.

ISO 200 • 1 sec. • f/16 • 9–18mm lens

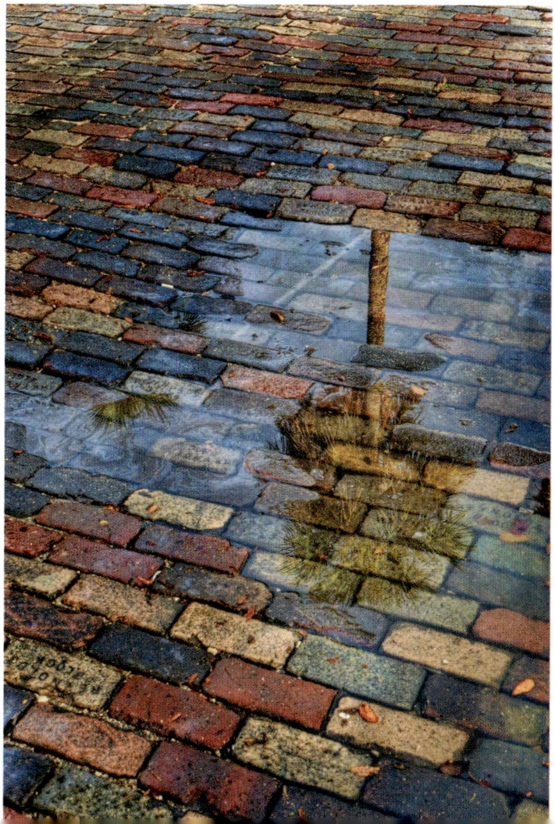

Figure 9.3
Getting a distant subject in focus in a reflection, along with the reflective surface itself, requires a small aperture.

ISO 200 • 1/60 sec. • f/16 • 24–70mm lens

Photographing reflections

A mirror is a two-dimensional surface, so why do you have to focus at a different distance for the image in the mirror? The answer is pretty simple, and it has to do with light. When you focus your lens, you are focusing on the light being reflected off a surface onto your camera sensor. So if you wanted to focus on the mirror itself, it would be at one distance, but if you wanted to focus on the subject being reflected, you would have to take into account the distance that the object is from the mirror. Remember that the light from the subject has to travel all the way to the mirror and then to your lens. This is why a smaller aperture can be required when shooting reflected subjects. Sit in your car and take a few shots of objects in the sideview mirrors to see what I mean.

Angles

Having strong angular lines in your image can add to the composition, especially when they are juxtaposed to each other (**Figure 9.4**). This can create a tension that is different from the standard horizontal and vertical lines that we are so accustomed to seeing in photos.

Point of View

Sometimes the easiest way to influence your photographs is to simply change your perspective. Instead of always shooting from a standing position, try moving your camera to a place where you normally would not see your subject. Try holding the camera over your head, getting down on your knees, or even lying on the ground. The tilting LCD and EVF on the GX7 make it easy to compose photos from many different angles. A different point of view can completely change how you view your subject and can create a new interest in common subjects (**Figure 9.5**).

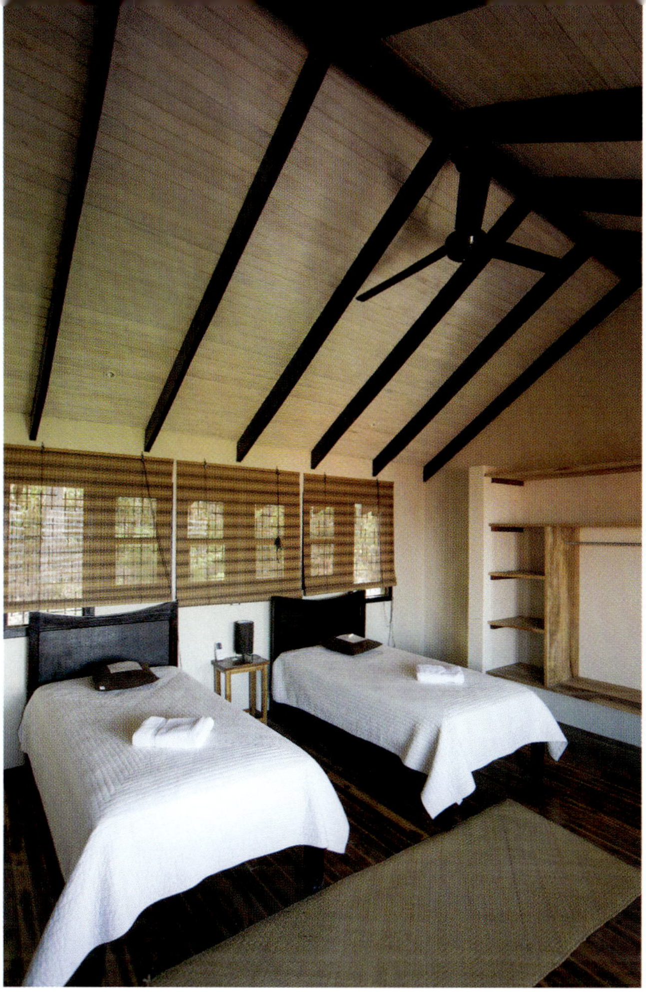

Figure 9.4

The strong diagonal lines of the ceiling beams contrast with the center beam and the angle of the windows to create a dynamic composition.

ISO 400 • 1/13 sec. • f/8 • 7–14mm lens

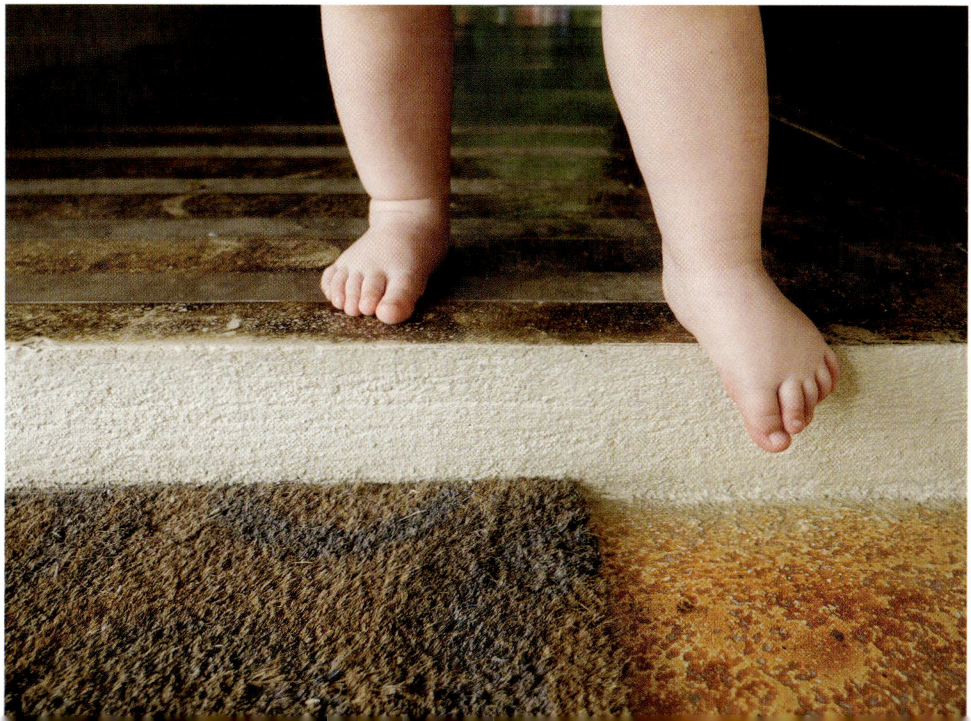

Figure 9.5

Put your camera into a position that presents an unfamiliar view of your subject.

ISO 320 • 1/60 sec. • f/2.8 • 12–35mm lens

Patterns

Rhythm and balance can be added to your images by finding the patterns in everyday life and concentrating on the elements that rely on geometric influences. Try to find the balance and patterns that often go unnoticed (**Figure 9.6**).

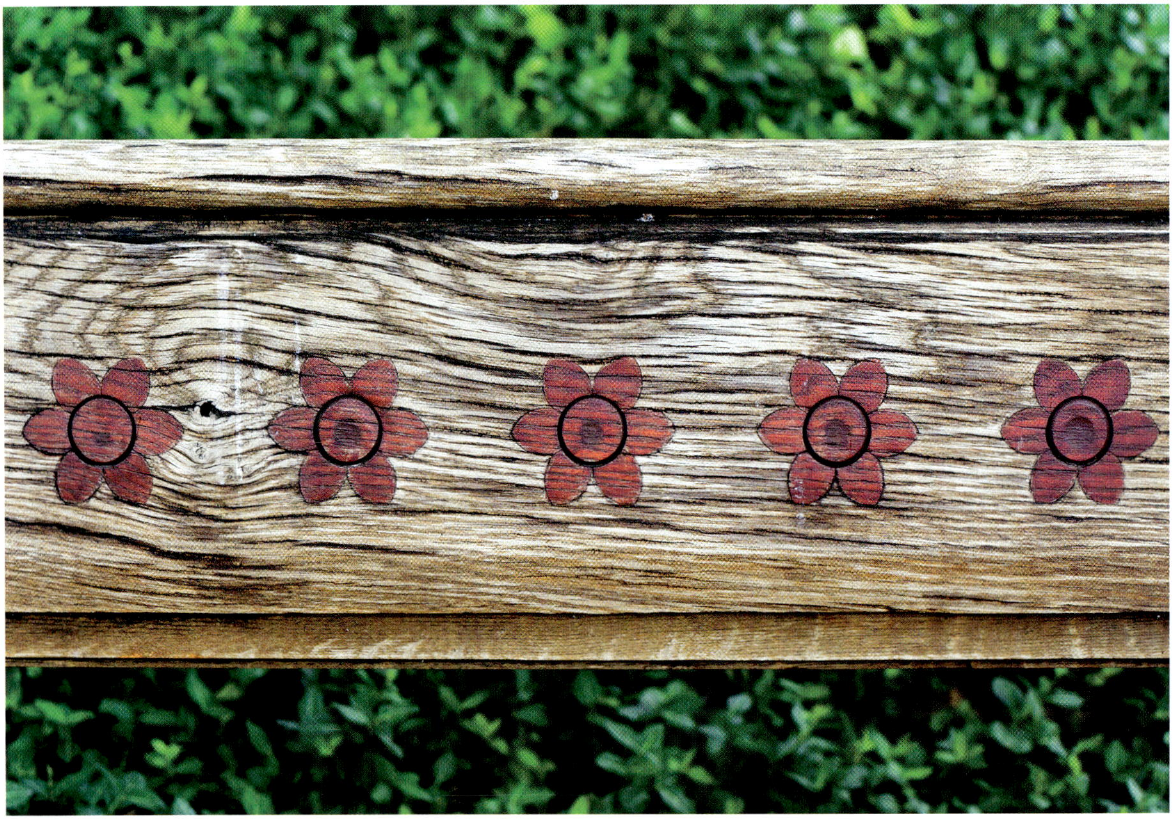

Figure 9.6 **Pay attention to small details. This simple graphic composition incorporates the repeating flower pattern, along with contrasting warm and cool colors.**

ISO 800 • 1/100 sec. • f/5.6 • 70–300mm lens

Color

Color works well as a tool for composition when you have very saturated colors to work with. Some of the best colors are those within the primary palette. Reds, greens, and blues, along with their complementary colors (cyan, magenta, and yellow), can all be used to create visual tension. This tension between bright colors will add visual excitement, drama, and complexity to your images when combined with other compositional elements.

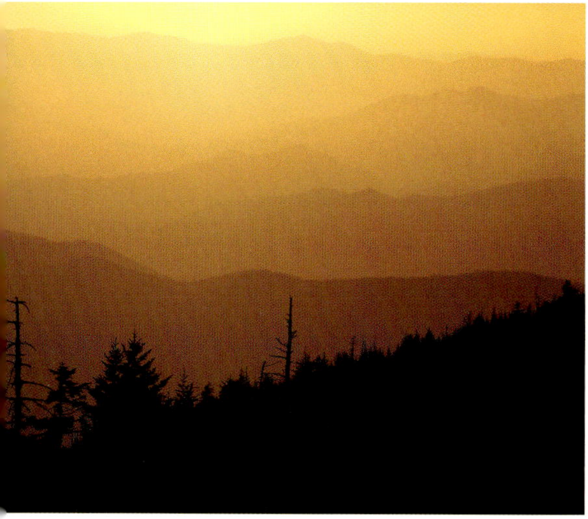

Figure 9.7 **The oranges and yellows in this sunset give the viewer a sense of warmth, even though it was about 30 degrees when I made this shot.**

ISO 200 • 1/800 sec. • f/8 • 35–100mm lens

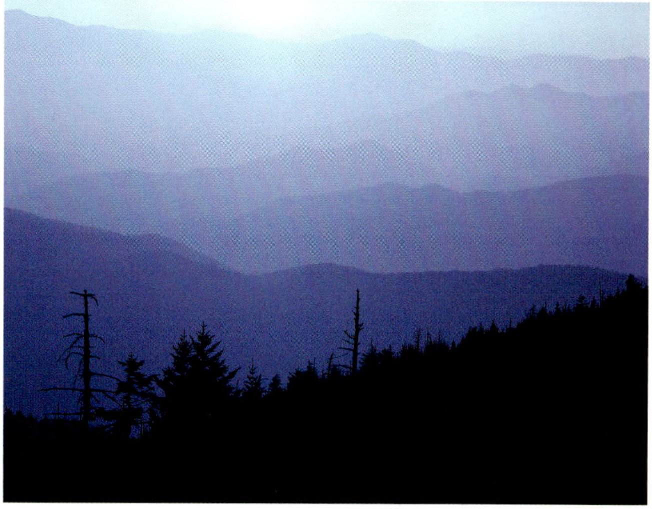

Figure 9.8 **Here's the same shot with the white balance adjusted from yellow to blue. I think this looks more like a sunrise, and it conveys the feeling of the cold weather I was shooting in.**

ISO 200 • 1/800 sec. • f/8 • 35–100mm lens

These two images are the same except for the white balance (**Figures 9.7** and **9.8**). Do you think one looks like a sunset and the other looks like a sunrise? The color in an image can change the mood of the photo or even the time of day. Sometimes it's important to capture the correct colors in a scene, but sometimes it's fun to get creative with color to tell a different story.

Contrast

We just saw that you can use color as a strong compositional tool. One of the most effective uses of color is to combine two contrasting colors that make the eye move back and forth across the image (**Figure 9.9**). There is no exact combination that will work best, but consider using dark and light colors, like red and green or blue and yellow, to provide the strongest contrasts.

You can also introduce contrast through different geometric shapes that battle (in a good way) for the attention of the viewer. You can combine circles and triangles, ovals and rectangles, curvy and straight, hard and soft, dark and light, and so many other elements (**Figure 9.10**). You aren't limited to just one contrasting element either. Combining more than one element of contrast will add even more interest. Look for these contrasting combinations whenever you are out shooting, and then use them to shake up your compositions.

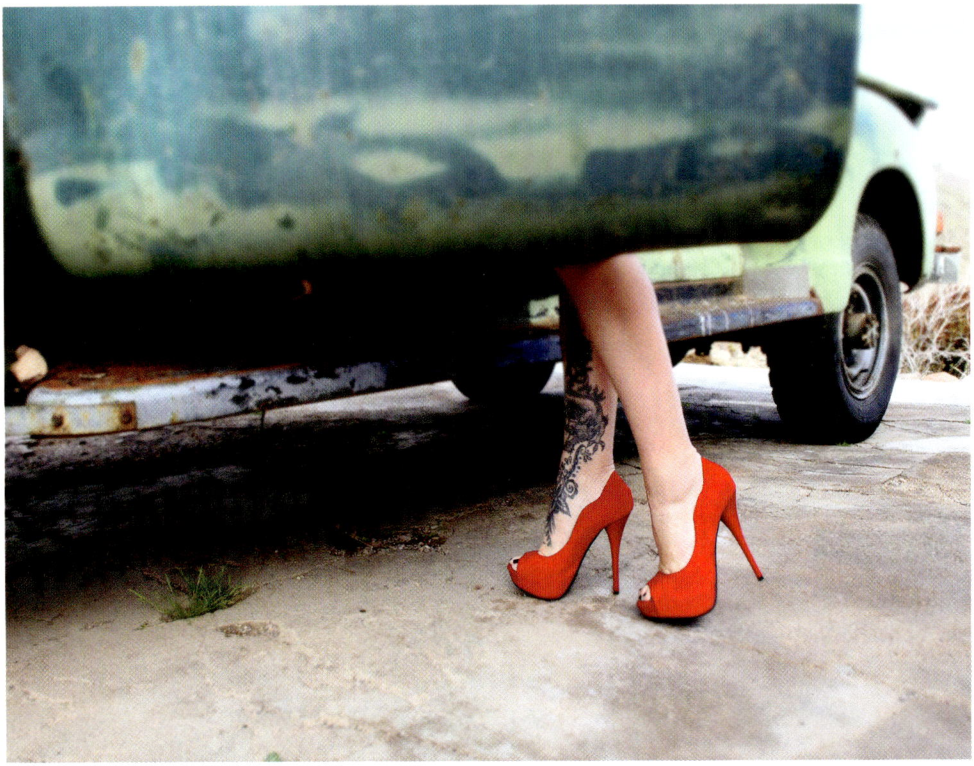

Figure 9.9
The red shoes stand out dramatically from the green truck. The dark green on the truck's door visually recedes, even though it is actually in front of brighter red shoes.

ISO 400 • 1/200 sec. • f/8 • 12mm lens

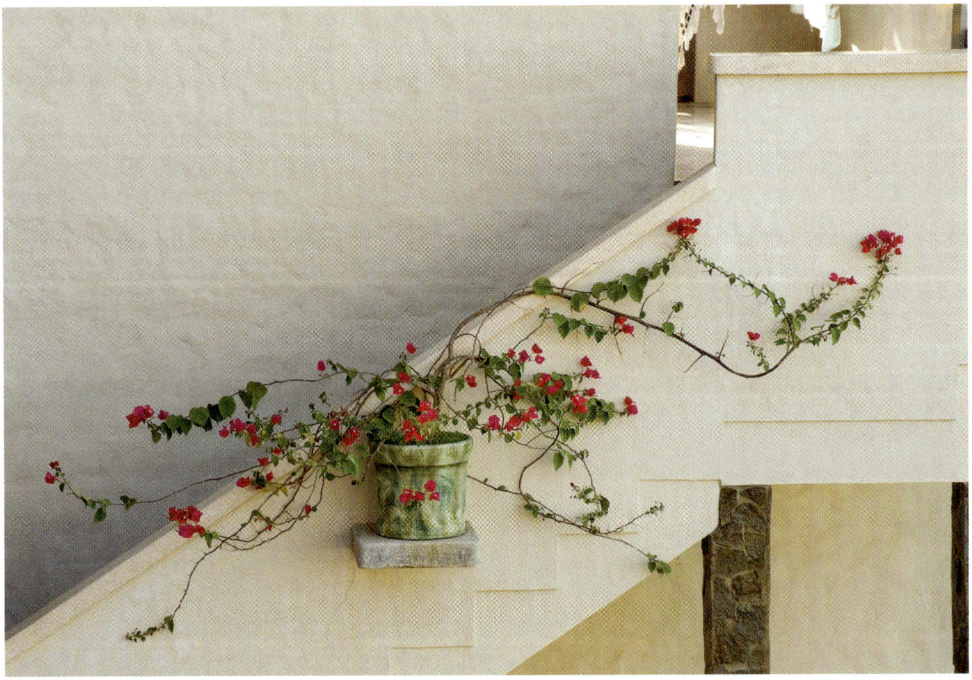

Figure 9.10
There are several contrasts at work in this image. The straight lines of the building contrast with the organic shapes of the plant, and the monochromatic background contrasts with the bright flowers in the foreground.

ISO 400 • 1/200 sec. • f/8 • 70–300mm lens

Leading Lines

One way to pull a viewer into your image is to incorporate leading lines. Sometimes these are elements that come from the edge of the frame and lead into the image toward the main subject (**Figure 9.11**). At other times, the lines may lead your eye from point to point within the image. This can be the result of vanishing perspective lines (which converge at what is commonly known as a vanishing point), an element such as a river, or some other feature that is used to move the eye toward the heart of the image.

Splitting the Frame

Generally speaking, splitting the frame right down the middle is not your best option. While it may seem more balanced, it can actually be pretty boring. You should utilize the rule of thirds when deciding how to divide your frame (**Figure 9.12**).

With horizons, a low horizon will give a sense of stability to the image. Typically, this is done when the sky is more appealing than the landscape below. When the emphasis is to be placed on the landscape, the horizon line should be moved upward in the frame, leaving the bottom two-thirds to the subject.

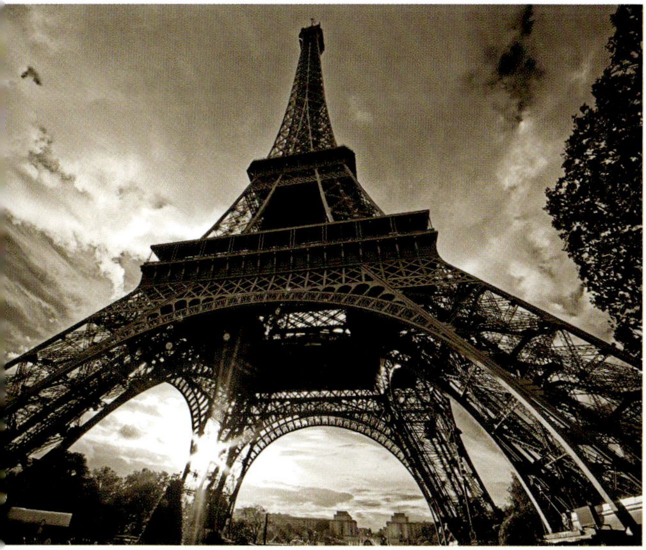

Figure 9.11 Sometimes leading lines are very literal, like in this shot of the Eiffel Tower. The legs of the tower pull your eye into the photo and up to the top of the tower.

ISO 100 • 1/15 sec. • f/22 • 10–22mm lens

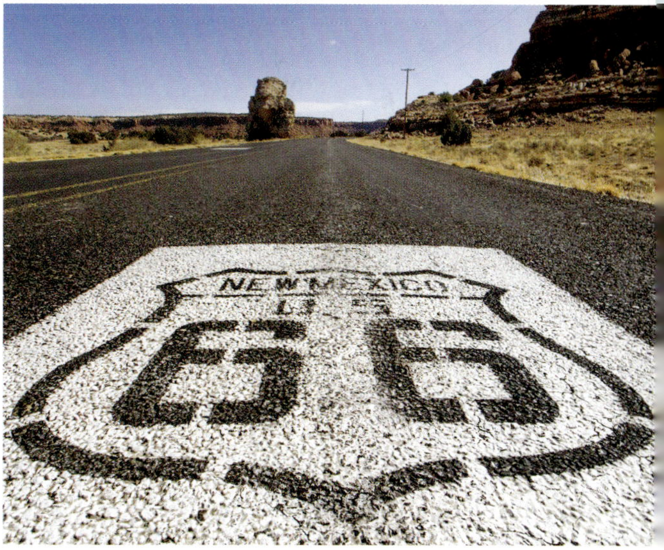

Figure 9.12 The boring sky is minimized by placing the horizon toward the upper third of the frame, driving more attention to the subject in the foreground.

ISO 200 • 1/1250 sec. • f/8 • 12mm lens

Frames Within Frames

Along with looking for leading lines, unique angles, and patterns, search for mechanisms in the composition that can visually frame your primary subject matter. Frames are useful when you want to drive attention toward a specific person, thing, or area in the photograph (**Figure 9.13**).

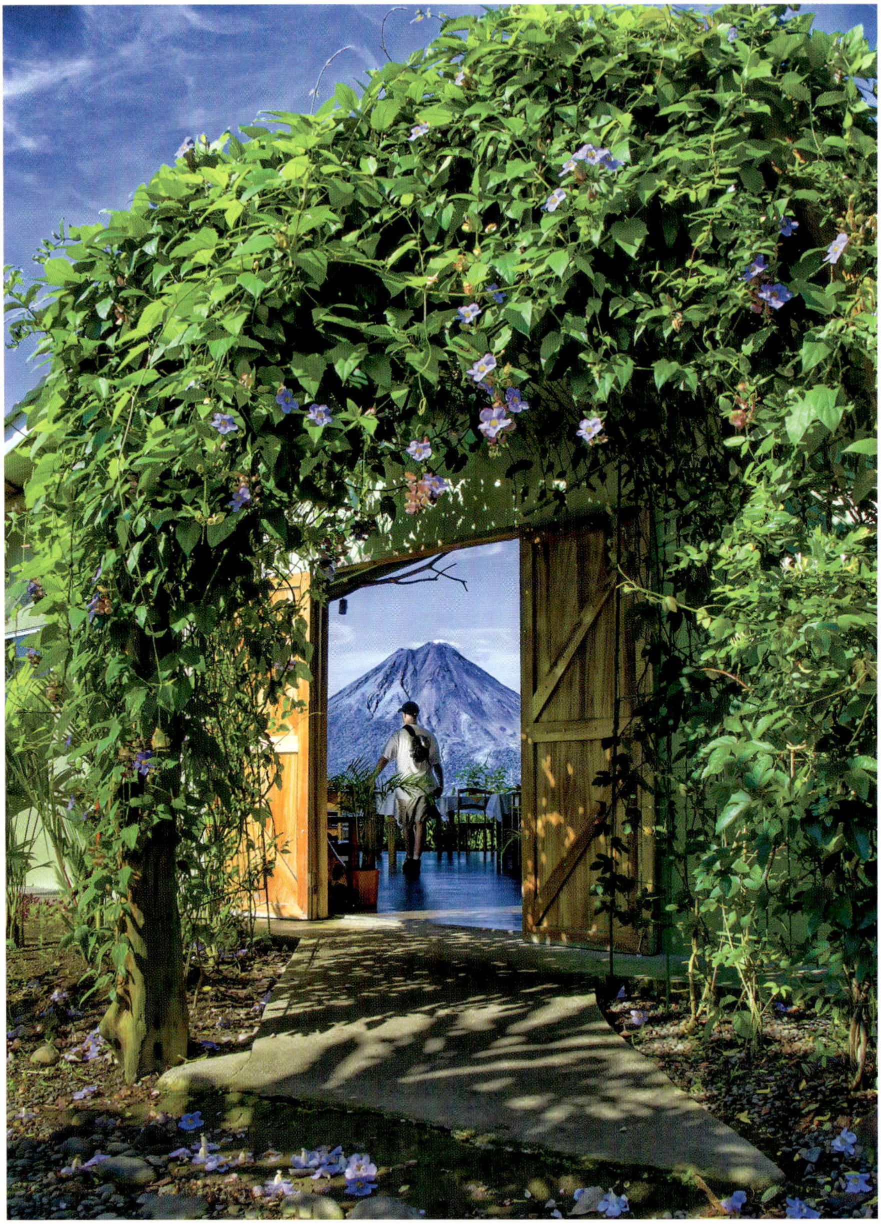

Figure 9.13
There are lots of frames within this frame. The flowers frame the door, which frames the volcano, which frames the man at the table.

ISO 1600 • 1/640 sec. • f/8 • 28–300mm lens

Focal Length and Composition

Different focal lengths provide various ways of seeing composition in a single environment. Wide-angle lenses accentuate the distance between the elements in a photo and help create a sense of depth (**Figure 9.14**). Telephoto focal lengths achieve the exact opposite, compressing foreground and background and making the elements seem closer together. This can be useful for creating patterns out of the landscape (**Figure 9.15** on the next page) or for depicting density in a crowd.

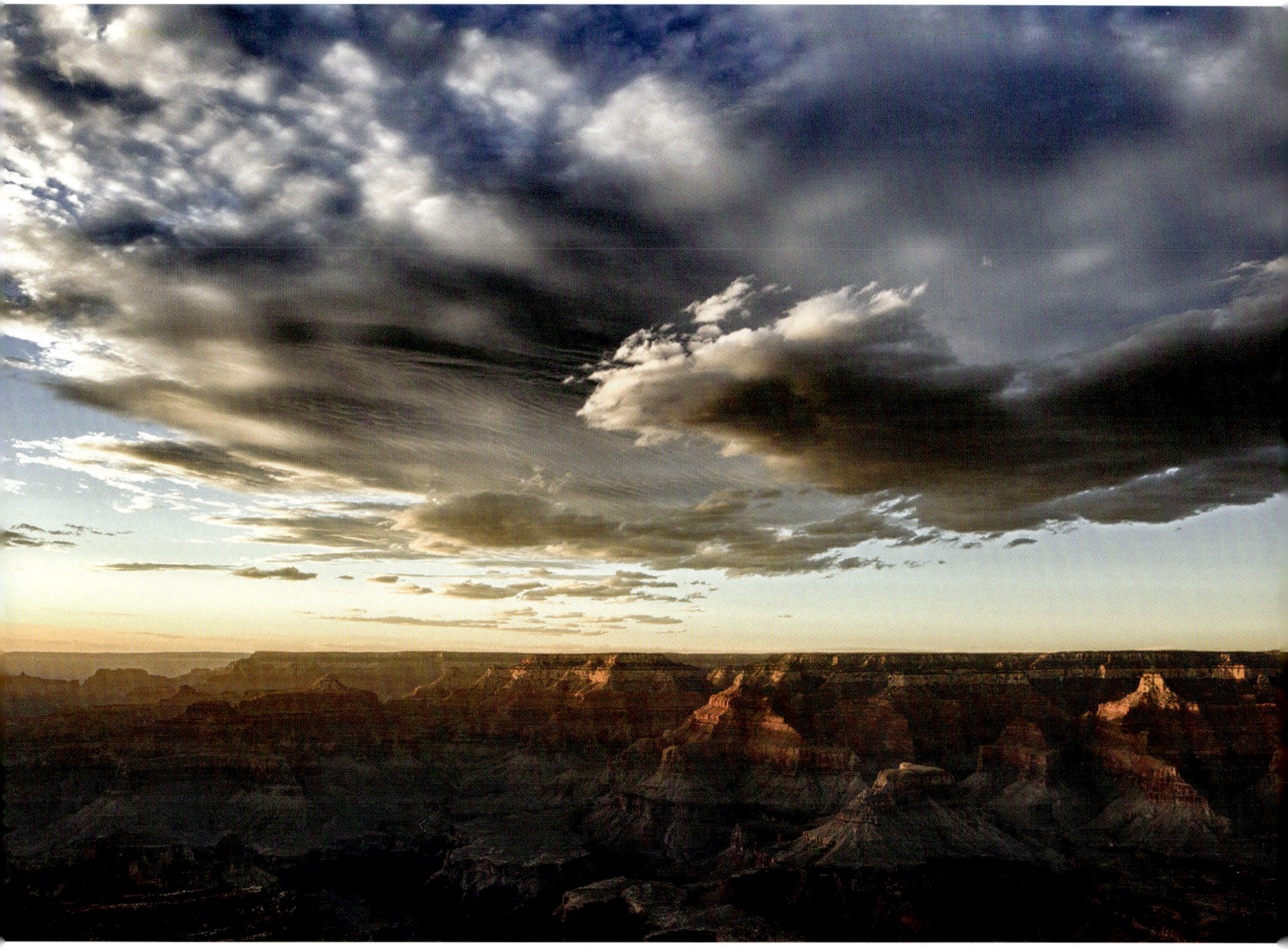

Figure 9.14 **The wide focal length creates a sense of depth and scale in this image of the Grand Canyon.**

ISO 200 • 1/40 sec. • f/16 • 24mm lens

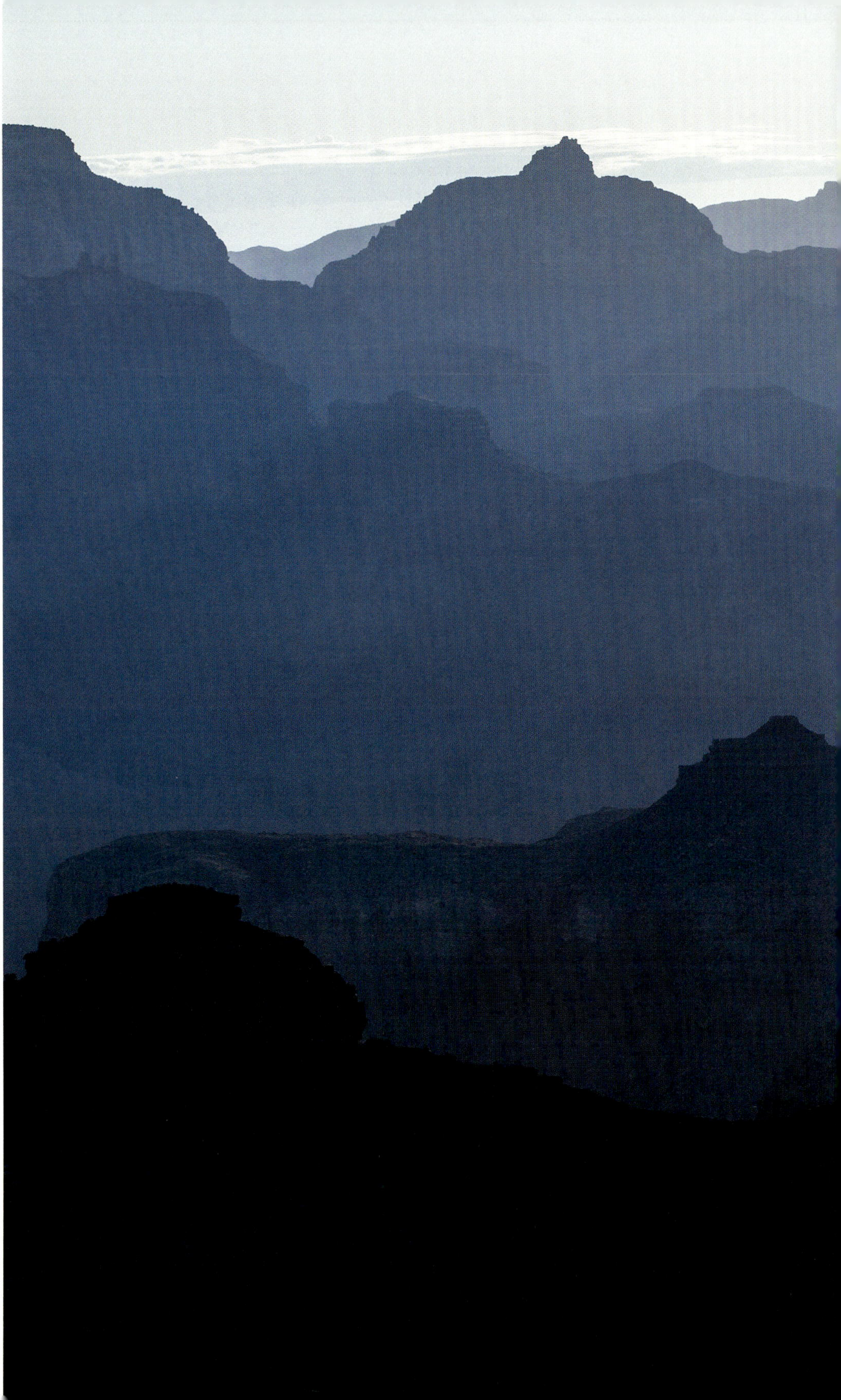

Figure 9.15
I used a telephoto lens in this frame to limit the sense of depth and compress the layers of the canyon into a much more graphic composition.

ISO 200 • 1/640 sec. • f/8 • 70–300mm lens

Chapter 9 Assignments

If you apply the shooting techniques and tools that you have learned in the previous chapters to these assignments, you'll improve your ability to incorporate good composition into your photos. Make sure you experiment with all the different elements of composition and see how you can combine them to add interest to your images. A great shot will usually illustrate more than one of these compositional ideas.

Learning to see lines and patterns

Take your camera for a walk around your neighborhood and look for patterns and angles. Don't worry as much about getting great shots as about developing an eye for details.

The ABCs of composition

Here's a great exercise that Vincent Versace suggests for those looking to advance their compositional vision: shoot the alphabet. This will be a little more difficult, but with practice you will start to see beyond the obvious. Don't just find letters in street signs and the like—instead, find objects that aren't really letters but that have the shape of letters.

Finding the square peg and the round hole

Circles, squares, and triangles. Spend a few sessions concentrating on shooting simple geometric shapes. Pick one shape to focus on for each session.

Using the aperture to focus attention

Depth of field plays an important role in defining your images and establishing depth and dimension. Practice shooting using your largest aperture for a shallow depth of field. Then find a scene that would benefit from extended depth of field, and use a very small aperture to give sharpness throughout the scene.

Leading them into a frame

Look for scenes where you can use elements as leading lines, and then look for framing elements that you can use to isolate your subject and add both depth and dimension to your images.

Share your results with the book's Flickr group!
Join the group here: flickr.com/groups/panasonicGX7_fromsnapshotstogreatshots

ISO 400 • 1/800 sec. • f/4.8 • 70–300mm lens

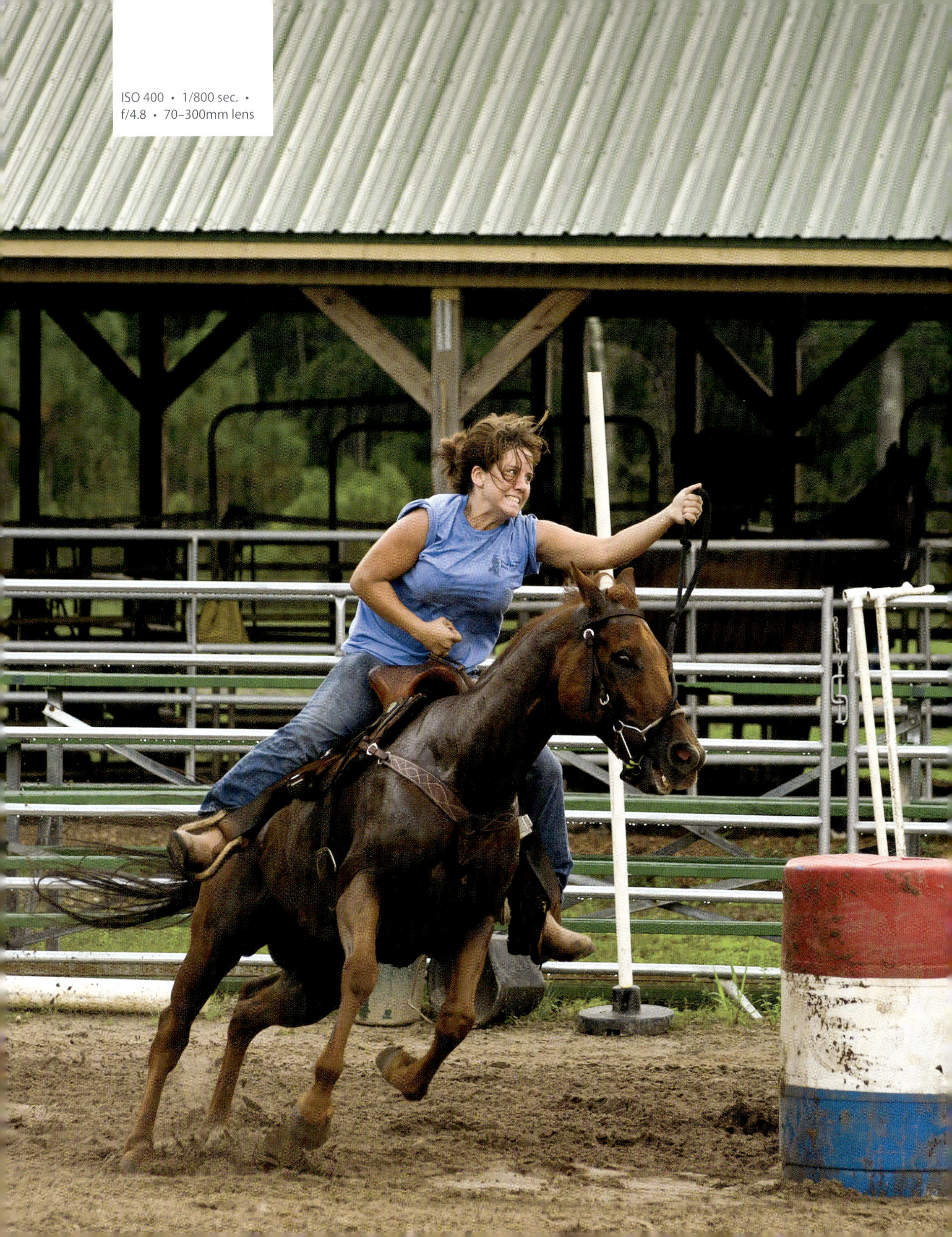

10

Lights, Camera, Action!

Getting Professional-looking Video from Your LUMIX camera

One of the reasons you purchased the GX7 or GM1 might have been its ability to capture HD video. Lumix cameras are known for their excellent video quality, and the GX7 and GM1 are no exception. Video capture is not just for moviemakers. Many photographers are blending video and still photography to create more interesting and engaging ways to display their work. I'll cover the basic settings you need to know to start capturing great video with your Lumix camera, and I'll give you some ideas for editing and sharing your videos.

Video recording is a feature you can access at any time by simply pressing the red Motion Picture button; it's behind the shutter button on the GX7 (**Figure 10.1**) and on the upper right of the back panel on the GM1. No matter what LCD display mode you are using, press the Motion Picture button once to start recording and then press it again to stop. Once Movie mode is active, the camera will focus on the focus point in your frame if it is set to autofocus.

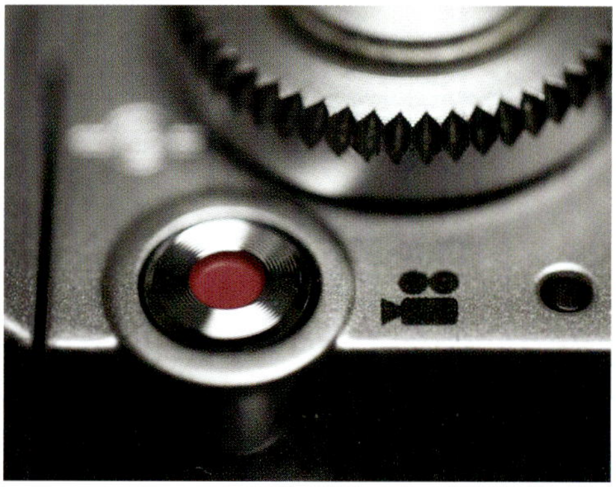

Figure 10.1 The Motion Picture button on the GX7, easily accessible with your right index finger

When the camera begins recording, there will be a flashing red dot in the upper-right corner of the LCD. The duration of the video clip in minutes and seconds appears on the upper left to let you know that the camera is in active record mode. The available recording time is shown in the lower-right corner.

Your video will be recorded in Program Auto (P) mode unless the Mode dial is set to Creative Video mode (the movie camera icon). Any exposure compensation setting will carry over from your still shooting. Your JPEG settings—like photo style, Highlight/Shadow, i.Dynamic, and i.Resolution—will stay the same when you switch from stills to video. This is a handy feature if you plan to combine video clips with your still images, because everything will match right out of the camera.

Framing your video

When the camera is in any mode but Creative Video, the EVF (GX7 only) and LCD will display the image in whatever aspect ratio you have set for still photos (4:3, 3:2, 16:9, or 1:1). Your video will be recorded in 16:9 no matter what aspect ratio the camera is set to, and the screen will change to reflect that (**Figure 10.2**). It can be a bit jarring to see your screen jump from 4:3 to 16:9 when you press the Motion Picture button. Keep in mind that your screen will be "letter-boxed" when you switch from stills to video. If the switch is too distracting, change the monitor to show the 16:9 video frame by pressing Menu/Set > Custom > Rec Area and choosing Motion Picture.

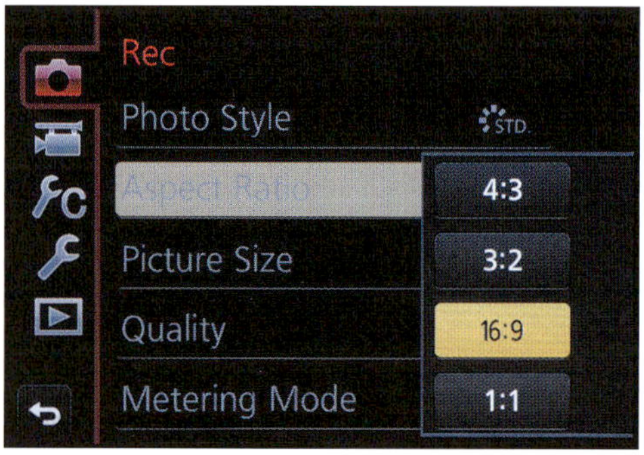

Figure 10.2 Your GX7/GM1 records video in the 16:9 aspect ratio.

Creative Control modes for video

Remember all of those cool Creative Control filter effects in Chapter 3? We can apply most of those effects to motion pictures as well. To record a video with creative control filters, simply set up the filter you want in Creative Control mode and then press the motion picture button. Maybe you want to shoot a classic car—use the Old Days filter to give your video a vintage look. You can create your own film noir by using one of the black-and-white settings. The great thing about using the creative control filters is that you will see the effect right on your LCD screen as you record, so you will know exactly what your video is going to look like. Keep in mind that ISO, white balance, and exposure will be set to auto, but you can still use exposure compensation for video.

Format, Size, and Frame Rate

The GX7 and GM1 have two video formats to choose from. According to Panasonic, AVCHD is the best choice if you plan to view your video on an HDTV, and MP4 is best for viewing on a PC. The video quality between the two should be very similar. MP4 files are self contained and easy to drag and drop onto your computer, whereas AVCHD files are easier to deal with if you're importing them into video editing software. AVCHD files are smaller than MP4 files, so you can fit more video on your memory card when you use the AVCHD format. Each format offers multiple choices for video size and frame rate.

Recording quality

You will find the options for video size and frame rate in the Rec Quality tab in the Motion Picture menu. The choices vary depending on whether you're using AVCHD or MP4, and the monitor will display a description of the settings as you scroll through them (**Figure 10.3**). The first numbers you see will be the video dimensions in pixels, such as 1920x1080. The second number is the frame rate, or how many frames of video will be captured per second. For example, 60p means sixty frames per second with progressive scanning (see the "Progressive scan" sidebar). The last number you see is the bit rate in megabits per second (Mbps).

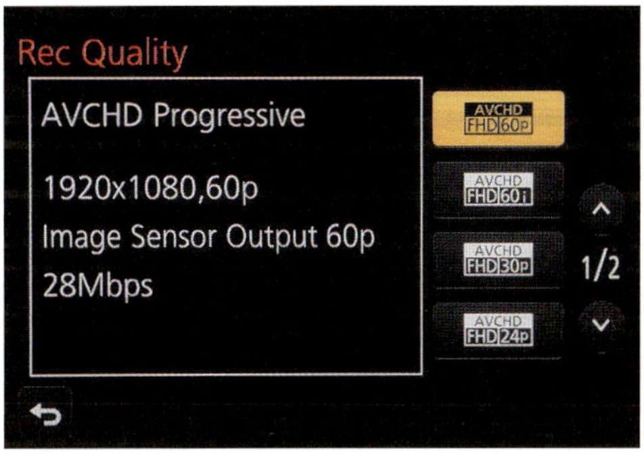

Figure 10.3 The monitor displays the size, frame rate, and bit rate for each video setting.

Let's start with the AVCHD format. The GX7 and GM1 will capture AVCHD video in two sizes: 1280x720 (HD) and 1920x1080 (Full HD). You can capture HD video in 60p, and Full HD video in 60p, 30p, or 24p. The GX7 also has the option Full HD 60i.

Both cameras will capture MP4 video in three sizes. The GM1 captures Full HD video at 30p, HD video at 30p, and VGA video (640x480) at 30p. The GX7 has the same options, plus Full HD 60p. If you are recording for the Internet or standard-definition TV, you might consider using the VGA resolution. The benefit of VGA is that it requires less physical storage since it contains a smaller pixel count. This means that you will fit more video on your storage card, and it will take less time to upload the video to the Internet.

I use AVCHD Full HD 24p for most of the video that I shoot because 24p video has a cinematic look that I like for my nature and travel videos. I also use Full HD 60p when I'm shooting subjects like wildlife. The higher frame rate captures fast-moving subjects more clearly, and it makes smooth slow motion footage when you slow it down in your editing software.

Flicker Decrease

It is common practice to set your shutter speed to twice the frame rate to replicate the characteristic look of a film movie camera. For 24p video, that means setting the shutter speed to 1/50 of a second for a smooth, cinematic look. You can set your shutter speed higher for a more staccato look (think *Saving Private Ryan*), or lower for more motion blur. Whatever shutter speed you choose, it is a good idea to use the same shutter speed for an entire project so that all the video clips have the same feel.

You can use the Flicker Decrease function to control your shutter speed when you are not using Creative Video mode. Navigate to Flkr Decrease in the Motion Picture menu, and select a shutter speed that is twice the frame rate you are using (**Figure 10.4**). Now when you press the Motion Picture button you will know that your video will have a consistent shutter speed.

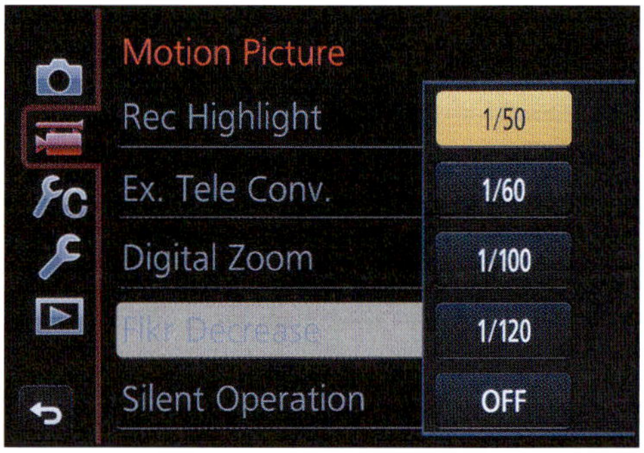

Figure 10.4 **The Flicker Decrease setting keeps your video looking consistent.**

Progressive scan

Two terms are associated with the quality of the video and how it is captured and displayed on a monitor/screen: progressive and interlaced. The two terms describe how the video is drawn per line for each frame. Video frames are not displayed all at once like a photograph. In progressive video, the lines are drawn in sequence from top to bottom. Interlaced video draws all of the odd-numbered lines and then all of the even-numbered lines. This odd-even drawing can present itself as screen flicker, which is why the progressive video standard is preferred, especially when viewing high-definition video. Even though you have the option of shooting interlaced video at 60 fps, I encourage you to stay with progressive video.

Setting the format and quality

1. To change the video format, press Menu/Set and select the Motion Picture menu.
2. Select Rec Format and choose AVCHD or MP4 (**A**).
3. Select Rec Quality in the Motion Picture menu to select the video size and frame rate (**B**).
4. Press the shutter button halfway to return to shooting.

A

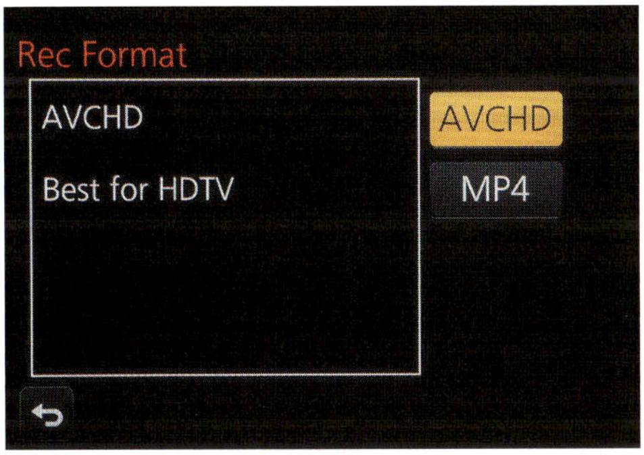

B

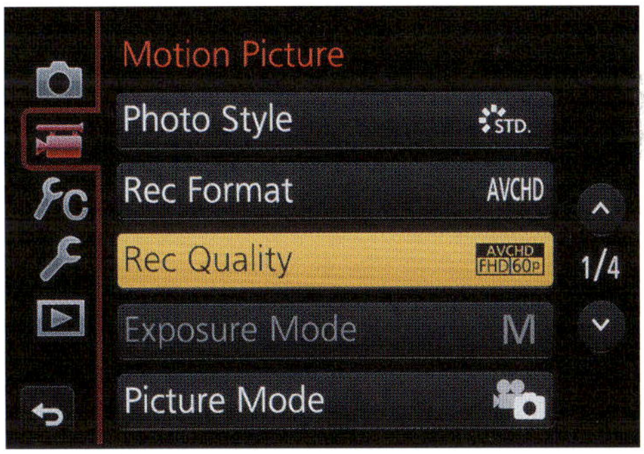

The format and recording quality settings you choose in the Motion Picture menu do not reset when you change modes or turn off the camera.

Focus Settings for Video

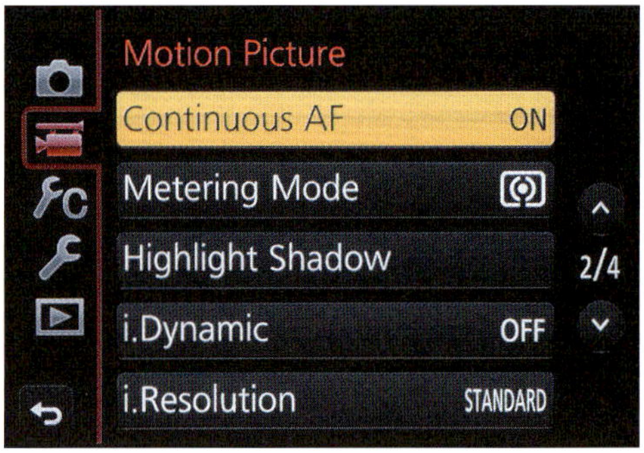

Figure 10.5 Use the Continuous AF setting in the Motion Picture menu to control autofocus for video recording.

The GX7 and GM1 have the same fast autofocus performance whether they are shooting still photos or videos. Use the touchscreen to choose your focus point for video just as you would if you were making a photo. All of the AF Area modes are available when recording a video, and Face Detection AF works extremely well. If you want to change the AF behavior for video, you use the Continuous AF setting in the Motion Picture menu (**Figure 10.5**).

With Continuous AF on, the camera will automatically adjust focus while it is recording. You can even touch the screen while you are shooting to change the focus point, and the camera will smoothly rack focus from one subject to another. With Continuous AF off, the focus is locked when you begin recording a video.

You can also manually focus for video recording by switching the Focus Mode lever to MF. Focus peaking is a very handy feature for manually focusing your videos. In fact, focus peaking is a feature that was originally developed for professional videography equipment. The MF Assist zoom feature works well to set your focus before shooting, but you probably wouldn't use it during video recording.

For stationary subjects I usually use manual focus, but I regularly use AF for video as well. Continuous AF can help you track a moving subject and keep it in focus. Continuous AF combined with Face Detection AF does a remarkable job when you are shooting people.

Creative Video Mode

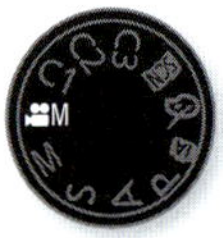

You can push the red Motion Picture button to record HD video with your GX7/GM1 no matter what mode the camera is in. The camera will record a movie with your format, size, and frame rate settings, but it will default to the Program Auto mode for exposure. If you want to take more control over your video, you need to switch the Mode dial to Creative Video mode.

There are a few settings in the Motion Picture menu that only apply in Creative Video mode. Press Menu/Set and select the Motion Picture menu to access all of your video settings. You can change your exposure mode for motion pictures by selecting Exposure Mode. Then choose M, A, S, or P mode, the same way you would for still photos (**Figure 10.6**).

Navigate to Rec Highlight and turn it on to see a live highlight overexposure warning (**Figure 10.7**). With the "blinkies" turned on, you can adjust your exposure before you record your video to avoid clipping your highlights. This is especially important with video because you don't have the editing leeway that you have with a RAW file.

Another handy feature in Creative Video mode is Silent Operation. With this feature turned on, you can adjust the aperture, shutter speed, exposure compensation, ISO, and mic level by using the touchscreen (**Figure 10.8**). That way the internal microphone won't pick up the sound of buttons pressing or dials turning when you make adjustments while recording.

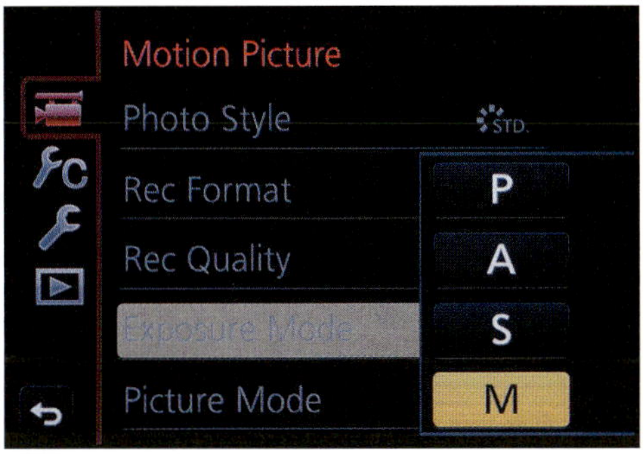

Figure 10.6 Select your exposure mode for motion pictures.

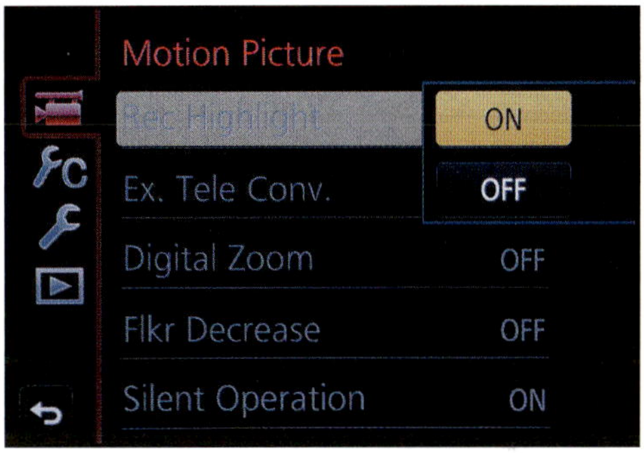

Figure 10.7 Turn on the "blinkies" under Rec Highlight.

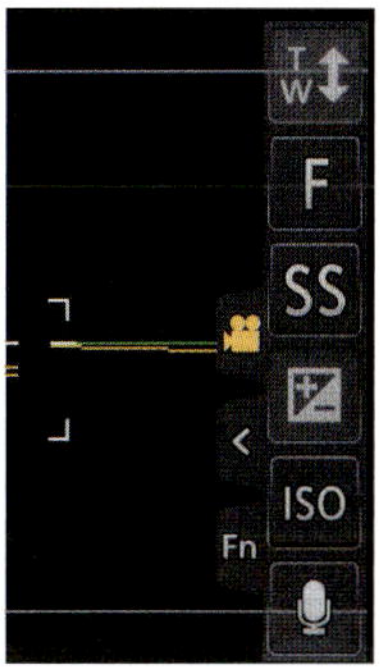

Figure 10.8 Use the touchscreen to make adjustments silently.

Manage your ISO

When shooting video, especially in the professional modes (P, A, S, M), you have control over your ISO level as part of the exposure formula. If you would rather not worry about manipulating one more control while managing other technical aspects of shooting video, you can use Auto ISO (Auto ISO is not available in Manual exposure mode). Doing so lets the camera determine the lowest ISO level needed, leaving you free to compose your shot.

Tips for Better Video

Shoot short clips

Even though your camera can record fairly long video sequences, you should probably limit your shooting time to short clips and then edit them together. Here's the deal: Most professional video shot today is actually made up of very short video sequences that are edited together. If you don't believe me, watch any TV show and see how long you actually see a continuous sequence. I am guessing that you won't see any clip that is longer than about 10 seconds. You can thank music videos for shortening our attention span, but the reality is that your video will look much more professional if you shoot in shorter clips and then edit them together.

Stage your shots

If you are trying to produce a good-looking video, take some time before you begin shooting to determine what you want to shoot and from where you want to shoot it. You can mark the floor with tape to give your "actors" a mark to hit. You can also use staging to figure out where your lens needs to be set for correct focus on these different scenes.

Avoid the quick pan

While recording video, your camera uses something called a rolling shutter, which, as the name implies, rolls from the top to the bottom of the frame. If you are panning quickly from one side to another, you will see your video start to jiggle as if it were being shot through Jell-O. This is something that can't be overcome except by using a slower panning motion. If you are going to be shooting a fast subject, consider using a faster frame rate (such as the 60 frames per second options) to get a faster frame rate and smoother motion. The more frames you record, the smoother the video will look when played back.

Use a fast memory card

Your video will be recording at up to 60 frames per second, and as it is recording, it's placing the video into a buffer, or temporary holding spot, while the camera writes the frames to your memory card. If you are using a slower memory card, it might not be able to keep up with the flow of video—with the result being dropped frames. The camera will actually not record some frames because the buffer will fill up before the images have time to be written. This will be seen as small skips in the video when you watch it later. You can prevent this from happening by using an SD card that has a speed rating of Class 10 or higher (**Figure 10.9**). These cards have faster writing speeds and will keep the video moving smoothly from the camera to the card.

Although the manufacturer suggests Class 4 or faster media, my recommendation is that you use only Class 10 cards for video applications.

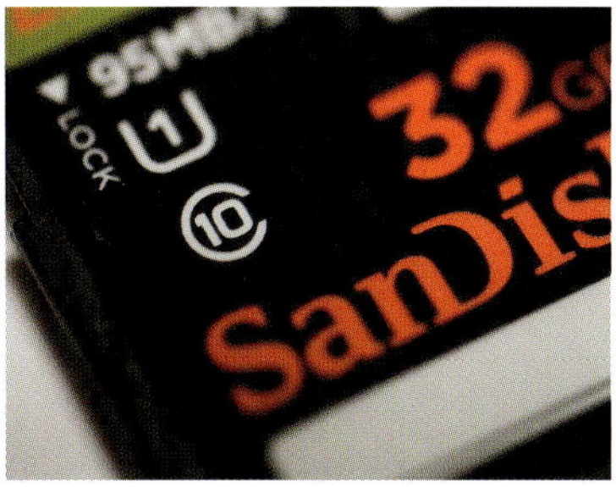

Figure 10.9
A fast card, such as this Sandisk SDHC Class 10, will help capture more of your video frames.

Better sound for your movies

If you want to eliminate the camera noise that comes with recording sound with your camera, you should consider using an external microphone. You can have much more control over the quality of the audio because you are using a device whose sole purpose is to record audio. Since there is no other external audio input, I suggest doing what the pros do: Record sound separately and sync it later using software. This does take a bit more time, but it also provides you the best sound. Several manufacturers sell separate audio recorders that produce high-quality sound at an affordable price, such as the Zoom H1, which retails for about $100. I prefer the H1's bigger brother, the H4n ($270) because it includes two XLR inputs, which allow the use of a variety of specialized high-quality microphones, such as a more sensitive dynamic or condenser mic, or a shotgun mic that can reach out and grab audio from far away.

Turn off the sound

If you don't have an external mic hooked up to your camera, your only audio option is to use the built-in microphone on the camera. The truth is that the microphone does not produce audio that is up to the quality of the video. To make your videos stand out, try turning it off and then adding a music soundtrack. You will be amazed at how the right music can enhance a video. Of course, you will need to do this on your computer, which will require special video editing software, which leads us to our next section.

Neutral density filters

Shooting in bright daylight conditions can sometimes overwhelm any attempts at using a larger aperture and, thus, a shallow depth of field. To help combat this problem, you might want to employ a neutral density filter to darken the scene. The filters come in varying densities, or darkness values, so you will need to determine how much light you need to cut down to get the effect you desire. A variable ND filter is a great option for controlling your video exposure. These filters allow you to you vary the amount of density by up to eight stops. Just dial in the amount of density you want and start recording. Be sure to get the right size filter to screw onto your lens. Most Lumix lenses take either 46mm or 58mm filters, but check your lenses to make sure.

Tripods

The use of a tripod for video is not quite the same as for still image applications. When you are shooting video, you want to present a nice, smooth video scene that is fairly free of camera shake. One particular case for this is the pan shot. When you are following a subject from side to side, you will want the viewer's attention to be focused on the subject, not the shaky look of the video. To help in this cause, your tool of choice should be a tripod with a fluid head. A fluid head looks a little different than a standard tripod head, in that it usually has one long handle for controlled panning. To really make things smooth, the head uses a system of small fluid cartridges within the panning mechanisms so that your panning movements are nice and smooth. For a compact system you can use a small fluid head like the Gitzo 2180 along with standard tripod legs. There is no need to use a large video-specific tripod with your small, lightweight equipment.

Watching and Editing Your Video

Watching video

There are a few ways to watch your videos. Actually, there are three:

- In your camera
- On your TV
- On your computer

To watch video clips on your camera, simply press the Playback button and then touch the Play button on the screen. Pretty simple.

To watch on your TV, you can purchase an HDMI cable to make a connection between camera and TV. This will allow you to view your video in HD, as long as your TV can display at least 720 HD resolution. Make sure that you purchase a Mini-HDMI-to-HDMI (GM1: HDMI micro to HDMI) cable since the camera does not use a standard-sized HDMI jack for outputting video (**Figure 10.10**). You can find them at

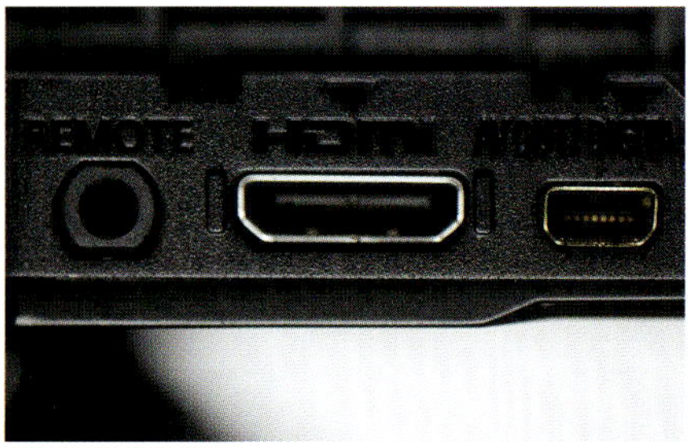

Figure 10.10 The mini-HDMI port on the GX7

most electronics stores that sell HD cameras and TVs. (Here's a little hint for purchasing a Mini-HDMI cable: Search the Internet for the best prices. Most electronics stores have huge mark-ups on cables, and you can usually find a suitable one online for about a third of the price of those in your local store.) Once you have the cable hooked up to your TV, tune it to the channel used for HDMI input, and use the same camera controls that you used for watching the video on the LCD screen to view it on the larger screen.

If you would like to watch your video on your computer, you will first need to download the files or access them using an SD card reader. For Mac owners, you can use Apple's QuickTime Player to watch the MP4 videos that you record. If it is too large for your screen, try pressing Command- – (minus) to decrease the size of the video frame, or Command-3 to fit the frame to your screen.

The easiest way to view AVCHD clips is to import the videos into a compatible editing program, such as Adobe Photoshop Lightroom (version 4 and later) or iMovie ('08 version or later). It is best to import the files from the SD card, since the software uses the entire file and folder structure of the AVCHD format to import the video. Copying just the .mts files to your computer and trying to import will unfortunately not work. You can also convert the AVCHD files to MP4 or another Mac-compatible format by using software, such as iSkysoft Video Converter for Mac.

For Microsoft Windows users, it is possible to view the MP4-formatted video, but you will need to download the Media Player Codec Pack. Instead, try downloading QuickTime for Windows from Apple (www.apple.com/quicktime). The basic player is free and will allow you to view your movie files. The latest versions of Windows Movie Maker and Windows Media Player 12 are capable of playing your AVCHD files.

Editing video

If you are a Mac owner, you can edit both high-definition MP4 and AVCHD video using the current version of iMovie. The most recent version of Windows Movie Maker is also capable of working with both file formats. Windows Movie Maker allows you to edit your video, and it also provides you a way to upload your finished videos to places like YouTube and Facebook. If you don't already have Movie Maker on your system, try this link for more information on how to download and install the free program: http://windows.microsoft.com/en-US/windows-live/movie-maker-get-started.

There are many other Mac and Windows video-editing applications, such as Adobe Premiere Elements 12 and its big brother Premiere Pro CC. You can find more information and download trial versions at www.adobe.com.

Hybrid photography

Hybrid photography is the blending of still photography with motion pictures. Some commercial photographers are working with stills and video to create hybrid eProducts for their clients. I like to add short video clips to my slideshows to augment and support my still photography. I use these hybrid "eScapes" to display my work and promote my classes and workshops. You would be amazed how just a few short moving pictures can spice up your presentations. Most people are viewing photography on a computer, smartphone, or tablet these days, so why not take advantage of the medium and add some motion?

I use software called ProShow Web to combine my images and videos into compelling hybrid eScapes. ProShow Web runs in a web browser and works on both Macs and Windows computers. You can also use a video-editing program like iMovie or Adobe Premiere Pro to combine stills and video, but I enjoy the simplicity and ease of use that ProShow Web offers. You can find out more about it at www.photodex.com.

Expanding your knowledge

I have given you a few quick tips and suggestions in this chapter to get you started with your moviemaking, but if you really want to get serious, there is a lot more you need to know. Videography can be a complex endeavor, and there is much to learn and know if you want to move beyond the simple video capture of the kids in the backyard or the trip to the amusement park. If you really want to explore all that your camera has to offer in the way of video moviemaking, then I suggest you read *Creating DSLR Video: From Snapshots to Great Shots* (Peachpit Press, 2012). Even though the GX7 and GM1 are mirrorless cameras, the same principles of moviemaking apply (and there's not much difference in operating the two camera platforms). The author, Rich Harrington, is a true master at shooting and editing digital video, and he is a top-notch instructor and author. This book is packed solid with everything you need to know about taking your video making to the next level and beyond.

Chapter 10 Assignments

You don't have to be a filmmaker to take advantage of the video functions in the GX7/GM1. Next time you're out shooting, try pressing the red button.

Get creative with filters

Choose your favorite filter in the Creative Control mode and record some stylized video clips. Try to choose a filter that is appropriate for the subject matter. Experiment and notice how different effects give your movies a different feel.

Try different Rec Quality settings

Find a moving subject and make short video clips using different frames. Try the exercise a few times with subjects moving at different speeds. Pay attention to the differences between 60p, 30p, and 24p. Try different Flicker Decrease settings to see the effect on the look of your videos.

Take control with Creative Video mode

Use the Creative Video mode and set your video exposure manually. First set the shutter speed to affect the look of your video, and then adjust the aperture value and ISO to dial in the exposure.

Share your results with the book's Flickr group!
Join the group here: flickr.com/groups/panasonicGX7_fromsnapshotstogreatshots

Index

T

U

V

W

Z